Communications
in Computer and Information Science 2402

Rationale
The CCIS series is devoted to the publication of proceedings of computer science conferences. Its aim is to efficiently disseminate original research results in informatics in printed and electronic form. While the focus is on publication of peer-reviewed full papers presenting mature work, inclusion of reviewed short papers reporting on work in progress is welcome, too. Besides globally relevant meetings with internationally representative program committees guaranteeing a strict peer-reviewing and paper selection process, conferences run by societies or of high regional or national relevance are also considered for publication.

Topics
The topical scope of CCIS spans the entire spectrum of informatics ranging from foundational topics in the theory of computing to information and communications science and technology and a broad variety of interdisciplinary application fields.

Information for Volume Editors and Authors
Publication in CCIS is free of charge. No royalties are paid, however, we offer registered conference participants temporary free access to the online version of the conference proceedings on SpringerLink (http://link.springer.com) by means of an http referrer from the conference website and/or a number of complimentary printed copies, as specified in the official acceptance email of the event.

CCIS proceedings can be published in time for distribution at conferences or as post-proceedings, and delivered in the form of printed books and/or electronically as USBs and/or e-content licenses for accessing proceedings at SpringerLink. Furthermore, CCIS proceedings are included in the CCIS electronic book series hosted in the SpringerLink digital library at http://link.springer.com/bookseries/7899. Conferences publishing in CCIS are allowed to use Online Conference Service (OCS) for managing the whole proceedings lifecycle (from submission and reviewing to preparing for publication) free of charge.

Publication process
The language of publication is exclusively English. Authors publishing in CCIS have to sign the Springer CCIS copyright transfer form, however, they are free to use their material published in CCIS for substantially changed, more elaborate subsequent publications elsewhere. For the preparation of the camera-ready papers/files, authors have to strictly adhere to the Springer CCIS Authors' Instructions and are strongly encouraged to use the CCIS LaTeX style files or templates.

Abstracting/Indexing
CCIS is abstracted/indexed in DBLP, Google Scholar, EI-Compendex, Mathematical Reviews, SCImago, Scopus. CCIS volumes are also submitted for the inclusion in ISI Proceedings.

How to start
To start the evaluation of your proposal for inclusion in the CCIS series, please send an e-mail to ccis@springer.com.

Huimin Lu
Editor

Artificial Intelligence and Robotics

9th International Symposium, ISAIR 2024
Guilin, China, September 27–30, 2024
Revised Selected Papers, Part I

 Springer

Editor
Huimin Lu
Southeast University
Nanjing, China

ISSN 1865-0929 ISSN 1865-0937 (electronic)
Communications in Computer and Information Science
ISBN 978-981-96-2910-7 ISBN 978-981-96-2911-4 (eBook)
https://doi.org/10.1007/978-981-96-2911-4

This Springer imprint is published by the registered company Springer Nature Singapore Pte Ltd.
The registered company address is: 152 Beach Road, #21-01/04 Gateway East, Singapore 189721, Singapore

If disposing of this product, please recycle the paper.

Preface

The integration of artificial intelligence and robotic technologies has become a topic of increasing interest for both researchers and developers from academic fields and industries worldwide. It is foreseeable that artificial intelligence will be the main approach of the next generation of robotics research. These proceedings include high-quality original research papers presented at the 9th International Symposium on Artificial Intelligence and Robotics (ISAIR 2024), which was successfully held in Guilin, China from September 27 to September 30, 2024. The symposium was planned to welcome participants from all over the world to meet physically in beautiful Guilin to exchange ideas, as we did in our past ISAIR conferences. The conference was held in a hybrid format allowing for both on-site and virtual participation. With all your participation and contributions, we believe ISAIR 2024 was a special and memorable event in the conference's history!

ISAIR 2024 was the 9th conference of the series since it was first held in Wuhan, China in 2016, followed by ISAIR 2017 in Kitakyushu, Japan, ISAIR 2018 in Nanjing, China, ISAIR 2019 in Daegu, South Korea, ISAIR 2020 in Kitakyushu, Japan, ISAIR 2021 in Fukuoka, Japan, ISAIR 2022 in Shanghai, China and ISAIR 2023 in Beijing, China. As we know, ISAIR was initiated to promote artificial intelligence and robotic technologies throughout the world. Over the years, it has welcomed authors from all over the world.

ISAIR 2024 focused on three important areas of pattern recognition: artificial intelligence, robotics and Internet of Things, covering various technical aspects. It received 164 submissions. The program chairs invited 40 program committee members and more additional reviewers. Each paper was single-blindly reviewed by at least two reviewers, and most papers received three reviews each. Finally, 61 papers were accepted for presentation in the program, resulting in an acceptance rate of 37.20%.

The technical program of ISAIR was scheduled in three days (21–23 October 2024) including 4 keynote speeches, 4 invited speeches, 6 oral Presentation sessions and 2 poster Presentation sessions.

Organizing a large event is a challenging task, requiring intensive teamwork. We would like to thank all members of the organizing committee for their hard work, with guidance from the steering committee. The general chairs, program chairs, publicity chairs, award chairs and area chairs all led their respective committees and worked together closely to make ISAIR 2024 successful. Our special thanks go to the many reviewers, who we could not name one by one, for constructive comments to improve the papers. We thank all the authors who submitted their papers, which is the most important part of a scientific conference. Finally, we would like to acknowledge the student volunteers from our local organizers.

Tohru Kamiya
Zongyuan Ge
Huimin Lu
Rushi Lan
Dong Wang
Quan Zhou
Xing Xu
Yuchao Zheng

Organization

Steering Committee

M. Malek (Editor-in-Chief)   Cognitive Robotics Journal, USA
S. Serikawa   Kyushu Institute of Technology, Japan
H. Luk   Southeast University, China

General Chairs

Tohru Kamiya   Kyushu Institute of Technology, Japan
Zongyuan Ge   Monash University, Australia
Huimin Lu   Southeast University, China

Program Chairs

Rushi Lan   Guilin University of Electronic Technology, China
Dong Wang   Dalian University of Technology, China
Quan Zhou   Nanjing University of Posts and
                                Telecommunications, China
Xing Xu   University of Electronic Science and Technology
                                of China, China
Yuchao Zheng   Kyushu Institute of Technology, Japan

Publicity Chairs

Jože Guna   University of Ljubljana, Slovenia
Guangwei Gao   Nanjing University of Posts and
                                Telecommunications, China
Shota Nakashima   Yamaguchi University, Japan

Award Chairs

Ruijun Liu   Beijing Technology and Business University,
                                China
Jihua Zhu   Xi'an Jiaotong University, China

Zhibin Yu   Ocean University of China, China
Weihua Ou   Guizhou Normal University, China

Area Chairs

Xin Jin   Beijing Electronic Science and Technology
                                 Institute, China
Csaba Beleznai   Austrian Institute of Technology, Austria
Hao Gao   Nanjing University of Posts and
                                 Telecommunications, China
Ainul Akmar Mokhtar   Universiti Teknologi Petronas, Malaysia
Ting Wang   Nanjing University of Technology, China
Wenpeng Lu   Qilu University of Technology, China
Shenglin Mu   Ehime University, Japan
Amit Kumar Singh   National Institute of Technology Patna, India
Zhe Chen   Hohai University, China

Program Committee Members

Chiew-Foong Kwong   University of Nottingham, UK
Dario Lodi Rizzini   University of Parma, Italy
Danijel Skocaj   University of Ljubljana, Slovenia
Donald Dansereau   University of Sydney, Australia
Guangxu Li   Tianjin Polytechnic University, China
Giancarlo Fortino   Università della Calabria, Italy
Hossein Olya   University of Sheffield, UK
Iztok Humar   University of Ljubljana, Slovenia
Jianru Li   Tongji University, China
Jinjia Zhou   Hosei University, Japan
Keshav Seshadri   Carnegie Mellon University, USA
Levis Mei   Agilent California Research Center, USA
Limei Peng   Kyungpook National University, South Korea
Liao Wu   University of New South Wales, Australia
Li He   Qualcomm Inc., USA
Mario G. C. A. Cimino   University of Pisa, Italy
M. Shamim Hossain   King Saud University, Saudi Arabia
Matjaz Perc   University of Maribor, Slovenia
Oleg Sergiyenko   Autonomous University of Baja California,
                                 Mexico
Sangeen Khan   COMSATS University, Pakistan

Shuai Chen	Chinese Academy of Sciences, China
Wendy Flores-Fuentes	Universidad Autónoma de Baja California, Mexico
Xin Li	Shanghai Jiao Tong University, China
Xinliang Liu	Beijing Technology and Business University, China
Yin Zhang	Zhongnan University of Economics and Law, China
Yichuan Wang	University of Sheffield, UK
Haitao Cheng	Nanjing University of Posts and Telecommunications, China
Fang Hu	Hubei University of Chinese Medicine, China
Xipeng Pan	Guilin University of Electronic Technology, China
Yun Liu	Southwest University, China
Huadeng Wang	Guilin University of Electronic Technology, China
Haigang Zhang	Shenzhen Polytechnic, China
Xianfeng Wu	Jianghan University, China
Zhihao Xu	Qingdao University, China
Junfei Wang	Jianghan University, China
Zhongyuan Lai	Jianghan University, China
Jianming Zhang	Changsha University of Science and Technology, China
Xiwang Xie	Dalian Maritime University, China
Heng Liu	Anhui University of Technology, China
Fenglian Li	Taiyuan University of Technology, China

Contents – Part I

Contents – Part II

Segmentation of Crack Disaster Images Based on Deep Learning Neural Network Method

Gengkun Wu[1,2] (iD), Letian Wang[2(✉)] (iD), Tossou Akpedje[1,2], C. F. Ingrid Hermilda[2], Zengwei Liang[2], and Jie Xu[2]

[1] Shandong Province Key Laboratory of Wisdom Mine Information Technology, Shandong University of Science and Technology, Qingdao 266590, China

[2] College of Computer Science and Engineering, Shandong University of Science and Technology, Qingdao 266590, China

wlt000122@gmail.com

Abstract. Automatic identification and early warning of surface cracks have become urgent for mine safety. The precise segmentation of mine crack images is a challenging task due to the complex nature of their content. The segmentation precision can be hindered by the presence of complex environmental backgrounds, such as crack sizes, illumination, slope, and vegetation, which can all interfere with the accuracy of the detection process. In this paper, a deep learning based mine crack segmentation method is proposed, which includes data preprocessing, crack image and non-crack image classification, and crack segmentation. The segmentation network is different from the existing DeeplabV3 Plus, Segformer, etc. It extricates three distinct scales of features within the encoder and proposes a unique multi-feature fusion and attention approach to fuse these three features in the encoder. We have also constructed a unique mine crack dataset. Experimental results on this dataset show that our method obtains 83.48% mIoU and 90.34% F1-score, demonstrating higher segmentation accuracy than other state-of-the-art methods.

Keywords: Semantic Segmentation · Image Classification Mine Crack · Multi-scale Fusion · Attention module

1 Introduction

Automatically and efficiently detecting mine cracks remains challenging due to crack size, vegetation, light, and mine slope effects. In recent years, the domain of artificial intelligence has witnessed an accelerated ascension and evolution [1, 2]. Deep learning neural networks are excellent in processing images [3, 4]. Deep learning methods have become popular for crack segmentation such as: [5–7], and they have shown more promising results than traditional segmentation algorithms. Inspired by the above work, we propose a new method that includes image preprocessing, crack and non-crack image classification, and crack image segmentation. Our dataset comes from real mine images collected by UAVs, and due to the large working surface area, choosing the whole image

H. Lu (Ed.): ISAIR 2024, CCIS 2402, pp. 1–9, 2025.
https://doi.org/10.1007/978-981-96-2911-4_1

for crack detection will increase the hardware cost. Therefore, we crop the image, which contains a 600m*600m mine landscape, into a bunch of 400*400 resolved images. Given that the cropped images without cracks contribute little to the segmentation training, we applied the Resnet50 classification network to obtain cropped images containing cracks that positively guide the subsequent segmentation training process. These images are eventually fed into our proposed segmentation network to train through a fully supervised way. The process of our work is shown in Fig. 1.

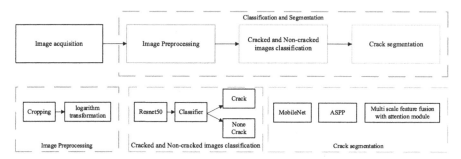

Fig. 1. Flowchart for detecting mine cracks.

The paper is structured as follows. Section 2 presents the details of the experimental methodology. The experiments and results are presented in Sect. 3. Finally, Sect. 4 concludes the paper.

2   Methods

2.1   Classification Network

During our research, we extensively evaluated the classification abilities of several different networks utilizing our dataset. Ultimately, we determined that constructing a classification network based on Resnet50 was the optimal choice, given its superior performance. The structure of the ResNet50 network is illustrated in Fig. 2. The overall architecture is shown on the left, while the middle section shows the specific structure of the network. On the right, two unique residual network structures are presented. Due to the dissimilarity between these residual edges, the Convolutional Blocks vary the width and height of the output feature layer and the number of channels, and the Identify Blocks serve the purpose of deepening the network.

2.2   Crack Semantic Segmentation Network

For the segmentation of crack images, we developed an end-to-end semantic segmentation network comprising an encoder and decoder. We extracted three different levels of feature maps from the backbone network and fed them into the decoder for more comprehensive feature information. At the end of the encoder, we utilized the Atrous Spatial Pyramid Pooling (ASPP) module to capture high-level semantic information. In the decoder, we introduce two suitable attention modules to weigh the extracted three distinct feature maps. We subsequently perform multi-scale feature fusion to enable the model to comprehend crucial information in the input feature maps, resulting in more precise output predictions. Figure 3 depicts our proposed network model for semantic segmentation of mine cracks. The model utilizes a single image of a mine crack as input and generates a corresponding segmentation mask image as output.

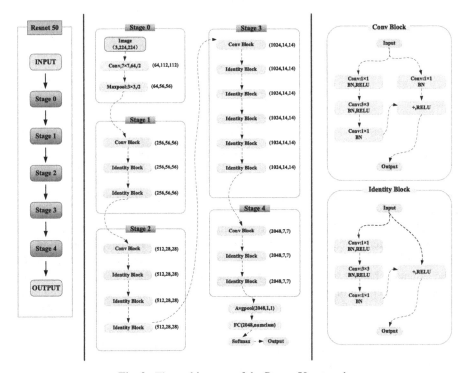

Fig. 2. The architecture of the Resnet50 network.

We build the backbone network of encoders based on MobileNetV2 [13]. The dimensions of the input image are 256*256*3. The final feature map size is 32*32*320, representing the extracted high-level feature map M_{high}. Meanwhile, the mid-level feature map M_{mid} has dimensions of 32*32*160, and the low-level feature map M_{low} has dimensions of 64*64*24. These three feature maps are then passed to the decoder.

The ASPP module was first introduced in the Deeplab network series. It improves the receptive field of the network by incorporating dilated convolutions with varying dilation rates, allowing it to capture features of different scales more effectively. The formula for dilated convolutions is as follows.

$$y[i] = \sum_{k=1}^{K} x[i + r \cdot d \cdot k] \cdot w[k] \tag{1}$$

Where $x[i]$ represents the pixel intensity value of either the input image or the feature map, $w[k]$ denotes the weight value of the k-th position in the convolutional kernel,

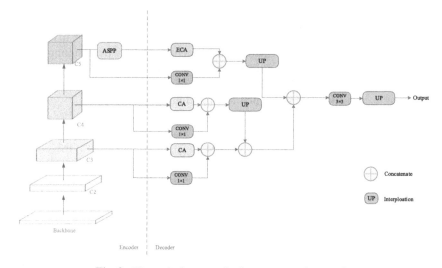

Fig. 3. The main framework of our proposed network.

r represents the stride, d represents the dilation rate, and k denotes the size of the convolutional kernel.

Employing multi-scale features in semantic segmentation yields feature maps amenable to different scales, which can then be fused to extract richer information and recover finer details. Inspired by Wang et al. [8], we have devised decoders grounded in the Efficient channel attention (ECA) module and Coordinate attention (CA) module to weigh the attention of the extracted feature maps, enhancing their expressive power and generalization performance. The following contents will discuss the ECA and CA modules in more details.

ECA-Net. The ECA module eliminates the fully connected layer of the original SENet module and instead deploys global average pooling without dimensionality reduction. The ECA module learns the features after global average pooling by a 1D convolution of convolution size k, where k denotes the extent of coverage of local cross-channel interactions.

Coordinate Attention. The CA module makes better use of the target position information of the image, resulting in improved localization and detection of the model. Specifically, the CA module encodes the input feature tensor in two different directions with 1D features, allowing the model to capture long-range dependencies between channels while retaining target location information. The target location information is then embedded in the generated attention map. The structure of the CA module is depicted in Fig. 4.

For a task such as mine crack segmentation, information may need to be extracted from various scales of features due to the relatively subtle features of the cracks. Therefore, the combined utilization of CA and ECA modules allows for the consideration of both detail and semantic information, which can better meet the requirements of the mine crack segmentation task.

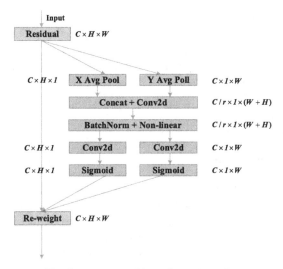

Fig. 4. Structure of Coordinate Attention.

Drawing the idea of residual connections, the feature map obtained by passing the input through a 1×1 convolution and the feature map obtained by passing the input through an attention module are added together along the channel dimension. Then, the M_{high} and M_{mid} are upsampled and fused with the M_{low}. The final result of the fusion is shown in Eq. (2).

$$O = U(M_{high} + M_{bhigh}) + U(M_{mid} + M_{bmid}) + (M_{low} + M_{blow}) \tag{2}$$

where O denotes the output, U represents the upsampling operation, and M_{bhigh} denotes the high-level feature map acquired from the backbone feature extraction network without further processing from other modules. The final output O is subjected to a convolution with a 3×3 and 1×1 kernel to resize the image to 256*256*2, and after bilinear difference, the image is reduced to a prediction map of size H*W.

2.3 Loss Function

In the task of segmenting mine cracks, there is a significant imbalance in pixels between the background (mine scenes) and the foreground (cracks). Imbalanced datasets can result in instability when training a well-constructed, generative, and discriminative model. To solve this issue and enhance the performance of the dice coefficients, we incorporate both the cross-entropy and dice loss functions.

$$L_{CE} = L(y_i, p_i) = -\sum_{i=1}^{n} y_i log(p_i) \tag{3}$$

$$L_{Dice} = 1 - Dice = 1 - \frac{2|X \cap Y|}{|X| + |Y|} \tag{4}$$

where $|X \cap Y|$ represents the size of the intersection set between X and Y, while $|X|$ and $|Y|$ represent the number of elements in X and Y, respectively. The p_i represents the predicted probability and y_i represents the true labeled value.

In the training stage, the loss function is obtained by summing the cross-entropy loss and the Dice loss as follows.

$$L = L_{CE} + L_{Dice} \tag{5}$$

3   Results and Discussion

In this section, we evaluate the performance of the present classification network on our dataset and compare our proposed network with existing segmentation networks to demonstrate the effectiveness of our approach. The evaluation metrics we use in this section include Accuracy (Acc), Precision (Pr), Recall (Re), F1-score (F1) and mean Intersection of Union (mIoU). The semantic segmentation training set consisted of 600 samples, while the validation set contained 230 samples.

3.1   Results of Classification Network

We constructed the classification network based on Resnet50 and compared it with several other classical neural networks while ensuring some hyperparameters remained consistent, such as the learning rate. The test results are illustrated in Table 1. When distinguishing between images that feature a crack and those that do not, the model achieved an accuracy rate of 95.16%, demonstrating that it is better suited for mine crack datasets than other models.

Table 1. Comparison of Resnet50 with other classification networks on the mine dataset.

Method	Precision (%)	Recall (%)	F1-score (%)
Vgg13	90.66	90	90.33
Vgg16	92.17	91.82	91.99
Vgg19	92.95	92.73	92.84
MobileNetV2	91.13	90.91	91.02
Vit	90.96	90.91	90.93
Mobile VIT	93.65	93.64	93.64
Resnet50	**96.43**	**96.36**	**96.39**

3.2   Results of Semantic Segmentation Network

Figure 5 compares the performance of our proposed segmentation network with the other four segmentation networks on the small mine crack dataset. Small cracks are susceptible

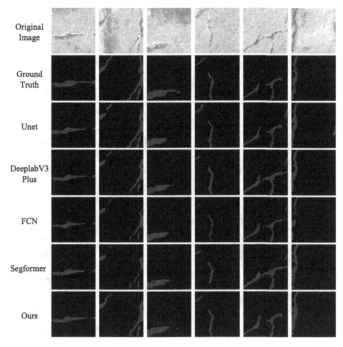

Fig. 5. Results of the comparison of datasets for small cracks in mine.

to vegetation and slope noise. The experimental results show that our proposed network can reduce the noise effect and thus provide more accurate segmentation of mine crack images compared to other algorithms. For instance, in the original image in column 2, a crack can be observed on the left side, with weeds and other vegetation covering its middle. However, our network can accurately segment the whole crack, proving its noise immunity. Figure 6 compares the performance of our proposed segmentation network with the other four segmentation networks on the datasets for large cracks in mine. Large cracks are susceptible to light. The experimental results show that our proposed network can segment the images of large cracks in mine more accurately. For instance, column 1 images display a visible crack and a depressed ground surface. Other networks misinterpret the depression as non-cracked, leading to inaccurate segmentation. Our network effectively mitigates this issue, ensuring accurate crack segmentation.

Based on the above analysis, it is evident that the three different scales of features extracted by our segmentation network, in conjunction with the multi-scale feature fusion attention method, allow the network to discern the background and target regions more nuancedly. Additionally, this approach effectively removes the influence of correlated noise while enhancing the details of various features to enable more precise segmentation of crack images.

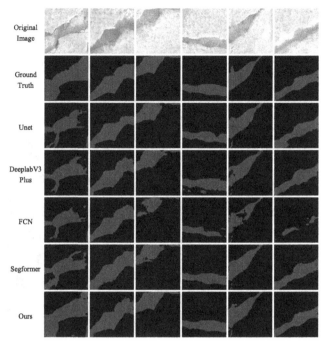

Fig. 6. Results of the comparison of datasets for large cracks in mine.

Table 2 shows experimental results comparing our semantic segmentation network with other models. Our model achieves superior performance with 90.81% recall, 97.6% accuracy, and 83.48% mIoU, surpassing all previous methods. Despite a slightly lower accuracy compared to some segmentation networks like Unet and FCN, our method obtained the highest F1 score (90.34%) by measuring the performance of the model in terms of recall and accuracy.

Table 2. Comparison of our method with previous methods on mine crack datasets.

Method	Accuracy	mIoU	Recall	Precision	F1-score
Unet	96.92	77.96	83.32	90.11	86.35
DeeplabV3+	97.19	80.08	85.86	90.33	87.94
Segformer	96.98	79.07	85.57	89.02	87.2
FCN	96.9	76.5	80.33	**92.36**	85.19
PSPnet	95.77	68.63	72.52	89.25	78.27
Lraspp	95.3	64.0	67.07	90.94	73.44
Ours	**97.6**	**83.48**	**90.81**	89.92	**90.34**

4 Conclusion

In this paper, we propose a novel approach for mine crack segmentation. Our approach begins with image preprocessing to create a distinctive mining dataset. We then use a Resnet50-based classification network to identify images containing cracks. Finally, our segmented network is employed to segment the identified crack-containing images. Our segmentation network extracts three different scales of features using the encoder and applies a distinct multi-scale attention feature fusion method in the decoder. Our proposed segmentation network exhibits the highest mIoU and F1-score compared to other segmentation networks, reaching 83.48% and 90.34%, respectively, as demonstrated by experimental results. While the current dataset is vast, the professionally annotated data is still limited, prompting us to consider semi-supervised or unsupervised segmentation algorithms in future work.

Acknowledgment. The authors are grateful for the collaborative funding support from the Shandong Natural Science Foundation of China (ZR2021MD063) and the University Youth Innovation Team Foundation of Shandong Province (2022KJ319).

References

1. Lu, H., Guizani, M., Ho, P.H.: Editorial introduction to responsible artificial intelligence for autonomous driving. IEEE Trans. Intell. Transp. Syst. **23**(12), 25212–25215 (2022)
2. Lu, H., Zhang, Y., Li, Y., Jiang, C., Abbas, H.: User-oriented virtual mobile network resource management for vehicle communications. IEEE Trans. Intell. Transp. Syst. **22**(6), 3521–3532 (2020)
3. Lu, H., Li, Y., Uemura, T., Kim, H., Serikawa, S.: Low illumination underwater light field images reconstruction using deep convolutional neural networks. Futur. Gener. Comput. Syst. **82**, 142–148 (2018)
4. Lu, H., Zhang, M., Xu, X., Li, Y., Shen, H.T.: Deep fuzzy hashing network for efficient image retrieval. IEEE Trans. Fuzzy Syst. **29**(1), 166–176 (2020)
5. Yang, L., Bai, S., Liu, Y., Yu, H.: Multi-scale triple-attention network for pixelwise crack segmentation. Autom. Constr. **150**, 104853 (2023)
6. Hamishebahar, Y., Guan, H., So, S., Jo, J.: A comprehensive review of deep learning-based crack detection approaches. Appl. Sci. **12**(3), 1374 (2022)
7. Chen, G., Teng, S., Lin, M., Yang, X., Sun, X.: Crack detection based on generative adversarial networks and deep learning. KSCE J. Civ. Eng. **26**(4), 1803–1816 (2022)
8. Wang, Z., Wang, J., Yang, K., Wang, L., Su, F., Chen, X.: Semantic segmentation of high-resolution remote sensing images based on a class feature attention mechanism fused with Deeplabv3+. Comput. Geosci.Geosci. **158**, 104969 (2022)

Numerical Calculation and Identification of 3D Time-Invariant Freak Waves Based on JONSWAP Spectrum and Donelan Direction Function

Geng-Kun Wu[1] ⓘ, Ruo-Yu Li[2](✉) ⓘ, Li-Chen Han[1] ⓘ, and Bin Liu[1] ⓘ

[1] College of Computer Science and Engineering, Shandong University of Science and Technology, Qingdao 266590, China
[2] Shandong Province Key Laboratory of Wisdom Mine Information Technology, Shandong University of Science and Technology, Qingdao 266590, China
ruoyuli67@gmail.com

Abstract. The results of recent maritime accident investigations show that many shipwrecks are related to the attack of freak waves, which can sink ships instantaneously with colossal energy. To identify and forecast freak waves accurately and avoid the danger of freak waves to marine structures and people, we have conducted further research on three-dimensional(3-D) freak waves. In this paper, we propose an efficient computational modeling of time-invariant 3-D freak waves and simulate the time-series evolution process of 3-D freak waves. We study the scattering characteristics of time-invariant 3-D freak waves and obtain a more explicit identification of their scattering differences. And we calculate the electromagnetic scattering view of the temporal evolution of 3-D freak waves through experiments. The experiments show that the research in this paper can identify and predict 3-D freak waves more effectively, further improve the forecast accuracy of future freak waves. It also have some application value for 3-D freak wave risk warnings.

Keywords: 3-D freak waves · numerical calculation · time series evolution · electromagnetic scattering

1 Introduction

Oceans of the world are vast and rich in resources, but the internal environment of the oceans is more complex, resulting in frequent marine disasters. As the research on the sea becomes more and more advanced, disaster prevention and mitigation of the ocean are also essential. Freak waves are particularly extreme waves in the sea. Freak waves are usually defined as waves with Hmax≥2Hs (where Hmax is the maximum wave height and Hs is the significant wave height). Freak waves have distinctive nonlinear characteristics, short duration, concentrated energy, and surprising destructive power [1]. The generation of freak waves is random and appears not only in the open ocean but also in the coastal

H. Lu (Ed.): ISAIR 2024, CCIS 2402, pp. 10–17, 2025.
https://doi.org/10.1007/978-981-96-2911-4_2

area. Its appearance is often accompanied by deep holes in the sea and continuous large waves. The extreme impact of freak waves on marine structures and ships has led to ship damage and loss of personnel [2]. Therefore, it is essential to study the freak waves further.

The current development of 3-D vision has a wide range of applications, especially for current intelligent systems, including drones, autonomous driving, etc. [3–6], This opens up greater possibilities for acquiring 3-D data in the future. This paper focuses on 3-D freak wave vision and its scattering image characteristics. 3-D modeling is the foundation of 3-D vision technology, 3-D computer modeling technology has created significant economic benefits for various aspects of society, and with the development of technologies such as big data, 3-D modeling will have higher research and utilization value [7]. In this article, we combine 3-D modeling technology with the ocean field, use computer simulation to simulate 3-D freak waves, and use the two-scale method(TSM) [8] to calculate the backscattering coefficient of 3-D freak waves on the sea surface. Then, we compare the electromagnetic scattering characteristics of various stages in the temporal evolution process of 3-D freak waves.

2 Numerical Calculation Method for 3-D Freak Wave

The occurrence of freak waves is an unpredictable chance event, and there is minimal information about the measured data of freak waves. Therefore, the mechanism of freak wave generation still needs to be well established. Based on the current research of scholars on the generation mechanism of freak waves, wave energy focusing and modulation instability are considered fundamental mechanisms [9, 10]. This experiment adopts the method of wave energy focusing and chooses a two-wave train superposition model, on which adaptations are made.

The experiment generates freak waves at specific locations. A 3-D random sea surface with an area range of 800 m × 800 m is used as the experimental background. The parameters of the JONSWAP spectrum are set to γ=7, F=13 km, U10=17 m/s. According to the Gaussian distribution, the freak wave was chosen to be generated at (200, 200), and the results are shown in Figure 1:

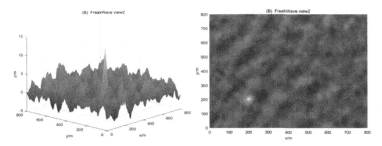

Fig. 1. 3-D Freak Wave Sea Surface.

Figure 1 shows that the experiments obtained wave height anomalies at (200, 200), where the wave height far exceeds the background wave height. The above experiment uses the two-wave train superposition model in the wave energy focusing method. Moreover, the reproduction of the 3-D freak wave is achieved quickly by the linear mechanism.

Selecting the appropriate wave spectrum and the energy distribution based on the wave spectrum and direction function and the overall section of the part of the high-energy region for energy focus can reduce the number of computer calculations and improve the calculation's efficiency. In the following experiment, we first choose the JONSWAP wave spectrum, based on the angular frequency [0.3,1.3] and directional angle $[-\pi/2, \pi/2]$, and then again choose a specific range of angular frequency and directional angle and change the peak elevation factors of the JONSWAP spectrum to do experiments, and then choose the PM spectrum to compare with it. The experiments are shown in Figure 2:

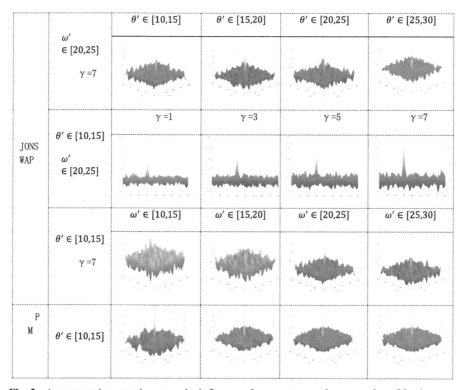

Fig. 2. A comparative experiment on the influence of parameters on the generation of freak waves using JONSWAP and PM spectra.

From Figure 2 we can see that the experiments were performed under the selected JONSWAP wave spectrum conditions, and when we set the angular frequency subinterval $\omega' \in [20,25]$, and the spectral peak elevation factor $\gamma = 7$, we can clearly conclude that the directional angular sub-generates freak waves in the range of 10-30. And when the maximum value of wave height is set in the interval $\theta' \in [20,25]$, the form of freak waves is more prominent. This is because the Donelan direction function has a maximum value of $\omega' = 24$ for a specific parameter of the wave spectrum, thus leading to a more significant value of the wave height of the freak wave. We change γ under the condition of other parameters constant, and the experimental results in the table's third row show that the freak wave's height increases with the increase of γ. The last two rows of the table vary the angular frequency subinterval range under the condition of the same parameters of the direction function and do the comparison experiments of the PM spectrum and JONSWAP spectrum to observe the wave states brought by the change of angular frequency interval of different wave spectra. The results show that the angular frequency ω' in the interval $[10,20]$ does not meet the parameter requirements of the freak wave when the JONSWAP spectrum is used with the same direction function and the spectral peak elevation factor $\gamma=7$, and the freak wave cannot be generated. Moreover, the interval of $[20,30]$ can generate a freak wave with a noticeable effect. When using the PM spectrum, the freak waves generated by ω' in the interval $[10,30]$ are similar. The change in angular frequency has little effect on the experimental results, and the wave heights of the generated freak waves are lower. The reason is that the wave spectrum belongs to the non-narrow band spectrum under the current experimental conditions. The energy is relatively average, and overall energy changes slowly, making the generated wave patterns more stable. In contrast, in the random sea surface of freak waves simulated using the JONSWAP spectrum, the wavelengths of individual waves are shorter, and the number of waves is greater, which is because the wave spectrum belongs to the narrow-band spectrum and its energy distribution is concentrated with a large number of low-energy constituent waves as well as a few high-energy constituent waves, which makes the generated wave shape present instability.

3 Identification of 3-D Time-Invariant Freak Waves

3.1 Electromagnetic Scattering from Rough Sea Surfaces with 3-D Freak Waves

The harm of freak waves to marine platforms is enormous. Establish a reliable electro-magnetic scattering model so that we can effectively identify the freak waves. It can also provide weather warning services for ships to take countermeasures in advance, which can effectively reduce the impact of marine disasters. This section explores the feasibility of introducing electromagnetic scattering technology into the research related to the 3-D freak wave sea surface, investigate the electromagnetic scattering characteristics of the freak wave sea surface and construct a 3-D freak wave scattering calculation model.

The experiment uses the numerical simulation to generate the 3-D freak wave and calculates the electromagnetic scattering coefficient of the 3-D freak wave rough sea surface by the TSM method. The wind speed is selected as $U_{10} = 17m/s$ and the relative permittivity of seawater is $Y = 81.5$. We chose the HH polarization method because the HH polarization is more accessible to detect the freak waves from the background sea surface than the VV polarization, and the radar wave number incidence angle θ is set as $70°$.

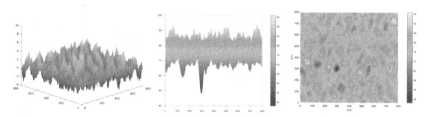

Fig. 3. Experimental results of electromagnetic scattering from 3-D freak wave sea surface.

The first image in Figure 3 represents the sea surface state at t = 14 s during the time series evolution of the 3-D freak wave surface, and the next two images show the characteristic distribution of the backward scattering of the 3-D freak wave at that moment in time using the TSM method. The green region in the figure indicates that the scattered field inside this region is relatively weak and is obscured by the adjacent waves. The scattered field in the dark blue region is relatively strong. The freak wave generated at (300,300) can be observed.

The method approximates the background wave and the freak wave as a superposition of two scales of size, and the results obtained can detect and identify freak waves. This is of great importance for the research work on freak waves. It can be seen from the figure that the lowest value of electromagnetic scattering coefficient NRCS is at the location where the freak wave generates, which has a large gap compared to the background sea surface. We record the lowest NRCS values for the background and freak waves in a single experiment and calculate the average value of NRCS inside a giant area with a side length of 100 m from the origin. We performed 20 experiments to derive the mean value of NRCS. The experimental data are shown in the following table:

Table 1. NRCS values of freak waves and background waves.

Type	Freak Wave	Background Wave	Difference
NRCS Minimum Value	7.5864	14.5167	6.9303
Average NRCS	8.3103	15.5005	7.1902

According to the experimental results in Table 1, we can see that the NRCS value is the lowest at the generation position of the freak wave, and this value is significantly different from the NRCS of the background waves. The electromagnetic scattering values of the two waves can be used as a basis for judging and identifying freak waves.

3.2   Effects of Different Wind Speeds, Incidence Angles and Wave Spectra on the Electromagnetic Scattering of 3-D Freak Waves

The experiments use the sea surface state at t=14 s in the time-series evolution model of 3-D freak waves constructed above. A significant freak wave is generated at the sea surface at that moment. We vary the wind speed and radar incidence angle while keeping the values of the other parameters fixed. The wind speed is chosen from Beaufort wind levels 5-9, i.e., $U_{10}= 8.0 \sim 24.4$, radar incidence angle $\theta = 45° \sim 85°$, and the wave spectrum is chosen from the JONSWAP and PM spectrum. The results of the comparison experiments are shown in Figure 4:

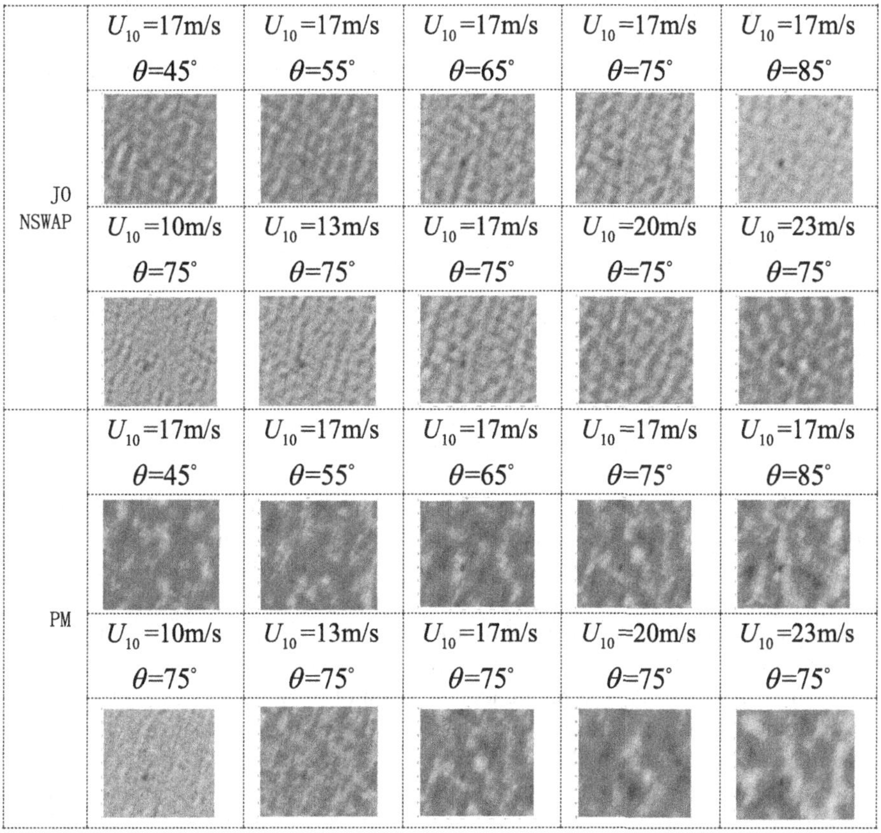

	U_{10}=17m/s θ=45°	U_{10}=17m/s θ=55°	U_{10}=17m/s θ=65°	U_{10}=17m/s θ=75°	U_{10}=17m/s θ=85°
JO NSWAP	U_{10}=10m/s θ=75°	U_{10}=13m/s θ=75°	U_{10}=17m/s θ=75°	U_{10}=20m/s θ=75°	U_{10}=23m/s θ=75°
PM	U_{10}=17m/s θ=45°	U_{10}=17m/s θ=55°	U_{10}=17m/s θ=65°	U_{10}=17m/s θ=75°	U_{10}=17m/s θ=85°
	U_{10}=10m/s θ=75°	U_{10}=13m/s θ=75°	U_{10}=17m/s θ=75°	U_{10}=20m/s θ=75°	U_{10}=23m/s θ=75°

Fig. 4. Comparison of electromagnetic scattering of different wave spectra at different wind speeds and incident angles.

The first two rows of Figure 4 show the generation of the freak wave sea surface electromagnetic scattering using the JONSWAP spectrum. The first row gives the effect of different radar incidence angles on the NRCS values of the freak wave electromagnetic scattering at the same moment and the sea surface state with a wind speed of 17 m/s. It can be seen that as the incidence angle increases, the green area of the sea surface electromagnetic scattering decreases and the orange area increases, the contrast between the blue freak wave position and the background sea surface becomes more and more apparent, and the NRCS value between the freak wave and the background wave increases continuously. The second row gives the effect on the NRCS value of the electromagnetic scattering of the freak wave at the same moment, 75° radar incidence angle, and under different wind speeds of the sea. As the wind speed increases, the area of the orange region decreases, and the area of the blue region increases, resulting in the dark blue region of the freak wave becoming less noticeable. As the wind speed increases, extreme waves begin to appear in the background waves, with higher wind speeds producing more extreme waves in the experimental wind speed interval. The overall wave height increases with it, causing interference in the recognition of the freak wave. The NRCS of the background wave is taken as the average NRCS value inside a rectangular area with a side length of 20 m centered on the position of the freak wave. The overall data of the JONSWAP spectrum generation freak wave sea surface electromagnetic scattering experiment are shown in Table 2:

Table 2. NRCS values under different wind speeds and incident angle.

NRCS	Wind speed 17m/s at different angles					Angle 75 °, different wind speeds				
	45°	55°	65°	75°	85°	10	13	17	20	23
freak wave	−0.5548	1.1164	4.2344	20.9550	259.0646	22.7397	22.6495	20.9550	19.9174	20.1361
Background wave	0.7579	2.2803	4.9758	23.4531	273.2144	25.6041	24.2586	23.4531	22.7845	23.0319
D-value	1.3127	1.1647	0.7414	2.4981	14.1498	2.8744	1.6091	2.4981	2.8671	2.8958

From the experimental data in Table 2, it is concluded that both the sea surface wind speed and the radar incidence angle affect the NRCS values derived from the electromagnetic scattering of freak waves. The increase in wind speed leads to the appearance of extreme waves in the background sea surface, which interferes with the study of the detection and identification of freak waves. However, with the decreasing incidence angle, the scattering difference between the freak and background waves is also gradually reduced. Therefore, the identification of freak waves by electromagnetic scattering characteristics should be judged under a large incidence angle, which has a more vital anti-interference ability and more reliable identification work.

According to the comparison between the experimental results of generating freak wave sea surface electromagnetic scattering using the PM spectrum and using the JONSWAP spectrum in Figure 4, it is concluded that the scattering difference between the freak wave and the background sea surface increases with the increasing radar incidence angle under the same wind speed condition. However, the freak wave recognition effect is not apparent. Even when the radar incidence angle is 85°, the background sea surface has a large blue area and will produce many waves with considerable wave height, causing significant interference to the electromagnetic scattering results. Under the condition of a larger radar incidence angle, the wave spectrum is influenced by the wind speed due to this wave spectrum. The higher the wind speed, the color of the location of the freak wave deepens. However, with the increasing wind speed, the background wave starts to appear as extreme waves, which affects the recognition effect of electromagnetic scattering. Overall, under the same wind speed and same radar parameters, the JONSWAP spectrum simulates the sea surface with more yellow areas and more uniform sea surface state changes, The difference effect of electromagnetic scattering of freak waves under large incidence angle conditions is obvious, and the identification of freak waves is better.

4 Conclusion

The extreme randomness of 3-D freak waves and the limitations of observation techniques make the study of freak wave-related work of great scientific significance and practical value. In this paper, we focus on the numerical simulation of 3-D freak waves and calculating electromagnetic scattering from the sea surface of freak waves. Firstly, this paper establishes a reliable 3-D freak wave through the two-wave train superposition wave energy focusing model of numerical simulation method. At the same time, the time-series evolution of the 3-D freak wave generation process is simulated for the characteristics of the time-series dynamics of the random sea surface. Then, we use the two-scale method to calculate the electromagnetic scattering of 3-D freak wave sea surfaces simulated by different wave spectra and compare and analyze the electromagnetic scattering characteristics of varying sea surfaces. The experimental results show that the freak waves generation location has the lowest value of NRCS, which verifies the feasibility of identifying anomalous waves by judging the electromagnetic scattering characteristics of the sea surface.

References

1. Wang, L., Ding, K., Zhou, B., Li, J., Liu, S., Tang, T.: Quantitative prediction of the freak wave occurrence probability in co-propagating mixed waves. Ocean Eng. **271**, 113810 (2023)
2. Didenkulova, E., Didenkulova, I., Medvedev, I.: Freak wave events in 2005–2021: statistics and analysis of favourable wave and wind conditions. Natural Hazards and Earth System Sci. **23**(4), 1653–1663 (2023)
3. Lu, H., Li, Y., Mu, S., Wang, D., Kim, H., Serikawa, S.: Motor anomaly detection for unmanned aerial vehicles using reinforcement learning. IEEE Internet of Things J. **5**(4), 2315–2322 (2017)
4. Lu, H., Guizani, M., Ho, P.H.: Editorial introduction to responsible artificial intelligence for autonomous driving. IEEE Trans. Intelligent Transportation Syst. **23**(12), 25212–25215 (2022)
5. Lu, H., Zhang, Y., Li, Y., Jiang, C., Abbas, H.: User-oriented virtual mobile network resource management for vehicle communications. IEEE Transactions on Intelligent Transportation Syst. **22**(6), 3521–3532 (2020)
6. Lu, H., Li, Y., Uemura, T., Kim, H., Serikawa, S.: Low illumination underwater light field images reconstruction using deep convolutional neural networks. Future Generation Computer Syst. **82**, 142–148 (2018)
7. Yan-lin, S., Ai-ling, Z., You-bin, H., Ke-yan, X.: 3D geological modeling and its application under complex geological conditions. Procedia Eng. **12**, 41–46 (2011)
8. Zheng, H., Zhang, J., Zhang, Y., Khenchaf, A., Wang, Y.: A modified TSM for better prediction of hh polarized microwave backscattering coefficient from sea surface. Remote Sensing Letters **11**(12), 1137–1146 (2020)
9. Sand, S.E., Hansen, N.O., Klinting, P., Gudmestad, O.T., Sterndorff, M.J.: Freak wave kinematics. Water Wave Kinematics, pp. 535–549 (1990)
10. Kharif, C., Pelinovsky, E., Slunyaev, A.: Rogue waves in the ocean. Springer Science & Business Media (2008)

Enhanced Computing for Marine Disaster Based on the Prior Dark Channel Scenes, Precise Depth Estimation and Channel-Dependent Compensation Method

Geng-Kun Wu[1] , Qing-Xin Sun[2](✉) , Jie Xu[1] , and Bei-Ping Zhang[1]

[1] College of Computer Science and Engineering, Shandong University of Science and Technology, Qingdao 266590, China
[2] Shandong Province Key Laboratory of Wisdom Mine Information Technology, Shandong University of Science and Technology, Qingdao 266590, China
qingxinsun0329@gmail.com

Abstract. Due to uneven lighting, unknown suspended particle deposition, and rapid movement of cells in seawater, harmful algal bloom (HABs) micro-images collected in real-time marine engineering suffer from a series of issues such as poor clarity, blurred cell contours, and distorted textures. To solve these issues, this paper introduces an image enhancement method, which is based on image blurriness and multi-channel color compensation, and is developed using the Underwater Image Blurriness and Light Absorption approach. Considering the critical role of depth estimation in transmission estimation and image restoration, we first enhance the image by Gaussian blurring and proportionally merging it with the original image to improve edges and details, thus resulting in a sharpened image. Then, we utilize the relative global histogram stretching (RGHS) operation on white-balanced images to enhance image contrast, significantly improving the accuracy of depth and transmission estimation. Furthermore, we estimate the three color channels and use an appropriate transmission map estimation method. For instance, if the red channel is missing, indicating a bias towards cyan and green colors will estimate the missing components using the red channel, ensuring the method remains applicable to other color biases. We incorporate adaptive estimation of image brightness and darkness to achieve a more reasonable distribution of image brightness in image enhancement, avoiding excessively bright or dim results. Through experiments, our method's enhancement of algal cell features surpasses that of other methods.

Keywords: Underwater Image Enhancement · Depth Estimation · Channel-Dependent Compensation · Adaptive Estimation

1 Introduction

With the acceleration of industrialization [1, 2], large amounts of domestic sewage are discharged, leading to increasing pollution in the marine environment [3]. In recent years, the eutrophication of seawater has intensified, resulting in frequent HABs disasters and

H. Lu (Ed.): ISAIR 2024, CCIS 2402, pp. 18–26, 2025.
https://doi.org/10.1007/978-981-96-2911-4_3

posing a severe threat to the marine ecological environment and human health. However, due to uneven lighting [4], unknown suspended particle deposition, and rapid movement of cells in seawater, the acquired micro-images of HABs suffer from color deviations. Consequently, using cell textures and overall unclear images for the identification system may affect the results of algal classification and the accuracy of determining HABs content in the water. Therefore, to solve the identification difficulties caused by image distortion [5], in this paper, we make use of image blurriness and variations in red light absorption to estimate background light (BL), underwater scene depth, and the transmission map (TM), aiming to enhance restoration performance in low-light conditions. During the TM estimation, we enhance the edge features of the input image to make it clearer, thereby improving the reliability of the TM. Finally, we incorporate adaptive estimation of image brightness and darkness adjustment to mitigate overexposure or underexposure in the processed images, ensuring the final image achieves optimal brightness. The proposed method follows the workflow depicted in Fig. 1.

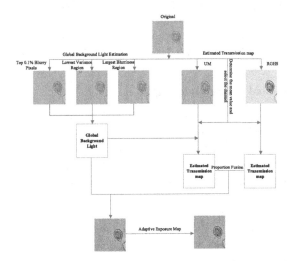

Fig. 1. The flowchart of our channel compensation method.

Our proposed image enhancement model involves the following steps:

i) Estimating the global BL: We utilize the DCP method, and the light blurriness to estimate the atmospheric light intensity. Then, we perform fusion to combine these estimations.

ii) Assessing the color deviation in the input image: If the image contains strong red and orange components, we can use the blue or green channel to estimate the other channel's component image.

iii) Estimating the image TM: We enhance the input image using the RGHS method for color enhancement and the UM method for sharpening to enhance image details. We then estimate TM separately and combine them in a proportional fusion process.

iv) Adaptive estimation of image brightness and darkness: We adjust the image's brightness and contrast to achieve a balanced image.

2 A Method Based on the Prior Dark Channel Scenes, Precise Depth Estimation and Channel-Dependent Compensation.

2.1 Related Work

We propose an underwater enhancement computing approach based on prior dark channel scenes, precise depth estimation, and channel-dependent compensation, providing more accurate transmission and depth estimation. Firstly, we select the BL from the blurry regions of the underwater image. Subsequently, using the BL, we derive the depth map and TM to recover the scene radiance.

The imaging model for underwater image restoration based on the Dark Channel Prior (DCP) can be described as follows [6]:

$$I^c(y) = J^c(y)t^c(y) + B^c\big(1 - t^c(y)\big), c \in \{r, g, b\} \tag{1}$$

In the equation, *y denotes a pixel*, $I(y)$ refers to the original image, $J(y)$ represents the final restored output image, B indicates the background-light, $I(y)\in [0,1]$ signifies the medium TM, which shows the proportion of scene radiance that reaches the camera. The objective of dehazing is to recover $J(y)$, B, and $t(y)$ from the $I(y)$.

2.2 Estimating Global Background Light

In the dark channel, we select the brightest 0.1% of pixels and choose the brightest pixels from three dark channels in the input image I as the BL I. Next, we employ the quadtree splitting method to partition the image into blocks and choose the sub-block with the smallest pixel variance for the next splitting. Finally, the average values of the sub-image blocks obtained after partitioning are considered as the values for the RGB components of the BL II. Then, we proceed with the estimation of image blur. Finally, the image blur estimation is performed, according to Yan-Tsung Peng et al. in [7], and then based on the quad-tree algorithm using the image blurring for stepwise segmentation to obtain the blur-based BL estimation, as the BL III. After determining the three candidate BL, the exact background light B is obtained by identifying the pixels with higher intensity in the image and by generating weights using an S-shaped function [7].

The Image Pre-processing Includes Two Steps: UM and RGHS. We noted that clear images yield superior results for depth maps compared to those that are blurry. As a result, we initially apply the Unsharp Masking (UM) algorithm to improve the edge and detail characteristics of the image. The sharpening operation using the UM method is illustrated in Fig. 2.

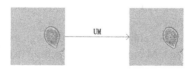

Fig. 2. Unsharp Masking (UM) processing of red tide algal images.

From the above Fig. 2, one can observe a significant improvement in the clarity of the algae images after UM processing. Similarly, we apply the RGHS algorithm for brightness space adjustment and smoothing to reduce noise and clutter in the image. By improving brightness, we enhance the visibility of textures, which ultimately elevates image quality and recognition capabilities, leading to more accurate depth maps. Figure 3 shows a comparison of our method with the IBLA method in terms of channel processing.

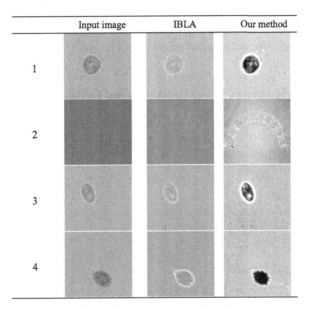

Fig. 3. Comparison of the red channel images.

The processed channel images using our method show enhanced clarity. For instance, in analyzing the red channel image, we examine how the red channel TM, derived from the light transmission characteristics of the red and blue-green channels, influences the final results. The clearness of the red-channel indicates the level of haze present; more distinct details correlate with a precise representation of light intensity. This improved representation in the red-channel leads to a more reliable TM, which also positively affects the blue-green channels' TM and the overall dehazing effect. The total TM is calculated from the depth map, influenced by the red channel TM. A well-defined red-channel yields a precise TM, enhancing the depth map's output. Since the overall TM dictates the extent of the dehazing process and controls the estimation of the transmission rate, the quality of the red channel image is crucial for improving the accuracy and effectiveness of the dehazing algorithm.

TM Estimation. We compute the TM for the images processed with RGHS and UM techniques applied to the original image. By considering light absorption and image blurriness, Then we can use the formula to calculate the TM:

$$t^r(y) = e^{-\beta^r d(y)} \tag{2}$$

where β^r represents the red channel attenuation coefficient $d(y)$the scene depth, $\beta^r \in \left[\frac{1}{8}, \frac{1}{5}\right]$. We set the Optical ranges for red-channel, green-channel, and blue-channel as $\lambda^r = 620$nm, $\lambda^g = 540$nm, and $\lambda^b = 450$nm. We also merge the TM generated by RGHS and UM through a weighted overlay method. Through our tests, we find that the best result is achieved when using a weight ratio of 0.1:0.9.

The above method estimates the green and blue channels based on the red channel, which is suitable when the red channel experiences the most attenuation. However, we also introduce a judgment based on the mean values of the input image's color channels. If there are harmful red tide algae with orange or red components in the image, we can use the blue or green channel to estimate the other channel's components.

2.3 Adaptive Estimation of Image Brightness and Darkness

Following image processing, the dark and bright areas may become too dim or overly illuminated. We enhance the image quality by incorporating the adaptive estimation of image brightness and darkness.

$$OutputExp = J^c(y) * s(y), c \in \{r, g, b\} \tag{3}$$

Here, J^c represents the restored output image, while s(y) denotes the adaptive exposure map.

3 Experimental Results

This chapter outlines the experimental results of our proposed method and offers a comparison with other underwater enhancement techniques based on various image objective metrics, such as image enhancement intensity, contrast, and similarity. The images we used are derived from underwater microscopic images of harmful red tide algae, which play a crucial role in marine ecosystems. These red tide algae often proliferate significantly under specific environmental conditions, thereby impacting the ecological balance of the water body. By analyzing these microscopic images, we can gain deeper insights into the morphological characteristics and growth behaviors of red tide algae, which is vital for studying the ecological health of aquatic environments and implementing appropriate management measures. We deliberately select images exhibiting different levels of clarity, with blurred cell boundaries and distorted textures. This paper uses these images to evaluate the proposed method compared to more advanced enhancement methods.

We apply our enhancement algorithms to three hundred HABs images. Due to space limitations, we present a subset of the images, comparing them with the aforementioned classic and state-of-the-art methods, as shown in Fig. 5.

Based on the six algal images shown in Fig. 4, it is evident that the enhancement technique we employed results in processed images with significantly clearer contrast. This improved contrast not only highlights the detailed features of the algal cells but also enhances the overall visual effect, making it easier for observers to identify and analyze the morphology and structure of these tiny organisms.

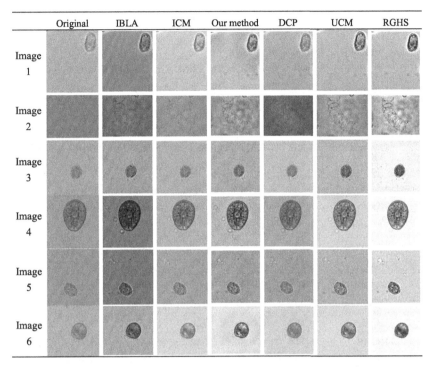

Fig. 4. Experimental results of image enhancement on other algae images.

This paper introduces objective evaluation metrics for image enhancement, including Enhanced Measurement of Enhancement (EME), Edge-based Measurement of Enhancement (EMEE), Mean Structural Similarity Index (MSSIM), Mean Squared Error (MSE), Image Entropy, Contrast, and Image Clarity Gradient. Using these parameters for performance evaluation, an increase in EME and EMEE indicates better image enhancement quality, while a smaller MSE value indicates a lower error between the two images. Values of Entropy, Contrast, and Gradient should also increase to enhance image details and achieve better underwater image quality.

The objective evaluation metric data are presented in Table 1, with the best-performing data highlighted. In all the metrics of image enhancement, our method is improved in comparison with the original image. These results are attributed to the use of UM and RGHS for pre-processing the images, resulting in a more accurate estimation of the depth map and the fusion of TM. This approach effectively preserves the details of the red tide algae while maintaining proximity to the original image. It also enhances image quality, making the structure clear and easy to recognize, leading to better performance in objective evaluation metrics such as EME, EMEE, and MSSIM. Furthermore, the optimization provided by the adaptive estimation of image brightness and darkness improves the brightness structure of the image, resulting in better contrast, image entropy, and image clarity gradient.

Table 1. Evaluation metrics

Image	Method	Quantitative analysis					
		EME	EMEE	MSSIM	Entropy	Contrast	Gradient
Image 1	Original	0.706	0.338	-	3.120	1.919	1.01
	IBLA	2.586	0.441	0.950	4.650	9.670	2.617
	ICM	1.260	0.369	**0.983**	3.837	5.770	1.689
	Our method	**3.832**	**0.511**	0.853	**5.563**	20.190	**4.483**
	DCP	1.722	0.394	0.961	4.582	6.063	2.448
	UCM	2.863	0.457	0.923	4.876	16.025	3.212
	RGHS	3.693	0.504	0.854	5.379	**26.357**	4.472
Image 2	Original	1.1962	1.1962	-	3.813	3.593	1.405
	IBLA	6.140	0.639	0.828	5.777	43.209	5.192
	ICM	1.932	0.405	**0.975**	4.583	10.047	2.378
	Our method	**7.157**	**0.738**	0.664	**6.909**	69.013	**8.834**
	DCP	5.058	0.577	0.876	5.840	23.633	4.158
	UCM	6.162	0.640	0.728	6.199	73.038	6.857
	RGHS	6.914	0.708	0.542	6.844	**163.712**	7.902
Image 3	Original	0.783	0.342	-	2.985	2.764	0.913
	IBLA	2.468	0.434	0.917	4.682	16.175	2.708
	ICM	1.121	0.361	**0.993**	3.436	4.889	1.250
	Our method	**3.048**	**0.495**	0.898	**5.100**	12.294	3.007
	DCP	1.365	0.374	0.962	4.430	6.166	1.885
	UCM	2.577	0.440	0.906	4.759	18.403	2.942
	RGHS	2.650	0.467	0.823	4.986	**26.892**	**3.911**
Image 4	Original	2.360	0.429	-	4.207	7.050	1.781
	IBLA	8.311	0.756	0.858	5.842	25.449	3.962
	ICM	3.422	0.489	**0.985**	4.594	12.682	2.396
	Our method	**8.365**	**0.769**	0.853	**5.960**	**36.269**	**4.833**
	DCP	3.076	0.469	0.980	5.030	9.865	2.404
	UCM	4.335	0.539	0.980	5.038	22.080	3.181
	RGHS	5.201	0.590	0.921	4.832	30.183	3.364
Image 5	Original	0.989	0.354	-	3.132	3.405	1.021
	IBLA	3.877	0.514	0.887	4.947	16.197	3.036
	ICM	1.375	0.376	**0.994**	3.437	5.775	1.280

(*continued*)

Table 1. (*continued*)

Image	Method	Quantitative analysis					
		EME	EMEE	MSSIM	Entropy	Contrast	Gradient
	Our method	**3.258**	**0.483**	0.864	**5.204**	15.542	3.546
	DCP	1.721	0.394	0.968	4.341	6.210	1.917
	UCM	1.927	0.404	0.959	4.256	12.402	2.109
	RGHS	3.122	0.479	0.842	5.184	**25.825**	**3.721**
Image 6	Original	0.777	0.777	-	2.956	2.098	0.956
	IBLA	3.222	0.473	0.878	5.095	17.557	3.610
	ICM	1.440	0.379	**0.979**	3.781	6.092	1.681
	Our method	**3.631**	**0.506**	0.902	4.751	**18.968**	**2.646**
	DCP	1.725	0.394	0.949	4.644	6.971	2.540
	UCM	2.004	0.409	0.945	4.303	11.638	2.366
	RGHS	3.071	0.470	0.881	**4.927**	16.684	2.472

4 Conclusion

This paper proposes a method for enhancing the detailed features of microscopic images. The proposed enhancement technique relies on image blurring and light absorption, incorporating RGHS, UM, and background color estimation. Furthermore, adaptive estimation of image brightness and darkness correction is applied to enhance the overall image quality. By using RGHS and UM, the finer details of the image are emphasized, which leads to more accurate depth map estimation and improved image enhancement. Experimental results indicate that our approach surpasses other advanced methods in terms of objective metrics, such as detail preservation, contrast, and clarity.

References

1. Lu, H., Guizani, M., Ho, P.H.: Editorial introduction to responsible artificial intelligence for autonomous driving. IEEE Trans. Intell. Transp. Syst. **23**(12), 25212–25215 (2022)
2. Lu, H., Zhang, Y., Li, Y., et al.: User-oriented virtual mobile network resource management for vehicle communications. IEEE Trans. Intell. Transp. Syst. **22**(6), 3521–3532 (2020)
3. Wu, G.K., Xu, J., Zhang, Y.D., et al.: Underwater enhancement computing of ocean HABs based on cyclic color compensation and multi-scale fusion. Multimedia Tools and Applications, pp. 1–25 (2023)
4. Lu, H., Li, Y., Uemura, T., et al.: Low illumination underwater light field images reconstruction using deep convolutional neural networks. Futur. Gener. Comput. Syst. **82**, 142–148 (2018)
5. Lu, H., Zhang, M., Xu, X., et al.: Deep fuzzy hashing network for efficient image retrieval. IEEE Trans. Fuzzy Syst. **29**(1), 166–176 (2020)

6. Narasimhan, S.G., Nayar, S.K.: Chromatic framework for vision in bad weather. In: Proceedings IEEE Conference on Computer Vision and Pattern Recognition. CVPR 2000 (Cat. No. PR00662). IEEE, **1**, pp. 598–605 (2000)
7. Peng, Y.T., Zhao, X., Cosman, P.C.: Single underwater image enhancement using depth estimation based on blurriness. In: 2015 IEEE International Conference on Image Processing (ICIP). IEEE, pp. 4952–4956 (2015)

Semi-supervised Learning-Based Passive Visible Light Positioning Using Solar Irradiation

Tian Wen[1], Gaofei Sun[2(✉)], Miaomiao Zhu[2(✉)], and Lifeng Zhang[1(✉)]

[1] Kyushu Institute of Technology, Kitakyushu, Japan
wen.tian843@mail.kyutech.jp, zhang@elcs.lyutech.ac.jp
[2] Changshu Institute of Technology, Suzhou, China
{gfsun,zhumm}@cslg.edu.cn

Abstract. With the advent of passive methods, the scope of applications for visible light positioning (VLP) systems has expanded. However, the diverse light sources present in various rooms necessitate improvements to ensure consistent deployment of passive VLP (PVLP) technology. In this paper, we propose an approach to passive VLP based on solar irradiation, which incorporates a preprocessing algorithm and a semi-supervised positioning model. The algorithm refines the Hilbert transform envelope using a dual threshold, taking into consideration both weather conditions and human activity patterns. The model employs supervised learning for solar irradiance in one room, while unsupervised learning enhances it in another. The experiments were conducted in two buildings with similar lighting conditions. The results demonstrate that our model effectively mitigates environmental and activity-related noise, achieving a mean of 86% positioning accuracy. Furthermore, the experiments indicate precise positioning in different rooms with a margin of error below 14.9 cm and maintain a pre-labeling accuracy of 84%.

Keywords: Passive Visible Light · Indoor Positioning · Solar Irradiation · Semi-supervised Learning · Internet of Things

1 Introduction

The emergence of the Internet of Things (IoT) has significantly propelled the growth of the sensor market. Forecasts predict an increase from USD 69.2 billion in 2020 to USD 236 billion by 2025 [1]. Sensor location technology is crucial in enabling a wide range of applications for IoT devices [19, 20], such as in the realm of indoor robotics. The primary conventional indoor localization techniques include Wi-Fi [2], Wireless Radio Frequency [3], and Ultra-wideband [4]. Notably, these methods demonstrate superior positioning accuracy compared to the Global Positioning System (GPS) in various settings, though they are associated with higher costs [5]. Furthermore, Visible Light Positioning (VLP) has emerged as a significant area of research due to the widespread presence of active lighting [6]. Despite its popularity, VLP faces challenges including the need for infrastructure modifications, user inconveniences, and inherent complexity [7]. A novel branch within VLP research focuses on utilizing passive light sources,

H. Lu (Ed.): ISAIR 2024, CCIS 2402, pp. 27–34, 2025.
https://doi.org/10.1007/978-981-96-2911-4_4

such as natural sunlight and engineered illumination, to convey location information. This approach offers advantages in terms of device compatibility, energy efficiency, and security, owing to its reliance on passive light sources.

In their research within the Passive Visible Light Positioning (PVLP) field, Singh et al. [8] made notable contributions. The Smartwall system, a 2D localization framework, utilizes extensive fingerprinting techniques and has been tested over an area of 3.4 by 2.2 m, achieving an accuracy of 7.9 cm [9]. Fieldlight, another 2D localization system, operates under the assumption of a constant background ambient light above Photodiodes (PDs). This system's testbed covered 4.8 by 9.6 m, yielding an accuracy of 68 cm [10]. These methods predominantly rely on Received Signal Strength (RSS). However, the long-term reliability and stability of RSS-based data remain significant concerns [11]. It is important to note the potential application of sunlight, a form of passive light, in PVLP systems. Solar Irradiation (SI) demonstrates robust signal strength, minimizing the impact of minor interferences. The positioning capabilities utilizing SI have been explored to a lesser extent. Botero-Valencia et al. [12] implemented nine light sensors to ascertain sensor positioning, while Lee et al. [13] employed a light sensor atop a building, utilizing an SI diffuse model for indoor positioning. Recent advancements have seen the integration of Machine Learning models to enhance the robustness of PVLP systems [17, 18]. This involves encoding light based on intensity levels and analyzing the encoded data through frequency and time domain methods [14]. Consequently, features representing location are extracted based on light performance, and a Machine Learning model is applied to adapt the system for use in different rooms. Semi-supervised models have shown to be particularly effective in these scenarios [15]. The process includes preparing data, where unlabeled data are automatically categorized using initially labeled data and a Machine Learning model.

In our proposed method, we address indoor environmental challenges, including obstacles and RSS signal interference, as noted in [11]. We combine supervised and unsupervised learning into a Semi-supervised algorithm. The outdoor SI data noise filter algorithm from [12] is adapted for indoor use. Ye et al. [16] inspire our approach to use peak values for location inference and pre-label data with unsupervised learning, specifically the Restricted Boltzmann Machine (RBM). Our aim is to refine this approach, incorporating more features [18] for a robust Semi-supervised model applicable in various indoor settings.

2 Passive Visible Light Positioning

In this paper, we designed and tested a novel SI-based PVLP system in a realistic indoor scenario, where position estimates were obtained using a semi-supervised learning framework, as depicted in Fig. 1. The room was assumed to be a 2D plane. The position of the object is denoted as $A_{x,y}$, where x represents the horizontal coordinate and y represents the vertical coordinate. The sensor value is denoted as $A_{x,y}^T = V$, where T denotes the timestamp, and V represents the SI intensity. At a specific time point n, the sensor value is denoted as $A_{x,y}^n = v_n$.

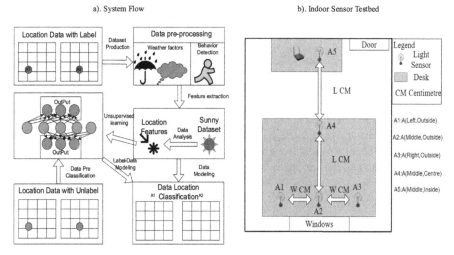

Fig. 1. Overview of system architecture.

2.1 Data Pre-processing

Weather conditions cause high frequencies in the signal. We followed the Botero-Valencia et al. [12] using the Hilbert transform envelope algorithm to extract the peak value and filtered the weather noise. In addition, we noted that indoor human significantly affect the correctness of the collected light, causing the light value to drop. The pattern is formed in Eq. (1),

$$\zeta = \frac{A_{x,y}^c}{A_{x,y}^{c+1}} \tag{1}$$

where ζ represents the rate of change and c represents the timestamp. Furthermore, the curve trend reflects the drop and the rise. The curve trend change during the human activities is formed as,

$$\delta = \frac{A_{x,y}^{c+1} - A_{x,y}^c}{(c+1) - c} \tag{2}$$

where δ represents the slope. It is worth noting that, $\zeta_{drop}in\ (0,1)$ when dropping, and $\zeta_{rise}\ in\ (1, \infty)$ when rising; $\delta_{drop}in(-\infty, 0)$, and $\delta_{rise}in(0, \infty)$; $|\delta_{rise} * \zeta_{rise}| \in (0, \infty)$; $\left|\frac{\delta_{drop}}{\zeta_{drop}}\right| \in (0, \infty)$. Therefore, the human behavior recognition obtained by Eq. (3),

$$\gamma = |\delta_{rise} * \zeta_{rise}| + \left|\frac{\delta_{drop}}{\zeta_{drop}}\right| \tag{3}$$

where *drop* means the timestamp of drop value and *rise* means the rise. It is a double threshold algorithm based on the rate of change and the slope to amplify the change.

2.2 Feature Extraction

SI intensity is treated similarly to signal intensity in localization models. For horizontal and vertical sensor deployment, the time to peak value, as shown in Fig. 2, is used as a feature. Additionally, it was observed that both the mean and variance of the values vary with position. To describe the problem, we formed the equation as follows:

$$A_{x,y}^d = \{p_d, m_d, s_d, t_d\} \tag{4}$$

where p_d represents the peak value in a day, and d represent the date; m_d represents the mean value in a day; s_d represents the variance value in a day; and t_d represents the maximum time value. The correlation between light and sensor position is summarized as follows: the data at $A_{(Outside,Middle,Inside,y)}$ are expressed in variations p_d, m_d, s_d, and t_d, respectively. Then, we use the coefficient of variation (C) to measure the relationship between the mean and the variance.

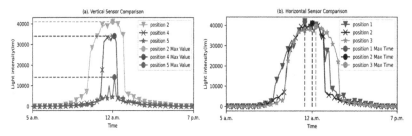

Fig. 2. Vertical and horizontal position light data display.

3   Semi-supervised Learning

3.1   Positioning Model Construction

After expressing the relationship between position and light, linear fitting was used to obtain the relationship between eigenvalues and positions [14]. We derived Eq. (5) based on the relationship,

$$A_{x,y}^d = \begin{cases} x = k_1 * t_d \\ y = p_d * k_2 + C_d * k_3 \end{cases} \tag{5}$$

where x represents the horizontal position and y represents the vertical position. k_1 is the parameter, with the solution obtained by Eq. (6),

$$\lim_{i \to n} |L_x| = \frac{1}{2} \sum_{i=1}^{n} (x - x_i)^2 \tag{6}$$

$$\lim_{i \to n} |L_y| = \frac{1}{2} \sum_{i=1}^{n} \left(\frac{(y - y_i)^2}{\partial C_d} - \frac{(y - y_i)^2}{\partial p_d} \right)$$

where x_i and y_i represent the ground truth, and L represent the L2 norm loss function.

3.2 Restricted Boltzmann Machine

The input data corresponds to the "Visible layer" of the RBM and the feature values to the "Hidden layer". The parameters (v, h) for the "Visible layer" and "Hidden layer", and RBM has the following energy equation,

$$E(v, h) = -\sum_{i\in visible} a_i v_i - \sum_{j\in hidden} b_j h_j - \sum_{i,j} v_i h_j w_{ij} \tag{7}$$

where v_i and h_j represent visible and hidden layer units with binary data types. a_i and b_j represent data biases of the visible and hidden layers, and $w_i j$ represents data weights connecting the visible and hidden layers.

The network assigns a probability to each possible pair of visible and hidden vectors by the energy function in the Eq. (8),

$$p(v, h) = \frac{1}{Z} e^{-E(v,h)}. \tag{8}$$

According to Eq. (4), three feature values were chosen. We prefer the output h_j and input v_i of the network for a single feature in the x-direction to be $v_i in [Left, Middle, Right]$, $and h_j in [p(Left), p(Middle), p(Right)]$. The output h_j and input v_i of the network for two features in the y-direction are $v_i in [C_v^p, t_d]$, $and h_j in [p(C_v^p), p(t_d)]$. From Eq. (7) and (8), the conclusion is drawn that the input of actual value and the output of probability type. However, the RBM only accepts binary input and output.

Therefore, the input data need to be transformed into a smaller range of discrete data, and the probability distribution of each category is mapped on the basis of the binarized output. Then, the input data v_i needs standardized,

$$E(v, h)! = -\sum_{i\in visible} a_i \frac{v_i - \mu}{\sigma} - \sum_{j\in hidden} b_j h_j - \sum_{i,j} \frac{v_i - \mu}{\sigma} h_j w_{ij} \tag{9}$$

where μ is the mean value of the data set and σ is the standard deviation of the data set. Hence, Eqs. (9) were the solution for the model.

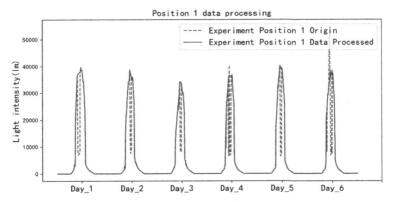

Fig. 3. Data preprocessing on filtering the effect of human behavior on light and data recovery.

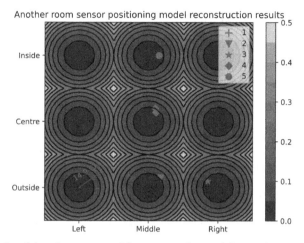

Fig. 4. The results of the other room model reconstruction, and the maximum error of the linear model.

Table 1. Comparison of RSS-based indoor positioning methods using

Framework Comparison	$\frac{Precision(cm)}{RoomSize(m^2)}$	Need other source	Portability
[10]	1.05	✓	✗
[11]	1.47	✗	✗
Ours	1.5	✗	✓

4 Experiment Verifications

The framework proposed above was validated in this section. The data set represents the office in the Changshu Institute of Technology building. The arrangement of the light sensors is shown in Fig. 1. The sensors collected light data at a frequency of 1 time every 10 min. Data from 180 days were selected.

4.1 Data Pre-processing and Positoning Model Verifications

We filtered the complex weather by Hilbert transform envelope. Then, the noise of human behavior was detected by Eq. (3), as shown in Fig. 3. The detected time nodes and data were eliminated, and the missing values were filled by the median insertion algorithm.

Secondly, we constructed a localization linear model using three feature values. The X orientation model was tested, and the result accuracy is 91%. The accuracy of the equation for the Y orientation was derived by extracting the p_d and the C_d, and the result accuracy is 82%.

4.2 Semi-supervised Learing Verifications

The first RBM model was used to pre-label in the x-direction of the room. The network fit when the number of iterations is 1500 and the learning rate is 0.6. The pre-labeled correct rate is 84%. The second RBM model was used to test the sensors in the y-direction of the room. The network fit when the number of iterations is 1500 and the learning rate is 0.6. The pre-labeled results were compared with the actual results, and the correct rate is 88%.

Sensor data in the N6 academic building of Changshu Institute of Technology was chosen as the test set for model reconstruction, in which the room size is 5 m * 10 m. The data were pre-labeled with the same parameters. As shown in Fig. 4, model error is within 14.9 cm. We achieved the best performance compared to previous studies, as shown in Table 1. The experiment shows that our framework makes the positioning model feasible in another room, providing a new approach to portable indoor positioning.

5 Conclusion

This paper introduces a portable PVLP framework, utilizing passive visible light features to develop a centimeter-level accurate localization model. The proposed algorithm filters weather noise, restores SI, and opens new avenues in visible light localization through pre-processing and feature extraction. Employing semi-supervised learning, the model achieves the mean of 86% accuracy with a location error within 14.9 cm. The model effectively filters indoor human activity noise, showing practical feasibility. It also demonstrates expanded applicability in different rooms. Compared to similar studies, our framework performs best, and future work will focus on developing a 3D PVLP framework with movable sensors.

References

1. Farahsari, P.S., Farahzadi, A., Rezazadeh, J., Bagheri, A.: A survey on indoor positioning systems for IoT-based applications. J. IEEE Internet of Things J. **147**, 7680–7699 (2022). https://doi.org/10.1109/JIOT.2022.3149048
2. Zhu, X., Qu, W., Qiu, T., Zhao, L., Atiquzzaman, M., Wu, D.O.: Indoor intelligent fingerprint-based localization: Principles, approaches and challenges. J. IEEE Communications Surveys Tutorials. **22**, 2634–2657 (2020). https://doi.org/10.1109/COMST.2020.3014304
3. Alam, F., Faulkner, N., Parr, B.: Device-free localization: a review of non-RF techniques for unobtrusive indoor positioning. J. IEEE Internet of Things J. **8**, 4228–4249 (2020). https://doi.org/10.1109/JIOT.2020.3030174
4. Mohanty, S., Tripathy, A., Das, B.: An overview of a low energy UWB localization in IoT based system. In: 2021 International Symposium of Asian Control Association on Intelligent Robotics and Industrial Automation (IRIA), pp. 293–296. IEEE, India (2021). https://doi.org/10.1109/IRIA53009.2021.9588718
5. Chen, P., Pang, M., Che, D., et al.: A survey on visible light positioning from software algorithms to hardware. J. Wireless Communications and Mobile Comput. **2021**, 1–20 (2021). https://doi.org/10.1155/2021/9739577
6. Almadani, Y., Plets, D., Bastiaens, S., et al.: Visible light communications for industrial applications—challenges and potentials. J. Electronics. **9**(12), 2157 (2020)

7. Zhuang, Y., Hua, L., Qi, L., et al.: A survey of positioning systems using visible LED lights. J. IEEE Communications Surveys Tutorials **20**(3), 1963–1988 (2018). https://doi.org/10.1109/COMST.2018.2806558

8. Singh, J., Raza, U.: Passive visible light positioning systems: an overview. In: Proceedings of the Workshop on Light Up the IoT, pp. 48–53. ACM (2020)

9. Faulkner, N., Alam, F., Legg, M., et al.: Smart wall: passive visible light positioning with ambient light only. In: 2019 IEEE International Instrumentation and Measurement Technology Conference (I2MTC). pp. 1–6. IEEE, New Zealand (2019)

10. Konings, D., Faulkner, N., Alam, F., et al.: FieldLight: device-free indoor human localization using passive visible light positioning and artificial potential fields. J. IEEE Sensors J. **20**(2), 1054–1066 (2019). https://doi.org/10.1109/JSEN.2019.2944178

11. Tran, H.Q., Ha, C.: Machine learning in indoor visible light positioning systems: a review. J. Neurocomputing **491**, 117–131 (2022). https://doi.org/10.1016/j.neucom.2021.10.123

12. Botero-Valencia, J.S., Valencia-Aguirre, J., Gonzalez-Montoya, D., et al.: A low-cost system for real-time measuring of the sunlight incident angle using IoT. J. HardwareX **11**, e00272 (2022). https://doi.org/10.1016/j.ohx.2022.e00272

13. Lee, D.S., Jo, J.H.: Application of simple sky and building models for the evaluation of solar irradiance distribution at indoor locations in buildings. J. Building and Environment. **197**, 107840 (2021). https://doi.org/10.1016/j.buildenv.2021.107840

14. Torres-Sospedra, J., Huerta, J.: A meta-review of indoor positioning systems. J. Sensors. **19**(20), 4507 (2019)

15. Qian, W., Lauri, F., Gechter, F.: Supervised and semi-supervised deep probabilistic models for indoor positioning problems. J. Neurocomputing **435**, 228–238 (2021). https://doi.org/10.1016/j.neucom.2020.12.131

16. Ye, H., Sheng, L., Gu, T., et al.: Seloc: collect your location data using only a barometer sensor. J. IEEE Access. **7**, 88705–88717 (2019). https://doi.org/10.1109/ACCESS.2019.2925460

17. Lu, H., Wang, T., Xu, X., et al.: Cognitive memory-guided autoencoder for effective intrusion detection in internet of things. J. IEEE Trans. Industrial Informatics **18**(5), 3358–3366 (2021). https://doi.org/10.1109/TII.2021.3102637

18. Zheng, Q., Zhu, J., Tang, H., et al.: Generalized label enhancement with sample correlations. J. IEEE Transactions on Knowledge and Data Engineering **35**(1), 482–495 (2021). https://doi.org/10.1109/TKDE.2021.3073157

19. Lou, R., Wang, W., Li, X., et al.: Prediction of ocean wave height suitable for ship autopilot. J. IEEE Transactions on Intelligent Transportation Systems **23**(12), 25557–25566 (2021). https://doi.org/10.1109/TITS.2021.3067040

20. Li, Y., Zhu, X., Zheng, Y., et al.: Underwater visibility enhancement iot system in extreme environment. J. IEEE Internet of Things J. (2023). https://doi.org/10.1109/ACCESS.2022.3150093

Multi-Teacher Knowledge Distillation via Student's Reflection

Xin Cheng[1], Jinjia Zhou[1(✉)], and Wei Weng[2]

[1] Hosei University, Koganei-Shi, Tokyo, Japan
zhou@hosei.ac.jp
[2] Kanazawa University, Kanazawa City, Japan

Abstract. Multi-teacher knowledge distillation utilizes diverse information from multiple teacher models to guide the student model's training. Traditional methods of knowledge distillation in multi-teacher scenarios typically follow a one-way approach, where teachers pass on their knowledge, compelling the student to replicate their output predictions. However, the student's reflective process is an essential element of human learning in real-world scenarios. In this paper, we propose multi-teacher knowledge distillation with student's reflection (MKD-SD), which integrates self-distillation to promote the student's reflective learning process. Additionally, to further enhance the student network's performance, we apply a decoupled knowledge distillation technique, which breaks down the standard loss function into two independent components. To maintain stability during training, we use intermediate layer features as the transferred knowledge. The effectiveness of MKD-SD was rigorously assessed using the CIFAR-100 benchmark. For example, the ShuffleNetV2 model trained with MKD-SD achieved a top-1 accuracy of 77.86% when a pretrained WideResNet40–2 model was used as the teacher, marking an absolute improvement of 4.97% compared to the model trained independently. Moreover, it consistently surpasses all existing state-of-the-art methods across different teacher-student model combinations.

Keywords: Knowledge Distillation · Self-Distillation · Multiple Teachers · Image Classification · Model Compression

1 Introduction

Over the past few years, deep neural networks [8, 11, 20] have made significant strides in various visual tasks such as image classification, object detection, and semantic segmentation. As performance continues to improve, model designs are experiencing an exponential increase in the number of parameters. For example, AlexNet [6] contains eight weight layers and six convolutional layers, totaling about 60 million parameters. VGG13 [13], which has 13 convolutional and fully connected layers, boasts around 138 million parameters. In contrast, ViT-Large [1] contains billions of parameters or even more. Deploying these complex models on edge devices with limited resources and computing power presents considerable challenges. To address this issue, researchers have extensively explored model compression techniques, including network pruning,

H. Lu (Ed.): ISAIR 2024, CCIS 2402, pp. 35–43, 2025.
https://doi.org/10.1007/978-981-96-2911-4_5

parameter quantization, low-rank decomposition, and knowledge distillation. Of these techniques, knowledge distillation has garnered widespread attention due to its simplicity and high efficiency. The primary objective of knowledge distillation is to transfer knowledge from a large, cumbersome teacher model to a more lightweight student model, ensuring that the student achieves similar generalization capabilities as the teacher.

Inspired by the notion that "The collective wisdom of a group exceeds that of even the most intelligent individual," a significant body of research has investigated the use of multi-teacher knowledge distillation to improve student model performance. Various approaches [3, 14] have been introduced to tackle the issue of assigning equal weights to all teachers, thereby overlooking the importance of diverse teacher contributions. Several methods have been developed to more effectively integrate multi-teacher knowledge. For instance, EBKD [7] assigns weights to teachers based on the information entropy of their predicted logits. AMTML-KD [10] calculates the importance of teachers using their latent factors. AEKD [2] delves into the diversity of multiple teachers by analyzing their gradient space. CA-MKD [16] differentiates the significance of each teacher by measuring the confidence of their predictions through the cross-entropy between the prediction logits and ground-truth labels. However, previous methods have primarily focused on a one-way teaching process from teachers to students, without considering a reflective phase for the student itself.

In this paper, we propose a novel method named multi-teacher knowledge distillation via student's reflection (MKD-SD). Unlike traditional approaches, our method integrates self-supervision, allowing the student model to review and refine the knowledge it has learned, thereby enhancing its performance. Additionally, DKD [19] demonstrates the coupling of traditional knowledge distillation loss functions, and we adopt similar techniques to further improve the network's performance. To ensure training stability, we also use intermediate layer features as distilled knowledge. Comprehensive experiments reveal that our proposed method consistently outperforms comparable state-of-the-art techniques. Our contributions are as follows:

- We introduce a novel multi-teacher knowledge distillation framework that incorporates both the traditional teaching stages from the teachers and a student reflection stage for further knowledge refinement.
- To enhance the student model's performance, we apply a decoupled distillation technique. Furthermore, we utilize distilled intermediate feature knowledge to ensure training stability.
- Extensive experiments on the CIFAR-100 benchmark validate the effectiveness of our proposed method, consistently showing improvements over state-of-the-art techniques across various teacher-student model pairs.

2   Related Work

Multi-teacher Knowledge Distillation (MKD) The MKD technique utilizes the diverse knowledge provided by multiple teachers to train a lightweight student model, aiming to enable the student to perform on par with its teachers. Several approaches have been developed to incorporate the knowledge from multiple teachers [3, 14]. However, these methods treat all teachers equally, assigning uniform weights without considering the varying importance of each teacher. To overcome this limitation, various techniques have been proposed. For instance, EBKD [7] assigns weights to teachers based on the information entropy of their predicted logits, while AMTML-KD [10] calculates teacher importance using latent factors. AEKD [2] investigates teacher diversity by analyzing the gradient space, and CA-MKD [16] differentiates teacher importance by assessing prediction confidence through cross-entropy between prediction logits and ground-truth labels. MMKD [17] employs a meta-weight network to integrate the output predictions and features from multiple teachers. However, none of these methods account for the student's reflection stage.

Self Knowledge Distillation (SDK). Unlike traditional knowledge distillation, which involves transferring knowledge between networks by requiring the student network to mimic the output predictions of a pre-trained teacher, self-knowledge distillation (SKD) distills knowledge within the network itself. The first work on SKD can be traced back to Born Again Neural Networks (BAN) [4], which introduced a serial-distillation process where teachers with the same architecture guide students, who in turn guide sub-students. The final output is produced by averaging the predictions of all students. Similarly, BYOT [18] introduced a multi-exit neural network architecture, where the final output is used to update the shallow layers. Moreover, prior studies [9, 15] have further improved the performance of SKD by utilizing more advanced regularization techniques.

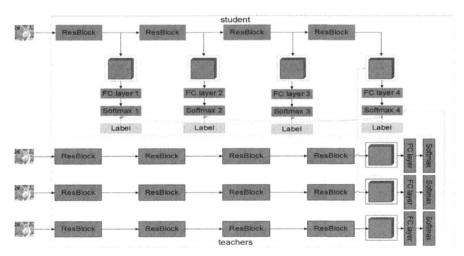

Fig. 1: An overview of our MKD-SD. The yellow curve depicts the student's self-reflection stage, while the green lines and blue lines illustrate the multi-teacher knowledge distillation, with green representing knowledge distillation based on features and blue corresponding to distillation based on logits.

3 Method

In this section, we present our proposed multi-teacher knowledge distillation framework, as shown in Fig. 1. The framework is primarily composed of three stages: the multi-teacher teaching stage, the ground-truth label learning stage, and the student self-reflection learning stage.

3.1 The Multi-Teacher Teaching

Knowledge distillation (KD) is a method for transferring knowledge from a complex teacher model to a simpler, lightweight student model by minimizing the Kullback-Leibler (KL) divergence between their softened output predictions [5]. Building on the ideas presented in DKD [19], we propose a multi-teacher loss function based on logits, defined as follows:

$$L_{KD} = \frac{1}{K} \sum_{i=1}^{K} (aTCKD + bNCKD). \tag{1}$$

The first component of our framework, termed target class knowledge distillation (TCKD), transfers knowledge regarding the "difficulty" of training samples and reflects the similarity in the target class prediction distributions between the student and teacher models. The second component, known as non-target class knowledge distillation (NCKD), focuses on the non-target classes and captures the similarity between the predictions made by the teacher and the student for these classes. As a result, the distillation loss function is reformulated as follows. For detailed derivations, please refer to DKD [19], as space is limited. The importance of TCKD and NCKD can be balanced by adjusting the weights a and b, while K denotes the number of teachers.

Features play a crucial role in representation learning. FitNets [12] have demonstrated, through experimental validation, that utilizing features from the teacher's hidden layers as transferred knowledge can enhance the performance of the student model in knowledge distillation. Feature distillation enables the student to replicate the intermediate features of the teacher. For the sake of simplicity, our method employs the L2 loss function directly.

$$L_{inter} = \frac{1}{K} \sum_{i=1}^{K} ||F_{T_k} - r(F_s)||_2^2. \tag{2}$$

The function $r(\cdot)$ is employed to align the dimensions of student and teacher features, $F \in R^{c \times h \times w}$ is the feature of a convolutional layer. Furthermore, to minimize computational requirements, we utilize only the features from the last convolutional layer as the distilled knowledge.

3.2 Student's Self-Reflection Learning

In the real-world teaching process, students not only benefit from direct instruction by teachers but also need to engage in reflection to better assimilate the knowledge they have acquired. In our study, we implement self-distillation to enhance the students' reflective learning processes. Specifically, we partition the student network into multiple sections; for instance, we divide the ResNet50 into four segments based on its residual blocks. Each segment is linked to a classifier comprising a bottleneck layer and a fully connected layer. These branches are utilized solely during training and can be eliminated during inference, ensuring that the model's prediction time remains unaffected.

To further improve the student model's performance via self-reflection, we introduce two distinct loss functions. The first loss is the Kullback-Leibler (KL) divergence calculated between the output predictions of each branch and those of the student. The formula for this loss is as follows:

$$L_{sd\_kd} = \sum_{i=1}^{B} KL(P_i^{\tau} || P_s^{\tau}) \quad (3)$$

where B represents the number of sections of the network divided. P_i^{τ} and P_s^{τ} denote the probability distribution of the output predictions of the i-th branch and those of the student model output predictions with temperature τ, respectively.

The second loss measures the discrepancy between the branches' outputs and the ground-truth labels. This loss encourages students to engage in reflective learning based on accurate predictions, thereby preventing erroneous reflective operations. The calculation for this loss is as follows:

$$L_{sd\_ce} = \sum_{i=1}^{B} CE(P_i, Y) \quad (4)$$

Thus, we summarize the total losses associated with the students' self-reflection as follows:

$$L_{SD} = L_{sd\_ce} + \lambda L_{sd\_kd} \quad (5)$$

factor λ balances the two losses.

3.3 The Overall Loss

In addition to the aforementioned losses, a regular cross-entropy loss LCE between the ground-truth labels and student predictions is calculated. The overall loss function of the proposed MKD-SD is given as:

$$L_{overall} = \gamma L_{CE} + \alpha L_{KD} + \beta L_{inter} + \zeta L_{SD}, \quad (6)$$

Here, α, β, γ, and ζ are hyperparameters that balance the effects of each loss.

4 Experiments

4.1 Datasets and Implementation Details

Datasets. We perform comprehensive experiments using the CIFAR-100 dataset for image classification. This dataset consists of 32×32 pixel images across 100 categories, with the training set containing 50,000 images and the validation set comprising 10,000 images.

Table 1. Top-1 test accuracy (%) of different multi-teacher knowledge distillation methods applied to CIFAR-100, with teachers sharing the same architecture.

Teacher	WRN40-2 79.62 ± 0.17	ResNet56 73.19 ± 0.30	VGG13 74.89 ± 0.18	ResNet32x4 79.45 ± 0.19	ResNet32x4 79.45 ± 0.19
Student	ShuffleNetV2 73.07 ± 0.06	MobileNetV2 65.46 ± 0.10	MobileNetV2 65.46 ± 0.10	ShuffleNetV1 71.58 ± 0.30	VGG8 70.70 ± 0.26
AVER-KD [5]	76.98 ± 0.19	70.68 ± 0.11	68.89 ± 0.10	75.02 ± 0.25	73.51 ± 0.22
AVER-FitNet [12]	77.29 ± 0.14	70.63 ± 0.23	68.87 ± 0.06	74.75 ± 0.27	73.00 ± 0.16
AEKD [2]	77.02 ± 0.17	70.36 ± 0.19	69.07 ± 0.22	75.11 ± 0.19	73.21 ± 0.04
EBKD [7]	76.75 ± 0.13	69.89 ± 0.14	68.09 ± 0.26	74.95 ± 0.14	73.01 ± 0.01
CA-MKD [16]	77.64 ± 0.19	71.19 ± 0.28	69.29 ± 0.09	76.37 ± 0.51	75.02 ± 0.12
MKD-SD (Ours)	**77.86 ± 0.21**	**71.54 ± 0.12**	**70.23 ± 0.12**	**77.24 ± 0.14**	**75.29 ± 0.22**

Implementation Details. Our implementation closely follows the approach described in [16]. Specifically, we train all models for 240 epochs with a batch size of 64, utilizing Stochastic Gradient Descent (SGD) with a momentum of 0.9 and a weight decay of 0.0001. The initial learning rate is set to 0.05 (0.01 for ShuffleNet and MobileNet), which is reduced by a factor of 10 at epochs 150, 180, and 210. We conduct experiments with various representative CNN networks: VGG, ResNet, WideResNet, MobileNet, and ShuffleNet. For the sake of fairness, the temperature (τ) is set to 4, while ζ is set to 0.1. The values for α and γ are both set to 1, and β is fixed at 100 for all methods. All results are presented as means and standard deviations obtained from three runs with different random seeds.

4.2 Main Results

Results on Teacher Have Same Architecture. We evaluate our approach using teacher models that share the same architecture but differ in their initializations. The experimental results are presented in Table 1, demonstrating that our method consistently surpasses the competing approaches. Notably, in the case of the ResNet32x4-ShuffleNetV1 pair, our method achieves an absolute improvement of 0.87% compared to the second-best performing method.

Results on Teachers Have Different Architecture. To evaluate the flexibility of our approach, we utilized different teacher networks in the teacher-student pairs. Specifically, we selected ResNet8x4, ResNet20x4, and ResNet32x4 as the teacher networks, while VGG8 was designated as the student network. The comparative results for top-1 accuracy are shown in Table 2, which further emphasizes the superiority of our method over the compared state-of-the-art (SOTA) techniques.

Table 2. Top-1 test accuracy (%) of different multi-teacher knowledge distillation methods applied to CIFAR-100, utilizing teachers such as ResNet8x4 (72.69), ResNet20x4 (78.28), and ResNet32x4 (79.31).

VGG8	AVER-KD	FitNet-MKD	AEKD	EBKD	CA-MKD	MKD-SD (Ours)
70.70 ± 0.26	74.53 ± 0.17	74.38 ± 0.23	74.75 ± 0.21	74.27 ± 0.14	75.21 ± 0.16	**75.62 ± 0.14**

4.3 Ablation Study

Table 3 displays the results of the ablation experiments, clearly highlighting the effectiveness of each component of our approach.

Table 3. Ablation study conducted using the ResNet32-VGG8 pair on CIFAR-100.

Variants	L_{CE}	L_{KD}	L_{inter}	L_{SD}	Top-1
A	✓	✗	✗	✗	70.70 ± 0.26
B	✓	✓	✗	✗	73.51 ± 0.22
C	✓	✓	✓	✗	75.10 ± 0.18
D	✓	✓	✓	✓	$\mathbf{75.39 \pm 0.20}$

5 Conclusion

In this paper, we introduce an innovative framework for multi-teacher knowledge distillation that emphasizes self-distillation to enhance the reflective learning processes of students. Our method parallels the training of student networks with the real-world learning experiences of students. The student model assimilates knowledge from three crucial sources: ground-truth labels, multiple teachers, and its own introspection. In contrast to traditional knowledge distillation methods, which typically concentrate solely on the first two sources, our approach integrates the student's self-reflection as a vital component. To demonstrate the robustness of our proposed method, we perform extensive experiments, consistently showcasing its superior performance when compared to cutting-edge techniques.

References

1. Dosovitskiy, A., et al.: An Image is Worth 16x16 Words: Transformers for Image Recognition at Scale. arXiv preprint arXiv:2010.11929 (2020)
2. Du, S., et al.: Agree to disagree: adaptive ensemble knowledge distillation in gradient space. Advances in Neural Information Processing Systems **33**, 12345–12355 (2020)
3. Fukuda, T., Suzuki, M., Kurata, G., Thomas, S., Cui, J., Ramabhadran, B.: Efficient knowledge distillation from an ensemble of teachers. In: Interspeech, pp. 3697–3701 (2017)
4. Furlanello, T., Lipton, Z., Tschannen, M., Itti, L., Anandkumar, A.: Born again neural networks. In: International Conference on Machine Learning, pp. 1607–1616. PMLR (2018)
5. Hinton, G., Vinyals, O., Dean, J.: Distilling the Knowledge in a Neural Network. arXiv preprint arXiv:1503.02531 (2015)
6. Krizhevsky, A., Sutskever, I., Hinton, G.E.: Imagenet classification with deep convolutional neural networks. Advances in Neural Information Processing Systems **25** (2012)
7. Kwon, K., Na, H., Lee, H., Kim, N.S.: Adaptive knowledge distillation based on entropy. In: ICASSP 2020–2020 IEEE International Conference on Acoustics, Speech and Signal Processing (ICASSP), pp. 7409–7413. IEEE (2020)
8. Li, Y., Cai, J., Zhou, Q., Lu, H.: Joint semantic-instance segmentation method for intelligent transportation system. IEEE Transactions on Intelligent Transportation Systems (2022)
9. Liang, J., et al.: Efficient one pass self-distillation with zipf's label smoothing. In: European Conference on Computer Vision, pp. 104–119. Springer (2022)
10. Liu, Y., Zhang, W., Wang, J.: Adaptive multi-teacher multi-level knowledge distillation. Neurocomputing **415**, 106–113 (2020)
11. Lu, H., Wang, T., Xu, X., Wang, T.: Cognitive memory-guided autoencoder for effective intrusion detection in internet of things. IEEE Trans. Industr. Inf. **18**(5), 3358–3366 (2021)

12. Romero, A., Ballas, N., Kahou, S.E., Chassang, A., Gatta, C., Bengio, Y.: Fitnets: Hints for Thin Deep Nets. arXiv preprint arXiv:1412.6550 (2014)
13. Simonyan, K., Zisserman, A.: Very Deep Convolutional Networks for Large-Scale Image Recognition. arXiv preprint arXiv:1409.1556 (2014)
14. You, S., Xu, C., Xu, C., Tao, D.: Learning from multiple teacher networks. In: Proceedings of the 23rd ACM SIGKDD International Conference on Knowledge Discovery and Data Mining, pp. 1285–1294 (2017)
15. Yuan, L., Tay, F.E., Li, G., Wang, T., Feng, J.: Revisiting knowledge distillation via label smoothing regularization. In: Proceedings of the IEEE/CVF Conference on Computer Vision and Pattern Recognition, pp. 3903–3911 (2020)
16. Zhang, H., Chen, D., Wang, C.: Confidence-aware multi-teacher knowledge distillation. In: ICASSP 2022–2022 IEEE International Conference on Acoustics, Speech and Signal Processing (ICASSP), pp. 4498–4502. IEEE (2022)
17. Zhang, H., Chen, D., Wang, C.: Adaptive Multi-Teacher Knowledge Distillation with Meta-Learning. arXiv preprint arXiv:2306.06634 (2023)
18. Zhang, L., Song, J., Gao, A., Chen, J., Bao, C., Ma, K.: Be your own teacher: Improve the performance of convolutional neural networks via self distillation. In: Proceedings of the IEEE/CVF International Conference on Computer Vision, pp. 3713–3722 (2019)
19. Zhao, B., Cui, Q., Song, R., Qiu, Y., Liang, J.: Decoupled knowledge distillation. In: Proceedings of the IEEE/CVF Conference on Computer Vision and Pattern Recognition, pp. 11953–11962 (2022)
20. Zheng, Y., Li, Y., Yang, S., Lu, H.: Global-pbnet: a novel point cloud registration for autonomous driving. IEEE Trans. Intell. Transp. Syst. **23**(11), 22312–22319 (2022)

Construction and Application of Protein-Protein Interaction Knowledge Graph

Jing Xiong[1,3]([✉]) [iD], Xiaohong Wang[2] [iD], Fangkun Dou[4], Haowei Cao[5,6],
Tenglong Hong[7], Zhiwei Li[8], and Xiaoli Jing[9] [iD]

[1] School of Computer Science, Qufu Normal University, Rizhao 276827, China
jingxiong125@gmail.com
[2] Shandong Foreign Trade Vocational College, Qingdao 266100, China
[3] Rizhao-Qufu Normal University Joint Technology Transfer Center, Rizhao 276827, China
[4] Institute of Oceanology, Chinese Academy of Sciences, Qingdao 266071, China
[5] Key Laboratory of Computing Power Network and Information Security, Ministry of
Education, Shandong Computer Science Center, Qilu University of Technology (Shandong
Academy of Sciences), Jinan 250101, China
[6] Shandong Provincial Key Laboratory of Computing Power Internet and Service Computing,
Shandong Fundamental Research Center for Computer Science, Jinan 250101, China
[7] China Everbright Bank Qingdao R&D Center, Qingdao 266071, China
[8] Rizhao Medical Insurance Service Center, Rizhao 276826, China
[9] Department of Information Research, Qingdao Marine Science and Technology Center,
Qingdao 266237, China

Abstract. With the rapid advancement of emerging technologies such as high-
throughput sequencing, cryo-electron microscopy, mass spectrometry, and artificial intelligence, our understanding of protein interactions has deepened significantly, leading to an increasing demand for effective data integration. This study
tackles the complexity of protein interaction networks and the challenges associated with data integration by employing a top-down approach. It utilizes a protein
ontology as the semantic framework, integrates resources from the BioGRID and
UniProt databases, and constructs a comprehensive protein-protein interaction
knowledge graph (PPIKG). This knowledge graph not only provides an intuitive,
graphical interface for visualizing intricate protein interactions but also serves
as a centralized platform for downloading protein interaction data. It acts as a
one-stop solution for scientists aiming to explore and comprehend the complex
landscape of protein interactions. With its user-friendly visualization and efficient download tools, the knowledge graph simplifies the data acquisition process,
thereby fostering a deeper, holistic understanding of protein interaction networks
among researchers. This innovative approach to data integration is set to accelerate
scientific discovery and enhance our comprehension of biological systems.

Keywords: Protein–protein interaction · Knowledge graph · Semantic
mapping · Data integration

H. Lu (Ed.): ISAIR 2024, CCIS 2402, pp. 44–53, 2025.
https://doi.org/10.1007/978-981-96-2911-4_6

1 Introduction

Biological data are often heterogeneous as they stem from a wide range of experiments involving many different types of information, such as genetic sequences, protein interactions and findings in medical records [1]. In past decades, amount of protein and gene database has been built. In order to make consistent functional and conceptual descriptions of protein and related gene products in various data base, different protein and gene ontology has been proposed. These digital protein resources contain a wealth of knowledge, which can support protein and gene data integration and sharing. However, the lack of protein interaction data led to low utilization of resources and hinders the study of regulatory cells and their signaling in the pathway. The related protein interaction knowledge resources are scattered and disconnected, like a set of "knowledge silos".

Knowledge graph is an emerging technology for massive knowledge management and intelligent services in the big data era [2]. A knowledge graph is a structured dataset that is compatible with the RDF model and has an ontology as its schema. Knowledge graphs are often used to represent the various entities and their relationships with a set of "subject-predicate-object" triples. It can capture and present the intricate relationships among the domain concepts, and connect the fragmented pieces of knowledge in various information systems.

Building a Protein-Protein Interaction Knowledge Graph (PPIKG) is an effective solution that, by integrating knowledge resources of protein interactions, helps to address the issue of "knowledge silos" and enhances the capacity for new knowledge discovery. PPIKG represents proteins and their interrelationships in a graphical format, supporting functions such as querying, reasoning, and intelligent analysis, thus providing a powerful tool for research in the field of biomedicine.

2 Related Work

PPIKG serve as a critical research tool in systems biology and bioinformatics, providing a visual and analytical framework for understanding the complex interplay of proteins within biological systems. These knowledge graphs, consisting of nodes representing proteins and edges representing interactions between them, have played a pivotal role in elucidating biological processes such as cell signaling, gene expression regulation, and metabolic pathways. Furthermore, the Protein-Protein Interaction (PPI) networks have facilitated the discovery of new protein functions and regulatory mechanisms, which may not be fully characterized in existing databases and literature [3]. In the realm of drug development, PPI knowledge bases have been instrumental in identifying potential drug targets by pinpointing key proteins within disease-associated pathways [4]. Additionally, PPI knowledge bases have the potential to inform personalized medicine strategies by tailoring therapeutic interventions based on an individual's specific protein interaction profile [5]. By comparing PPI Networks in healthy versus diseased states, researchers can gain deeper insights into disease mechanisms, paving the way for innovative preventive, diagnostic, and therapeutic strategies [6]. Moreover, the study of PPI networks has fostered interdisciplinary collaboration between biologists, bioinformaticians, and statisticians, driving advancements in technology and methodology. Finally,

PPI networks have been crucial in uncovering new mechanisms of action for existing drugs, opening avenues for the repurposing and expanded application of pharmaceuticals [7].

Classic PPI knowledge bases include STRING [8], BioGRID [9], IntAct [10], HuRI [11], and the Pan-plant Protein Complex Map [12]. These resources provide comprehensive maps of protein interactions, elucidating the complex networks that underlie biological processes. STRING integrates multiple types of evidence to predict protein associations, while BioGRID curates experimentally validated interactions from published studies. IntAct focuses on binary protein interactions and offers detailed annotations. HuRI specializes in high-quality human protein interactome data, and the Pan-plant Protein Complex Map aims to capture the protein complex landscape across plant species. These invaluable resources have significantly advanced our understanding of biological systems. However, these knowledge bases share several common limitations: incomplete database coverage, lack of functional annotations and data integration challenges.

Addressing these challenges this paper presents an innovative solution: establishing deep semantic links between the PPI data from the BioGRID database and the high-quality data from the Uniprot [13], protein database. This association not only facilitates intuitive visualization through knowledge graphs but also provides data in CSV format for comprehensive analysis. This method offers two key advantages:

(1) This addresses the limitation of the BioGRID network, which lacks direct access to the attribute information of interacting proteins.
(2) While maintaining the original visualization benefits of the BioGRID, it introduces access to PPI subgraphs and enables data download functions, significantly enhancing both functionality and user experience.

3 Protein-Protein Interaction Knowledge Graph Construction

This study aims to construct the PPIKG to aid biologists in understanding the connections between proteins and their related partners within specific pathways. There are primarily two methods for constructing a knowledge graph: top-down and bottom-up. The top-down approach is appropriate for entities with well-defined semantic descriptions, starting with the establishment of a semantic model from the ontology library, followed by mapping the extracted data to these models. Conversely, the bottom-up approach is employed in scenarios where semantics are ambiguous or the domain is highly specialized. Given the meticulous efforts of experts in the biopharmaceutical field, the data storage structure in this domain is relatively organized, and most data adheres to storage standards such as OWL and XML, facilitating straightforward extraction of attributes and relationships. Consequently, this study adopts the top-down construction method, which involves eight specific steps, as shown in Fig. 1, with subsequent sections detailing each step.

3.1 Data Source Obtaining

Biological data often stems from a variety of experiments and exhibits heterogeneity, encompassing information such as gene sequences, protein interactions, and medical

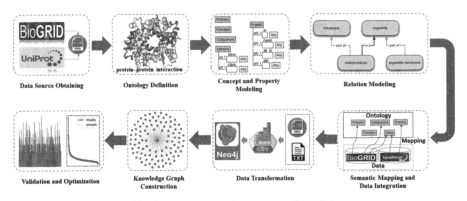

Fig. 1. The construction process of PPIKG.

records. The BioGRID and UniProtKB/Swiss-Prot databases serve as crucial resources for knowledge graphs. BioGRID is an open-access database dedicated to organizing and storing interactions among proteins, genes, and chemicals across major biological models and humans. In contrast, UniProtKB/Swiss-Prot represents the manually annotated and expert-reviewed segment of the UniProt knowledge base, boasting over 550,000 sequences. These databases utilize a relatively standardized storage structure, with most data conforming to specific storage standards, which facilitates the extraction of entity attributes and relations (Table 1).

Table 1. The data sources of PPIKG.

Data source	Entities	Entity Types	Date
BioGRID	104,563	Genes, Proteins	27-Aug-2019
Uniprot-Swiss-Prot	560,275	Proteins, Protein sequences	8-May-2019

BioGRID provides a comprehensive dataset that can be downloaded at https://downlo ads.thebiogrid.org/BioGRID/LatestRelease/. And UniProtKB offers access to various datasets for download at https://www.uniprot.org/downloads.

3.2 Ontology Definition

Ontology definition involves determining the domain and scope of the ontology, specifying the field it covers, its intended uses, the types of information it contains, and its potential users. The protein ontology is centered on the biomedical domain, particularly within molecular biology and bioinformatics, to describe and analyze protein interactions. Its primary purpose is to offer a structured representation of these interactions, which aids in computational processing and enhances understanding for subsequent biological analyses. This ontology encompasses various aspects, including interactor, biological process, subcellular location, interaction type, biological function, and detection method. It serves as a valuable knowledge resource for bioinformaticians, researchers, and bioengineers.

3.3   Concept and Property Modeling

Concept and property modeling involves the meticulous definition and refinement of concepts and properties within the ontology. The objective is to ensure that these elements accurately map to and describe entities within the domain, thereby enhancing the precision and detail of the knowledge graph's representation.

Due to the standardization, comprehensiveness, and authority of the data in Uniprot KB, we extracted the schema from Uniprot as the primary entities such as "Name", "Synonym", and "TaxId" and attributes such as "has-Basic Infor", "has-Sequence", "has-Organism", "has-Keywords", "has-Feature" in the protein ontology. Entities and attributes from other data sources such as BioGRID and Uniprot are aligned with the protein ontology model. If entities or attributes not yet covered by the model, we refine the concepts and properties within the protein ontology to ensure that they accurately describe the facts.

3.4   Relation Modeling

Relation modeling is essential for defining the various interactions between entities, such as one-to-one and one-to-many relationships. This process uncovers the intricate dynamics among entities, enhancing our understanding of protein networks. It involves not merely categorizing entities but also exploring their interrelationships, which is vital for constructing the complex structure of knowledge graphs. For instance, a many-to-many mapping exists between Uniprot and BioGRID. As shown in the Fig. 2.

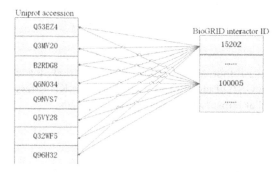

Fig. 2. Mappings between Uniprot and BioGRID.

When integrating BioGRID with protein ontology, the following steps should be taken: 1) Verify whether the BioGRID protein is listed in Uniprot. If an entry is found in the "accession" field of Uniprot, proceed to the next step; if not, expand the entry for the BioGRID protein. 2) Integrate the "shortLabel" values, retain the "Name" value in the protein ontology, and add the BioGRID "shortLabel" to the ontology's "Synonym" field, provided they are different. 3) For synonym integration, if the "Synonym" from BioGRID matches that in the ontology, keep the ontology's "Synonym"; otherwise, merge BioGRID's synonyms with those in the ontology, deduplicate them, and store the results in the ontology. 4) Finally, expand the BioGRID protein by mapping BioGRID's "shortLabel" to the ontology's "Name", linking "ncbiTaxId" to "TaxId", and aligning "alias" with the ontology's "Synonym".

3.5 Semantic Mapping and Data Integration

This stage involves aligning data from existing sources with the concepts and properties outlined in the ontology. This process transforms raw data into nodes and edges that conform to the ontology format, thereby converting data into knowledge. An example of semantic mapping and data integration between Uniprot-Swiss-Prot, BioGRID and ontology is shown in Fig. 3.

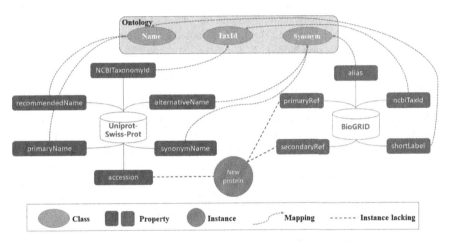

Fig. 3. Semantic mapping and data integration example.

In Fig. 3, the tags <recommendedName> and <primaryName> of Uniprot-Swiss-Prot are mapped to the "Name" in the protein ontology; The tags <alternationName> and <synonymName> are mapped to "Synonym"; The tag <NCBITaxonomyId> is mapped to "TaxId". Proteins and their properties are preserved as instances of the protein ontology, ensuring that all proteins and properties in Uniprot-Swiss-Prot are fully integrated.

We first establish a mapping between the "primaryRef" and "secondaryRef" fields in BioGRID and UniProt, in order to integrate the protein attribute information of BioGRID into the protein ontology. For example, in BioGRID, for proteins with a "short tag" of "HSPA5", their "secondaryRef" values include "Q9UK02", "Q2EF78", "B0QZ61", and "Q9NPF1". Through mapping, we can find the corresponding UniProt protein, thus achieving the integration of the two.

If the <primaryRef> or <secondaryRef> values in BioGRID are not recorded in the <accession> of UniProt, it indicates that the ontology instance is missing the relevant protein and a new instance needs to be added. In addition, the instance layer of this embodiment is extended through semantic mapping, including mappings between "shortLabel" and "Name", "ncbiTaxId" and "TaxId", and "alias" and "Synonym".

3.6 Data Transformation

It includes the processes of cleaning, integrating, and converting data to ensure quality and consistency while transforming it into a suitable format and structure for inclusion in the knowledge graph. Due to the variability and diversity in protein naming conventions, data inconsistency and redundancy are prevalent. We addressed this by removing duplicate information and assigning species classification to each protein. Additionally, we enriched the synonyms of proteins with organism taxonomic information. This enhancement provides stronger semantic support for protein queries based on the PPIKG in subsequent studies.

In terms of data format, the data sources we obtain are mainly in XML format. Additionally, we employ professional documents to aid in data cleaning, entity recognition, and relationship extraction. The final extracted entities are stored in a CSV file, facilitating future import into Neo4J.

3.7 Knowledge Graph Construction

The knowledge graph construction involves organizing the transformed data in accordance with the ontology's structure to create a well-defined knowledge graph. Based on the aforementioned operations, a comprehensive knowledge graph, PPIKG, has been constructed using protein ontology. The PPIKG encompasses 582,635 proteins from 13,718 species and includes 2,005,416 associated interactions. It serves as a powerful tool for knowledge discovery, reasoning, and application within the domain. The PPIKG is accessible through the protein query website mentioned in Sect. 4.

3.8 Validation and Optimization

During the validation and optimization stage, a thorough verification of the knowledge graph is performed to ensure its accuracy and completeness. Based on this foundation, necessary optimizations and adjustments are implemented to achieve peak performance and effectiveness.

4 Application

The protein query website (http://43.153.4.4:8000/protein_search) is constructed to provide one-stop data retrieval without considering the diversity of protein nomenclature and species, as shown in Fig. 4.

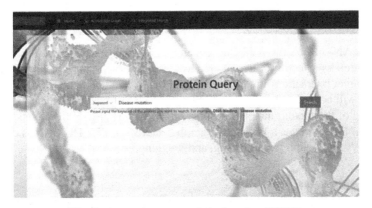

Fig. 4. A protein query website based on PPIKG.

4.1 Protein Search Based on PPIKG

Based on the PPIKG, a condition query interface (http://43.153.4.4:8000/ppi) is developed. The search box is designed on the left side where users can customize the query criteria for head node, tail node and attribute relation respectively. Construction of query criteria follows the property graph query patterns. The system will combine query statements in triples of "*(head node)-[relation condition]-(tail node)*", and return the results as a subgraph on the right side. As shown in Fig. 5.

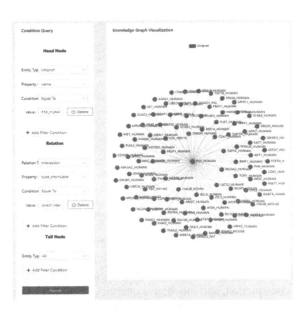

Fig. 5. An example of the P53_HUMAN search.

Using P53_HUMAN retrieval as an example, users need first establish filtering conditions for the head node. After selecting "Uniprot" as the entity type, the system will automatically generate blank attribute filtering conditions. Next, users should choose "name" from the attribute drop-down menu, select "Equal to" as the condition, and input "P53_HUMAN" in the value field. Subsequently, users need to create filtering conditions for the relation by selecting "interaction", followed by "type_shortLabel", "Equal To", entering "direct interaction" in the value field. Finally, by clicking the "Search" button, the system will compile all query conditions into a single query statement, resulting in the retrieval of the protein interaction subgraph of P53_HUMAN from Neo4J. On the right side of the interface, a knowledge graph centered on P53_HUMAN is displayed, which allows for zooming, rearranging, and dragging.

4.2   Data Access Based on PPIKG

In the PPIKG on the right side of the page, users can discover which proteins interact with "p53_HUMAN" by clicking on the relevant links (as shown in Fig. 6). Additionally, they can expand the information card to view detailed data about the selected protein. Interaction protein information can be downloaded in CSV format via the "Download" button.

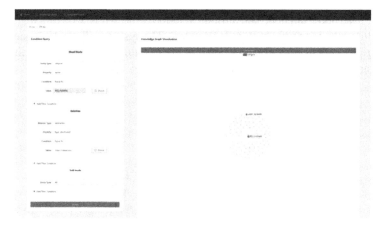

Fig. 6. Primary information of one specific protein in PPIKG.

5   Conclusion

This study integrates protein data from Uniprot and BioGRID databases to address incomplete information and the lack of the capability for direct access to the attribute information of interacting proteins in BioGRID's network. It focuses on data fusion, knowledge graph construction, and interactive querying. The study harmonizes diverse protein naming conventions and provides a comprehensive visualization and download platform for protein interactions. This study is invaluable for life science researchers, consolidating protein data and their attributes. It allows biologists to map protein connections within biological pathways, facilitating drug target discovery, elucidating mechanisms, and revealing new functions for established proteins.

Despite the limited size and scope of the platform's data, it provides a crucial foundation for our future research aimed at refining the knowledge graph and integrating additional biological entities into the data repository. Furthermore, updating and synchronizing this data will be a primary focus of our upcoming efforts.

Acknowledgement. This work was supported by Shandong Provincial Natural Science Foundation of China (ZR2020MF145), the Key Technology Project of Henan Educational Department of China (22ZX010), Shandong Province Key R&D Program Soft Science Project (2023RKY02009), and Henan Provincial Department of Science and Technology Research Project (212102310295).

References

1. Marx, V.: The big challenges of big data. Nature **498**(7453), 255–260 (2013)
2. Pan, J.Z., Vetere, G., Gomez-Perez, J.M., et al.: Exploiting Linked Data and Knowledge Graphs in Large Organisations. Springer, Switzerland (2017)
3. Rümplera, F., Theißena, G., Melzera, R.: Sequence features of MADS-domain proteins that act as hubs in the protein-protein interaction network controlling flower development. Cold Spring Harbor Laboratory (2017)
4. Rout, T., Mohapatra, A., Kar, M.: A systematic review of graph-based explorations of PPI networks: methods, resources, and best practices. Netw. Model. Anal. Health Inform. Bioinform. **13**(1), 29 (2024)
5. Holzinger, A.: Trends in interactive knowledge discovery for personalized medicine: cognitive science meets machine learning. IEEE Intell. Inform. Bull. **15**(1), 6–14 (2014)
6. Wang, X., Gulbahce, N., Yu, H.: Network-based methods for human disease gene prediction. Brief. Funct. Genomics **10**(5), 280–293 (2011)
7. Barabási, A., Gulbahce, N., Loscalzo, J.: Network medicine: a network-based approach to human disease. Nat. Rev. Genet. **12**(1), 56–68 (2011)
8. Szklarczyk, D., Gable, A.L., Lyon, D., et al.: STRING v11: protein-protein association networks with increased coverage, supporting functional discovery in genome-wide experimental datasets. Nucleic Acids Res. **47**(D1), D607–D613 (2019)
9. Oughtred, R., Rust, J., Chang, C., et al.: The BioGRID database: a comprehensive biomedical resource of curated protein, genetic, and chemical interactions. Protein Sci. **30**(1), 187–200 (2021)
10. Orchard, S., Ammari, M., Aranda, B., et al.: The MIntAct project—IntAct as a common curation platform for 11 molecular interaction databases. Nucleic Acids Res. **42**(D1), D358–D363 (2014)
11. Luck, K., Kim, D., Lambourne, L., et al.: A reference map of the human binary protein interactome. Nature **580**(7803), 402–408 (2020)
12. McWhite, C.D., Papoulas, O., Drew, K., et al.: A pan-plant protein complex map reveals deep conservation and novel assemblies. Cell **181**(2), 460–474 (2020)
13. The UniProt Consortium.: UniProt: the universal protein knowledgebase. Nucleic Acids Res. **46**(5), 2699 (2018)

A Learning-Based Monitoring System for Factory Assembly Behavior

Yi Liu[1], Hao Wang[2], Xiaodong Liu[1], Man Jiao[1], Wenchang Li[1], Xiaochuan Wang[2], and Ruijun Liu[1(✉)]

[1] Beijing Research Institute of Automation for Machinery Industry Co., Ltd., Beijing, China
liuruijun@buaa.edu.cn
[2] Beijing Technology and Business University, Beijing, China

Abstract. With the advancement of deep learning, industries are now demanding higher standards for assembly product quality and efficiency. This study integrates temporal action localization, human pose estimation, and graph comparison algorithms, utilizing a multi-thread concurrency mechanism to facilitate real-time monitoring and assessment of assembly behavior. Such an approach enables monitoring personnel to focus solely on videos depicting abnormal behavior, thereby enhancing the overall quality and efficiency of the assembly process. In Sect. 2, we conduct an overview of factory assembly behavior techniques. Subsequently, we introduce the technology roadmap integrated into our system, present the architecture, demonstrate experimental results on our dataset, and draw conclusions.

Keywords: Assembly Behavior · Temporal Action Localization · Action Quality Assessment · Human Pose Estimation · Learning-based Method

1 Introduction

Despite technological limitations hindering automated machine assembly, manual assembly remains the predominant method in mass customization production. The quality and efficiency of product assembly heavily depend on individual contributions. Deviations from standard assembly actions by workers can significantly impede workshop production efficiency, product quality, and safety. Therefore, monitoring and assessing assembly actions are crucial components within industrial manufacturing enterprises and intelligent production systems [17], particularly in assembly workshops employing a substantial workforce.

Conventional assembly motion monitoring relies on remote cameras transmitting videos to a central monitoring center, where they are manually assessed by monitoring personnel. However, achieving comprehensive and real-time monitoring becomes challenging in sizable workshops, compounded by the potential for monitoring personnel fatigue-induced attention lapses. Consequently, traditional

H. Lu (Ed.): ISAIR 2024, CCIS 2402, pp. 54–68, 2025.
https://doi.org/10.1007/978-981-96-2911-4_7

manual monitoring approaches struggle to adapt to the demands of large-scale workshop assembly.

With advancements in artificial intelligence [18], research has increasingly focused on monitoring and evaluating human behavior using deep learning neural networks. Leveraging the capabilities of these networks allows effective detection and evaluation of workers' assembly behavior. This study employs temporal action localization, human pose estimation, and graph comparison algorithms for automated monitoring and evaluation of workers' assembly behavior.

2   Related Work

2.1   Production Workshop Assembly Monitoring

The assembly manufacturing workshop serves as a cornerstone within mechanical manufacturing enterprises, encompassing production equipment, personnel, and management divisions. Here, production staff meticulously adhere to defined processing sequences for product manufacturing. Nevertheless, the inherent complexities often introduce uncertainties, especially when workers employ non-standard assembly practices. These challenges notably impede workshop efficiency and product quality. Hence, monitoring assembly in disrupted environments becomes critical for improving the management standards of production systems.

Employing intelligent identification monitoring serves as a foundational tool for manufacturing enterprises to craft production plans and management strategies. Wang et al. [1] proposed a comprehensive blueprint outlining the design of a workshop data acquisition and monitoring system. This blueprint centers on a tripartite network structure comprising an Ethernet management network, a data transmission network, and a real-time data acquisition device network. This amalgamation of software and hardware facilitates swift and accurate transmission of diverse workshop production line data to the monitoring and management system. Empirical evidence highlights the efficacy of this approach in enhancing production efficiency and generating favorable results, indicating substantial potential for early-stage assembly monitoring research.

On the other hand, Chen et al. [2] utilized a deep learning model to differentiate between the quantity of assembly operations and the corresponding action types performed by assembly workers. The implementation of the pose estimation algorithm CPM facilitated the extraction of human joint point coordinates, allowing for the quantification of repetitive assembly operations. The use of the YOLO algorithm [11] enabled the identification of assembly tool types, leading to the categorization of assembly actions with an impressive recognition rate of 92%. Nonetheless, it's important to note that this approach has limitations in recognizing subtle human movements, which consequently hampers its efficiency.

2.2   Assembly Behavior Action Recognition

Assembly action recognition encompasses identifying and categorizing assembly workers' actions and behaviors to detect and analyze the assembly process

[33]. Predominant methods in action recognition fall into two main categories: those using two-stream convolutional architectures [12] and those employing 3D convolutional approaches, including the (2+1)D variant.

Video Action Recognition Method Based on Dual Stream Convolutional Architecture. The video action recognition method employing the two-stream convolutional architecture is based on the Two-Stream CNN [12]. This approach entails training CNN networks using motion images and employing dual streams to classify motion. Simonyan et al. introduced the dual-stream convolutional network, performing spatial feature extraction on RGB frames in the spatial domain and temporal feature extraction on optical flow information within the temporal domain. While employing a multi-task training approach has yielded favorable recognition results on publicly available datasets, the computationally intensive nature of optical flow extraction, both spatially and temporally, renders it impractical for deployment in enterprise settings.

Video Recognition Method Based on 3D Convolution and Variant (2+1) D Convolution. The video action recognition method based on 3D convolution, including the (2+1)D convolution variant, extracts features from video frames using convolutional operations. For capturing temporal information, researchers have employed 3D CNN methods. Tran et al. [13] introduced the C3D network, utilizing three-dimensional convolutional kernels to comprehend spatiotemporal features from action images. Carreira et al. [14] expanded on the two-stream architecture and 3D convolutional networks with the I3D architecture. This model extends 2D convolutional kernels and filters into a 3D framework through the Inflated operation, merging the strengths of the two-stream network and the wide receptive field of 3D convolutions. As a result, it demonstrates robust performance in video classification and offers flexibility in deployment and engineering considerations.

Assembly Behavior Action Evaluation. In engineering, evaluating the quality of assembly actions represents a vital research focus. Its objective is to monitor and assess action behaviors during assembly, ensuring precision and quality. Research methods for assessing action quality can generally be categorized into two groups.

The first category encompasses video-based action quality assessment. In this method, models directly use RGB video streams as input and employ techniques such as 3D convolutional neural networks (CNNs) to extract human motion features. These features are then used for regression to predict scores. Inspired by action recognition, Shi et al. [3] propose a multi-task quality assessment model that utilizes the C3D-LSTM method for feature extraction and employs SVM regression for score prediction. Zhou et al. [4] propose a multi-task quality assessment model capable of simultaneously learning tasks like action description and action scoring, consequently improving interpretability and performance.

Apart from direct score regression, Wang et al. [5] utilize siamese networks to compute the similarity between input action videos and reference videos. This allows for relative score prediction through comparative regression.

The second category of methods relies on human pose estimation. Initially, a pose estimation algorithm is used to identify the human skeletal structure and gather keypoint information. Subsequently, the 2D human skeletal information undergoes feature extraction using graph convolutional neural networks. Jiang et al. [6] introduces the Spatial-Temporal Pyramid Graph Convolutional Network (ST-PGN) for human pose estimation and action quality assessment. This model utilizes a pyramid network to extract skeletal features at multiple hierarchical levels. Wu et al. [7] develops a trainable skeletal joint relation graph and suggests joint commonality and joint distinctiveness modules for learning joint kinematics.

3 Technology Roadmap

Given the substantial distance between cameras in the workshop assembly environment and the monitoring area, along with the requirement to process multiple camera video streams concurrently, necessitating high computational power, this study employs a Client/Server architecture. The Server, housing a high-performance computing unit, is dedicated to executing the core algorithms for workshop action monitoring and assessment. It stores exceptional event information and manages client requests. Conversely, the client, any network-enabled terminal, interacts with the server, transmitting requests and receiving respective outcomes. The computational layout for this system is illustrated in Fig. 1.

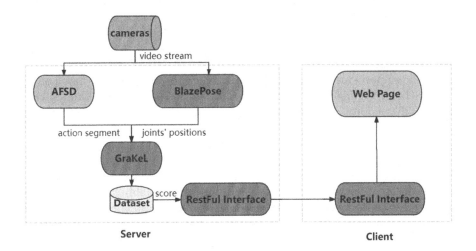

Fig. 1. System Technology Roadmap

The server-side process commences by receiving video streams from cameras. A dedicated thread responsible for reading camera feeds then segments these video streams into fixed-length video segments. Following this, another thread is engaged in processing these video segments through the AFSD module [9], overseeing temporal action localization. This step results in the classification of human actions within the video segment, providing the corresponding start and end times for each action.

Simultaneously, the BlazePose module [8], designed specifically for human pose estimation, extracts the coordinate positions of key joints involved in human motion. A graph is formed by comparing the reference key points of a specific action category with those extracted from the video segment. This graph undergoes the GraKeL [10] graph comparison algorithm, generating an evaluation score for the respective action category. Finally, information pertaining to exceptional actions is stored on the server.

To maintain real-time responsiveness, the system utilizes multiple threads, enabling concurrent execution of tasks such as reading camera frames and processing video segments. This approach ensures and upholds system efficiency.

The client side utilizes RESTful interfaces. Clients can initiate or terminate the operation of specific IP-addressed cameras through POST requests. Additionally, clients have the ability to retrieve video information that contains details of anomalous actions.

4   Architecture

4.1   Temporal Action Localization

Focusing on the aforementioned requirements, our approach begins by employing action temporal localization [21–23] techniques to identify and recognize worker actions within assembly videos. Action temporal localization is a critical and challenging task in video behavior understanding, aiming to predict action categories present in extended untrimmed videos, along with the initiation and cessation times for each action.

Action temporal localization can be classified into two categories based on the use of anchors, leading to methods known as anchor-based [27–29] and anchor-free [30–32] temporal action localization, respectively. The former requires predefined anchors for precise prediction of action temporal locations, resulting in redundant parameters and additional processing time. In contrast, the latter involves direct prediction, enhancing efficiency but requiring additional processing to ensure the accuracy of regression predictions.

Considering the real-time demands of workshop assembly behavior monitoring, our study opts for a more efficient anchor-free method [9], which does not rely on predefined anchors. This approach encompasses several key modules as outlined in Figure 2.

4.2   Human Pose Estimation

The task of human pose estimation [24–26] focuses on localizing key points on individuals within video frames, such as wrists, neck, and ankles. Deep

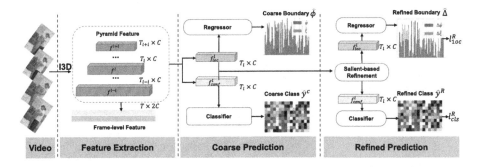

Fig. 2. AFSD architecture

learning-based human pose estimation can generally be categorized into two types: keypoint-based methods and heatmap-based methods.

Keypoint-based methods predict the locations of human keypoints in images to achieve pose estimation. Common keypoint-based methods include OpenPose [15], Stacked Hourglass [16] and so on. Heatmap-based methods, on the other hand, forecast pose heatmaps for pose estimation. These pose heatmaps consist of specialized images where each keypoint is depicted by a 2D Gaussian distribution centered on the keypoint location. Heatmap-based methods can often manage occlusions and intricate backgrounds more effectively by predicting the distribution of keypoints without explicitly pinpointing their exact positions. Common heatmap-based methods encompass SimpleBaseline [19] and HRNet [20].

In this study, BlazePose, an exceptionally efficient human pose estimation model developed by Google, is utilized. It emphasizes single-person keypoint prediction and boasts real-time functionality on mobile devices. BlazePose stands out for its efficiency, lightweight design, one-stage detection, context fusion, and scalability. The architecture of BlazePose is depicted in Fig. 3.

The efficient real-time operation of BlazePose is primarily grounded in two key insights. Initially, upon detecting a human presence in a video stream, the model utilizes the Face Detector module to predict the bounding box encompassing the individual. In subsequent video frame processing, the model refines the bounding box coordinates using the coordinates from the previous frame, eliminating the necessity of re-executing the Face Detector module. Secondly, during the training phase, the model employs both the two-dimensional coordinates of keypoints and heatmap representations of those keypoints. The heatmap representation involves a two-dimensional Gaussian distribution centered on the coordinates of the keypoint. Using both these representations during training enhances the accuracy of regressing keypoints. However, during actual inference, the model discards the heatmap representation and exclusively utilizes the two-dimensional coordinates of keypoints, skipping the keypoint heatmap prediction step. Collectively, these two insights significantly reduce the model's complexity, facilitating BlazePose's real-time operation.

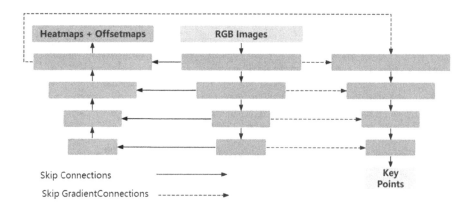

Fig. 3. BlazePose architecture

BlazePose demonstrates real-time performance and maintains prediction accuracy when compared to OpenPose on both the AR Dataset and Yoga Dataset.

4.3 Action Quality Assessment

Human action quality assessment is primarily employed to evaluate the efficacy and effectiveness of human movements and actions. This paper amalgamates the aforementioned human pose estimation algorithm with graph comparison methods to achieve action quality scoring.

GraKeL [10] (Graph Kernels Library) is a Python library specifically tailored for graph data, designed to offer an array of graph kernel functions and tools for processing and analyzing graph data structures. These graph kernel functions serve as methods that gauge the similarity between two graphs.

In this study, graphs are formulated based on the human pose topology extracted from both standard and real-life videos. The ShortestPath function offered by GraKeL is utilized to compute the shortest path kernel between two graphs. This process involves computing the shortest path length for each pair of nodes in the graph using a shortest path algorithm such as Dijkstra's algorithm. The ShortestPath function offered by GraKeL is utilized to compute the shortest path kernel between two graphs. This process involves computing the shortest path length for each pair of nodes in the graph using a shortest path algorithm such as Dijkstra's algorithm. The ShortestPath function offered by GraKeL is utilized to compute the shortest path kernel between two graphs. This process involves computing the shortest path length for each pair of nodes in the graph using a shortest path algorithm such as Dijkstra's algorithm.

4.4   Network Communication Interface

In this paper, the server is built using the Flask framework, and MySQL is utilized for storing exceptional data. The communication between the client and server is established using the RESTful (Representational State Transfer) interface style. The system incorporates the following interfaces, illustrated in Table 1:

Table 1. Interface

Interface Name	Description
POST /startSeat	The system receives video streams from designated IP cameras and initiates the algorithms.
POST /endSeat	Terminate the reception of video streams from designated cameras and halt algorithms.
POST /videoList	List the detailed information of all videos with abnormal actions.
POST /videoCount	Compute the number of videos containing abnormal actions within the specified time segment.

5   Experiment Result

5.1   Experiment Settings

The system's employed database structure is designed as follows, capturing video streams showcasing worker actions during printer inspection. The process entails two distinct steps:

Step One: Opening the printer cover for visual inspection, followed by closing the cover.

Step Two: Opening the paper tray for visual examination, followed by closing the tray.

The visual representations of Step One and Step Two are illustrated in the accompanying Fig. 4.

In the annotations, Step One and Step Two are denoted as "One" and "Two," respectively, along with the indicated start and end times for each action. The training dataset comprises 78 videos containing both Step One and Step Two actions, while the validation dataset consists of 56 videos.

The experiments were conducted on an Ubuntu 22.04.2 LTS system, utilizing an AMD Ryzen 9 7950X processor and an NVIDIA GeForce RTX 4090 graphics processor for computation.

Fig. 4. Visual representation of Step One(left) and Step Two(right)

Table 2. AFSD on public datasets

Type	Model	Backbone	THMOUS14					
			0.3	0.4	0.5	0.6	0.7	Avg
Anchor-based	SSAD	TS	43.0	35.0	24.6	-	-	-
	TURN	C3D	44.1	34.9	25.6	-	-	-
	R-C3D	C3D	44.8	35.6	28.9	-	-	26 .8
	CBR	TS	50.1	41.3	31.0	19.1	9.9	-
	TAL	I3D	53..2	48.5	42.8	33.8	20.8	38.2
	GTAN	P3D	57.8	47.2	39.8	-	-	52.6
Actionness	CDC	-	40.1	29.4	23.3	13.1	7.9	22.8
	SSN	TS	51.0	41.0	29.8	-	-	-
	BSN	TS	53.5	45.0	36.9	28.4	20.0	36.8
	BMN	TS	56.0	47.4	38.8	29.4	20.5	38.5
	DDG	TS	57.8	49.4	12.8	33.8	21.7	41.1
	G-TAD	TS	54.5	47.6	40.2	30.8	23.7	39.3
	BU-TAL	I3D	53.9	50.7	45.4	38.0	28.5	43.3
	BC-GNN	TS	57.1	49.1	40.4	31.2	23.1	40.2

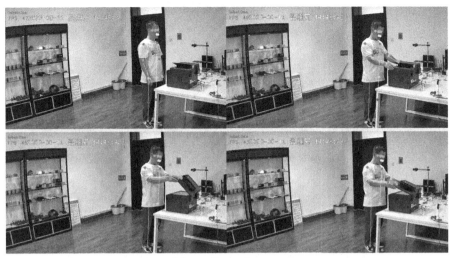

(a) result on step one

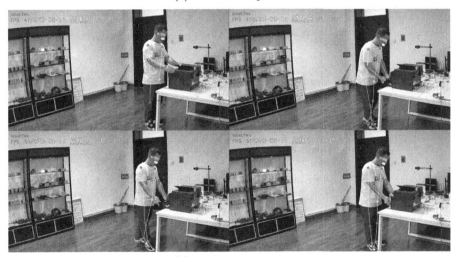

(b) result on step two

Fig. 5. Performance of AFSD on our dataset

5.2 Experimental Results of Temporal Action Localization

The performance of AFSD on public datasets is shown in Table 2.

The effect of AFSD running on our dataset is shown in Figure 5, where steps One and Two are labeled as one and two respectively:

The experimental results indicate that AFSD successfully identifies the action intervals.

The IoU calculated in this data set is shown in Fig. 6.

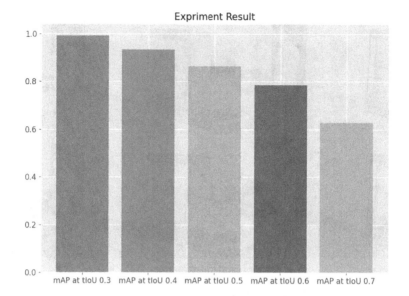

Fig. 6. Performance of AFSD on our dataset

5.3   Experimental Results of Human Pose Estimation

The performance of BlazePose on public datasets is as Table 3:

Table 3. BlazePose on public datasets

Model	FPS	AR Dataset, PCK@0.2	Yoga Dataset, PCK@0.2
OpenPose(body only)	0.4	87.8	83.4
BlazePose FULL	10	84.1	84.5
BlazePose Lite	31	79.6	77.6

The effect of OpenPose and BlazePose running on our dataset is depicted in Figs. 7 and 8.

As illustrated in Figs. 7 and 8, the result graphs from OpenPose and BlazePose demonstrate precise prediction of the coordinates for human body nodes by both algorithms. Meanwhile, the BlazePose algorithm excels in real-time applications due to its effectiveness.

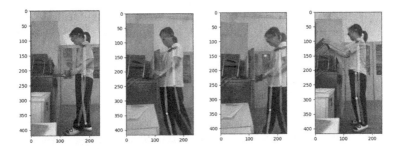

Fig. 7. Performance of OpenPose on our dataset

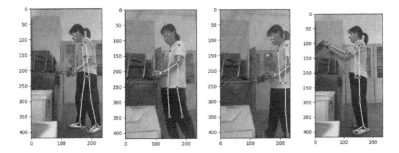

Fig. 8. Performance of BlazePose on our dataset

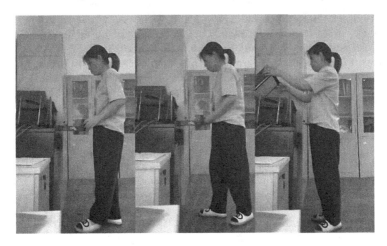

Fig. 9. Figures from left to right are denoted as (a), (b), (c)

5.4 Experimental Results of Action Quality Assessment

Use Fig. 9(a) as the action base, using the topological structure of the key points in the graph to construct the graph and comparing it with the GraKeL graph, the score obtained is $s(a, a) = 1.0, s(a, b) = 0.05597, s(a, c) = 0.00373$.

The scoring results reveal a distinction between standardized and non-standard actions through a comparison of actual actions against a benchmark action skeleton graph using the GraKeL algorithm.

6   Conclusion

The study accomplished automated recognition and assessment of assembly behaviors through action temporal localization [21–23], human pose estimation [24–26], and graph comparison algorithms [10]. As a result, efficient identification and localization of assembly anomalies were achieved, significantly enhancing the quality and efficiency of assembly operations. However, it's essential to acknowledge certain constraints within the proposed system. Specifically, the performance of temporal action localization might be limited due to insufficient training data. Additionally, enhancements in both keyframe extraction and graph comparison algorithms are necessary to bolster system efficiency.

Addressing these constraints and further refining the system is expected to yield improved performance and broader applicability in real-world scenarios.

References

1. Wang, J., et al.: Real-time Workshop information acquisition and monitoring system based on three-layer network. In: 3rd International Conference on Electric and Electronics. Atlantis Press (2013)
2. Chen, C., et al.: Repetitive assembly action recognition based on object detection and pose estimation. J. Manuf. Syst. **55**, 325–333 (2020)
3. Parmar, P., Morris, B.T.: Learning to score Olympic events. In: Proceedings of the IEEE Conference on Computer Vision and Pattern Recognition Workshops (2017)
4. Dong, L.-J., et al.: Learning and fusing multiple hidden substages for action quality assessment. Knowl. Based Syst. **229**, 107388 (2021)
5. Wang, S., et al.: TSA-net: tube self-attention network for action quality assessment. In: Proceedings of the 29th ACM International Conference on Multimedia (2021)
6. Parsa, B., Dariush, B.: Spatio-temporal pyramid graph convolutions for human action recognition and postural assessment. In: Proceedings of the IEEE/CVF Winter Conference on Applications of Computer Vision (2020)
7. Balcan, M.-F., Liang, Y., Gupta, P.: Robust hierarchical clustering. J. Mach. Learn. Res. **15**(1), 3831–3871 (2014)
8. Bazarevsky, V.: BlazePose: On-device Real-time Body Pose tracking. arXiv preprint arXiv:2006.10204 (2020)
9. Lin, C., et al.: Learning salient boundary feature for anchor-free temporal action localization. In: Proceedings of the IEEE/CVF Conference on Computer Vision and Pattern Recognition (2021)
10. Siglidis, G., et al.: Grakel: a graph kernel library in python. J. Mach. Learn. Res. **21**(54), 1–5 (2020)
11. Redmon, J., et al.: You only look once: Unified, real-time object detection. In: Proceedings of the IEEE Conference on Computer Vision and Pattern Recognition (2016)

12. Simonyan, K., Zisserman, A.: Two-stream convolutional networks for action recognition in videos. In: Advances in Neural Information Processing Systems, vol. 27 (2014)
13. Tran, D., et al.: Learning spatiotemporal features with 3d convolutional networks. In: Proceedings of the IEEE International Conference on Computer Vision (2015)
14. Carreira, J., Zisserman, A.: Quo vadis, action recognition? A new model and the kinetics dataset. In: Proceedings of the IEEE Conference on Computer Vision and Pattern Recognition (2017)
15. Cao, Z., et al.: Realtime multi-person 2d pose estimation using part affinity fields. In: Proceedings of the IEEE Conference on Computer Vision and Pattern Recognition (2017)
16. Newell, A., Yang, K., Deng, J.: Stacked Hourglass Networks for Human Pose Estimation. In: Leibe, B., Matas, J., Sebe, N., Welling, M. (eds.) ECCV 2016. LNCS, vol. 9912, pp. 483–499. Springer, Cham (2016). https://doi.org/10.1007/978-3-319-46484-8_29
17. Ma, C., et al.: Visual information processing for deep-sea visual monitoring system. Cogn. Robot. **1**, 3–11 (2021)
18. Krizhevsky, A., Sutskever, I., Hinton, G.E.: Imagenet classification with deep convolutional neural networks. In: Advances in Neural Information Processing Systems, vol. 25 (2012)
19. Martinez, J., et al.: A simple yet effective baseline for 3d human pose estimation. In: Proceedings of the IEEE International Conference on Computer Vision (2017)
20. Sun, K., et al.: Deep high-resolution representation learning for human pose estimation. In: Proceedings of the IEEE/CVF Conference On Computer Vision and Pattern Recognition (2019)
21. Yan, S., Xiong, Y., Lin, D.: Spatial temporal graph convolutional networks for skeleton-based action recognition. In: Proceedings of the AAAI Conference on Artificial Intelligence, vol. 32. No. 1 (2018)
22. Wang, L., et al.: Temporal segment networks: towards good practices for deep action recognition. In: Leibe, B., Matas, J., Sebe, N., Welling, M. (eds.) Computer Vision – ECCV 2016. LNCS, vol. 9912. Springer, Cham (2016). https://doi.org/10.1007/978-3-319-46484-8_2
23. Lin, T., Zhao, X., Su, H., Wang, C., Yang, M.: BSN: boundary sensitive network for temporal action proposal generation. In: Ferrari, V., Hebert, M., Sminchisescu, C., Weiss, Y. (eds.) ECCV 2018. LNCS, vol. 11208, pp. 3–21. Springer, Cham (2018). https://doi.org/10.1007/978-3-030-01225-0_1
24. Zheng, C., et al.: 3d human pose estimation with spatial and temporal transformers. In: Proceedings of the IEEE/CVF International Conference On Computer Vision (2021)
25. Zhao, Q., et al.: Poseformerv2: exploring frequency domain for efficient and robust 3d human pose estimation. In: Proceedings of the IEEE/CVF Conference on Computer Vision and Pattern Recognition (2023)
26. Li, W., et al.: MHFormer: multi-hypothesis transformer for 3d human pose estimation. In: Proceedings of the IEEE/CVF Conference on Computer Vision and Pattern Recognition (2022)
27. Gao, J., et al.: Turn tap: Temporal unit regression network for temporal action proposals. In: Proceedings of the IEEE International Conference on Computer Vision (2017)
28. Gao, J., Yang, Z., Nevatia, R.: Cascaded boundary regression for temporal action detection. arXiv preprint arXiv:1705.01180 (2017)

29. Long, F., et al.: Gaussian temporal awareness networks for action localization. In: Proceedings of the IEEE/CVF Conference on Computer Vision and Pattern Recognition (2019)

30. Shou, Z., et al.: CDC: convolutional-de-convolutional networks for precise temporal action localization in untrimmed videos. In: Proceedings of the IEEE Conference on Computer Vision and Pattern Recognition (2017)

31. Zhao, P., Xie, L., Ju, C., Zhang, Y., Wang, Y., Tian, Q.: Bottom-up temporal action localization with mutual regularization. In: Vedaldi, A., Bischof, H., Brox, T., Frahm, J.-M. (eds.) ECCV 2020. LNCS, vol. 12353, pp. 539–555. Springer, Cham (2020). https://doi.org/10.1007/978-3-030-58598-3_32

32. Xu, M., et al.: G-tad: sub-graph localization for temporal action detection. In: Proceedings of the IEEE/CVF Conference on Computer Vision and Pattern Recognition (2020)

33. Koga, S., et al.: Optimizing food sample handling and placement pattern recognition with YOLO: advanced techniques in robotic object detection. In: Proceedings of Cognitive Robotics (2024)

A Two-Stage Generative Adversarial Approach for Domain Adaptive Semantic Segmentation

Chen Li, Jingbo Deng, Xinchen Xie, Yixiao Xiang, and Lihua Tian[✉]

Xi'an Jiaotong University, Xi'an, China
lhtian@xjtu.edu.cn

Abstract. The abundance of light and the wide range of object colors in the image datasets gathered in daylight situations make it simpler for semantic segmentation networks to extract useful image information. Nevertheless, the existing model trained in the daytime setting struggles to accurately discriminate distinct objects in the nighttime scenes. To solve this problem, we suggest a two-stage generative adversarial network-based unsupervised domain adaptive semantic segmentation algorithm. In the first stage, a circular generative adversarial network (RoundGAN) based on cycle consistency is proposed to transform the annotated daytime images in the source domain into a style similar to that of nighttime images in the target domain. A new semantic segmentation network training architecture (SDNet) is proposed in the second stage, which is based on the concept of an adversarial network. In this architecture, the conventional semantic segmentation network is used as a sub-module of the training network, and an adversarial loss function is added. A combination of fully supervised and unsupervised training techniques is used to train the segmentation network. Experiments show that the final trained model can effectively segment classes in nighttime images.

Keywords: Domain adaptation · Semantic segmentation · Generative adversarial network

1 Introduction

With the tremendous advancement of artificial intelligence and computer science in past few years, computer vision technology has also advanced significantly. In the subject of autonomous driving, computer vision techniques have also been applied to the recognition and understanding of various scenarios, such as vehicle and pedestrian detection and recognition, lane detection, and traffic sign recognition.

Semantic segmentation [1, 2] is a pixel-level classification task and aims to forecast each pixel in an image and identify the class to which it belongs by assigning a label to each pixel. Due to the growth of deep neural network technology, deep learning-based semantic segmentation algorithm [3] is currently a widely used technique.

Semantic segmentation of nighttime scenes is as important as that of daytime images [4]. To address this issue, we propose a two-stage unsupervised domain adaptive semantic segmentation algorithm based on generative adversarial networks. To begin with, a cyclic

H. Lu (Ed.): ISAIR 2024, CCIS 2402, pp. 69–81, 2025.
https://doi.org/10.1007/978-981-96-2911-4_8

consistency-based cyclic generative adversarial network is proposed in the first stage. In this stage, we convert the source daytime images into nighttime images. Then, in the next stage, a new semantic segmentation network training architecture is proposed based on the idea of adversarial network, using the target domain daytime images, target domain nighttime images and generated source domain nighttime images from the first stage. It is demonstrated that the proposed cyclic generative adversarial network in the first stage can generate high-resolution labeled nighttime image data, and the semantic segmentation network training architecture based on adversarial network in the second stage can further improve the semantic segmentation network's capacity for nighttime feature extraction. The model performs well on the Dark Zurich and Nighttime Driving datasets.

These are the key contributions made by our work:

1) We propose a cyclic generative adversarial network to more effectively synthesize night images with high resolution and fewer defects.
2) We introduce discriminator network in the process of semantic segmentation, input high-dimensional image features for discrimination, and avoid the impact of mislabeling on the segmentation model through the cross-entropy loss of static objects.

The remaining sections of the paper are structured as follows. Previous research on semantic segmentation and domain adaptation are discussed in Sect. 2. Our proposed method is given in Sect. 3. The experimental results are shown in Sect. 4. Finally, conclusions are provided in Sect. 5.

2 Related Works

2.1 Domain Adaptation

The current mainstream unsupervised domain adaptation methods are founded on minimizing the difference in data distribution between intermediate features or output features of source and target domain. Such differences can be measured by metrics such as the maximum mean difference [5], H-scatter [2], or implicitly measured by domain invariant features [6], domain confusion [7], and gradient inversion [8]. Another recently emerged unsupervised approach is the introduction of self-supervised training to domain adaptation tasks, the core idea of which is to generate pseudo-labels by pre-training the model so that the model can be trained under supervision [9–12]. There are also approaches based on generative adversarial networks [13–15], which aim to reduce the difference between source and target directly on the input space, enabling the model to perform supervised learning on the source.

Hoffman et al. [13] are the first to combine adversarial learning methods with unsupervised domain-adaptive semantic segmentation algorithms. They train the network to learn domain-invariant features for semantic segmentation using pixel-level adversarial loss functions. Tsai et al. [14] propose a multilevel adversarial network with adversarial learning in the output space to align the features in the output space over the data distribution. In addition to above, image translation and image style migration techniques [15] are also widely used for unsupervised domain adaptation methods. Several works have shown that transforming source images to target images can obtain domain-invariant features of image. Chang et al. [16] propose a domain-invariant feature extraction framework that decomposes images into domain-invariant structures and domain-specific texture representations.

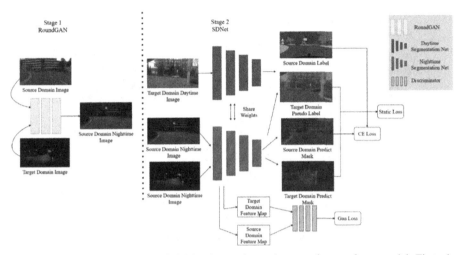

Fig. 1. Our network design in brief. The figure shows the two phases of our model. First, the source images are converted to nighttime images. The segmentation network and the discriminator network are then given the source and target pictures, respectively.

2.2 Semantic Segmentation

Deep learning semantic segmentation algorithms have received a lot of attention from industry and academia in recent years. The FCN algorithm [3] is the first proposal to apply neural networks for image classification task to semantic segmentation task. The PSPNet [17] and the DeepLab series [13, 18–20] use the FCN's encoder-decoder design. Their encoder network reuse pre-training models that perform well in image classification, such as ResNet, VGG, etc. The design of the decoder is then the main focus of these traditional methods. To improve the segmentation accuracy, a more complex network structure is used, resulting in the overall network.

3 Methods

3.1 Network Architecture

The lack of labeled data makes it impossible for the semantic segmentation network to be trained under supervision. Therefore, in the first stage, the source labeled daytime images are firstly synthesized into nighttime images by a generative model based on generative adversarial network. The model's second step combines the semantic segmentation network with the discriminator network based on the adversarial network's training procedure. Let the image feature distributions of the two domains extracted by the encoder gradually approximate, and finally enable the decoder to process the image features located in the same feature space. The approach suggested overall network architecture is depicted in Fig. 1.

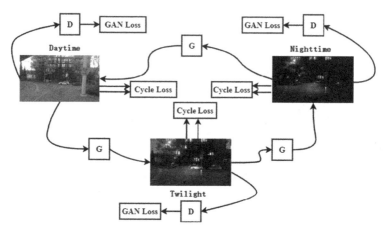

Fig. 2. RoundGAN Architecture. The twilight image is included as an intermediate domain.

3.2   Cyclic Consistency-Based Round Generative Adversarial Network (RoundGAN)

RoundGAN Network Architecture. With a view to resolving the issue that there are many defects in the generated images due to the large difference of daytime and nighttime images, and to make the transition from daytime to nighttime images smoother, this study proposes the Ring Generative Adversarial Network RoundGAN, which is based on CycleGAN. Figure 2 displays RoundGAN's architecture. When converting from a daytime image to a nighttime image, instead of generating a nighttime image directly, an intermediate image is generated between the two domains. In addition to the target image, the discriminator also collects the created source nighttime image to calculate the adversarial loss. Finally, the source daytime image is obtained by sending the source nighttime image to another generator network. To make sure that the generator network maintains the image's precise information as the image style migrates, a cyclic consistency loss between the generated image and input can be calculated. The intermediate and target images are processed by the same manner as the source daytime image. The adversarial loss is calculated for the images generated after two generator networks, and the cyclic consistency loss is calculated for the images generated after the third generator network. In Fig. 2, the generator network is referred to as G, D stands for the discriminator network, cycle loss refers to the cycle consistency loss of the image generated after one cycle with the original image, and GAN loss refers to the adversarial loss generated by the discriminator network for the discriminated results of the original and synthetic images.

Loss Function of RoundGAN. In CycleGAN, its network structure fits only two mapping functions, a mapping function $G: X \rightarrow Y$ from source domain to target domain and a mapping function $F : Y \rightarrow X$ from target domain to source domain, where X denotes the source data, Y denotes the target data, and G and F represent the mapping functions, respectively. The objective function of CycleGAN is shown in (1) where, L_{GAN} denotes the adversarial loss, L_{cyc} denotes the cyclic consistency loss, and λ is a constant.

$$
\begin{aligned}
L(G, F, D_X, D_Y) &= L_{GAN}(G, D_Y, X, Y) \\
&+ L_{GAN}(F, D_X, Y, X) + \lambda L_{cyc}(G, F)
\end{aligned} \tag{1}
$$

In the proposed RoundGAN, compared with CycleGAN, a generator network is inserted between G and F, and an intermediate domain X_2 is introduced between the source domain X_1 and the target domain Y, such that G is decomposed into G_1 and G_2, $G_1: X_1 \rightarrow X_2$, $G_2: X_2 \rightarrow Y$, $F : Y \rightarrow X$. That is, G_1 migrates the daytime image to intermediate images, G_2 migrates intermediate images to nighttime images, and F migrates nighttime images to daytime images. Then the adversarial loss of RoundGAN from X_1 to Y is shown in (2), and the cyclic consistency loss function between target and source is shown in (3). Adding weights to the loss values from X_1 to Y, X_2 to X_1, and Y to X_2, and combining with the cyclic consistency loss, the objective function of RoundGAN is shown in (4). The weight of the adversarial loss is shown by λ_{gan}, while which of the cyclic consistency loss is indicated by λ_{cyc}.

$$
\begin{aligned}
L_{GAN}(G_1, G_2, D_Y, X, Y) &= E_{y \sim P_{data(y)}} \left[\log(D_Y(y)) \right] + \\
&E_{x \sim P_{data(x)}} \left[\log(1 - D_Y(G_2(G_1(x)))) \right]
\end{aligned} \tag{2}
$$

$$
\begin{aligned}
L_{cyc}(G_1, G_2, F) &= E_{x_1 \sim P_{data(x_1)}} [F(G_2(G_1(x_1))) - x_1] + \\
&E_{x_2 \sim P_{data(x_2)}} [G_1(F(G_2(x_2))) - x_2] + \\
&E_{y \sim P_{data(y)}} \left[G_2(G_1(F(y))) - y \right]
\end{aligned} \tag{3}
$$

$$
\begin{aligned}
L(G_1, G_2, F, D_1, D_2, D_Y, X_1, X_2, Y) &= \lambda_{gan} L_{GAN}(G_1, G_2, D_Y, X_1, Y) + \\
&\lambda_{gan} L_{GAN}(F, G_1, D_2, Y, X_2) + \\
&\lambda_{gan} L_{GAN}(G_2, F, D_1, X_2, X_1) + \\
&\lambda_{cyc} L_{cyc}(G_1, G_2, F)
\end{aligned} \tag{4}
$$

3.3 An Unsupervised Semantic Segmentation Plus Discriminator Network Based on Feature Space Consistency (SDNet)

SDNet Network Architecture. The architecture of SDNet is displayed in Fig. 3, where the semantic segmentation network can be replaced with a network based on the FCN 18 codec architecture, and the discriminator network consists of a single layer of convolutional layers. Unlike general generative adversarial networks, SDNet introduces target daytime images as input data in addition to source daytime images and target nighttime images to the network. The image features are first extracted using the encoder, and the image features are used as the input of the decoder and the discriminator, respectively.

The decoder outputs the segmentation mask, and the discriminator network determines whether the image features originate from the source domain or the target domain. The segmentation mask calculates the cross-entropy loss of static objects and of all objects, respectively, and discriminant result calculates the adversarial loss.

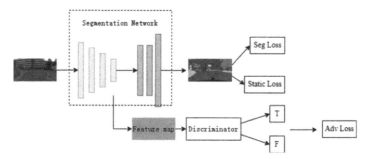

Fig. 3. SDNet Architecture

Loss Function of SDNet. In SDNet, there are two outputs, a semantic segmentation result P and an output result D of the discriminator network. The provenance of the input image is indicated by a label, either source or target, so that the semantic segmentation result P can be subdivided into the source segmentation result PS and the target segmentation result PT. In the Dark Zurich dataset, although daytime images and nighttime images have one-to-one annotation, only static objects, such as buildings, trees, and roads, are constant in the photos taken at the same location in the scene, and objects such as pedestrians, bicycles, and cars in the scene are changing. Directly using the segmentation results of daytime images as the annotation of nighttime scenes will have a considerable degree of mislabeling, because the annotation of dynamic objects is not stable. Therefore, inspired by the literature 4, for the segmentation result PT, when calculating the cross-entropy loss of multiple classifications, the weight of dynamic object loss value is set to 0 in this paper, i.e., the loss value of dynamic objects is ignored. As shown in (5), α_k is the weight of each category, and the cross-entropy loss is noted as $L_{t\,arg\,et}$. As for the source domain segmentation result PS, it is normal to calculate the multiclassification cross-entropy loss, calculated as in (6), we note it as L_{seg}.

$$L_{target} = -\sum_{k=1}^{K} \alpha_k y_k \log(\hat{y}_k) - \sum_{k=1}^{K} \alpha_k (1 - y_k) \log(1 - \hat{y}_k) \tag{5}$$

$$L_{seg} = -\sum_{k=1}^{K} y_k \log(\hat{y}_k) - \sum_{k=1}^{K} (1 - y_k) \log(1 - \hat{y}_k) \tag{6}$$

As important as loss of the segmentation results is the calculation of the discriminator's loss so that the features extracted by the encoder approximate the same distribution. The discriminator's loss, denoted as L_{adv} or L_{dis}, is used to calculate the cross-entropy loss of the binary classification for the feature map D generated from the discriminator network.

In summary, the optimization objectives of SDNet in the second stage are shown in (7), where the λ in is the weight of the antagonistic loss.

$$L_G = \begin{cases} L_{seg} + \lambda L_{adv}; \textit{Source Images} \\ L_{target} + \lambda L_{adv}; \textit{Target images} \end{cases}$$

$$L_D = L_{dis}$$

(7)

4 Experiment

4.1 Dataset

Cityscapes Dataset. Cityscapes is a streetscape dataset widely used in academia today. The dataset consists of 5000 images of 2048×1024 pixels in size. 2975 photos were used for the training set, 500 for the validation set, and 1525 for the test set. The objects in the images are labeled with a total of 19 categories.

Dark Zurich Dataset. The Dark Zurich dataset has 8377 images collected in the city of Zurich as the training set, including 3041 daytime images, 2930 twilight images, and 2416 nighttime images, each with a resolution size of 1920×1080.

Nighttime Driving Dataset. The Nighttime Driving dataset is also a dataset of images in nighttime scenes, but due to privacy policy, it is only available as a test set for testing. There are 50 annotated images of nighttime scenes in the test set. In this paper, this dataset is tested to evaluate our model in nighttime scenes.

Data Pre-processing. For the source domain, the image resolution is first randomly adjusted to 1–1.5 times the initial size, and a random crop to 1024×512 size is used.

For the target data, first randomly adjusting the image resolution to 1 to 1.5 times the initial size and using random cropping to 960×540 size.

The images will be trained using regularization techniques like random level flipping, and the images will be normalized before being fed into the network to prevent from overfitting. In this study, we set the three RGB channels' respective averages at 123.675, 116.28, and 103.53, and their variances at 58.395, 57.12, and 57.375.

4.2 General Settings

In the first phase of experiments, for training the generator network, the Adam [23] is used, with momentum $= 0.9$. For discriminator, the Adam [23] is used with same parameters as generator. The small batch gradient descent method is used, and the size of one small batch is set to 1. A total of 250,000 iterations are used for training.

In the second stage, for PSPNet, the SGD [24] is used to optimize the model. The initial learning rate $= 0.01$ and is gradually reduced using a polynomial decay of the order of 0.9. For Segformer, the AdamW [25] is used to optimize the model with offsets set to 0.5 and 0.999 and the weight decay rate $= 0.01$. λ_adv is set to 0.001.

4.3 Evaluation Metric

To compare it fairly to alternative techniques and intuitively analyze the effectiveness of the algorithm, this paper uses mIOU to evaluate the performance of the algorithm.

mIOU denotes the mean intersection over union, n_{ij} denotes the number of pixels in category i predicted as category j, n_c denotes the number of categories, the number of pixels in category i is indicated by t_i, and the label of each image is $\sum_{i}^{n_c} t_i$.

4.4 Compare with State-of-the-Art

The selected comparison methods include AdaptSegNet [14], ADVENT [26], BDL [15], DMAda [27], and CIConv [28]. For the fairness of the experimental comparisons, the comparison methods all use semantic segmentation networks with comparable performance.

In the experimental results in Table 1, as can be observed, the domain adaptation approach outperforms the model trained on the source domain only, and thus domain adaptation is necessary for the semantic segmentation task in cross-domain scenarios. Meanwhile, the results of the Segformer model show that when the model performs well on the source domain, it also has better results on the target domain. Comparing with the more cutting-edge unsupervised domain adaptive methods now used, the proposed domain adaptive segmentation network can lead to the best outcomes, which can finally reach 42.6 mIoU on the Dark Zurich test set, which, when compared to other approaches, represents a significant performance boost.

Our models were also tested on the Nighttime Driving dataset. Since the Nighttime Driving dataset does not provide training data, the tested models were trained using Cityscapes and Dark Zurich datasets, and only the test set of Nighttime Driving was used to evaluate the model performance. From the results in Table 2, as can be shown, the strategy presented in this paper considerably enhances the semantic segmentation model's performance for nighttime datasets like Nighttime Driving.

Some randomly selected visualization results are shown in Fig. 4, and each group of images from left to right are the original image, the original image roughly labeled, the Segformer segmentation results trained on the source domain only, and the Segformer segmentation results trained in two stages. It has been proved that as compared to the model trained on the source domain only, the visualization outputs of our domain adaptive segmentation network are closer to the actual image semantic labels.

4.5 Ablation Study

This subsection shows the results of the ablation experiments on the Cityscapes-to-DarkZurich task in the nighttime scene, and investigates the contributions of RoundGAN, the second stage training network, and the custom loss function to the result. We use Segformer as the base for semantic segmentation in unsupervised domain adaptive task, and the results are shown in Table 3.

Table 1. Results of Cityscapes-to-DarkZurich on Dark Zurich Validation Set

Method	Road	Side	Building	Wall	Fence	Pole	Light	Sign	Vegetation	terrain	Sky	Person	Rider	Car	Truck	Bus	Train	Motor	Bike	mIoU
PSPNet	43.0	0.86	9.75	1.87	2.72	5.05	1.58	7.49	31.8	7.37	0.03	14.0	0.16	6.53	0.03	0.0	15.7	0.34	0.42	28.8
DeepLabV2	49.4	7.69	10.3	5.11	5.59	11.4	2.19	9.27	18.4	12.8	0.08	20.8	11.2	13.6	0.02	0.09	25.7	0.90	5.69	28.6
Segformer-b2	81.6	19.0	51.2	15.5	10.6	30.3	28.9	22.0	56.7	13.3	20.8	38.2	21.8	52.1	1.6	0.0	53.2	23.2	10.7	34.3
AdaptSegNet	86.1	44.2	55.1	22.2	4.8	21.1	5.6	16.7	37.2	8.4	1.2	35.9	26.7	68.2	45.1	0.0	50.1	33.9	15.6	30.4
ADVENT	85.8	37.9	55.5	27.7	14.5	23.1	14.0	21.1	32.1	8.7	2.0	39.9	16.6	64.0	13.8	0.0	58.8	28.5	20.7	29.7
BDL	85.3	41.1	61.9	32.7	17.4	20.6	11.4	21.3	29.4	8.9	1.1	37.4	22.1	63.2	28.2	0.0	47.7	39.4	15.7	30.8
DMAda	75.5	29.1	48.6	21.3	14.3	34.3	36.8	29.9	49.4	13.8	0.4	43.3	50.2	69.4	18.4	0.0	27.6	34.9	11.9	32.1
CiConv	-	-	-	-	-	-	-	-	-	-	-	-	-	-	-	-	-	-	-	34.5
PSPNet-R(ours)	91.0	60.3	55.0	32.0	11.7	42.9	39.5	41.1	39.0	19.7	0.12	44.6	37.7	69.4	10.1	7.0	11.4	33.9	22.5	35.2
Segformer-R(ours)	91.0	59.0	61.2	38.2	13.6	41.2	42.3	46.5	38.3	12.0	0.16	48.5	53.0	76.1	25.8	1.60	68.9	36.9	22.3	**42.6**

Fig. 4. Visualization results of nighttime images segmentation.

Table 2. Results of Cityscapes-to-DarkZurich on Nighttime Driving Validation Set

Method	Ref.	Training Dataset	mIoU
PSPNet [17]	CVPR 2017	Cityscapes	7.06
Segformer [22]	NeurIPS 2021	Cityscapes	34.3
AdaptSegNet [14]	CVPR 2018	Cityscapes-DZ	34.5
ADVENT [26]	CVPR 2019	Cityscapes-DZ	34.7
BDL [15]	CVPR 2019	Cityscapes-DZ	34.7
DMADA [27]	ITSC 2018	Cityscapes-DZ	36.1
DANNet [4]	CVPR 2021	Cityscapes-DZ	47.7
MGCDA [29]	TPAMI 2020	Cityscapes-DZ	49.4
Segformer-R(ours)	–	Cityscapes-DZ	**49.64**

The results of the ablation experiments demonstrate that the semantic segmentation model trained using the images generated by CycleGAN segmented the nighttime images is poor at segmenting nighttime images and can barely classify image pixels correctly. In contrast, the nighttime images generated using the RoundGAN proposed in this paper are capable of producing high-quality, high-resolution nighttime images, and the semantic segmentation network can be trained properly on the synthesized image data. Network's performance is further enhanced after the second stage of SDNet implementation, demonstrating that the SDNet suggested in this paper can cause the source and target features extracted by the segmentation network to converge to the same feature space and ultimately enhance the model's performance.

Some randomly selected nighttime images generated by RoundGAN are shown in Fig. 5, where the original image is shown on the left and the generated nighttime image is shown on the right.

Table 3. Ablation Results of the two Stages Method on Dark Zurich Validation Set

Model	Stage 1	Stage 2	mIoU
Segformer	None Additional Modification	None Additional Modification	34.3
Segformer	CycleGAN	None Additional Modification	2.02
Segformer	RoundGAN	None Additional Modification	40.9
Segformer	RoundGAN	SDNet	**42.6**

Fig. 5. Images generated by RoundGAN. The original image is shown on the left and the generated nighttime image is shown on the right

5 Conclusion

The task of unsupervised domain-adaptive semantic segmentation is problematic in nighttime scenes, and we propose a solution. We first introduce the background of the task and the issues with the current approach. We propose a two-stage unsupervised domain-adaptive semantic segmentation method based on generative adversarial networks. Different from traditional methods, a discriminator network is introduced to train the semantic segmentation model to enhance model performance. We demonstrate the effectiveness of the method through comparative experiments.

Although the method improves the classification accuracy of nighttime images, there is still a gap in segmentation performance between nighttime and daytime scenes, and image blur will affect the segmentation effect. In addition, there are other difficult vision tasks in night scenes, such as object detection, image classification, and lane line detection, which deserve further research.

Acknowledgment. This work was supported by the National Natural Science Foundation of China under Grant No. 61901356 and the HPC Platform, Xi'an Jiaotong University.

References

1. Chen, L.-C., et al.: Rethinking atrous convolution for semantic image segmentation. arXiv preprint arXiv:1706.05587 (2017)
2. Ros, G., et al.: The synthia dataset: a large collection of synthetic images for semantic segmentation of urban scenes. In: Proceedings of the IEEE Conference on Computer Vision and Pattern Recognition (2016)
3. He, K., et al.: Deep residual learning for image recognition. In: Proceedings of the IEEE Conference on Computer Vision and Pattern Recognition (2016)
4. Wu, X., et al.: DANNet: a one-stage domain adaptation network for unsupervised nighttime semantic segmentation. In: Proceedings of the IEEE/CVF Conference on Computer Vision and Pattern Recognition (2021)
5. Long, M., et al.: Learning transferable features with deep adaptation networks. In: International Conference on Machine Learning. PMLR (2015)
6. Tzeng, E., et al.: Adversarial discriminative domain adaptation. In: Proceedings of the IEEE Conference on Computer Vision and Pattern Recognition (2017)
7. Tzeng, E., et al.: Simultaneous deep transfer across domains and tasks. In: Proceedings of the IEEE International Conference on Computer Vision (2015)
8. Ganin, Y., et al.: Domain-adversarial training of neural networks. J. Mach. Learn. Res. 17(1), 2096–2030 (2016)
9. Zou, Y., et al.: Unsupervised domain adaptation for semantic segmentation via class-balanced self-training. In: Proceedings of the European Conference on Computer Vision (ECCV) (2018)
10. Zou, Y., et al.: Confidence regularized self-training. In: Proceedings of the IEEE/CVF International Conference on Computer Vision (2019)
11. Zhang, P., et al.: Prototypical pseudo label denoising and target structure learning for domain adaptive semantic segmentation. In: Proceedings of the IEEE/CVF Conference on Computer Vision and Pattern Recognition (2021)
12. Hoyer, L., Dai, D., Gool, L.V.: DAFormer: improving network architectures and training strategies for domain-adaptive semantic segmentation. In: Proceedings of the IEEE/CVF Conference on Computer Vision and Pattern Recognition (2022)
13. Hoffman, J., et al.: FCNs in the wild: pixel-level adversarial and constraint-based adaptation. arXiv preprint arXiv:1612.02649 (2016)
14. Tsai, Y.-H., et al.: Learning to adapt structured output space for semantic segmentation. In: Proceedings of the IEEE Conference on Computer Vision and Pattern Recognition (2018)
15. Li, Y., Yuan, L., Vasconcelos, N.: Bidirectional learning for domain adaptation of semantic segmentation. In: Proceedings of the IEEE/CVF Conference on Computer Vision and Pattern Recognition (2019)
16. Chang, W.-L., et al.: All about structure: adapting structural information across domains for boosting semantic segmentation. In: Proceedings of the IEEE/CVF Conference on Computer Vision and Pattern Recognition (2019)
17. Chen, L.-C., et al.: Semantic image segmentation with deep convolutional nets and fully connected CRFs. arXiv preprint arXiv:1412.7062 (2014)
18. Long, J., Shelhamer, E., Darrell, T.: Fully convolutional networks for semantic segmentation. In: Proceedings of the IEEE Conference on Computer Vision and Pattern Recognition (2015)
19. Chen, L.-C., et al.: DeepLab: semantic image segmentation with deep convolutional nets, atrous convolution, and fully connected CRFs. IEEE Trans. Pattern Anal. Mach. Intell. 40(4), 834–848 (2017)
20. Chen, L.-C., et al.: Encoder-decoder with atrous separable convolution for semantic image segmentation. In: Proceedings of the European Conference on Computer Vision (ECCV) (2018)

21. Zhu, J.-Y., et al.: Unpaired image-to-image translation using cycle-consistent adversarial networks. In: Proceedings of the IEEE International Conference on Computer Vision (2017)
22. Xie, E., et al.: SegFormer: simple and efficient design for semantic segmentation with transformers. Adv. Neural Inf. Process. Syst. **34**, 12077–12090 (2021)
23. Kingma, D.P., Ba, J.: Adam: a method for stochastic optimization. arXiv preprint arXiv:1412. 6980 (2014)
24. Zhang, N., Lei, D., Zhao, J.F.: An improved Adagrad gradient descent optimization algorithm. In: 2018 Chinese Automation Congress (CAC). IEEE (2018)
25. Loshchilov, I., Hutter, F.: Decoupled weight decay regularization. arXiv preprint arXiv:1711. 05101 (2017)
26. Vu, T.-H., et al.: Advent: adversarial entropy minimization for domain adaptation in semantic segmentation. In: Proceedings of the IEEE/CVF Conference on Computer Vision and Pattern Recognition (2019)
27. Dai, D., Gool, L.V.: Dark model adaptation: semantic image segmentation from daytime to nighttime. In: 2018 21st International Conference on Intelligent Transportation Systems (ITSC). IEEE (2018)
28. Lengyel, A., et al.: Zero-shot day-night domain adaptation with a physics prior. In: Proceedings of the IEEE/CVF International Conference on Computer Vision (2021)
29. Sakaridis, C., Dai, D., Gool, L.V.: Map-guided curriculum domain adaptation and uncertainty-aware evaluation for semantic nighttime image segmentation. IEEE Trans. Pattern Anal. Mach. Intell. **44**(6), 3139–3153 (2020)
30. Zhao, H., et al.: Pyramid scene parsing network. In: Proceedings of the IEEE Conference on Computer Vision and Pattern Recognition (2017)

LCRNet: Unsupervised Non-rigid Point Cloud Registration Network Based on Local Correspondence Relationships

Yiqi Wu[1,2], Tiantian Zhang[2], Lixiang Liu[1], Ronglei Hu[2], Yidong Yang[1], Yanli Li[3], and Boxiong Yang[1(✉)]

[1] School of Information and Intelligence Engineering, University of Sanya, Sanya, China
boxiongyang@sanyau.edu.cn
[2] School of Computer Science, China University of Geosciences, Wuhan, China
[3] Department of Information Engineering, Ordos Vocational College, Ordos, China

Abstract. Currently, the registration of non-rigid 3D objects remains a challenging task. This paper proposes an unsupervised non-rigid point cloud registration network based on local correspondence relationships, namely the LCRNet. By learning the partial matching matrix to obtain more accurate point cloud correspondences and optimizing the matrix in combination with the Sinkhorn algorithm, we successfully eliminate the noise and outliers in the initial matching. In addition, through the adaptive learning of the transformer network and using complex geometric properties, we realize the deformation of non-rigid point clouds. The experiments on multiple datasets indicate that the LCRNet achieves accurate unsupervised non-rigid object registration, outperforming comparative methods.

Keywords: Point cloud · Non-rigid registration · Correspondence · Deep learning

1 Introduction

Non-rigid point cloud registration is important for applications like 3D reconstruction [18], human posture estimation [25], autonomous driving [28], and robot navigation [12]. However, it poses challenges with shape variations, noise, and outliers. Current methods struggle with non-rigid transformations and noise. This paper presents an unsupervised method for non-rigid point cloud registration, using local region correspondences to enhance accuracy and robustness.

Recent studies prompt a rethinking of point cloud registration and shape alignment by exploring the correspondence of points relation. Some research [6, 19] prioritize shape correspondence over internal point-to-point structure. Zeng et al. [24]

Supported by Hainan Province Science and Technology Special Fund (No. ZDYF2022GXJS005), the specific research fund of The Innovation Platform for Academician of Hainan Province (No. YSPTZX202144), and Inner Mongolia Autonomous Region Higher Education Scientific Research Project (No. NJZY21164).

proposed Corrnet3D for point cloud correspondence, however, it lacks effectiveness in learning shape correspondence. Inspired by these insights, we propose a network, namely LCRNet, which employs a two-step strategy: first, internal learning of point-to-point correspondences, followed by shape similarity learning. To resolve internal differences and enhance understanding, we introduce a correspondence detection module that emphasizes the internal details of the point cloud, using a combination of soft and hard matching methods to deal with the point cloud correspondence. During shape transformations, through self-attention and cross-attention mechanisms, we accurately capture local structures and features within the point cloud.

This paper makes the following main contributions:

1. An unsupervised non-rigid point cloud registration method guided by local region correspondences is introduced, addressing challenging issues in point cloud registration, including shape similarity, noise, and outliers.
2. A shape-adaptive registration module is proposed, achieving accurate capture of local structures and features within the point cloud through adaptive learning of local shape variations.

The rest of this article is arranged as follows. In Sect. 2, related work is carried out to review the point cloud registration methods. In Sect. 3, the model Method and loss function are presented. In Sect. 4, the performance of the proposed method is demonstrated through qualitative and quantitative experiments. The conclusion is given in Sect. 5.

2 Related Works

2.1 Traditional Point Cloud Registration Methods

Probability-based point cloud registration methods. Myronenko et al. [14] proposed CPD (Coherent Point Drift), using Gaussian mixture model to consider the overall point cloud distribution. Yew et al. [23] improved robustness against noise and outliers through soft assignment and the expectation-maximization algorithm for fuzzy point matching. Feature-based point cloud registration methods are effective in handling non-rigid deformations [22]. For example, Steder et al. [17] achieved point cloud registration by identifying significant regions on the point cloud surface and computing features aligned with normal.

2.2 Point Cloud Registration Based on Deep Learning

With the rise of deep learning, there is a continuous exploration of its applications across various tasks [10], such as intelligent transportation [7, 9], image processing [11, 27], and point cloud registration. Aoki et al. [1] proposed the PointNetLK network, using PointNet [16] to implement end-to-end registration for local feature matching. Choy et al. [3] enhanced large-scale point cloud registration with global characteristics. Trappolini et al. [19] utilized a transformer structure for the shape registration of the point cloud. Wang et al. [21] improved the registration effect of large-scale point cloud data by introducing global features. Corrnet3D [24] proposed to find the correspondence between points for point cloud registration.

3 Method

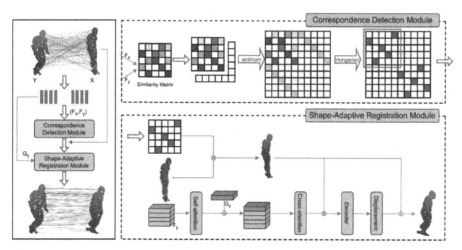

Fig. 1. The proposed architecture involves local relation-guided 3D point cloud registration. The point clouds X and Y are input into the corresponding detection module after extracting features to obtain the replacement matrix. The point cloud X is transformed and input into the shape-adaptive registration module to obtain a point cloud similar to Y.

As shown in Fig. 1, LCRNet is mainly composed of a feature embedding module, a corresponding detection module, and a shape-adaptive registration module. The source point cloud X and target point cloud Y to be registered are processed by the feature embedding module, respectively, using DGCNN [15] for this step. DGCNN [15] captures and integrates a broader local geometry through multiple iterations of the edge-conv layer. At each layer, additional neighboring point information is incorporated $f_i^{(l+1)} = \sum_{f_j^l \in \Omega_i^l} M_l\left(f_i^l, f_j^l - f_i^l\right)$, where $f_i^l \in R^{(1 \times d)}$ represents the feature representation of point i fed into the l-th edge-conv. Then, corresponding local feature vectors $F_x \in R^{(n \times d)}$ and $F_y \in R^{(n \times d)}$ are generated, where d represents the feature dimension. Subsequently, these feature vectors $F_x \in R^{(n \times d)}$ and $F_y \in R^{(n \times d)}$ are input into the correspondence detection module. We introduce a corresponding permutation matrix and perform partial matching and outlier optimization. After successfully obtaining an effective permutation matrix P, X is transformed to ensure a one-to-one correspondence with Y. After that, the transformed point cloud $\tilde{X}$ and Y are input into the shape-adaptive registration module for shape matching. Point cloud registration is realized by learning the shape features between the source point cloud and the target point cloud.

3.1 Correspondence Detection Module

After extracting the point features, the module initially applies a feature set matching algorithm to quantify the semantic similarity features between the source and target point clouds, generating an initial similarity matrix $S = [s_{ij}]_{N_x \times N_y}$, where each s_{ij} represents the similarity between $x_i \in X$ and $y_j \in Y$.

However, relying solely on the initial correspondences may neglect global optimization, which would result in a local optimum. Inspired by S2H [26], we incorporate the Sinkhorn [4] algorithm, introducing the concept of a "dumpster" by adding a row and a column. This effectively partitions the matching weights of outliers. Subsequently, an enhanced profit matrix strategy is employed to increase row and column maximization to resolve uncertain or ambiguous situations. We employ the Hungarian algorithm to obtain the final correspondence matrix P. Later, we use the corresponding matrix P, sorting X to $\tilde{X} = P^T X$, which makes the x_i correspond to the y_j.

3.2 Shape-Adaptive Registration Module

After obtaining the true correspondence between X and Y, we proceed with the shape deformation of the point clouds. Initially, $F_y \in R^{(n \times d)}$ is fed into an encoder, effectively capturing both global and local attributes. The detailed features are concatenated with the global features $G_y \in R^{(n \times d)}$ of point cloud Y. The decoder takes the permuted $\tilde{X}$ and the detailed point cloud information from the encoder as inputs. During decoding, the attention mechanism at each layer focuses on capturing the inter-dependencies between different points. By learning adaptive feature coding and information propagation of local and global features of the target point cloud, the source point cloud is deformed to obtain the final generated point cloud.

3.3 Unsupervised Loss Function

To ensure the shape similarity between the target point cloud and the generated point cloud, we employ the point-to-point Euclidean distance L_1 supervision, expressed as:

$$L_1 = ||X - \tilde{X}||_F^2 + ||Y - \tilde{Y}||_F^2, \tag{1}$$

In addition, in the correspondence learning module, we specifically focus on the generation of the correspondence matrix, expressed as:

$$L_2 = ||PP^T - I_n||_F^2, \tag{2}$$

where P is the generated permutation matrix, and I is the unit matrix. In the third part, the learning process of the matrix P is facilitated by a fine analysis of the calculated input point cloud and the local geometry of each layer of the point cloud, expressed as:

$$L_3 = \sum_{i=1}^{n} \left(\sum_{k \in \Omega_i^y} \frac{||P_i X - P_k X||_2^2}{||y_i - y_k||_2^2} + \sum_{s \in \Omega_i^x} \frac{||P_i Y - P_s Y||_2^2}{||x_i - x_s||_2^2} \right), \tag{3}$$

where P_i denotes the i-th row of P, Ω_i^x denotes the k nearest neighbors of x_i.

The final loss function is formulated as:

$$L = L_1 + \alpha L_2 + \beta L_3, \tag{4}$$

here, α and β are balance parameters.

4 Experiments

4.1 Dataset and Experiment Settings

For the dataset, the training and testing datasets are from Surreal [6] and Shrec [5], respectively. In addition, to further validate our method, we conduct experiments on a synthetic dataset. We implement it on the NVIDIA RTX A4000 using the PyTorch framework. The learning rate is set to 1e−4, and the batch size is 8. The experiment is evaluated according to the accuracy corresponding to the point set, expressed as:

$$Acc = \frac{1}{n}|P \odot P_{gt}|_1, \tag{5}$$

where $\odot$ is the Hadamard product of matrices, $|\cdot|_1$ is the l_1 norm of a matrix, and P_{gt} encodes the ground-truth correspondence. This paper establishes accuracy in point correspondences at various tolerant errors to compare the effectiveness of the proposed method. Expressed as: $Acc_{rate} = \frac{r}{\max\{||x_i - x_j||_2 \forall i,j\}}$, where r represents the tolerant radius.

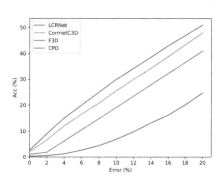

Fig. 2. Comparison of the corresponding accuracy of different non-rigid registration methods.

4.2 Experiments on Surreal Dataset

Figure 2 shows the advantage of our network in the accuracy of correspondence, especially when compared with F3D [8] and CPD [14]. There are also improvements in comparing Corrnet3D [24]. Figure 3 presents a visualization of the accuracy of LCRNet in correspondence. Figure 4 shows that LCRNet is closer to the target point cloud in shape registration.

4.3 Experiments on Synthetic Dataset

We use Thin Plate Spline [2] to deform some flexible 3D point clouds in different degrees to form a synthetic dataset. We use the chamfer distance as a measure of similarity evaluation. Table 1 shows the advantage of our method in shape similarity. Visualization results are shown in the Fig. 5.

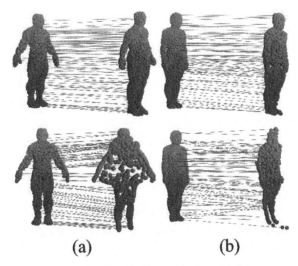

Fig. 3. Learned correspondence visualized by lines and colors. (a), (b) are two sets of point clouds, the left side of each pair is the target, and the right is the generation. The first row is our result, while the second is by Corrnet3D.

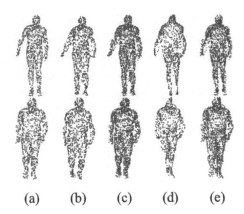

Fig. 4. Visual comparison of shape registration by different methods. (a) Mutual targets and sources. (b) Our generation. (c) Our registration effectiveness. (d) Corrnet3D generation. (e) Corrnet3D registration effect.

4.4 Ablation Study

Ablation study is performed on the Surreal [6] dataset. Table 2 compares the correspondence accuracy between the Shape-Adaptive Registration Module and the Deformer from Corrnet3D [24] at different error tolerances, while keeping other factors constant.

Table 1. Compare the chamfer distance of different methods under different deformation levels (D.L.).

D.L	0.5	0.7	0.8
PR-Net [20]	0.00354	0.00433	0.00592
CPD-Net [14]	0.00301	0.00442	0.00497
PC-Net [13]	0.00291	0.00408	0.00511
Our	0.0015	0.0015	0.0016

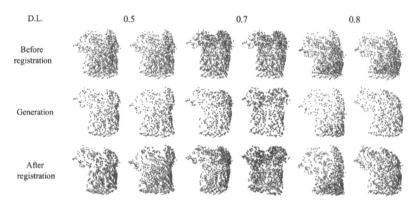

Fig. 5. Visualization of registration results under different deformation levels.

Table 2. Comparison of methods at different error tolerances (E.T.).

Method	0% E.T.	4% E.T.	8% E.T.	12% E.T.
Deformer	13.75	46.55	71.76	82.83
Our	19.29	55.10	79.07	87.96

5 Conclusions

An unsupervised non-rigid point cloud registration with local correspondence relationships is proposed by us. By combining soft and hard matching, shape registration, and local geometric relationships, our method not only enhances registration accuracy but also improves the model's adaptability to complex scenes and noisy environments. Experiments are conducted on both public and synthetic datasets. The Visualization results and quantitative comparisons indicate that our method can effectively learn correspondences among points for registration, successfully achieving non-rigid point cloud registration. In future work, we can extend correspondence finding to the hierarchical refinement of point clouds and optimize the amount of computation, which we believe can improve the registration accuracy of non-rigid point clouds. At the same time, we believe that our method can help with large-scale point cloud registration, medical image processing, and robot navigation.

References

1. Aoki, Y., Goforth, H., Srivatsan, R.A., Lucey, S.: PointNetLK: robust & efficient point cloud registration using PointNet. In: Proceedings of the IEEE/CVF Conference on Computer Vision and Pattern Recognition, pp. 7163–7172 (2019)
2. Bookstein, F.L., Green, W.: A thin-plate spline and the decomposition of deformations. Math. Methods Med. Imaging **2**(14–28), 3 (1993)
3. Choy, C., Dong, W., Koltun, V.: Deep global registration. In: Proceedings of the IEEE/CVF Conference on Computer Vision and Pattern Recognition, pp. 2514–2523 (2020)
4. Cuturi, M.: Sinkhorn distances: lightspeed computation of optimal transport. In: Advances in Neural Information Processing Systems, vol. 26 (2013)
5. Donati, N., Sharma, A., Ovsjanikov, M.: Deep geometric functional maps: robust feature learning for shape correspondence. In: Proceedings of the IEEE/CVF Conference on Computer Vision and Pattern Recognition, pp. 8592–8601 (2020)
6. Groueix, T., Fisher, M., Kim, V.G., Russell, B.C., Aubry, M.: 3D-coded: 3D correspondences by deep deformation. In: Proceedings of the European Conference on Computer Vision (ECCV), pp. 230–246 (2018)
7. Li, Y., Cai, J., Zhou, Q., Lu, H.: Joint semantic-instance segmentation method for intelligent transportation system. IEEE Trans. Intell. Transp. Syst. (2022)
8. Liu, X., Qi, C.R., Guibas, L.J.: Flownet3D: learning scene flow in 3 Dpoint clouds. In: Proceedings of the IEEE/CVF Conference on Computer Vision and Pattern Recognition, pp. 529–537 (2019)
9. Lu, H., Teng, Y., Li, Y.: Learning latent dynamics for autonomous shape control of deformable object. IEEE Trans. Intell. Transp. Syst. (2022)
10. Lu, H., Wang, T., Xu, X., Wang, T.: Cognitive memory-guided autoencoder for effective intrusion detection in internet of things. IEEE Trans. Industr. Inf. **18**(5), 3358–3366 (2021)
11. Lu, H., Zhang, M., Xu, X., Li, Y., Shen, H.T.: Deep fuzzy hashing network for efficient image retrieval. IEEE Trans. Fuzzy Syst. **29**(1), 166–176 (2020)
12. Ma, C., et al.: Visual information processing for deep-sea visual monitoring system. Cogn. Robot. **1**, 3–11 (2021)
13. Ma, J., Wu, J., Zhao, J., Jiang, J., Zhou, H., Sheng, Q.Z.: Nonrigid point set registration with robust transformation learning under manifold regularization. IEEE Trans. Neural Netw. Learn. Syst. **30**(12), 3584–3597 (2018)
14. Myronenko, A., Song, X., Carreira-Perpinan, M.: Non-rigid point set registration: coherent point drift. In: Advances in Neural Information Processing Systems, vol. 19 (2006)
15. Phan, A.V., Le Nguyen, M., Nguyen, Y.L.H., Bui, L.T.: DGCNN: a convolutional neural network over large-scale labeled graphs. Neural Netw. **108**, 533–543 (2018)
16. Qi, C.R., Su, H., Mo, K., Guibas, L.J.: PointNet: deep learning on point sets for 3D classification and segmentation. In: Proceedings of the IEEE Conference on Computer Vision and Pattern Recognition, pp. 652–660 (2017)
17. Steder, B., Rusu, R.B., Konolige, K., Burgard, W.: NARF: 3D range image features for object recognition. In: Workshop on Defining and Solving Realistic Perception Problems in Personal Robotics at the IEEE/RSJ International Conference on Intelligent Robots and Systems (IROS), vol. 44, p. 2. Citeseer (2010)
18. Tan, X., Zhang, D., Tian, L., Wu, Y., Chen, Y.: Coarse-to-fine pipeline for 3D wireframe reconstruction from point cloud. Comput. Graph. **106**, 288–298 (2022)

19. Trappolini, G., Cosmo, L., Moschella, L., Marin, R., Melzi, S., Rodol'a, E.: Shape registration in the time of transformers. In: Advances in Neural Information Processing Systems, vol. 34, pp. 5731–5744 (2021)
20. Wang, L., Chen, J., Li, X., Fang, Y.: Non-rigid point set registration networks. arXiv preprint arXiv:1904.01428 (2019)
21. Wang, Y., Solomon, J.M.: Deep closest point: learning representations for point cloud registration. In: Proceedings of the IEEE/CVF International Conference on Computer Vision, pp. 3523–3532 (2019)
22. Yang, S., Lu, H., Li, J.: Multifeature fusion-based object detection for intelligent transportation systems. IEEE Trans. Intell. Transp. Syst. 24(1), 1126–1133 (2022)
23. Yew, Z.J., Lee, G.H.: RPM-Net: robust point matching using learned features. In: Proceedings of the IEEE/CVF Conference on Computer Vision and Pattern Recognition, pp. 11824–11833 (2020)
24. Zeng, Y., Qian, Y., Zhu, Z., Hou, J., Yuan, H., He, Y.: Corrnet3D: Unsupervised end-to-end learning of dense correspondence for 3D point clouds. In: Proceedings of the IEEE/CVF Conference on Computer Vision and Pattern Recognition, pp. 6052–6061 (2021)
25. Zhang, D., Wu, Y., Guo, M., Chen, Y.: Deep learning methods for 3D human pose estimation under different supervision paradigms: a survey. Electronics 10(18), 2267 (2021)
26. Zhang, Z., Sun, J., Dai, Y., Zhou, D., Song, X., He, M.: End-to-end learning the partial permutation matrix for robust 3D point cloud registration. In: Proceedings of the AAAI Conference on Artificial Intelligence, vol. 36, pp. 3399–3407 (2022)
27. Zhao, F., Zhao, W., Lu, H., Liu, Y., Yao, L., Liu, Y.: Depth-distilled multi-focus image fusion. IEEE Trans. Multimedia (2021)
28. Zheng, Y., Li, Y., Yang, S., Lu, H.: Global-PBNet: a novel point cloud registration for autonomous driving. IEEE Trans. Intell. Transp. Syst. 23(11), 22312–22319 (2022)

Point Cloud Completion via Trigonometric Encoding and Self-attention Based Feature Fusion

Yiqi Wu[1,2], Weijun Peng[2], Yidong Yang[1], Huachao Wu[2], Lixiang Liu[1], Yanli Li[3], and Boxiong Yang[1][✉]

[1] School of Information and Intelligence Engineering, University of Sanya, Sanya, China
boxiongyang@sanyau.edu.cn
[2] School of Computer Science, China University of Geosciences, Wuhan, China
[3] Department of Information Engineering, Ordos Vocational College, Ordos, China

Abstract. Recovering a complete point cloud from a partial point cloud is a critical and challenging task for many 3D applications. In this paper, we propose a point cloud completion network that focuses on improving the point cloud feature extraction and the initial generated point cloud in the encoding phase. We highlight the local details of the original point cloud by introducing trigonometric positional embedding for point cloud encoding. Moreover, a self-attention mechanism for feature fusion is proposed to facilitate the generation of a complete point cloud. The experiments on multiple public datasets demonstrate that our network effectively achieves 3D point cloud completion with strong generalization, outperforming recent point cloud completion methods.

Keywords: Point cloud completion · Feature extraction · Trigonometric embedding · Self-attention

1 Introduction

Point cloud, as a primitive but information-rich 3D representation, is widely used in fields such as 3D modeling, autonomous driving, and virtual reality [1, 8, 13, 23, 24]. However, point clouds are often sparse and incomplete due to occlusions, reflection differences, and sensor limitations. The absence of geometric and semantic information in the point cloud will affect the subsequent 3D task. Repairing this incompleteness is critical for downstream tasks [4, 19, 27]. Current completion methods are mainly divided into three categories: geometric methods [9, 26], alignment-based methods [5, 10] and learning-based methods. Geometric methods utilize geometric information but have limited effectiveness when dealing with complex shapes. Alignment-based methods require matching a reference model, and both methods have certain limitations. In

Supported by Hainan Province Science and Technology Special Fund (No. ZDYF2022GXJS005), the specific research fund of The Innovation Platform for Academician of Hainan Province (No. YSPTZX202144), and Inner Mongolia Autonomous Region Higher Education Scientific Research Project (No. NJZY21164).

H. Lu (Ed.): ISAIR 2024, CCIS 2402, pp. 91–99, 2025.
https://doi.org/10.1007/978-981-96-2911-4_10

comparison, point cloud completion methods based on deep learning have strong generalizations. Traditional learning-based completion methods focus on extracting global features, which makes it difficult to capture local details, hence the generated results are often too smooth. The effective extraction of the geometric details and structural information of point clouds remains a challenge in the field of 3D completion.

We propose a point cloud completion network to address the above problems. Unlike existing methods, we focus on optimizing the input point cloud feature extraction in the encoding stage and the initial generated point cloud. In the Experiments on the PCN (Point cloud Completion) dataset [22] and the ShapeNet-34 dataset [21] demonstrate that our network performs better compared to existing algorithms. Our main contributions can be summarized as follows:

1. We innovatively combine trigonometric positional coding and traditional coding methods to emphasize the local details of the original point cloud and improve the effectiveness of the decoder in generating a complete point cloud.
2. We introduce a new seed point cloud generation and refinement module, which fuses the features extracted by the trigonometric encoder and the predicted seed point cloud through a self-attention mechanism, effectively optimizing the generated point cloud results.

The rest of this article is organized as follows. In Sect. 2, related work on point cloud completion is reviewed to provide the necessary background and literature support. In Sect. 3, we describe in detail the structure of the designed network and its individual modules. In Sect. 4, we focus on experiments to validate the performance of the proposed method by comparing it with state-of-the-art completion methods on the PCN and ShapeNet-34 datasets. Section 5 summarizes and gives the conclusion.

2   Related Work

Voxel-Based Shape Completion. 2D convolutional neural networks perform well in image processing [7, 25]. Early attempts to use 3D convolution to map disordered point clouds to ordered volumes to complement the point cloud suffered from missing information [6, 29]. In addition, the high computational and memory overhead of 3D volume representation and the limited characterization of the surface features of 3D shapes lead to the consumption of large computational resources during feature extraction and sampling.

Point Cloud Completion. With the success of PointNet [11] and its subsequent work [12], directly processing point cloud coordinates became a mainstream method. PCN (Point Cloud Completion) [22] realizes point cloud completion from coarse to fine through the encoder-decoder architecture. Huang et al. [3] introduce a multi-resolution encoder, pyramid decoder, and adversarial loss function to improve the completion effect. Yu et al. [21] adopts the Transformer encoder-decoder structure and introduces a geometry perception module to better model local set relationships. Xiang et al. [17] introduced a novel method inspired by the snowflake splitting process, gradually restoring missing details through multi-stage point cloud.

3 Method

Our network's overall architecture, shown in Fig. 1, receives a partial point cloud as input and outputs a complete and dense point cloud after an encoder-decoder structure. Our network consists of three modules: composite encoder feature extraction module, seed generation and refinement module, and point generation module. In the following sections, we will introduce our method in detail.

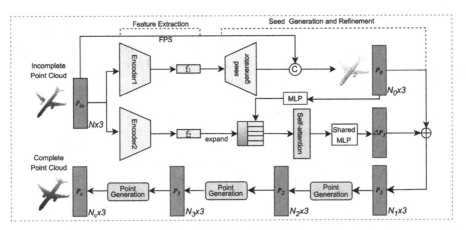

Fig. 1. The overall architecture of the network. We first feed the partial point cloud into a parallel composite encoder to extract features, then perform prediction and refinement of the seed point cloud, and finally feed it into a multi-stage point generation module.

3.1 Composite Encoder Feature Extraction Module

As shown in Fig. 1, the composite encoder feature extraction module consists of two encoders that avoid interfering with each other by having two independent paths in parallel. The module takes the partial point cloud $P_{in} = \{P_i | i = 1, 2, ..., N\} \in R^{N \times 3}$ as input. The module performs positional embedding through MLP (Multi-layer Perceptron), and by three consecutive set abstractions, each layer uses the FPS (Farthest Point Sampling) to get a smaller subset of the point cloud, and then clusters attachment k points with the subset as the center point. The points are continuously reduced at each layer to finally obtain a global feature vector f_1 of size $1 \times C$. At each layer of the set abstraction, we integrate a trigonometric positional encoding to extract the relative distances and positional relationships in the original point cloud. For each original point P_{in}, we upgraded its 3D coordinates into a C-dimensional vector, taking the x-axis as an example:

$$pos_x(p_{inx}, 2i) = sin(\frac{\alpha p_{in}}{\beta^{\frac{2i}{c}}}) \qquad (1)$$

$$pos_x(p_{inx}, 2i+1) = cos(\frac{\alpha p_{in}}{\beta^{\frac{2i}{c}}}) \qquad (2)$$

where α and β control the amplitude and wavelength, respectively, and i is used to assign information of different frequencies in the embedding vector. In this way, fine-grained semantics can be captured in 3D space. Then we select a subset $\{g_1, g_2, \ldots, g_K\}$ of the original point by FPS, and use a multi-stage k-NN and pooling operation to aggregate the local features. Finally the global feature f_2 of size $1 \times C$ is obtained.

3.2 Seed Generation and Refinement Module

We use the global shape feature f_1 to predict a rough but complete seed point cloud p_0 of size $N_0 \times 3$ ($N_0 = 512$). We convert f_1 to point features using the 1D deconvolution with the same kernel size and step size, and then generate seed points by integrating f and point features through MLP. We further concatenate the seed points and the incomplete point cloud P_{in} and then downsample the points to P_0 by FPS.

The trigonometric extracted features f_2 is then used to complement each other with it, The per-point features of the seed point P_0 extracted by PointNet are integrated with f_2 through shared-MLP to generate feature vector h. To enhance the positional linkage in the local features, we introduce a self-attention module that takes h as an input, followed by a linear transformation to generate the query matrix Q, the key matrix K, and the value matrix V. Then, the query matrix Q is multiplied with the transpose of the key matrix K to obtain the attention weight matrix.

$$F_{Attention} = soft \max\left(\frac{QK^T}{\sqrt{d_k}}\right)V \tag{3}$$

$$Q, K, V = (\text{Expand}(\text{H}(\text{seed}))) \oplus (\text{Expand}(f_2)) \oplus (\text{seed})\mathbf{x}(W_q, W_k, W_v) \tag{4}$$

where softmax is a normalized exponential function, the seed is the seed point predicted in the previous stage, H is the extraction based on PointNet [11], and W_q, W_k and W_v are linear transformation matrices.

Then, the dimension of the final features is reduced to the original point cloud $N_0 \times 3$ through a shared MLP. Subsequently, they are normalized using the hyperbolic tangent activation function to generate point displacements ΔP_i. These displacements are then added to the initial coarse seed point cloud P_0 for point offset refinement,

$$\Delta P_i = \tanh(\text{SMLP}(F_{Attention})) \tag{5}$$

$$P_1 = P_0 + \Delta P_i. \tag{6}$$

3.3 Point Generation Module

The point generation module adopts SnowflakeNet's SPD (Snowflake Point Deconvolution) [17] module. Each SPD layer takes the previous point cloud as input and simulates the growth process of a snowflake in 3D space. In each SPD layer, the point cloud from the previous step is split to generate multiple sub-nodes, as in the process of a snowflake splitting into more sub-nodes in 3D space. Multiple SPD layers are superimposed so that each seed node is gradually split in space to form more child nodes. Each SPD layer is equipped with a Skip-Transformer [17] to capture regional shape features. This design ensures that the splitting of points conforms to local features while prompting neighboring SPD layers to work in concert to ensure the consistency of multi-step point splitting.

3.4 Loss Function

The generation phase of our network consists of two parts: the first one generates the primitive seed point cloud P_0 and the second one produces several progressively denser point clouds $\{P_1, P_2, P_3, P_c\}$. We downsample the ground truth point cloud to maintain the same density as the predicted point cloud at each stage. The loss function consists of two parts: the difference between the shape of the multiple refined point clouds including the seed point cloud and the ground truth point cloud, and the difference between the shape of the predicted complete point cloud and the ground truth point cloud. In training, Chamfer Distance (CD) is used as the point cloud metric to calculate the average nearest distance. This is defined as follows:

$$L_{CD_2}(\mathbf{X}, \mathbf{Y}) = \sum_{\mathbf{x} \in \mathbf{X}} \min_{\mathbf{y} \in \mathbf{Y}} \|\mathbf{x} - \mathbf{y}\|_2^2 + \sum_{\mathbf{y} \in \mathbf{Y}} \min_{\mathbf{x} \in \mathbf{X}} \|\mathbf{y} - \mathbf{x}\|_2^2$$

$$L_{\text{completion}} = L_{CD}(P_c, P_{gt}) + \sum_{i=0}^{3} L_{CD}(P_i, P_i'). \tag{7}$$

4 Experiments

To validate the effectiveness of our method, we conducted comprehensive experiments on two widely used datasets PCN [22] and the newly proposed ShapeNet34 [21] to evaluate the network's completion capabilities. Our methods are implemented in the Python language and the Pytorch framework, and all the work is trained on two NVIDIA GeForce GTX A4000 GPUs with a batch size of 24. We use the Adam optimizer to train our network with the learning rate initially set to 1e−4.

4.1 Performance on the PCN Dataset

Dataset. The PCN dataset is one of the most widely used point cloud completion datasets and contains a total of 30,974 CAD models in 8 classes. The full point cloud for each instance contains 16,384 points, while the partial point cloud contains 2,048 points. We used the same experimental setup as for PCN [22] and compared it to state-of-the-art methods.

Results. The results are shown in Table 1. We report the Chamfer Distance for the L1 criterion and also provide detailed results for each category, and our method exhibits the highest performance among all the evaluated methods. As shown in Fig. 2, we selected three typical point cloud completion methods (PCN [22], PoinTr [21], Snowflakenet

Table 1. Point cloud completion results on the PCN dataset in terms of per-point L1 Chamfer Distance × 1000 (lower is better).

Methods	Average	Plane	Cabinet	Car	Chair	Lamp	Couch	Table	Boat
FoldingNet [20]	14.31	9.49	15.80	12.61	15.55	16.41	15.97	13.65	14.99
TopNet [14]	12.15	7.61	13.31	10.90	13.82	14.44	14.78	11.22	11.12
AtlasNet [2]	10.85	6.73	11.94	10.10	12.06	12.37	12.99	10.33	10.61
PCN [22]	9.64	5.50	22.70	10.63	8.70	11.10	11.34	11.68	8.59
GRNet [18]	8.83	6.45	10.37	9.45	9.41	7.96	10.51	8.44	8.04
CRN [15]	8.51	4.79	9.97	8.31	9.49	8.94	10.69	7.81	8.05
PMP-Net [16]	8.73	5.65	11.24	9.64	9.51	6.95	10.83	8.72	7.25
PoinTr [21]	8.38	4.75	10.47	8.68	9.39	7.75	10.93	7.78	7.29
SnowflakeNet [17]	7.21	4.29	9.16	8.08	7.89	6.07	9.23	6.55	6.40
Ours	7.17	4.22	9.17	8.16	7.65	6.10	9.18	6.45	6.44

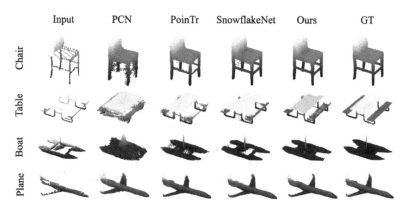

Fig. 2. Visualization of point cloud completion on the PCN dataset.

[17]) to compare with our network completion visual results. From the visual results, it can be inferred that our completion effect is better and the network has more advantages. For example, in the category of chairs and airplanes, the results of the other methods are surrounded by a lot of noise points, and in addition, it can be seen from the table and the boat that the complement of our method is more complete.

4.2   Performance on the ShapeNet-34 Dataset

Dataset. The ShapeNet-34 dataset covers more object categories and three different levels of incomplete point cloud patterns. We used the subset of Shapenet's 34 categories for training and the remaining 21 unseen categories for testing. The input partial point cloud is 2,048 points, and the complete point cloud is 8,192 points. During the test, we selected 8 fixed viewpoints and set the number of incomplete point clouds to 25%, 50%, and 75% of complete point clouds, which corresponds to the three difficulties of easy, medium, and difficult in the test stage level.

Table 2. Point cloud completion results on ShapeNet-34 dataset. Evaluated as L2 Chamfer Distance $\times$ 1000 (lower is better) and F-Score@1% (higher is better).

Methods	34 seen categories					21 unseen categories				
	CD-S	CD-M	CD-H	Avg	F1	CD-S	CD-M	CD-H	Avg	F1
FoldingNet [20]	1.86	1.81	3.38	2.35	0.139	2.76	2.74	5.36	3.62	0.095
PCN [22]	1.87	1.81	2.91	2.22	0.154	3.17	3.08	5.29	3.85	0.101
TopNet [14]	1.77	1.61	3.54	2.31	0.171	2.62	2.43	5.44	3.50	0.121
PFNet [3]	3.16	3.19	7.71	4.68	0.347	5.29	5.87	13.33	8.16	0.322
GRNet [18]	1.26	1.39	2.57	1.74	0.251	1.85	2.25	4.87	2.99	0.216
PoinTr [21]	0.76	1.05	1.88	1.23	0.421	1.04	1.67	3.44	2.05	0.384
SnowflakeNet [17]	0.60	0.86	1.50	0.99	0.422	0.88	1.46	2.92	1.75	0.388
SeedFormer [28]	0.48	0.70	1.30	0.83	0.452	0.61	1.07	2.35	1.34	0.402
ours	0.465	0.66	1.15	0.77	0.455	0.67	1.10	2.18	1.31	0.410

Results. We use 34 subcategories for training and the test also includes 21 training unseen categories. Our method achieved the best scores in all areas. As shown in Table 2, on the 34 seen categories and the 21 unseen categories, it achieved the best average F-score@1% of 0.455 and 0.410, respectively. This indicates that our network generates objects with a density distribution closest to the ground truth point cloud. In particular, when dealing with unseen objects, our network shows stronger generalization ability with an average Chamfer Distance of 1.31.

5 Conclusion

In this paper, we propose a novel point cloud completion network that emphasizes the integrity of point cloud structure and detail preservation. We integrated trigonometric positional encoding with traditional encoding methods, highlighting the local details of the original point cloud. Through the use of self-attention mechanisms, we effectively optimized the generated point cloud results by merging features extracted by the trigonometric encoding and the predicted seed point cloud. Through experiments on multiple public datasets and comparisons with current state-of-the-art methods, it is shown that our method can effectively complete the 3D shape and has superior generalization capabilities. In future work, the focus will be more on the decoder point cloud generation phase of the point cloud completion process to improve the completion effect. In addition, instead of limiting the process to only dealing with partial point clouds, image data will be introduced to complement the point cloud information more comprehensively.

References

1. Chen, J., Zhang, D., Wu, Y., Chen, Y., Yan, X.: A context feature enhancement network for building extraction from high-resolution remote sensing imagery. Remote Sens. **14**(9), 2276 (2022)
2. Groueix, T., Fisher, M., Kim, V.G., Russell, B.C., Aubry, M.: A Papier-Mâché approach to learning 3D surface generation. In: Proceedings of the IEEE Conference on Computer Vision and Pattern Recognition, pp. 216–224 (2018)
3. Huang, Z., Yu, Y., Xu, J., Ni, F., Le, X.: PF-Net: point fractal network for 3D point cloud completion. In: Proceedings of the IEEE/CVF Conference on Computer Vision and Pattern Recognition, pp. 7662–7670 (2020)
4. Li, Y., Cai, J., Zhou, Q., Lu, H.: Joint semantic-instance segmentation method for intelligent transportation system. IEEE Trans. Intell. Transp. Syst. (2022)
5. Li, Y., Dai, A., Guibas, L., Nießner, M.: Database-assisted object retrieval for real-time 3D reconstruction. In: Computer Graphics Forum, pp. 435–446 Wiley Online Library (2015)
6. Liu, Y., Fan, B., Xiang, S., Pan, C.: Relation-shape convolutional neural network for point cloud analysis. In: Proceedings of the IEEE/CVF Conference on Computer Vision and Pattern Recognition, pp. 8895–8904 (2019)
7. Lu, H., Zhang, M., Xu, X., Li, Y., Shen, H.T.: Deep fuzzy hashing network for efficient image retrieval. IEEE Trans. Fuzzy Syst. **29**(1), 166–176 (2020)
8. Ma, C., et al.: Visual information processing for deep-sea visual monitoring system. Cogn. Robot. **1**, 3–11 (2021)
9. Mitra, N.J., Pauly, M., Wand, M., Ceylan, D.: Symmetry in 3D geometry: extraction and applications. In: Computer Graphics Forum, pp. 1–23. Wiley Online Library (2013)
10. Nan, L., Xie, K., Sharf, A.: A search-classify approach for cluttered indoor scene understanding. ACM Trans. Graph. (TOG). **31**(6), 1–10 (2012)
11. Qi, C.R., Su, H., Mo, K., Guibas, L.J.: PointNet: deep learning on point sets for 3D classification and segmentation (2017). http://arxiv.org/abs/1612.00593
12. Qi, C.R., Yi, L., Su, H., Guibas, L.J.: PointNet++: deep hierarchical feature learning on point sets in a metric space. In: Advances in Neural Information Processing Systems, vol. 30 (2017)
13. Tan, X., Zhang, D., Tian, L., Wu, Y., Chen, Y.: Coarse-to-fine pipeline for 3D wireframe reconstruction from point cloud. Comput. Graph. **106**, 288–298 (2022)
14. Tchapmi, L.P., Kosaraju, V., Rezatofighi, H., Reid, I., Savarese, S.: TopNet: structural point cloud decoder. In: Proceedings of the IEEE/CVF Conference on Computer Vision and Pattern Recognition, pp. 383–392 (2019)
15. Wang, X., Ang Jr., M.H., Lee, G.H.: Cascaded refinement network for point cloud completion. In: Proceedings of the IEEE/CVF Conference on Computer Vision and Pattern Recognition, pp. 790–799 (2020)
16. Wen, X., et al.: PMP-Net: point cloud completion by learning multi-step point moving paths. In: Proceedings of the IEEE/CVF Conference on Computer Vision and Pattern Recognition, pp. 7443–7452 (2021)
17. Xiang, P., et al.: SnowFlakeNet: point cloud completion by snowflake point deconvolution with skip-transformer. In: Proceedings of the IEEE/CVF International Conference on Computer Vision, pp. 5499–5509 (2021)

18. Xie, H., Yao, H., Zhou, S., Mao, J., Zhang, S., Sun, W.: GRNet: gridding residual network for dense point cloud completion. In: European Conference on Computer Vision, pp. 365–381. Springer, Cham (2020)

19. Yang, S., Lu, H., Li, J.: Multifeature fusion-based object detection for intelligent transportation systems. IEEE Trans. Intell. Transp. Syst. **24**(1), 1126–1133 (2022)

20. Yang, Y., Feng, C., Shen, Y., Tian, D.: FoldingNet: point cloud auto-encoder via deep grid deformation. In: Proceedings of the IEEE Conference on Computer Vision and Pattern Recognition, pp. 206–215 (2018)

21. Yu, X., Rao, Y., Wang, Z., Liu, Z., Lu, J., Zhou, J.: PoinTr: diverse point cloud completion with geometry-aware transformers. In: Proceedings of the IEEE/CVF International Conference on Computer Vision, pp. 12498–12507 (2021)

22. Yuan, W., Khot, T., Held, D., Mertz, C., Hebert, M.: PCN: point completion network. In: 2018 International Conference on 3D Vision (3DV), pp. 728–737. IEEE (2018)

23. Zhang, D., He, L., Luo, M., Xu, Z., He, F.: Weight asynchronous update: improving the diversity of filters in a deep convolutional network. Comput. Visual Media **6**, 455–466 (2020)

24. Zhang, D., Wu, Y., Guo, M., Chen, Y.: Deep learning methods for 3D human pose estimation under different supervision paradigms: a survey. Electronics 10(18), 2267 (2021)

25. Zhao, F., Zhao, W., Lu, H., Liu, Y., Yao, L., Liu, Y.: Depth-distilled multi-focus image fusion. IEEE Trans. Multimedia (2021)

26. Zhao, W., Gao, S., Lin, H.: A robust hole-filling algorithm for triangular mesh. Visual Comput. **23**, 987–997 (2007)

27. Zheng, Y., Li, Y., Yang, S., Lu, H.: Global-PBNet: a novel point cloud registration for autonomous driving. IEEE Trans. Intell. Transp. Syst. **23**(11), 22312–22319 (2022)

28. Zhou, H., et al.: SeedFormer: patch seeds based point cloud completion with upsample transformer. In: European Conference on Computer Vision, pp. 416–432. Springer, Cham (2022)

29. Zhou, Y., Tuzel, O.: VoxelNet: end-to-end learning for point cloud based 3D object detection. In: Proceedings of the IEEE Conference on Computer Vision and Pattern Recognition, pp. 4490–4499 (2018)

Research Progress of Exploring Intelligent Rehabilitation Technology Based on Human-Computer Interaction

Shuai Zhao[1], Wei Wei[1(✉)], and Lin Gan[2]

[1] School of Health Industry Management, University of Sanya, Sanya 572022, China
396871550@qq.com
[2] School of Information and Intelligent Engineering, University of Sanya, Sanya 572022, China

Abstract. In this paper, through the comprehensive analysis of human-computer interaction in the field of intelligent rehabilitation technology, introduces the human-computer interaction technology in the field of rehabilitation background, the basic theory and application and the intelligent rehabilitation technology based on human-computer interaction research, further points out that human-computer interaction technology is beneficial to improve the level of intelligent rehabilitation, the development of intelligent rehabilitation technology need to play the human-computer interaction in the field of rehabilitation, and on the basis of comprehensive analysis to promote the development of human-computer interaction technology and application to provide useful reference, actively promote the progress of rehabilitation medicine, improve the quality of life of rehabilitation patients.

Keywords: Intelligent Rehabilitation · Human-computer Interaction · Brain-computer Interface Technology · Motion Imagination · Electroencephalogram (EEG) Signal

1 Introduction

The field of intelligent rehabilitation is one of the research directions that have much attention in recent years. With the increasing trend of population aging and the number of patients with chronic diseases increasing year by year, more efficient and personalized rehabilitation treatment methods are needed to improve the quality of life of patients. In the traditional field of rehabilitation, doctors and rehabilitation teachers lead the rehabilitation training process, but there are some problems in this way, such as the long rehabilitation process and the limited effect. Therefore, people began to explore the use of human-computer interaction technology to improve the field of intelligent rehabilitation.

First, this paper comprehensively introduces the basic theory and application of human-computer interaction technology, the research on intelligent rehabilitation technology based on human-computer interaction, and the research on the interaction between human brain and computer signals. Secondly, this paper provides an important reference for the theory and practice of intelligent human-computer interaction technology through systematic summary and induction. Finally, the data collection, summary and analysis of human-computer interaction technology and its data in the field of intelligent rehabilitation can promote the cooperation and communication of multiple disciplines.

2 Overview of Human-Computer Interaction

As a multidisciplinary research field of computer science, anthropology and psychology, human-computer interaction plays an important role in the research of intelligent rehabilitation technology. This section will discuss the basic theory and application of human-computer interaction.

2.1 Basic Theory of Human-Computer Interaction

The basic theory of human-computer interaction studies the way of information exchange and interaction between human and computer. Among them, human cognitive process and behavior mode are one of the core problems of human-computer interaction. Human cognitive processes include perception, attention, memory, thinking, and problem solving. In the human-computer interaction rehabilitation technology, the monitoring and intervention of the patient's perception and attention can help the patient to improve the concentration and effect of the rehabilitation training. The study of memory and thinking also provides an important theoretical basis for the design of intelligent human-computer interaction rehabilitation technology.

The behavior mode of human-computer interaction studies the way and law of interaction between human and computer. In the intelligent rehabilitation Brain-Computer Interface (BCI) technology, understanding the behavior pattern of patients can provide a basis for the design of adaptive rehabilitation system. By monitoring and analyzing the behavior patterns of patients, the content and difficulty of rehabilitation training can be adjusted in real time to improve the rehabilitation effect.

In addition, the interface design and user experience of human-computer interaction are also one of the basic theoretical contents of human-computer interaction.

2.2 Application of Human-Computer Interaction

The application of human-computer interaction covers many fields, such as medical care, education, entertainment and so on. In the intelligent rehabilitation technology, the application of human-computer interaction mainly focuses on the rehabilitation evaluation and treatment.

In terms of rehabilitation evaluation, human-computer interaction can realize the collection and analysis of patients' EEG signals through brain-computer interface technology, so as to help doctors to timely, accurately and objectively understand the rehabilitation status of patients' recovery, conduct rehabilitation efficacy evaluation, and provide effective and objective data support for the adjustment of rehabilitation treatment plan.

In terms of rehabilitation treatment, human-computer interaction can improve the patient's participation and interest and increase the effect of rehabilitation training by designing the interactive interface and the gamified training mode. Through the technical means of human-computer interaction, rehabilitation training can be more personalized and intelligent to meet the needs of different patients.

In addition, the application of human-computer interaction can also be extended to auxiliary tools and intelligent devices in daily life. For example, through intelligent rehabilitation brain-computer interface technology, disabled people can use electrical signals to control electronic devices and improve their quality of life and autonomy.

Brain-computer interface technology applied by human-computer interaction is a kind of technology that directly connects and interacts with the human brain and external devices such as the computer. It can realize direct communication and control between human and machine by interpreting the signals of the human brain. The development of brain-computer interface technology originated in the 1960s, when scientists began to explore the use of EEG for human-computer interaction. As technology continues to advance, researchers are gradually shifting their attention from EEG to more sophisticated and accurate brain-computer interface technologies. In recent years, brain-computer interface technology has been widely used in the field of medical rehabilitation, especially in the rehabilitation treatment of neurological diseases such as stroke. Through the brain-computer interface technology, the rehabilitation treatment of patients with impaired motor function can be realized, especially in the stroke rehabilitation treatment, which can help patients recover the limb motor function and improve the quality of life. In addition, BCI technology can be applied to the treatment of motor neuron diseases, such as Parkinson's disease. Through the interpretation and analysis of BCI signals, it can realize the control and regulation of patients' muscle movements, reduce symptoms and improve the quality of life.

At present, the research of BCI technology mainly focuses on the following aspects. First, the researchers aim to improve the accuracy and stability of brain-computer interface systems. By improving the signal acquisition and processing algorithm, optimize the electrode material and design, and improve the accuracy of signal recognition and decoding. Second, researchers are also exploring how to achieve more natural and efficient interactions with brain-computer interfaces. For example, using artificial intelligence technologies such as deep learning can achieve accurate identification and prediction of multiple motion intentions, so as to achieve more flexible and accurate motion control. In addition, there are researchers working on non-invasive brain-computer interface technologies to reduce discomfort and risk.

In general, human-computer interaction technology has a wide application prospect in the field of medical rehabilitation, which will bring more accurate and effective methods for rehabilitation treatment, and provide strong support for patients to restore their functions and improve their quality of life.

3   Research on Intelligent Rehabilitation Technology Based on Human-Computer Interaction

3.1   Goal and Pathological Basis of Intelligent Rehabilitation

The goal and pathological basis of intelligent rehabilitation are important directions in the research of intelligent rehabilitation technology.

The goal of intelligent rehabilitation is to realize the personalized, accurate and efficient rehabilitation treatment through human-computer interaction technology. Human-computer interaction technology realizes the direct communication and control between human and machine by reading and parsing the brain neural activity information, and realizes the function of the recovery and improvement of the injured neural system. The main mechanism is to record the neural signals such as EEG, magnetoencephalography (MEG) and so on, and through the analysis of signal processing and pattern recognition algorithm, the neural activities of the brain are converted into control signals for external equipment, so as to realize the control of rehabilitation equipment. Intelligent rehabilitation technology has a wide range of applications, including limb rehabilitation, speech rehabilitation, cognitive rehabilitation and other directions. In terms of limb rehabilitation, human-computer interaction technology can recover and improve the motor function of patients with hemiplegia through the brain-computer interface. By reading the patient's EEG signal, it can be transformed into a control signal of external rehabilitation equipment to realize the motor training of the patient's limbs. In speech rehabilitation, human-computer interaction technology can help aphasia patients communicate through mental control computers or other auxiliary devices. In terms of cognitive rehabilitation, human-computer interaction technology can judge the cognitive state of patients and carry out corresponding rehabilitation training according to the results.

The pathological basis of intelligent rehabilitation mainly includes nervous system damage and functional impairment. Nervous system injury refers to the structural and functional abnormalities of the central nervous system, leading to neurological dysfunction. Common neurological injuries include stroke, brain trauma, spinal cord injury, etc. Functional dysfunction refers to the patient's various functions in daily life are affected, including movement, sensory, speech, cognition and other aspects.

3.2   Role of Human-Computer Interaction in Rehabilitation Treatment

Human-computer interaction technology refers to the technology of information exchange and operation between people and machines. It realizes the information transmission and instruction execution between people and machines through various input and output devices. Human-computer interaction technology plays an important role in rehabilitation treatment.

The Role of Human-Computer Interaction in Rehabilitation Patients in Rehabilitation Treatment. First, human-computer interaction technology can provide personalized treatment plans for rehabilitation patients according to their needs. By analyzing the basic conditions of patients' conditions and rehabilitation needs, a reasonable rehabilitation plan is designed based on big data. For example, for patients with different degrees of motor impairment, human-computer interaction technology can design corresponding motor training plans according to their motor ability and rehabilitation goals, so as to realize personalized rehabilitation treatment.

Secondly, human-computer interaction technology can provide timely feedback and guidance for rehabilitation patients in the rehabilitation training. In rehabilitation treatment, timely feedback and guidance is crucial for patients 'rehabilitation effect, human-computer interaction technology can be by monitoring the patient's movement state and posture, real-time feedback patients' movement, and provide corresponding guidance and adjustment advice, help patients to correct the wrong way of movement, strengthen the correct movement mode, improve the rehabilitation effect. You can also monitor your own health status by wearing portable devices, such as smart watches and bracelets, etc., to prevent the occurrence of myocardial infarction and cerebral infarction. Xiaoyong Chen advocated "pass forward" and "health first" early warning management, and pointed out that the human-machine interaction intelligent wearable device acquisition human pulse, heart rate, blood pressure and other important physiological indicators, using the existing medical diagnosis experience data of artificial intelligence deep learning model training and validation, to establish a new stroke prediction intelligent pathology model, reduce the risk of cardiovascular and cerebrovascular disease [1].

In addition, human-computer interaction technology can also increase the interest and participation of rehabilitation patients. The rehabilitation process often requires long periods of training and repeated practice, which may feel monotonous and boring to the patient. Human-computer interaction technology can increase patients' participation and enthusiasm through the design of interesting rehabilitation training games and interactive interfaces, and make the rehabilitation treatment process more pleasant and effective.

The Role of Human-Computer Interaction for Rehabilitation Physicians and Rehabilitation Therapists in Rehabilitation Treatment. First, human-computer interaction technology plays an important role in rehabilitation evaluation by rehabilitation physicians and rehabilitation therapists. Rehabilitation evaluation on the basis of rehabilitation treatment, through human-computer interaction technology can be collected to rehabilitation patients before treatment more objective and accurate functional data, for rehabilitation physicians and rehabilitation therapists comprehensive rehabilitation evaluation to provide data support, is conducive to the early rehabilitation plan, for late rehabilitation effect evaluation and program adjustment to provide objective data support.

Secondly, human-computer interaction technology is beneficial to rehabilitation doctors and rehabilitation therapists to evaluate and adjust the effect of rehabilitation treatment. Through human-computer interaction technology, rehabilitation treatment can be monitored and evaluated in real time, so that rehabilitation doctors can understand and master the rehabilitation progress and effect of patients in real time, and adjust and optimize the rehabilitation program according to the monitoring results. At the same time, human-computer interaction technology can record and save the rehabilitation data of patients, provide a basis for the follow-up rehabilitation evaluation, and help doctors to better understand and analyze the effect of rehabilitation treatment and make further treatment plans.

In addition, the human-computer interaction technology intelligent rehabilitation training setting is conducive to rehabilitation therapists in the process of rehabilitation treatment more time, energy and attention on patients, real-time observation of rehabilitation training found problems in time, guide and correct, to improve rehabilitation effect, at the same time, can strengthen the communication with patients, understand the patient's psychological state, psychological counseling in a timely manner.

4 Study of the Interaction Between Human Brain and Computer Signals

4.1 Human-Computer Interaction Technology of Asynchronous EEG

Research Status of Asynchronous EEG. Asynchronous EEG technology is a method based on interaction between human brain signal and computer, which has wide application prospect in the field of intelligent rehabilitation. This technology can realize the flexible communication and control between the human brain and the computer by recording and analyzing the EEG signals.

Yu Zhang et al. proposed a human-computer interaction technology based on asynchronous EEG, which analyzes the characteristics of EEG signals and uses the algorithm to transform them into interactive instructions that can be understood by the computer [2]. This research lays the foundation for the application of asynchronous EEG technology and provides new ideas for the development of the field of intelligent rehabilitation.

Kang Wang et al. explored the human-computer interaction technology based on asynchronous EEG by studying the perception algorithm of motor imagination EEG signals. They designed an algorithm that can sense motion and imagine EEG signals, and applied it to human-computer interaction. This study further broadens the application scope of asynchronous EEG technology in the field of intelligent rehabilitation [3].

JingweiYue et al. research analyzed the relationship between EEG signals and computer commands, and proposed a technical method for interaction. This study provides new ideas and methods for the human-computer interaction technology of asynchronous EEG [4].

In conclusion, by analyzing the characteristics of the EEG signals and designing the corresponding algorithms and technologies, it can realize the interaction and control between the human brain and the human computer, providing a more convenient and effective method for rehabilitation.

Application and Challenges of Asynchronous EEG in the Field of Rehabilitation. In the field of rehabilitation, asynchronous EEG technology also has a wide application.

Meiyu Zhong et al. designed and realized the YSU-lower limb rehabilitation robot intelligent interaction system, using brain-computer interface technology to achieve rehabilitation training and achieve good results [5]. In that study, Meiyu Zhong et al. used a lower limb rehabilitation robot, YSU-II, as a research platform, which mainly solved three key questions. First, a brain-computer interface system was designed to collect patient EEG signals and analyze them in real time. The analysis and processing of the EEG signals can enable the control of the robot motion. Secondly, a set of robot control algorithm is designed to transform EEG signals into robot motion commands. By modeling the relationship between EEG signals and robot motion. Finally, a set of human-computer interaction interface is designed to display the motion state and rehabilitation effect of the robot. Patients can understand their rehabilitation by observing the information on the interface. The experimental results of this study show that the YSU-II intelligent interaction robot system can effectively improve the movement recovery and rehabilitation effect of recovered patients. Through the use of asynchronous EEG technology, patients can feel the movement of the robot more intuitively, and control the movement of the robot according to their own rehabilitation needs, so as to improve the initiative and participation of rehabilitation.

Qingmin Li et al. summarized the research on EEG brain-computer interface, explored the application of rehabilitation, investigated the current application status of EEG-based brain-computer interface in rehabilitation, and discussed the applicability of different rehabilitation diseases. The results show that EEG CI has shown good results in the rehabilitation of Parkinson's disease, stroke and spinal cord injury [6].

However, there are still some challenges in the application process, which limit the further development and application of synchronous EEG technology in the field of rehabilitation. Qingchun Meng et al. pointed out that the current brain-computer information interaction technology still faces a variety of problems, such as the limitation of single-channel information acquisition, signal interference and noise, differences between individuals and other [7].

Researchers have proposed some solutions to solve the challenges in the application of asynchronous EEG technology. Taking the differences between individuals as an example, Chenxi Li et al. mentioned in their review that the adaptability and intelligence level of BCI system can be improved through personalized parameter adjustment and machine learning algorithms [7]. For the limitation of the single-channel information collection, Yu Zhang et al. proposed to improve the signal quality through the multi-channel information fusion and the noise reduction algorithm [2].

In conclusion, asynchronous EEG technology has wide application prospects in the field of intelligent rehabilitation. However, there are still some challenges that need to be overcome. Facing these challenges, the researchers have proposed some solutions, such as personalized parameter adjustment, multi-channel information fusion, and noise reduction algorithms. Future research work could further explore the effectiveness and feasibility of these programs to facilitate the development of asynchronous EEG technologies in the field of intelligent rehabilitation.

4.2 Application of the EEG Signal Sensing Algorithm in Human-Computer Interaction

Research Progress of EEG Signal Perception Algorithm for Motor Imagination.
The motor imagination EEG signal perception algorithm mainly measures and analyzes human EEG signals to realize the interaction between human thinking and intention and computer. In human-computer interaction, the research algorithm of motor imagination is as follows.

Yun Ma et al. developed a virtual reality rehabilitation training platform, which provides a variety of rehabilitation training modes, and realizes real-time monitoring and feedback of patients' movement status through EEG signal identification and movement intention decoding. The experimental results show that this platform can significantly improve the exercise capacity of patients with cerebral palsy [8].

Jinshu Zheng et al. designed a rehabilitation robot based on brain-computer interaction technology to provide precise guidance in rehabilitation treatment by capturing the activity signal of patients' brains and conducting real-time analysis. The results show that the brain-computer interface technology can promote the movement recovery and improve the rehabilitation effect [9].

Huaiwei Wu proposed a precise control method of the robotic arm by recognizing the motor intention of the brain. Experiments show that this method can effectively improve the quality of life and independence of exercise-restricted people [10].

The research progress of motor imagination EEG signal sensing algorithm in human-computer interaction is rich and varied, covering different methods and application fields. These studies provide important theoretical basis and technical support for the research of human-computer interaction to explore intelligent rehabilitation technology.

Application of the EEG Signal Sensing Algorithm in the Field of Rehabilitation. It is a human-computer interaction technology based on EEG signals. Through the recognition and analysis of the EEG signals, the direct interaction between human and computer can be realized. In the field of intelligent rehabilitation, the motor imagination EEG signal sensing algorithm is widely used in rehabilitation training and motor recovery, and some research progress has been made.

Junyu Wang et al. developed a rehabilitation prosthesis system based on brain-computer interface technology for stroke patients. Through the collection and processing of the EEG signals of the patients' big movement imagination, the accurate control of the prosthesis was realized. The results show that this system is effective in improving motor function and quality of life in stroke patients [11].

Jun Qin designed a wearable device that can collect EEG signals from stroke patients in real time and convert EEG signals into control commands through brain-computer interface technology. This wearable system is not only convenient and comfortable, but also can realize the personalization and flexibility of rehabilitation training [12].

Wei Sun carried out the movement of the brain control robot imagine EEG signal classification identification research, through the analysis of the EEG signal and movement imagination related EEG signal concentration frequency, the results show that the fusion-frequency-airspace feature extraction method can significantly improve the left and right hand movement imagine the classification of EEG signal identification rate, realize movement imagination EEG signal movement control of robot arm [13].

Wenwen Zhai et al. carried out a study on the brain-computer interface system of the upper limb rehabilitation training robot. Through the acquisition and processing of EEG signals, the intention of patients was transformed into instructions to control the movement of the robot, so as to realize the interaction between the patient and the robot [14].

The research progress of motor imagination EEG signal sensing algorithm in the field of intelligent rehabilitation has achieved some results. However, the algorithm still needs further research and improvement to improve the signal resolution ability and classification accuracy and achieve better human-computer interaction effect. First of all, we can further study and optimize the rehabilitation brain-computer interface technology algorithm to improve the accuracy and efficiency of signal processing and pattern recognition. Secondly, more advanced and intelligent technologies can be combined to explore rehabilitation brain-computer interaction. Moreover, the application of human-computer interaction technology in other neurological diseases and functional disorders can be explored to more fully play its role in the field of neurorehabilitation.

5 Conclusion

The research trend in the field of intelligent rehabilitation is toward the multimodal fusion, machine learning and artificial intelligence, the combination of virtual reality and augmented reality, and the direction of network and remote monitoring, through continuous exploration and innovation, will further push the human-computer interaction technology application in the field of intelligent rehabilitation, and provide more effective and personalized rehabilitation.

This study aims to explore the progress of intelligent rehabilitation technology through human-computer interaction, comprehensive introduction of the background and importance of human-computer interaction to explore intelligent rehabilitation technology, summarizes the progress of the human-computer interaction in intelligent rehabilitation technology research, put forward the practical practice and research direction, to promote the development and application of rehabilitation brain-computer interface technology provide useful reference, is conducive to further promote the progress of rehabilitation medicine, improve the quality of life of patients.

Conflicts of Interest. The authors declare that they have no conflicts of interest to report regarding the present study.

Funding Statement. This paper was supported by Hainan Province Science and Technology Special Fund (No. ZDYF2021SHFZ240).

References

1. Chen, B.X., et al.: Management for stroke intelligent early warning empowered by big data. Comput. Electr. Eng. **106**, 108602 (2023)
2. Zhang, Y.: Research on human-computer interaction technology based on asynchronous EEG. Southeast University (2020). https://doi.org/10.27014/d.cnki.gdnau.2020.00007
3. Wang, K., Zhai, D., Xia, Y.: Research on motor imagination for human-computer interaction. Unmanned Syst. Technol. **3**(01), 31–37 (2020)
4. Jingwei Yue, Y., Ge, Z.Z., et al.: Interaction technology in the brain-computer interface system. Comput. Meas. Control **08**, 1180–1183 (2008)
5. Zhong, M., Zhao, F., Dou, Y., et al.: Design and implementation of the YSU-lower limb rehabilitation robot. High Technol. Commun. **30**(09), 959–966 (2020)
6. Li, Q., Li, Z., Qiu, J., et al.: Current status of EEG CI-based research and its application in rehabilitation. Beijing Biomed. Eng. **36**(03), 310–316 (2017)

7. Li, C., Meng, Q., Yiyang, E., et al.: Summary of brain-computer information interaction technology. Comput. Knowl. Technol. **15**(03), 184–185 (2019). Academic Edition

8. Ma, Y., Wang, Y., Gao, X., et al.: Virtual reality rehabilitation training platform based on brain-machine interface technology. Chin. J. Biomed. Eng. **03**, 373–378 (2007)

9. Zheng, J., Wang, M., Zhu, Y., et al.: Clinical study on the rehabilitation treatment of post-stroke hemiplegia based on brain-machine interaction technology. J. External Treat. Tradit. Chin. Med. **30**(03), 3–5 (2021)

10. Wu, H.: 3D remote operation of the robotic arm based on a brain-computer interface. South China University of Technology (2018)

11. Wang, J., Wang, M., Xiang, W., et al.: On the rehabilitation of brain-computer interface prosthesis. World's Latest Med. Inf. Abstract **17**(45), 75–76 (2017)

12. Qin, H.: Research on a wearable brain-computer interface system for stroke rehabilitation. Shanghai Jiao Tong University (2020). https://doi.org/10.27307/d.cnki.gsjtu.2020.002277

13. Sun, W.: Classification and identification of motor EEG signals in a brain-controlled robot. Chongqing Jiaotong University (2021). https://doi.org/10.27671/d.cnki.gcjtc.2021.000884

14. Zhai, W., Yang, Y., Lu, S., et al.: Brain-computer interface system of upper limb rehabilitation training robot. Biomed. Eng. Res. **38**(03), 269–274 (2019)

Spectral Graph Neural Network: A Bibliometrics Study and Visualization Analysis via CiteSpace

Shelei Li[1,2] (ID), Yong Chai Tan[1], and Boxiong Yang[2](✉)

[1] Faculty of Engineering, Building Environment and Information Technology, SEGi University, 47810 Petaling Java, Malaysia
SUKD2202348@segi4u.my
[2] School of Information and Intelligence Engineering, University of Sanya, Sanya 572022, China
boxiongyang@sanyau.edu.cn

Abstract. Spectral Graph neural network has recently attracted increasing attention. Although it has been intensively research and widely applied in areas, such as link prediction, node classification, and clustering due to the powerful modeling capabilities of graph-structured data bioinformatics, 3D point cloud, Graph outlier detection, social network study, traffic networks and Hyperspectral image classification, the research of Spectral Graph Neural Network model is still in its infancy. CiteSpace was used as the tool to analyze the research hotspots and frontiers of Spectral Graph Neural Network. This study reviewed 3721 publications on Spectral Graph Neural Network between 2010 and 2023 from Web of Science Core Collection, using the appropriate keywords. CiteSpace was used to generate network maps and identify top authors, most productive country, core institutions, most high-frequency keywords, highly cited papers, and hot topics of research; and trends about co-author analysis, co-keyword analysis, co-citation analysis, and particularly cluster analysis ((Q = 0.8716)). Based on the CiteSpace outcomes, this domain is a hot topic with growing number of publications and close institutional and inter-country collaboration. Additionally, it integrates diverse disciplines and covers a wide range of topics. These results can be used by researchers and research groups' future research directions. In addition, beyond the current utilization of graph Fourier transform and spectral graph wavelet transform, more graph data analysis methods will be introduced in the future.

Keywords: Graph signal processing · Graph convolution network (GCN) · Spectral graph wavelet transform · Graph Fourier transform · CiteSpace · Intelligent Transportation System · Industrial Internet of Things (IIoT)

1 Introduction

Spectral Graph Neural Network (GNN) is a type of GNN that design graph signal filters in the spectral domain [1]. Currently, many researchers had reviewed literature in the field of spectral GNN from different perspectives, such as receptive field [2], deep Graph

Convolution Network (GCN) [3], graph wavelet frame [4], expressive power [1], etc. However, these reviews were based on the author's own understanding of the field, very few literatures were analyzed based on objective perspective using professional analysis tools. This paper provides a systematic and comprehensive analysis of the Spectral GNN related literature using CiteSpace.

Rapid growth of the Spectral GNN has drawn great interest from many researchers. In 2013, Bruna et al. [5] proposed a Spectral Graph Neural Network (spectral GNN) based on graph-Laplacian for the first time. However, the algorithm relies on the eigen decomposition of the Laplacian matrix which is time consuming. In addition, the convolution kernel is a global convolution kernel rather than a local one. To alleviate this limitation, Defferrard et al., [6] developed a method motivated by first-order approximation of spectral graph convolution [7]. This approach effectively addressed the huge computational overhead caused by Laplacian matrix decomposition by employing Chebyshev polynomial approximation. Graph Convolution Network (GCN) constructs a second-order approximation function for the Laplacian operator, which is equivalent to only considering 1-hop neighboring nodes [8]. This adjustment not only contributes to an expended receptive but also leads to a notable reduction in the model's running time, a critical aspect in spectral GNN research. Wu et al. [9] introduced simplifying graph convolutional networks that reduces running time consumption by optimizing the GCN model. Xu et al. [10] employed the wavelet basis derived by Hammond et al. [7] as a replacement for the Fourier transform basis. Additionally, Xu et al., introduced the heat kernel to address the challenges related to wavelet inverse transform [11]. This integration resulted in improvement in node classification performance to some extent. Veličković Petar [12] developed the Graph Attention Network (GAN), which introduce self-attention and multi-head attention. Graph Markov Neural Networks (GMNN) captures the combined probability distribution of object labels using a conditional random field, and this can be efficiently trained using the variational EM algorithm [13].

The above work focuses on node classification problems on graphs. There is also much research related to link prediction [14] and graph classification [15] problems.

In addition to the above-mentioned tasks (node classification, link prediction, graph classification), corresponding research has been carried out for different graph types, broadening the scope of applications. For instance, dynamic graph which is used to represent the transformation of graph structures over time. Such as, traffic flow prediction, vehicle trajectory prediction, daily runoff prediction, stock market index trend prediction, social behavior prediction. These applications all involve graph signal or structure changes over time, requiring algorithms to adapt to evolving structures [16]. Directed graph introduces the notion of edge directionality, influencing information flow and connectivity patterns. Hypergraph generalizes traditional graphs, allow for relationships between more than two nodes, posing additional challenges and opportunities for exploration [17, 18] which. Heterogeneous graph which deals with graphs with multiple node types or multiple edge types [19]. Hierarchical Graph can represent not only information in different levels but also their relationship [20].

Spectral GNN and its improved algorithms have been successful applied to various fields related to artificial intelligence, such as traffic flow forecasting [21], 3D point cloud

[22], recommender system [24, 33], hyperspectral image classification [25], anomaly detection [26], skeleton-based action recognition [27] etc.

These reviews analyzed the literature related to spectral GNN, offering valuable references to researchers engaged in Spectral GNN, aiding researchers in gaining a thorough understanding of the subject from diverse perspectives. Some of the contributions of this paper are as follows:

1. From the review analysis, it was discovered that only two data analysis methods, namely graph Fourier transform and graph wavelet transform, are currently employed in spectral GNN research for graph analysis. Other data analysis methods, such as the Hilbert-Huang transform, Empirical Orthogonal Function expansion (EOF), etc., have yet to be applied in graph structures analysis.
2. This review showcases the advancements in spectral GNN research from various perspectives (such as publication statistics, collaboration, co-citation, co-occurrence), offering valuable literature, dynamic visualizations, and insights for researchers.
3. Latest information of the current hotspots, trends, and potential research directions, offering specific technologies are provided in this review. This guidance is intended to help researchers to conduct research more efficiently in the ongoing exploration of this subject.

2 Data Acquisition and Bibliometric Analysis

2.1 Data Collection and Processing

The literature was retrieved from the Web of Science (WoS) Core Collection as of August 9, 2023. The search focused on the terms "spectral GNN", "graph convolution network", and "wavelet and graph". Based on retrieved document set, it was found that although spectral-domain and spatial-domain based convolutional neural networks on graphs were first proposed in 2013 [5], there were some related studies on graph neural networks as early as 2010 [28]. Therefore, this study reviews papers published between 2010 and 2023 to explore the trends of spectral GNN over the past decade.

2.2 Bibliometric Analysis Tool

CiteSpace, a Java-based bibliometric tool developed by Chen et al. [29] was used as the bibliometric analysis tool in this study as it offers diverse functionalities. These include identification of research fronts and hotspots, facilitation of knowledge dissemination and interdisciplinary interaction, and exploration the emerging trends.

3 Results

3.1 Statistical Analysis

A total of 3721 documents were obtained in the field of spectral GNN as of August 9, 2023. The annual and cumulative numbers of publications are depicted in Fig. 1. The number of publications has experienced a substantial increase since 2010. This clarifies the escalating interest in spectral GNN research. Publications were primarily categorized into four types of documents - article, review, proceeding paper, and book chapter. Articles constituted the predominant document publication type, followed by proceeding papers, review, and other publication types.

Number of Publications by Years. The yearly distribution of publications shows the historical dynamics of research in spectral GNN work and assists researchers to anticipate future development.

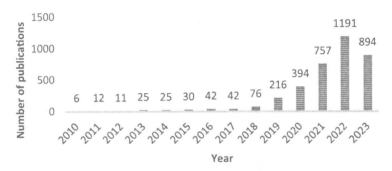

Fig. 1. Publication output performance during 2010–2023

Only a single-digit number of papers in spectral GNN were published in the year 2010 but the number of papers increased significantly until 2022, reaching 1191. The accumulated publications for the last three years (2019–2023) are 2842 (76.4% of the total reviewed), indicating that spectral GNN research is garnering increasing attention and generating more academic contributions. The count for 2023 is smaller than that of in 2022 due to only partial of publications captured till the month of August. Based on the result, the upward trend substantiates the ongoing prevalence of research on spectral GNN.

3.2 Collaboration Analysis

The collaboration network aims to understand the links among different institutions, countries, and authors on spectral GNN. Analyzing these collaboration links enables researchers to grasp the current research correlations and identify potential cooperation partners.

Institution Collaboration Network. Table 1 revealed the top 10 collaborative institutions in the globe by centrality (a key indicator for analyzing the importance of item). It's evident that most of the collaborative institutions are in China (6 institutions), and USA (3). This indicates a high level of engagement in the research on spectral GNN in these countries. However, the centrality of these top collaborative institutions tends to be relatively low except Chinese Academy of Sciences (0.31), Xidian University (0.11), University of California System (0.1).

114   S. Li et al.

Table 1. Institution collaboration

Ranking	Institution	Region	Count	Centrality	Year
1	Chinese Academy of Sciences	China	258	0.31	2013
2	Xidian University	China	67	0.11	2019
3	University of California System	USA	57	0.1	2011
4	Shanghai Jiao Tong University	China	95	0.06	2019
5	Beihang University	China	72	0.06	2019
6	University of Chinese Academy of Sciences	China	105	0.05	2019
7	Tsinghua University	China	80	0.05	2018
8	University of Southern California	USA	39	0.05	2011
9	Swiss Federal Institutes of Technology Domain	Swiss	35	0.05	2018
10	State University of New York (SUNY) System	USA	23	0.05	2015

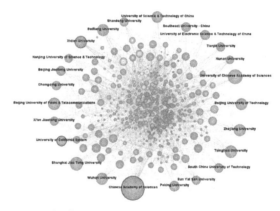

Fig. 2. Institutional cooperation network

Figure 2 showed the institutional cooperation network, which includes 669 nodes and 2717 cooperative links. Clearly, there is cooperation among institutions, and the existing institutional cooperations appear relatively tight, indicating that spectral GNN is a highly collaborated topic among these institutions.

Country Collaboration Network. Figure 3 illustrates the regional cooperation network, which include 72 nodes and 325 collaborative links. Node size corresponds to the citation frequency of the associated articles, serving as an indicator of the node's prominence. The presence of numerous regional links underscores the frequency of regional cooperation. Notable, significant nodes such as China, USA, Australia, United Kingdom, and India emerged in the network, indicating their substantial contributions and focus within the spectral GNN research landscape.

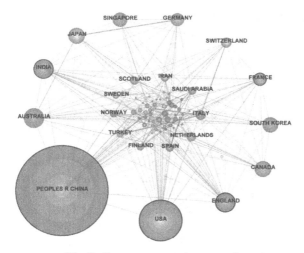

Fig. 3. Country cooperation network

Author Collaboration Network. Table 2 has shown that the top 10 authors collaborated with more than 10 authors in this field. The authors with the most collaborations are Ortega, Antonio and Yin, Baocai. Ortega, Antonio primarily collaborates on graph filter banks, while Yin, Baocai's collaboration focuses on application of graph convolution network (traffic flow prediction). However, the centrality is relatively low. The results suggested more collaboration is required between researchers according to their research interests.

Table 2. Author collaboration

Ranking	Author	Count	Centrality	Year
1	Ortega, Antonio	28	0.01	2010
2	Yin, Baocai	22	0	2021
3	Tanaka, Yuichi	20	0	2014
4	Gao, Junbin	17	0	2021
5	Sakiyama, Akie	16	0	2014
6	Yang, Jian	15	0.03	2019
7	Chen, Siheng	15	0	2013
8	Hu, Yongli	15	0	2021
9	He, Xiangnan	14	0	2019
10	Ribeiro, Alejandro	13	0	2019

3.3 Co-Citation Analysis

Conducting co-citation analysis enhances comprehension of the existing research landscape. It provides researchers with insights into highly reputed journals or literature, ongoing research focuses, and notable researchers or works in this field.

Reference Co-Citation Network. The most cited articles are usually regarded as landmarks due to their ground-breaking contributions, where two (8,10) and eight (1, 2, 3, 4, 5, 6, 7, 9) articles in the top 10 landmarks are from cluster #0 and #1 respectively (Fig. 7). Table 3 shows the top 10 cited literature on spectral GNN (a systematic review of block chain) which were cited no less than 420 times. Some publications lay the theoretical foundation of spectral GNN [5, 6, 8], and some publications offer improvement ideas, such as introducing attention mechanisms [12], drawing on the idea of signal processing on graph [31], or being inspired by stochastic optimization [32], inductive representation learning [33], deep residual learning [34]. In addition, the article from Hammond et al., 2011 provides possibilities for applying graph wavelet transform in graph neural networks.

Table 3. Top 6 articles with the most citation counts

Author	Frequency	DOI	Google Scholar citations
Thomas Kipf	2032	https://doi.org/10.1109/CVPR.2019.01157	29430
Michaël Defferrard	947	https://doi.org/10.5555/3157382.3157527	8185
Bruna J	690	https://doi.org/10.48550/ARXIV.1312.6203	5443
Velickovic P	679	https://doi.org/10.48550/arXiv.1710.10903	17347
William L Hamilton	673	https://doi.org/10.5555/3294771.3294869	12779
Diederik P Kingma	624	https://doi.org/10.48550/arXiv.1412.6980	166767
Ashish Vaswani	484	https://doi.org/10.5555/3295222.3295349	99816
David Kenric Hammond	446	https://doi.org/10.1016/j.acha.2010.04.005	2279
Shuman DI	426	https://doi.org/10.1145/2623330.2623732	4162
Zonghan Wu	426	https://doi.org/10.1109/TNNLS.2020.2978386	7455

Figure 4 illustrates a network of reference co-citation clusters comprising 2108 nodes and 9556 links aiming to represent the broadly focused topics related to spectral GNN.

As an indicator of homogeneity or consistency to measure the quality of a cluster, the silhouette score of the largest 10 clusters is all above 0.9, suggesting a reliable quality due to their closeness to the highest value of 1.00. The largest cluster is graph convolution network cluster (#0), which contains 236 member references. Notable findings within these clusters include: (a) Graph convolution network cluster (#0) is found to be the largest cluster representing the spectral graph neural network, graph signal processing cluster (#1) is representing the theoretical basic, while other clusters are representing the fields of application.

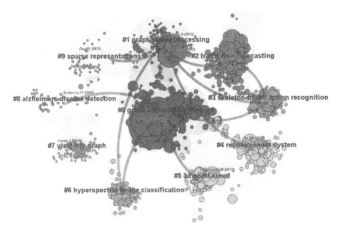

Fig. 4. Cluster view of co-citation network

Articles cited more than 100 times are mainly from cluster (#0) and cluster (#1), followed by skeleton-based action recognition cluster (#3) [35], traffic flow forecasting cluster (#4) [27, 36], 3D point cloud [29, 37], recommender system [37].

3.4 Hotspots Analysis

Analyzing hotspots enables researchers to identify the current trending research topics and potential directions in the field, offering valuable insights for research direction.

Keywords Co-Occurrence. Table 4 presents the top 10 keywords related to spectral GNN. Some notable details include: (a) Among the top 10 keywords, the 3 keywords with centrality exceeding 1.0 are GCN, spectral graph wavelet transform (SGWT), and graph signal processing. (b) Traffic flow forecasting, skeleton-based action recognition, and anomaly detection are fields that have a graph structure. These 3 fields are integrated with graph data processing. Along with the network in graph neural network, it is gradually applied to recommender system and hyperspectral image classification (HSIC). (c) Some keywords appeared more frequently, but the centrality value is low. Traffic flow forecasting has 310 occurrences, and attention mechanism has 199 occurrences, but their centrality is only 0.02 and 0.03 respectively. These keywords analysis provides a clear framework for pursuing targeted studies.

Table 4. Top 10 keywords co-occurrence

Ranking	Keyword	Count	Centrality	Year
1	Graph Convolution network (GCN)	2815	1.41	2015
2	Traffic flow forecasting	310	0.02	2010
3	Attention mechanism	199	0.03	2018
4	Spectral graph wavelet transform (SGWT)	187	0.31	2014
5	Skeleton-based action recognition	173	0.02	2015
6	Recommender system	137	0.01	2019
7	Graph signal processing (GSP)	128	0.14	2011
8	Hyperspectral image classification (HSIC)	125	0.03	2016
9	3D point cloud	115	0.03	2015
10	Anomaly detection	84	0.02	2010

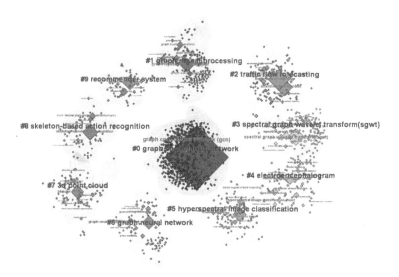

Fig. 5. Top 10 keyword clusters

The keyword clusters are analyzed by CiteSpace. Figure 5 illustrated the top 10 keyword clusters. Table 9 shows the top 5 keywords of each cluster. Upon comparing the top 10 clusters view of co-citation network (Fig. 4), it is evident that "spectral graph wavelet transform (SGWT)" has garnered attention in recent years and has rapidly developed into the 3rd largest cluster. At the same time, electroencephalogram (EEG) processing and hyperspectral image classification have also achieved rapid development and developed into the 4th and 5th largest clusters respectively, with the number of articles exceeding skeleton-based action recognition.

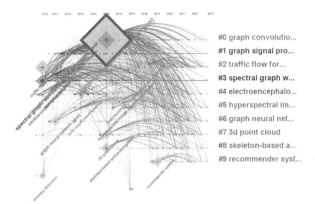

Fig. 6. The timeline view of keywords of top 10 clusters

The timeline view of keyword co-occurrence is designed to comprehend the evolution of most discussed topics and keywords (see Fig. 6). Some notable findings include: (a) The top 10 clusters have remained consistently active in recent years. (b) Research has evolved significantly in the field of graph convolution network, with the spectral graph wavelet transform following closely behind. (c) In terms of applications, research in traffic flow forecasting is thriving, and the combination of recommender system with spectral graph neural networks, though introduced relatively recently, is generating robust and dynamic exploration.

Keyword Bursts. The keywords citation bursts analysis is to delineate emerging trends within the domain. As illustrated in Fig. 7, the top 8 keywords exhibiting the highest citation intensity provide insights into the evolving hotspots in the realm of spectral GNN over time. The analysis yields several key findings: (a) The earliest keyword to manifest an intense citation burst was "spectral graph wavelet transform (SGWT)" a research endeavor that established a theoretical foundation for subsequent graph wavelet neural network (GWNN) models. The applications of the GWNN extend across diverse domains. (b) The top 5 keywords with the highest citation strength are "spectral graph wavelet transform (SGWT) (citation strength of 50.52)", "graph signal processing (citation strength of 29.46)", "spectral graph theory (citation strength of 11.3)", "graph wavelet filter bank (citation strength of 8.62)", and "graph filter bank (citation strength of 6.48)". These keywords revealed researchers' escalating attention towards various aspects of spectral GNN. These findings signify potential inflection points in the domain's hot topics, offering valuable insight into the popularity of specific research themes for researchers. These results served as valuable resources for new entrants in this research field, facilitating a swift understanding of current frontiers, prediction of future research directions, reduction of potential research costs, and initiation of research endeavors with greater efficiency and effectiveness.

References	Year	Strength	Begin	End	2010 - 2023
spectral graph wavelet transform(sgwt)	2010	50.52	2010	2018	
graph signal processing (gsp)	2012	29.46	2012	2019	
spectral graph theory	2011	11.3	2011	2018	
graph wavelet filterbank	2012	8.62	2012	2018	
graph filterbank	2014	6.48	2014	2019	
graph fourier transform	2013	4.3	2016	2018	
functional mri	2011	3.23	2011	2015	
community detection	2013	3.17	2013	2017	

Fig. 7. Top 8 keywords with the strongest citation bursts during 2010–2023

4 Conclusion and Perspectives

4.1 Conclusion

This paper reviewed 3721 articles related to spectral GNN on the Web of Science (WOS) Core Collection. The analysis was conducted using CiteSpace based on bibliographic records from the field of spectral GNN, which provides a unique and interesting snapshot of spectral GNN knowledge domain. Several conclusions can be drawn from the results. First, publication data revealed a remarkable surge in researchers' productivity from 2010 to 2022, witnessing a substantial growth in output from 6 to 1191. In 2023, as of August 9, a total of 898 articles were published. Spectral has become interdisciplinary according to the subject category distribution. Second, research on spectral GNN is dominated by China, USA, Australia, England, India, and Canada, all of which have the most productive authors and institutions. China and USA play important roles in stable cooperative relationships between themselves which have been established gradually over the past ten years. Third, the most influential authors are reasonably consistent with productive authors. The most cited articles mainly come from top international conferences (ICLR, NIPS, AAAI, CVPR) and top journals (IEEE T PATTERN ANAL, IEEE T NEUR NET LEAR) in computer vision and artificial intelligence. The hot topics in spectral GNN in recent years are focused on studying representation and learning of graphs with complex graph structures and dynamic graph.

4.2 Future Research Direction

The future trajectory of spectral GNN research may exhibit the following characteristics, offering valuable insights for researchers to conduct more impactful and effective research.

(a) Future studies may cover more topics. At present, it has been applied to several areas such as traffic flow prediction, drug performance prediction, Grap anomaly detection, human action recognition, etc. In the future, it could be expanded to many other application areas.
(b) Future studies may integrate more graph data analysis methods to address specific problems such as using Wigner-Ville distribution, Hilbert-Huang transform, evolutionary spectrum, empirical orthogonal function expansion (EOF), etc.

Funding. This study was supported by the Hainan Provincial Natural Science Foundation of China (No. 621MS058), the Hainan Province Science and Technology Special Fund (No. ZDYF2022GXJS005), the specific research fund of The Innovation Platform for Academician of Hainan Province (No. YSPTZX202144, No. YSPTZX202145).

References

1. Wang, X., Zhang, M.: How powerful are spectral graph neural networks. In: ICML, May 2022, pp. 23341–23362 (2022). http://arxiv.org/abs/2205.11172
2. Quan, P., Shi, Y., Lei, M., Leng, J., Zhang, T., Niu, L.: A brief review of receptive fields in graph convolutional networks. In: IEEE/WIC/ACM International Conference on Web Intelligence - Companion Volume, New York, NY, USA, pp. 106–110. ACM, October 2019. https://doi.org/10.1145/3358695.3360934
3. Bhatti, U.A., Tang, H., Wu, G., Marjan, S., Hussain, A.: Deep learning with graph convolutional networks: an overview and latest applications in computational intelligence. Int. J. Intell. Syst. **2023**, 1–28 (2023). https://doi.org/10.1155/2023/8342104
4. Zhou, J., Zhang, Z.: A brief survey of the graph wavelet frame. Complexity **2022**, 1–12 (2022). https://doi.org/10.1155/2022/8153249
5. Bruna, J., Zaremba, W., Szlam, A., LeCun, Y.: Spectral networks and locally connected networks on graphs. In: ICLR, December 2013. http://arxiv.org/abs/1312.6203
6. Defferrard, M., Bresson, X., Vandergheynst, P.: Convolutional neural networks on graphs with fast localized spectral filtering. NIPS, June 2016. http://arxiv.org/abs/1606.09375
7. Hammond, D.K., Vandergheynst, P., Gribonval, R.: Wavelets on graphs via spectral graph theory. Appl. Comput. Harmon. Anal. **30**(2), 129–150 (2011). https://doi.org/10.1016/j.acha.2010.04.005
8. Kipf, T.N., Welling, M.: Semi-supervised classification with graph convolutional networks. In: 5th International Conference on Learning Representations, September 2016. http://arxiv.org/abs/1609.02907
9. Wu, F., Zhang, T., de Souza, A.H., Fifty, C., Yu, T., Weinberger, K.Q.: Simplifying graph convolutional networks. In: ICML, February 2019. http://arxiv.org/abs/1902.07153
10. Xu, B., Shen, H., Cao, Q., Qiu, Y., Cheng, X.: Graph wavelet neural network. In: ICLR (2019)
11. Donnat, C., Zitnik, M., Hallac, D., Leskovec, J.: Learning structural node embeddings via diffusion wavelets. In: Proceedings of the 24th ACM SIGKDD International Conference on Knowledge Discovery & Data Mining, New York, NY, USA. ACM, July 2018, pp. 1320–1329 (2018). https://doi.org/10.1145/3219819.3220025
12. Petar, V.: Graph attention networks. ICLR (2018). https://doi.org/10.48550/arXiv.1710.10903
13. Qu, M., Bengio, Y., Tang, J.: GMNN: graph Markov neural networks, May 2019. http://arxiv.org/abs/1905.06214
14. Park, M., Geum, Y.: Two-stage technology opportunity discovery for firm-level decision making: GCN-based link-prediction approach. Technol. Forecast Soc. Change **183**, 121934 (2022). https://doi.org/10.1016/j.techfore.2022.121934
15. Bai, L., Cui, L., Jiao, Y., Rossi, L., Hancock, E.R.: Learning backtrackless aligned-spatial graph convolutional networks for graph classification. IEEE Trans. Pattern Anal. Mach. Intell. **44**(2), 783–798 (2022). https://doi.org/10.1109/TPAMI.2020.3011866
16. Yang, B., Cao, F., Ye, H.: A novel method for hyperspectral image classification: deep network with adaptive graph structure integration. IEEE Trans. Geosci. Remote Sens. **60**, 1–12 (2022). https://doi.org/10.1109/TGRS.2022.3150349
17. Hao, X., Li, J., Guo, Y., Jiang, T., Yu, M.: Hypergraph neural network for skeleton-based action recognition. IEEE Trans. Image Process. **30**, 2263–2275 (2021). https://doi.org/10.1109/TIP.2021.3051495

18. Nong, L., Wang, J., Lin, J., Qiu, H., Zheng, L., Zhang, W.: Hypergraph wavelet neural networks for 3D object classification. Neurocomputing **463**, 580–595 (2021). https://doi.org/10.1016/j.neucom.2021.08.006

19. Yu, L., Sun, L., Du, B., Liu, C., Lv, W., Xiong, H.: Heterogeneous graph representation learning with relation awareness. IEEE Trans. Knowl. Data Eng. 1 (2022). https://doi.org/10.1109/TKDE.2022.3160208

20. Zhu, W., Liu, Y., Wang, P., Zhang, M., Wang, T., Yi, Y.: Tri-HGNN: learning triple policies fused hierarchical graph neural networks for pedestrian trajectory prediction. Pattern Recognit. **143**, 109772 (2023). https://doi.org/10.1016/j.patcog.2023.109772

21. Zhao, L., et al.: T-GCN: a temporal graph convolutional network for traffic prediction. IEEE Trans. Intell. Transp. Syst. **21**(9), 3848–3858 (2020). https://doi.org/10.1109/TITS.2019.2935152

22. Wang, L., Huang, Y., Hou, Y., Zhang, S., Shan, J.: Graph attention convolution for point cloud semantic segmentation. In: 2019 IEEE/CVF Conference on Computer Vision and Pattern Recognition (CVPR), pp. 10288–10297. IEEE, June 2019. https://doi.org/10.1109/CVPR.2019.01054

23. He, X., Deng, K., Wang, X., Li, Y., Zhang, Y.D., Wang, M.: LightGCN: simplifying and powering graph convolution network for recommendation. In: SIGIR 2020 - Proceedings of the 43rd International ACM SIGIR Conference on Research and Development in Information Retrieval, pp. 639–648. Association for Computing Machinery, Inc, July 2020. https://doi.org/10.1145/3397271.3401063

24. Ying, R., He, R., Chen, K., Eksombatchai, P., Hamilton, W.L., Leskovec, J.: Graph convolutional neural networks for web-scale recommender systems. In: Proceedings of the ACM SIGKDD International Conference on Knowledge Discovery and Data Mining, pp. 974–983. Association for Computing Machinery, July 2018. https://doi.org/10.1145/3219819.3219890

25. Wan, S., Gong, C., Zhong, P., Du, B., Zhang, L., Yang, J.: Multiscale dynamic graph convolutional network for hyperspectral image classification. IEEE Trans. Geosci. Remote Sens. **58**(5), 3162–3177 (2020). https://doi.org/10.1109/TGRS.2019.2949180

26. Liu, Y., Li, Z., Pan, S., Gong, C., Zhou, C., Karypis, G.: Anomaly detection on attributed networks via contrastive self-supervised learning. IEEE Trans. Neural Netw. Learn. Syst. **33**(6), 2378–2392 (2021). https://doi.org/10.1109/TNNLS.2021.3068344

27. Zhu, Y., Shuai, H., Liu, G., Liu, Q.: Multilevel spatial-temporal excited graph network for skeleton-based action recognition. IEEE Trans. Image Process. **32**, 496–508 (2023). https://doi.org/10.1109/TIP.2022.3230249

28. Narang, S.K., Shen, G., Ortega, A.: Unidirectional graph-based wavelet transforms for efficient data gathering in sensor networks. In: 2010 IEEE International Conference on Acoustics, Speech and Signal Processing, pp. 2902–2905. IEEE (2010). https://doi.org/10.1109/ICASSP.2010.5496172

29. Chen, C.: Searching for intellectual turning points: progressive knowledge domain visualization. Proc. Natl. Acad. Sci. **101**(suppl_1), 5303–5310 (2004). https://doi.org/10.1073/pnas.0307513100

30. Geng, Y., Zhang, N., Zhu, R.: Research progress analysis of sustainable smart grid based on CiteSpace. Energ. Strat. Rev. **48**, 101111 (2023). https://doi.org/10.1016/j.esr.2023.101111

31. Shuman, D.I., Narang, S.K., Frossard, P., Ortega, A., Vandergheynst, P.: The emerging field of signal processing on graphs: extending high-dimensional data analysis to networks and other irregular domains. IEEE Signal Process. Mag. **30**(3), 83–98 (2013). https://doi.org/10.1109/MSP.2012.2235192

32. Kingma, D.P., Ba, J.: Adam: a method for stochastic optimization. In: ICLR, December 2015. http://arxiv.org/abs/1412.6980

33. Hamilton, W.L., Ying, R., Leskovec, J.: Inductive representation learning on large graphs. NIPS (2017). https://doi.org/10.5555/3294771.3294869

34. He, K., Zhang, X., Ren, S., Sun, J.: Deep residual learning for image recognition, December 2015. http://arxiv.org/abs/1512.03385

35. Li, M., Chen, S., Chen, X., Zhang, Y., Wang, Y., Tian, Q.: Actional-structural graph convolutional networks for skeleton-based action recognition. In: 2019 IEEE/CVF Conference on Computer Vision and Pattern Recognition (CVPR), pp. 3590–3598. IEEE, June 2019. https://doi.org/10.1109/CVPR.2019.00371

36. Lv, Y., Duan, Y., Kang, W., Li, Z., Wang, F.Y.: Traffic flow prediction with big data: a deep learning approach. IEEE Trans. Intell. Transp. Syst. 16(2), 865–873 (2015). https://doi.org/10.1109/TITS.2014.2345663

37. Charles, R.Q., Su, H., Kaichun, M., Guibas, L.J.: PointNet: deep learning on point sets for 3D classification and segmentation. In: 2017 IEEE Conference on Computer Vision and Pattern Recognition (CVPR), pp. 77–85. IEEE, July 2017. https://doi.org/10.1109/CVPR.2017.16

H_2L: High-Performance Multi-agent Path Finding in High-Obstacle-Density and Large-Size Maps

Chang Tang[1], Shitao Chen[2], Zhiqiang Tian[1], and Xuguang Lan[2(✉)]

[1] School of Software Engineering, Xi'an Jiaotong University, Xi'an, China
3121158002@stu.xjtu.edu.cn, zhiqiangtian@mail.xjtu.edu.cn
[2] National Key Laboratory of Human-Machine Hybrid Augmented Intelligence, National Engineering Research Center for Visual Information and Applications, and Institute of Artificial Intelligence and Robotics, Xi'an Jiaotong University, Xi'an, China
chenshitao@xjtu.edu.cn, xglan@mail.xjtu.edu.cn

Abstract. Multi-Agent Path Finding (MAPF) is vital for large-scale Multi-Agent Systems (MAS), where agents must plan collision-free paths to reach their goals. While Reinforcement Learning (RL) methods aim to enhance real-time performance and scalability over search-based approaches, their success on complex maps is limited. This is due to the use of independent RL algorithms, which fail to address the non-stationarity of the environment, and inappropriate reward functions that cause the agent's policy to worsen with greater distance to the goal. To tackle these issues, we propose a MAPF algorithm based on a new variant of the Value Decomposition Network (VDN), a multi-agent RL algorithm, and introduce a novel reward function. This VDN variant trains the network using agents within a specific agent's field of view, addressing non-stationarity and training challenges in large-scale MAS, unlike naive VDN, which considers all agents. We introduce a novel reward function using potential-based reward shaping, rendering the agent's policy independent of the map size. Additionally, we enhance the reward to alleviate congestion by preventing agents from stopping next to each other and by penalizing the following conflicts. Experiments show our planner has a notably higher success rate than other RL-based planners and slightly lower than the latest state-of-the-art search-based planner, LaCAM*, on complex maps. For instance, on a 160×160 map with 30% obstacle density and 1024 agents, our planner achieves an 88% success rate, while other RL-based planners achieve virtually 0%.

Keywords: Multi-agent path finding · Multi-agent path planning · Multi-agent deep reinforcement learning · Coordination and cooperation

1 Introduction

Multi-Agent Path Finding (MAPF) finds utility across diverse domains such as airport towing [1], logistics warehousing [2], electronic gaming [3], and numerous other applications. In these instances, agents are tasked with traversing from one location to another.

The classic MAPF problem involves finding conflict-free and optimal paths for agents from their starts to their goals [4]. However, MAPF is an NP-hard problem within the realm of combinatorial optimization. For search-based centralized planning algorithms, the computational complexity increases exponentially as the number of agents rises [4]. Additionally, variations in the number of agents and environmental changes can necessitate replanning of paths by the centralized scheduler, rendering centralized algorithms sometimes unable to meet real-time requirements [5, 6].

Recently, many methods based on Reinforcement Learning (RL) have been proposed to address the real-time and scalability issues. Unlike centralized planners, which require global information to plan a complete path, learning-based methods only need local observation to plan the next step and eventually reach the goal [7]. However, existing RL-based methods [5–7] underperform on the complex environments such as a random 160×160 map with 30% obstacle density and 1024 agents, according to our experiments. There are three problems with existing methods. The first problem is the use of independent RL algorithms, which fails to address the non-stationarity of the environment [8]. The non-stationarity arises from the fact that the policies of other agents change over time, and the agent cannot receive the same reward when executing the same action under the same observation [8]. This non-stationary nature makes it challenging for the agent's policy to converge, as it must continually adapt to the evolving behavior of other agents in the dynamic environment [8]. To address non-stationarity, Multi-Agent Reinforcement Learning (MARL) algorithms, like Value Decomposition Network (VDN) [9], train agents from a global perspective. However, as the map size and the number of agents increases, the team reward becomes sparser [10] because all agents need to blindly explore all possible paths. The joint value function becomes more complex [11] as the dimension of joint observation and joint action increases exponentially. Additionally, the memory required for training becomes larger because each agent has parameters and needs to participate in gradient backpropagation. These problems render the direct application of MARL algorithms less effective, as exemplified by [10]. However, current MAPF algorithms have not yet overcome these challenges. Second, existing methods exhibit a low success rate on large maps due to inherent flaws in their reward functions. For example, [6, 7] set a positive reward once all agents reach their goals; otherwise, they give a fixed negative reward to agents if there are no collisions. By doing so, the action-value function of an agent will be influenced by the distance from it to its goal. The action-value function is defined as $Q(s, a) = E\left[\sum_{t=0}^{T}\gamma^t R_{t+1}|S_0 = s, A_0 = a\right]$, where T is equal to the distance from goal. As the distance becomes large, the action-value function tends to a constant because $\gamma < 1$, and agents may struggle to recognize the correct directions. The best example is [12]. The success rate of [12] decreases when the map size increases, while keeping obstacle density and agent density constant. Our proposed reward function aims to break the link between the action-value function and the distance, enabling agents' policies to be independent of the map size. Third, partial observability [8] may lead to agent congestion [13]. This occurs because agents often make decisions based on incomplete or inaccurate information about the environment, which can result in suboptimal actions, such as crowding in certain areas or inefficient resource utilization, ultimately affecting overall performance.

To address these issues, we have implemented a series of improvements. Firstly, to overcome the challenges mentioned when using naive MARL algorithms, we propose a variant of VDN. We observed that in the MAPF problem, the actions of some agents become independent of others beyond a certain range. Therefore, we decompose the larger problem into smaller local path planning problems based on the distribution of agent positions. In this paper, our approach, H_2L—derived from High-performance, High-obstacle-density and Large-size—involves using variant VDN to train only the agents within a particular agent's Field Of View (FOV), rather than all agents. The reason why this approach works is that as the size of the agent team for training decreases, the team reward becomes denser, the joint action-value function becomes simpler, and the memory required for training becomes smaller. Secondly, to ensure that the algorithm's performance is not constrained by the map size, we adopt the potential-based reward reshaping method [14]. This method ensures that the action-value function is theoretically independent of the distance to the goal and varies for different actions. Thirdly, to alleviate congestion caused by partial observability, we further refine the reward function by avoiding agents stopping next to each other and by penalizing the following conflicts.

Our contributions are summarized as follows:

1. We proposed a MAPF algorithm based on a new variant of VDN, overcoming the challenges of training in large-scale multi-agent systems.
2. We designed a novel reward function to ensure the agent's policy remains independent of the distance to the goal.
3. We enhanced the reward function to alleviate congestion among agents, particularly in scenarios with partial observability.
4. Experiments show that our method significantly outperforms existing RL-based algorithms.

The rest of this paper is organized as follows. In Sect. 2, we briefly introduce the MAPF problem, how to formalize MAPF problem to decentralized partially observable markov decision process, some notations in multi-agent RL, the VDN algorithm and potential-based reward shaping. In Sect. 3, we present our MAPF method in details. In Sect. 4, comparative and ablation experiments are conducted to verify our method. Finally, Sect. 5 contains the conclusion.

2 Preliminary

2.1 MAPF Problem Definition

The classical MAPF problem with n agents is defines by an undirected graph $G = (V, E)$, a set of agents $N = \{1, 2, 3, \ldots, n\}$, a set of different starts $S = \left(s^i \in V\right)^{i \in N}$ and goals $\mathcal{G} = \left(g^i \in V\right)^{i \in N}$. Time is discretized into steps, with each agent capable of taking a single action per step. At each step, agents can wait at its current position or move to the adjacent position. A valid solution to a MAPF problem is a joint plan that guides all agents to their respective goals without collisions. There are three types of conflicts: the vertex conflict, the edge conflict, and the following conflict. A vertex conflict occurs when at least two agents occupy the same vertex at the same time step. An edge conflict occurs when two agents traverse the same edge at the same time step. A following conflict occurs when one agent occupies a vertex that was occupied by another agent in the previous time step. The optimization object is to maximize makespan (MS) or sum of costs (SOC). The MS is the number of time steps until all agents reach their goal. The SOC is the number of actions taken by all agents until they reach their goals. The action contributes to the SOC if an agent leaves its goal after reaching it.

2.2 Decentralized Partially Observable Markov Decision Process

We consider the partially observable scenario where agents only have partial observation of environment. We model this partially observable variant of MAPF as a Decentralized Partially Observable Markov Decision Process (Dec-POMDP) [15], defined as a 7-tuple $\langle S, A, \mathcal{P}, \mathcal{R}, O, \mathcal{O}, \gamma \rangle$. S is a set of global states. $A = \times_{i \in N} A^i$ is the set of joint actions, where $N = \{1, \ldots, n\}$ is the set of n agents and A^i is the set of actions available to agent i. At every time step t, each agent i takes an action a_t^i, leading to one joint action $a = (a^1, \ldots, a^n)$ at every time step. $\mathcal{P} : A \times S \to S$ is the transition probability function, which specifies $\Pr(s'|s, a)$, where $s, s' \in S$. $O = \times_{i \in N} O^i$ is the set of joint observations, where O^i is a set of observations available to agent i. $\mathcal{O} : A \times S \to O$ is the observation probability function, which specifies $\Pr(o|a, s)$, where $o \in O$. $\mathcal{R} : O \times A \to R$ is the immediate reward function, where R represents the set of real numbers. γ is the discounted factor.

2.3 Multi-agent Reinforcement Learning

The team goal is to maximize expected cumulative discounted team reward, $G_t = \sum_{t=1}^{\infty} \gamma^{t-1} \mathcal{R}_t$. The joint policy is $\pi : S \to \Pr(A)$. The team value function is $V^{\pi}(s) := E_{\pi} \left[\sum_{t=0}^{\infty} \gamma^t \mathcal{R}_{t+1} | S_0 = s \right]$ and the team action-value function is $Q^{\pi}(s, a) := E_{\pi} [\mathcal{R}_{t+1} + \gamma V^{\pi}(S_{t+1}) | S_t = s; A_t = a]$, where $s \in S$, $a \in A$. $V^*(s) := \sup_{\pi} V^{\pi}(s)$ is the optimal team value function and $Q : S \times A \to R$ is the optimal team action-value function. For a given action-value function $Q : S \times A \to R$, the deterministic greedy policy is $\pi(s) := \operatorname{argmax}_{a \in A} Q(s, a)$.

In Dec-POMDPs, agents only have partial observations, and the team value function can be defined as $Q(h, a)$, where $h = (h^1, h^2, \ldots, h^n)$, $a = (a^1, a^2, \ldots, a^n)$ and h^i is the historical observation substituting the global state s^i.

2.4 Value Decomposition Network

The Value Decomposition Network (VDN) is a effective multi-agent RL algorithm. It makes an assumption that the joint action-value function can be additively decomposed into value functions across agents, $Q(h, a) \approx \sum_{i=1}^{n} \tilde{Q}^i(h^i, a^i)$, where the $\tilde{Q}^i(h^i, a^i)$ depends only on each agent's local historical observations. VDN learns the single agent action-value function using neural networks parameterized by θ, represented as $\tilde{Q}^i(h^i, a^i; \theta)$. The optimal policy is trained by minimizing the loss

$$\mathcal{L} = E\left[\left(r + \gamma max_{a'}Q(h', a'; \overline{\theta}) - Q(h, a; \theta)\right)^2\right], \tag{1}$$

where $Q(h, a; \theta) \approx \sum\limits_{i=1}^{n} \tilde{Q}^i(h^i, a^i; \theta), \overline{\theta}$ is the target network parameter and is periodically updated by assigning the current network parameters θ to it. When executing, an agent i gets its deterministic greedy policy from $\tilde{Q}^i(h^i, a^i; \theta)$.

2.5 Potential-Based Reward Shaping

In single RL, the interaction between the agent and the environment is modeled as Markov Decision Process (MDP), denoted as $MDP = \langle S, A, \mathcal{P}, \mathcal{R}, \gamma \rangle$. Potential-based reward shaping [14] is a technique in RL that modifies the reward function to accelerate the learning process without changing the optimal policy. The potential-based reward shaping is that given a potential-based function $\mathcal{F}(s, a, s') = \gamma \Phi(s') - \Phi(s)$, then every optimal policy in $MDP' = \langle S, A, \mathcal{P}, \mathcal{R} + \mathcal{F}, \gamma \rangle$ will also be an optimal policy in MDP and vice versa, where $\Phi : S \rightarrow R$ is a potential function that maps each state to a real number, representing the "potential" or "energy" of that state. With this potential function, the relationship between the action-value functions of the two processes can be expressed as: $Q^*_{MDP'}(s, a) = Q^*_{MDP}(s, a) - \Phi(s)$ [14]. What we do in this paper is to set $\Phi(s) = V^*_{MDP}(s)$ and make $Q^*_{MDP'} \equiv 0$, which makes learning easy and renders the value-action function independent of the distance to the goal.

3   Method

In this section, the proposed algorithm, action space, observation space, reward function, and agent network structure will be covered in detail.

3.1   Algorithm: The Proposed Variant of VDN

When dealing with numerous agents and a large map size, applying naive VDN to all agents becomes challenging. However, by considering the distribution of agent positions, we can decompose the large problem into smaller, locally independent path planning problems. In this paper, we assume that the agents within a particular agent's FOV are independent from other agents and apply VDN to these agents. Nevertheless, since the number of agents can vary and sometimes be quite high, we only train the agent itself and no more than 7 other agents that are closest in Manhattan distance to it with in its FOV.

The local team reward for the variant of VDN is obtained from individual rewards, defined as $r(s_t, a_t) := \sum\limits_{i=1}^{M} r^i(o_t^i, a_t^i)$, where $r^i(o_t^i, a_t^i)$ is the reward of agent i, M is the number of agents in the training team.

Before deriving the loss function for the VDN variant, we need to derive the local team action-value function. We assume that M agents have been selected from those within a particular agent's FOV. Let the local team state be denoted as s, the joint action of M agents as a, and the joint policy of M agents as π. Then, the team Q-function can be expressed as follows:

$$Q^{\pi}(s, a) = E\left[\sum_{t=1}^{\infty} \gamma^{t-1} r(s_t, a_t)|s_0 = s, a_0 = a; \pi\right]$$

$$= \sum_{i=1}^{M} E\left[\sum_{t=1}^{\infty} \gamma^{t-1} r^i\left(o_t^i, a_t^i\right)|s_0 = s, a_0 = a; \pi\right]$$

$$= \sum_{i=1}^{M} Q^{\pi,i}(s, a)$$

$$\approx \sum_{i=1}^{M} Q^{\pi,i}\left(h^i, a^i\right), \tag{2}$$

where $Q^{\pi,i}(s, a)$ is the action-value function of agent i when agent i can observe the local team state and the team joint action, and $Q^{\pi,i}\left(h^i, a^i\right)$ is the action-value function of agent i when agent i uses recurrent neural network to store information from historical observations h^i to approximate (s, a).

We can derive the loss function of VDN variant as below:

$$\mathcal{L} = E\left[\left(\gamma \sum_{i=1}^{M} \max_{a^{i\prime}} Q^i\left(h^{i\prime}, a^{i\prime}; \overline{\theta}\right) + \sum_{i=1}^{M} r^i\left(o^i, a^i\right) - \sum_{i=1}^{M} Q^i\left(h^i, a^i; \theta\right)\right)^2\right], \tag{3}$$

where $\overline{\theta}$ is the target network same as the naive VDN.

3.2 Action Space

Agents perform discrete actions on a grid map. At each timestep, agents have five possible actions: moving up, down, left, right, or wait. According to [6], we assume that agents move simultaneously and remain in the environment after reaching their goals, which proves beneficial for agents in handling collisions. Unlike other RL-based methods [6, 7, 16] that overlook following conflicts, we consider vertex conflicts, edge conflicts, and following conflicts to achieve better coordination. During training or execution, agents may choose invalid actions, leading to collisions with obstacles or between agents. Upon collision detection, all colliding agents return to previous positions and receive a collision penalty. During training, we select one agent to use an ε-greedy strategy, while other agents employ a greedy strategy. During execution, all agents use the greedy strategy.

3.3 Observation Space

Each agent observes a limited area around it, set to 11×11. We utilize heuristic information proposed by [6] to design the observation space. To obtain this information, agents store the static map and use a flood-fill algorithm to determine optimal movement toward the goal at each point on the map. The heuristic information is represented as a 4-dimensional vector for the four directions at a map point. If moving in a certain direction brings the agent closer to the goal, the corresponding vector element is 1; otherwise, it is 0. With a map dimension of $L \times L$, the heuristic information dimension is $L \times L \times 4$.

The observation space for an agent is a tensor of size $11 \times 11 \times 57$, with 57 channels representing different features within an 11×11 observation range. These features include static obstacles, surrounding agents' positions, whether surrounding agents have reached their goals, distance to the goal for all agents in the FOV, intended movement direction for agents in the FOV (derived from their heuristic information), the agent's and surrounding agents' previous actions, and the heuristic information of agents in the FOV (see Table 1).

Table 1. Individual observation.

Feature	# of channels	Data type
Static obstacles	1	0/1
Agents	1	0/1
Whether agents are on goal	1	0/1
Agents' distance to goals	1	float
Intended direction of movement	8	0/1
Previous action	5	0/1
Heuristic information	5×8	0/1

In the Table 1, the fifth observation indicates the average direction of potential positions reachable within the next 10 timesteps based on heuristic information, rather than the direction toward the goal. This approach provides a more accurate orientation than simply aiming directly at the goal. The movement orientation is discretized into eight directions and represented using an eight-dimensional one-hot vector.

Regarding the representation of an agent's heuristic information, each agent occupies 5 channels. The first channel identifies positions within the 11×11 observation range, while the other 4 channels represent the agent's own heuristic information or that of the surrounding agents within this 11×11 range.

Each agent is required to pre-store the global static map and communicate with surrounding agents to acquire their heuristic information. We have set a limit that an agent can obtain heuristic information from a maximum of 7 surrounding agents. Additionally, there are scenarios where agents can obtain heuristic information without explicit communication. In such cases, each agent must be capable of recognizing surrounding agents without explicit communication, possibly through methods like object detection [17, 18], and should pre-store the global static map and the goals of other agents.

3.4 Reward Function

We define the reward function in Table 2. Due to the presence of heuristic information, we can set a more positive reward for moving towards the goal. Consequently, through potential-based reward shaping, we introduce this reward function: 0 for moving closer to the goal, -0.7 for moving away, and -0.35 for waiting. Although $\gamma < 1$ when training, $Q^*(s, a_1) \equiv 0$ and $Q^*(s, a_2) \equiv -0.7$ if in a single-agent environment, where action a_1 is to move closer to the goal and a_2 away the goal. It can be observed that the value function is independent of the discount factor γ and distance d. Hence, the reward function proposed in this article is not affected by the size of the map.

To reduce congestion in narrow passages, we have also improved the reward function. The motivation is to assign a larger negative reward (we set -1.05) when an agent stops and another agent also stops adjacent to it, thereby discouraging agents from stopping together and causing congestion. Furthermore, unlike other RL-based methods that do not penalize following conflicts, we penalize vertex conflicts, edge conflicts, and following conflicts. In the case of a following conflict, we penalize only the actively following agent and not the agent being followed. The reward for collision is set at -5.0. Experiments in our paper show that penalizing the following conflicts is helpful to alleviate congestion. Finally, once the agent and its surrounding agents have all reached the goals, a reward of 0 is given to encourage stopping at the goal.

Table 2. Individual reward.

Action	Reward
Move (Up, Left, Down, Right) towards the goal	0.0
Move (Up, Left, Down, Right) away from the goal	-0.7
Wait not at the goal, and there is no agent within a Euclidean distance of $\sqrt{2}$ that also stops	-0.35
Wait not at the goal, and there is at least an agent within a Euclidean distance of $\sqrt{2}$ who also stops	-1.05
Wait at the goal, and there is at least one agent in the FOV who is not at the goal. Additionally, no other agents within a Euclidean distance of $\sqrt{2}$ stop at posi-tions other than their goals	-0.35
Wait at the goal, and there is at least one agent in the FOV who is not at the goal. Additionally, there is at least an agent within a Euclidean distance of $\sqrt{2}$ that stops at a position other than its goal	-1.05
Wait at the goal, and surrounding agents in FOV are all at the goal	0.0
Collide (including out-of-bounds, collisions with obstacles, vertex conflicts, edge conflicts, and following conflicts)	-5.0

3.5 Agent Network Structure

We utilize neural networks to represent the action-value function of agents. The input sequentially passes through one convolutional module, followed by five SE-ResNet modules, a GRU (with a hidden state of 256 dimensions), and a Dueling Network structure to generate the action-value functions.

4 Experiments

In this section, we describe comparative and ablation experiments. We trained and tested our model on a server equipped with an AMD EPYC 7542 CPU and an NVIDIA GeForce RTX 3090 GPU. The models were trained for about 600K updates.

4.1 Experiment Setup

We provide an overview of the configuration for both the training and testing environments, including the training parameters and evaluation metrics.

Training Environment. We train our models in randomly generated environments where obstacles, starting positions, and goals are randomly placed. Before training each scenario, we randomly select the map size from 5×5 to 40×40. For a map size of 5, the number of agents ranges from 1 to 6. For a map size of 40, the number of agents varies from 1, 8, 16, 32, 64, to 256. Additionally, we utilize curriculum learning to expedite the learning process. The initial task settings include $(1,5 \times 5)$ and $(1,40 \times 40)$. For a map size of 5, if the success rate of task $(n, 5 \times 5)$ reaches 0.9, we introduce task $(n + 1,5 \times 5)$. For a map size of 40, if the success rates of both task $(n,40 \times 40)$ and task $(4,5 \times 5)$ reach 0.9 simultaneously, we increase the number of agents on the 40×40 map, where n represents the number of agents. The obstacle density follows a triangular distribution with a lower limit of 0, a mode of 0.33, and an upper limit of 0.5, as described in [6, 7].

Testing Environment. The test benchmark is a square grid map where we randomly select obstacles, starting positions, and goals for the agents. The map sizes are 20, 80, and 160. The number of agents is 32 and 64 for 20×20, 256 and 512 for 80×80, and 512 and 1024 for 160×160. The obstacle density is 30%.

Training Parameter. We train the agent network based on the Ape-X architecture, which involves multiple Actors interacting with the environment to generate experiences that are passed to the Learner. The Learner computes gradients, updates network parameters, and communicates the new network parameters back to the Actors. We have configured 39 actors to interact with the environment. The optimizer is Adam, with the following parameters: $lr = 1.0e{-}4$, $\beta_1 = 0.9$, $\beta_2 = 0.999$, $\varepsilon = 1e{-}7$. The learning rate decays every 10,000 steps with a base decay rate of 0.96. The batch size for training is set to 128. Actor network parameters are updated every 50 updates, and target network parameters are updated every 250 updates. The discount factor γ is sct to 0.95. Additionally, the agents are trained using the proposed variant of the VDN, with a maximum of 8 agents in each team. If there are more than 7 surrounding agents, we choose the 7 agents with the closest Manhattan distance to the center of the field of view.

Evaluation Metrics. We employ four evaluation metrics listed in Table 3. When calculating the average MS, unlike [5], we only consider successful planning instances of MAPF. This approach makes it easier to compare with traditional planners. Additionally, we do not use the definition of CR in [5], which defines CR $= K$/MS, because our definition intuitively indicates the probability of agents colliding with each other during each step of their movement in a specific environment setting.

4.2 Comparative Experiments

We have chosen various representative MAPF algorithms from different categories to compare with H$_2$L. For the traditional search-based algorithms, we selected the suboptimal algorithm inflated ODrM* [19], EECBS [20], and the state-of-the-art LaCAM* [21] for comparison. For the RL-based algorithms, we only choose the communication-based algorithms for comparison because our method involves either explicit or implicit communication. We selected four representative algorithms: DHC [6], PICO [5], SCRIMP [16], and CPL [10].

Table 3. Evaluation Metrics.

Metrics	Description
success rate (SR)	The probability of the planner successfully solving a MAPF problem
arrive rate (AR)	The proportion of agents in a MAPF problem that reach their respective goals
makespan (MS)	The number of time steps for a successfully solved MAPF problem
collision rate (CR)	CR $= K/(\text{MS} \cdot n)$, where K is the number of collision, n is the number of agents in the environment

Based on previous papers [6, 7], we set a maximum runtime limit of 60 s for CBSH2-RTC implemented in C++, and 300 s for ODrM* implemented in Python. Similarly, we determined the timestep limit for RL-based algorithms in test benchmark and are shown in Table 4.

The comparative experiment results presented in Table 4 demonstrate that our method, H$_2$L, consistently outperforms other RL-based methods across all four evaluation metrics. Specifically, H$_2$L achieves a significantly higher success rate (SR), approximately ten times better collision rate (CR), lower makespan (MS), and a higher average reward (AR) compared to other approaches. These results strongly validate the effectiveness of our MAPF method, H$_2$L, showcasing its superior performance in diverse scenarios.

4.3 Ablation Experiments

We conduct ablation experiments to investigate the impact of VDN variant on the coordination of agents, the influence of reward function on the performance of agents in

Table 4. Comparative results. *The environment format is $(n, s \times s, d, l)$, where n is the number of agents, s is the map size, d is the obstacle density, l is the maximum timestep for planning.*

Environment				$(64, 20 \times 20, 0.3, 256)$				$(512, 80 \times 80, 0.3, 512)$				$(1024, 160 \times 160, 0.3, 512)$			
				SR↑	AR↑	MS↓	CR↓	SR↑	AR↑	MS↓	CR↓	SR↑	AR↑	MS↓	CR↓
Search-based methods	ODrM*($\epsilon = 1.5$) (2015)			0.00	-	-	0.00	0.00	-	-	0.00	0.00	-	-	0.00
	ODrM*($\epsilon = 10$) (2015)			0.45	-	63.3	0.00	0.00	-	-	0.00	0.00	-	-	0.00
	EECBS($w = 1.2$) (2021)			0.21	-	40.4	0.00	0.01	-	175.0	0.00	0.01	-	320.0	0.00
	LaCAM* (2023)			0.97	-	49.3	0.00	0.95	-	176.2	0.00	0.97	-	289.3	0.00
RL-based methods	DHC (2021)			0.00	0.63	-	6.3e-2	0.00	0.61	-	5.4e-2	0.00	0.72	-	3.6e-2
	PICO (2022)			0.00	-	-	3.6e-2	-	-	-	-	-	-	-	-
	SCRIMP (2023)			0.6	0.96	120.25	4.9e-2	0.07	0.89	353.6	7.4e-2	-	-	-	-
	CPL (2023)			0.00	-	-	6.7e-3	-	-	-	-	-	-	-	-
	H₂L (Ours)			**0.88**	**0.99**	**87.0**	**2.4e-3**	**0.84**	**0.99**	**260.6**	**1.0e-3**	**0.88**	**0.99**	**377.0**	**4.0e-4**
Environment				$(32, 20 \times 20, 0.3, 256)$				$(256, 80 \times 80, 0.3, 384)$				$(512, 160 \times 160, 0.3, 512)$			
				SR↑	AR↑	MS↓	CR↓	SR↑	AR↑	MS↓	CR↓	SR↑	AR↑	MS↓	CR↓
Search-based methods	ODrM*($\epsilon = 1.5$) (2015)			0.68	-	37.2	0.00	0.21	-	145.9	0.00	0.29	-	290.4	0.00
	ODrM*($\epsilon = 10$) (2015)			0.98	-	44.5	0.00	0.79	-	160.5	0.00	0.92	-	302.2	0.00
	EECBS($w = 1.2$) (2021)			0.97	-	40.9	0.00	0.99	-	154.0	0.00	0.7	-	287.6	0.00
	LaCAM* (2023)			0.99	-	35.7	0.00	0.99	-	140.7	0.00	0.99	-	277.4	0.00
RL-based methods	DHC (2021)			0.49	0.94	118.9	1.7e-2	0.00	0.89	-	1.7e-2	0.00	0.95	-	8.2e-3
	PICO (2022)			0.00	-	-	1.0e-2	-	-	-	-	-	-	-	-
	SCRIMP (2023)			0.92	0.99	56.7	7.6e-3	0.74	0.99	232.4	1.2e-2	-	-	-	-
	CPL (2023)			0.00	-	-	5.6e-3	-	-	-	-	-	-	-	-
	H₂L (Ours)			**0.99**	**0.99**	**50.9**	**7.8e-4**	**0.96**	**0.99**	**173.2**	**3.4e-4**	**0.93**	**0.99**	**303.7**	**1.6e-4**

large maps, the effect of reward functions on agent congestion, and the influence of considering the following conflicts.

We analyze the role of VDN variant by comparing it with independent RL. Therefore, we will use the independent RL algorithm to train the agents. For a more intuitive presentation of results, we conduct training only in environments with a map size of 5, keeping other conditions constant. We analyze the impact of VDN variant by comparing the success rate of agents during training on maps of size 5×5 with 5 agents, and we name this approach H₂L-VDN.

We investigate the impact of the reward function on agent performance in large maps by contrasting it with the reward function in PRIMAL's style [7]. For a more intuitive presentation of results, we conduct training in environments with one agent and map sizes of 5, 10, 20, 40, 80, keeping other conditions constant. We analyzed the effect of reward functions by comparing the success rate of the agent on 80×80 maps during training, and we name this approach H₂L-Reward.

We analyze the impact of penalizing stopping next to each other on congestion by comparing it with a reward function without congestion optimization. We assess the success rates of both methods in various environments to comprehend the influence of reward functions on agent congestion. This approach is denoted as H₂L-Jam, implemented by excluding the fourth and sixth reward items as detailed in Table 2.

We investigate the influence of penalizing the following conflicts by comparing it with a reward function that does not consider following conflicts. We evaluate the success rates of both methods across different environments to understand the effect of considering the following conflicts, and we designate this approach as H₂L-F.

Figure 1 illustrates the crucial role of the VDN variant we proposed in coordinating agents. In Fig. 2, we observe that our proposed reward function demonstrates better generalization performance across varying map sizes. Table 5 emphasizes the effectiveness of penalizing stopping next to each other in addressing congestion, and Table 6 indicates the effectiveness of considering the following conflicts.

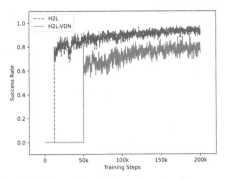

Fig. 1. Comparison between H₂L and H₂L-VDN.

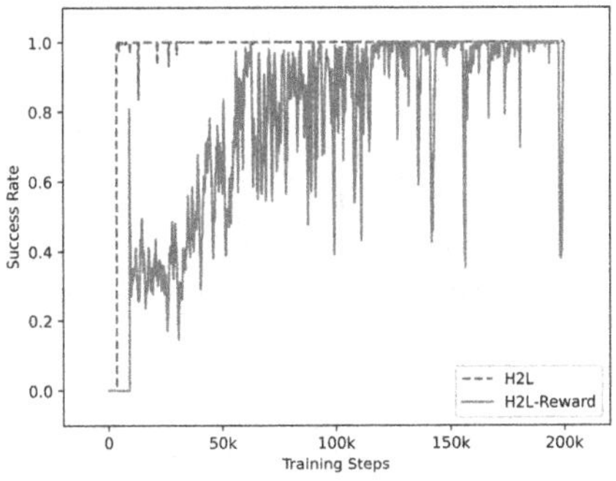

Fig. 2. Comparison between H₂L and H₂L-Reward.

Table 5. Comparison between H₂L and H₂L-Jam. *The obstacle density is 0.3.*

	(64, 20 × 20)	(512, 80 × 80)	(1024, 160 × 160)
H₂L-Jam	0.89	0.34	0.53
H₂L	0.88	0.84	0.88

Table 6. Comparison between H₂L and H₂L-F. *The obstacle density is 0.3.*

	(64, 20 × 20)	(512, 80 × 80)	(1024, 160 × 160)
H₂L-F	0.91	0.82	0.85
H₂L	0.88	0.84	0.88

5   Conclusion

We propose an RL-based MAPF algorithm, H₂L, which is trained centrally and executes in a decentralized manner. Agents need to communicate with neighboring agents to acquire information, and can also realize that without explicit communication through vision methods, such as object detection. We introduce a new variant of VDN, which overcomes the non-stationary of the environment and the challenges of training in large scale multi-agent system. We designed a novel reward function to ensure the agent's policy is independent of the map size. We also enhance the reward function to alleviate agent congestion. In experiments, we achieve higher success rate and lower collision rate than other RL-based methods.

H_2L is an important step towards the practical application of learning-based MAPF algorithms. In the future, we aim to apply H_2L in real-world scenarios and continue its improvement.

References

1. Morris, R., et al.: Planning, scheduling and monitoring for airport surface operations. In: AAAI Workshop: Planning for Hybrid Systems, pp. 608–614 (2016)
2. Wurman, P.R., D'Andrea, R., Mountz, M.: Coordinating hundreds of cooperative, autonomous vehicles in warehouses. AI Mag. **29**(1), 9 (2008)
3. Ma, H., Yang, J., Cohen, L., Kumar, T.K., Koenig, S.: Feasibilitystudy: moving non-homogeneous teams in congested video game environments. In: Proceedings of the AAAI Conference on Artificial Intelligence and Interactive Digital Entertainment, vol. 13, pp. 270–272 (2017)
4. Stern, R., et al.: Multi-agent pathfinding: Definitions, variants, and benchmarks. In: Proceedings of the International Symposium on Combinatorial Search, vol. 10, pp. 151–158 (2019)
5. Li, W., Chen, H., Jin, B., Tan, W., Zha, H., Wang, X.: Multi-agent path finding with prioritized communication learning. In: 2022 International Conference on Robotics and Automation (ICRA), pp. 10695–10701. IEEE (2022)
6. Ma, Z., Luo, Y., Ma, H.: Distributed heuristic multi-agent path finding with communication. In: 2021 IEEE International Conference on Robotics and Automation (ICRA), pp. 8699–8705. IEEE (2021)
7. Sartoretti, G., et al.: Primal: pathfinding via reinforcement and imitation multi-agent learning. IEEE Robot. Autom. Lett. **4**(3), 2378–2385 (2019)
8. Oroojlooy, A., Hajinezhad, D.: A review of cooperative multi-agent deep reinforcement learning. Appl. Intell. **53**(11), 13677–13722 (2023)
9. Sunehag, P., et al.: Value-decomposition networks for cooperative multi-agent learning. arXiv preprint arXiv:1706.05296 (2017)
10. Zhao, C., Zhuang, L., Huang, Y., Liu, H.: Curriculum learning based multi-agent path finding for complex environments. In: 2023 International Joint Conference on Neural Networks (IJCNN), pp. 1–8. IEEE (2023)
11. Wang, W., et al.: From few to more: large-scale dynamic multiagent curriculum learning. Proc. AAAI Conf. Artif. Intell. **34**, 7293–7300 (2020)
12. Song, Z., Zhang, R., Cheng, X.: Helsa: hierarchical reinforcement learning with spatiotemporal abstraction for large-scale multi-agent path finding. In: 2023 IEEE/RSJ International Conference on Intelligent Robots and Systems (IROS), pp. 7318–7325. IEEE (2023)
13. He, C., Yang, T., Duhan, T., Wang, Y., Sartoretti, G.: Alpha: attention-based long-horizon pathfinding in highly-structured areas. arXiv preprint arXiv:2310.08350 (2023)
14. Ng, A.Y., Harada, D., Russell, S.: Policy invariance under reward transformations: theory and application to reward shaping. In: ICML, vol. 99, pp. 278–287. Citeseer (1999)
15. Bernstein, D.S., Givan, R., Immerman, N., Zilberstein, S.: The complexity of decentralized control of markov decision processes. Math. Oper. Res. **27**(4), 819–840 (2002)
16. Wang, Y., Xiang, B., Huang, S., Sartoretti, G.: Scrimp: scalable communication for reinforcement-and imitation-learning-based multi-agent pathfinding. arXiv preprint arXiv:2303.00605 (2023)
17. Li, Y., Wang, M., Xie, X., Chai, W., Chen, X.: Brain-inspired perception feature and cognition model applied to safety patrol robot. IEEE Trans. Ind. Inform. (2023)

18. Yang, S., Huimin, L., Li, J.: Multifeature fusion-based object detection for intelligent transportation systems. IEEE Trans. Intell. Transp. Syst. **24**(1), 1126–1133 (2022)
19. Wagner, G., Choset, H.: Subdimensional expansion for multirobot path planning. Artif. Intell. **219**, 1–24 (2015)
20. Li, J., Ruml, W., Koenig, S.: EECBS: a bounded-suboptimal search for multi-agent path finding. Proc. AAAI Conf. Artif. Intell. **35**, 12353–12362 (2021)
21. Okumura, K.: Improving LaCam for scalable eventually optimal multi-agent pathfinding. arXiv preprint arXiv:2305.03632 (2023)

Stereo Image Super-Resolution via Disparity Estimation and Domain Diffusion

Wanjun Wang[1,3], Chunyan Ma[2,3(✉)], Hongjun Zhu[1,3], Kai Xu[1,3], and Huihui Han[1,3]

[1] School of Computer and Software Engineering, Anhui Institute of Information Technology,
WuHu 241199, China
[2] School of Artificial Intelligence, Department of Information, Hohai University,
NanJing 210024, China
1287861054@qq.com
[3] Platforms of Automotive Intelligent Software and Systems, Anhui Institute of Information
Technology, WuHu 241199, China

Abstract. Image super-resolution (SR) and disparity estimation are closely related in stereo images, with effective utilization of disparity maps enhancing SR performance. This paper proposes a stereo image super-resolution reconstruction network utilizing disparity estimation and a domain diffusion model. The network integrates disparity estimation with diffusion models for feature summation and domain space construction, enabling interaction between forward and backward diffusion memory units. To further improve reconstructed image quality, we introduce a novel memory unit inspired by long short-term memory concepts. Disparity loss and structural similarity are included in the loss function to achieve more accurate results. Experiments show that our method outperforms existing techniques.

Keywords: Super-resolution · Disparity Estimation · Domain Diffusion · Long Short-Term Memory

1 Introduction

With the pervasive utilization of dual-camera devices, enhancing the quality of captured images has become increasingly critical [1]. Single image super-resolution (SR) reconstruction harnesses the intrinsic relationships between pixels and their neighboring counterparts, effectively leveraging the inherent redundancy present in natural data. This technique enables the recovery of lost details from a single low-resolution (LR) image to generate a high-resolution (HR) output. In contrast, disparity maps derived from left and right images involve comparing two similar images to achieve sub-pixel displacements, utilizing cross-view information to improve reconstruction fidelity. Stereo imaging holds substantial potential for various applications, including smartphones, drones, and autonomous driving technologies [2].

In recent years, the rapidly evolving field of deep learning has attracted considerable attention for its applications in super-resolution [3]. The application of image super-resolution reconstruction to left and right disparity images has emerged as a crucial

H. Lu (Ed.): ISAIR 2024, CCIS 2402, pp. 138–145, 2025.
https://doi.org/10.1007/978-981-96-2911-4_14

area within deep learning methodologies. In these disparity images, given that each pixel corresponds to a specific depth map, the relationship between low-resolution and high-resolution images can be effectively learned through a feed-forward depth network, thereby facilitating successful image super-resolution reconstruction.

Kim et al. [4] proposed a method for achieving accurate image super-resolution through the use of very deep convolutional networks (VDSR), advancing beyond traditional approaches that focus on mapping relationships between low-resolution (LR) and high-resolution (HR) images. This methodology emphasizes learning from residual images and incorporates gradient clipping to restrict gradients within a specified range, thereby enhancing both the convergence rate and the quality of the reconstructed images. Lim et al. [5] further improved the quality of reconstructed images by eliminating redundant modules from conventional residual networks and optimizing their architectures. Zhang et al. [6] introduced an enhanced residual dense network (RDN) that effectively extracts abundant local features via densely connected convolutional layers while establishing a continuous memory mechanism for adaptive learning of more efficient features, aided by local feature fusion within a residual dense block (RDB). Dai et al. [7] presented a novel human resource differential information feedback (HRDIF) mechanism designed for constructing a disparity estimation feedback network (SSRDE-FNet), which iteratively enhances the quality of super-resolved images.

However, as network depth increases, the training efficiency of deep-layered models does not scale proportionately with the quality of the final images. This limitation renders them unsuitable for resource-constrained devices such as mobile and embedded systems. Currently, several stereo image super-resolution algorithms utilizing diffusion models have emerged, including SR3 [8] and the Nonlinear Activation Network (NAFNet) [2], among others. SR3 employs Denoising Diffusion Probabilistic Models (DDPM) [9] combined with denoising fraction matching techniques to achieve image super-resolution through iterative refinement. This approach generates conditional images by leveraging a denoising diffusion probabilistic model that iteratively refines noise outputs via a U-Net model trained across varying levels of noise.

In this paper, we introduce an approach for super-resolution reconstruction of stereo images, leveraging disparity estimation and domain diffusion. Our contribution are as follows: (1) The diffusion model enhances image details and texture by introducing smoothness, while the LSTM model improves contextual understanding, effectively capturing critical information to significantly enhance super-resolution outcomes. (2) Given the limited availability of high-resolution training data for stereo images, the sequence optimization capabilities of LSTM predict missing high-frequency components, yielding results that are closer to true high-resolution images. (3) This proposal incorporates a weighted loss function that integrates left-right disparity and structural similarity loss to bolster model robustness and generalization, thereby enabling efficient adaptation to various image types with improved accuracy.

2 Our Method

This section delineates a proposed network for image super-resolution reconstruction, leveraging disparity estimation and domain diffusion techniques. By utilizing the left and right disparity feature images derived from low-resolution inputs, the network constructs a zero space informed by the diffusion model. This approach enhances feature extraction and facilitates high-resolution image reconstruction through the interplay of forward and reverse diffusion spaces. The optimization process is guided by a loss function that integrates structural similarity loss alongside disparity loss, thereby refining overall network performance. In this context, we outline the network framework, elaborate on the domain diffusion model, and clarify the construction of the loss function. This methodology effectively addresses several limitations associated with current generative adversarial networks (GANs) in managing complex tasks while harnessing distinct advantages offered by disparity estimation and domain diffusion to advance state-of-the-art super-resolution techniques.

2.1 Disparity Estimation and Domain Diffusion Model

Given the distinct features perceived by the left and right human eyes, leveraging disparity between these two perspectives can significantly enhance image super-resolution reconstruction. Currently, most generative adversarial networks tend to excel in single tasks such as image super-resolution; however, they are often hindered by complex learning processes that make training challenging. To address this issue, we propose a disparity estimation and domain diffusion-based image super-resolution reconstruction network (DEDD), as illustrated in Fig. 1.

2.2 Domain Diffusion Model

Figure 1(b) shows the basic framework of the domain diffusion model presented in this paper, where the reverse diffusion process iteratively samples x_{t-1}^+ from $p(x_{t-1}^+|x_t^+, x_0^+)$ to generate a clean image $x_0^+ \sim q(x^+)$ from random noise $x_t^+ \sim N(0, I)$. However, this process is entirely random, and the intermediate state x_t^+ is noisy. In order to produce a pure intermediate state for the range zero spatial decomposition, the mean and variance variations of the diffusion distribution are defined as follows:

$$\mu_t(x_t^+, x_0^+) = \frac{\sqrt{\overline{\alpha}_{t-1}}\beta_t}{1 - \overline{\alpha}_t}x_0^+ + \frac{\sqrt{\overline{\alpha}_t}(1 - \overline{\alpha}_{t-1})}{1 - \overline{\alpha}_t}x_t^+,$$
$$\sigma_t^2 = \frac{1 - \overline{\alpha}_{t-1}}{1 - \overline{\alpha}_t}\beta_t \tag{1}$$

where x_0^+ is unknown, β_t representing a pre-determined parameter, $\alpha_t = 1 - \beta_t$, $\overline{\alpha} = \prod\limits_{i=0}^{t} \alpha_i$, We can predict noise $Z_\theta(x_t, t)$ from x_t and x_0 by forward diffusion, so we can build our zero space. We denote the estimate x_0 of the time step t as $x_{0|t}$, defined as follows:

$$x_{0|t} = \frac{1}{\sqrt{\overline{\alpha}_t}}(x_t - Z_\theta(x_t, t)\sqrt{1 - \overline{\alpha}_t}) \tag{2}$$

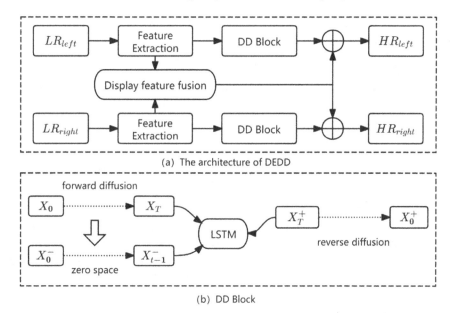

(a) The architecture of DEDD

(b) DD Block

Fig. 1. The architecture of DEDD. (a) Feature extraction is completed by three layers of 3×3 convolution. Feature fusion is performed by adding, and the intermediate memory units are changed over time. (b) The architecture of the domain diffusion model. Each part is connected by an LSTM structure.

In order to finally get an x_0 that satisfies $Ax_0 \equiv y$, We fix the range space as $A^- y$, and maintain a constant zero space, so as to get a estimate after correction $x_{0|t}^+$ as:

$$x_{0|t}^+ = A^- y + (I - A^- A)x_{0|t} \tag{3}$$

Therefore, we use the forward diffusion $x_{0|t}$ in (1) as an estimate of the zero space x_0^-, Thus only the zero space is allowed to participate in the backward diffusion process. Then we sampling to get x_{t-1}^+ from $p(x_{t-1}^+ | x_t^+, x_0^+)$:

$$x_{t-1}^+ = \frac{\sqrt{\overline{\alpha}_{t-1}}\beta_t}{1 - \overline{\alpha}_t}x_{0|t}^+ + \frac{\sqrt{\overline{\alpha}_t}(1 - \overline{\alpha}_{t-1})}{1 - \overline{\alpha}_t}x_t^+ + \sigma_t Z_\theta \tag{4}$$

Similarly we can obtain x_t^+ in the subsequent diffusion process. In order to solve the problem of noisy image restoration, We optimize the domain space distance Γ_t to obtain:

$$x_{0|t}^+ = x_{0|t} - \Gamma_t A^- (Ax_{0|t} - y) \tag{5}$$

where Γ_t should be as close to I as possible, to keep distance space correction $A^- (Ax_{0|t} - y)$ to the largest extent, so as to maximize consistency. Since LSTM has the function of long short-term memory in sequence modeling and other issues, the model can be optimized by combining the input parameters before and after. Inspired by this, we combined the forward and reverse direction diffusion model on the basis of denoising diffusion null space [10] to form a different domain diffusion model (DDNM). The intermediate parameters are as follows:

$$x_t = x_t - \Gamma_t A^-(Ax_t - y) \qquad (6)$$

The backward diffusion process can be used to obtain the desired x_{t+1}^+, so for the forward diffusion of the new state x_{new}, can be expressed as:

$$x_{new} = x_{t+1}^+ * \tanh(\eta_t)$$
$$\eta_t = x_{t-1}^+ * \eta_{t-1} + x_t * \tanh(x_t) \qquad (7)$$

where η_t denotes the intermediate state, which is used to alleviate the vanishing gradient.

2.3 Loss Function of Model

The optimization of the model includes a left-right disparity loss within the final loss function to account for the influence of disparity on image reconstruction. Furthermore, to address the varying applicability of data to the model, we incorporate a weighting mechanism for lower structural similarity scores in relation to image quality, which is also integrated into the final loss. This section outlines a comprehensive formulation of the specific loss function.

Left-right disparity loss is included in the overall loss function to reflect its impact on image reconstruction effectively. In addition, considering the diverse generality of data as it relates to model performance, lower structural similarity scores are weighted and incorporated into this final composition. The specific formulation of the loss function is expressed as follows:

$$Loss = L_{SR} + \gamma \cdot L_{Disp} + \lambda \cdot L_{SSIM} \qquad (8)$$

where γ and λ are constants, which are set to 0.1 and 0.01 respectively.

3 Experiment

3.1 Preparation

The experimental hardware setup consists of an Intel(R) Core(TM) i5 processor paired with a GTX 3060Ti graphics card, operating on Ubuntu 20.04 LTS and equipped with 16 GB of RAM. The deep learning framework utilized in this study is PyTorch, supported by CUDA 11.3 and cuDNN 8.0. For diffusion methods, we employed Denoising Diffusion Probabilistic Models (DDPM) as the standard sampling strategy without classifier guidance, using peak signal-to-noise ratio (PSNR), structural similarity index measure (SSIM), and the number of model parameters as key performance indicators.

This research was conducted on four publicly available datasets, specifically KITTI 2012. To maintain spatial resolution consistency with other methodologies, we performed double-cubic resampling on the Middlebury dataset to incorporate supplementary imagery. Furthermore, to ensure that the experimental results objectively reflect the effects described in this paper, objective metrics were measured and compared based on these approaches [4–8]. Subsequently, a stereoscopic super-resolution image was reconstructed for analysis; moreover, comparisons were made between both left and right view stereo images ((left + right)/2).

3.2 Comparisons of SOTA Methods

Our method is compared with VDSR [4], EDSR [5], RDN [6], RCAN [11] and SSRDE-FNet [7]. From the two aspects of objective metrics and subjective visual measures. To objectively show the comparative fairness between the proposed method and the SISR method, we retrain the models of these methods using the proposed training dataset.

Table 1. Quantitative result of different methods on KITTI 2012 datasets under the condition of scaling size of 2 and 4. The optimal results of PSNR and SSIM are shown in bold.

Method	Scale	Left	(Left + Right)/2
		KITTI 2012	KITTI 2012
VDSR	2	30.17/0.9062	30.30/0.9089
EDSR	2	30.83/0.9199	30.96/0.9228
RDN	2	30.81/0.9197	30.94/0.9227
RCAN	2	30.88/0.9202	31.02/0.9232
SSRDE-FNet	2	31.08/0.9224	31.23/0.9254
DEDD	2	**31.42/0.9341**	**31.48/0.9421**
VDSR	4	25.54/0.7662	25.60/0.7722
EDSR	4	26.26/0.7954	26.35/0.8015
RDN	4	26.23/0.7952	26.32/0.8014
RCAN	4	26.36/0.7968	26.44/0.8029
SSRDE-FNet	4	26.61/0.8028	26.70/0.8082
DEDD	4	**26.72/0.8132**	**26.75/0.8112**

As shown in Table 1, in terms of objective metrics, our method is due to these SR methods. In SISR and stereo image SR approach, Our DEDD method outperforms various SISR and stereo image SR approaches across all datasets and sampling factors of 2 and 4. This underscores DEDD's effectiveness and advancement over existing SR methods (Fig. 3).

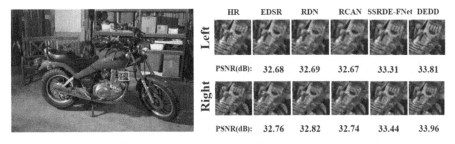

Fig. 2. Qualitative results (×2) on Test dataset.

Fig. 3. Qualitative results (×4) on Test dataset.

In Fig. 2, visual comparisons between the proposed method and alternative methods are presented, highlighting differences at magnifications of ×4. From the figures, it is evident that the majority of the compared SR methods fail to clearly delineate the edge information of the images. In contrast, our DEDD demonstrates the ability to reconstruct high-quality SR images, characterized by abundant details and sharp edges. This underscores the competitive advantage of DEDD.

4   Conclusion

We commenced our investigation with the hypothesis that disparity estimation is crucial for the effective reconstruction of stereo images. Building upon this premise, we developed an innovative super-resolution reconstruction model that leverages both disparity estimation and domain diffusion techniques. A notable innovation within our approach is the incorporation of memory unit feature representations into the diffusion process, employing a null space to integrate forward diffusion models. This amalgamation, in conjunction with features derived from disparity estimation, enables image super-resolution reconstruction through a feature fusion strategy inspired by LSTM networks. To enhance the applicability of our model across various imaging scenarios, we introduced a composite loss function that unites disparity loss with structural similarity metrics. This newly devised loss function aims to improve the super-resolution performance of our model significantly. Extensive experimental evaluations benchmarked against state-of-the-art methods have validated the superiority of our approach. The results consistently demonstrate advanced capabilities in enhancing the quality of super-resolution reconstructions achieved by our model. Notably, one highlight of this work is its application to underwater stereoscopic images' super-resolution reconstruction. This application not only illustrates the versatility of our model but also emphasizes its potential for overcoming unique challenges associated with underwater imaging yielding impressive results in this context.

References

1. Zhang, D., Huang, F., Liu, S., Wang, X., Jin, Z.: Swinfir: revisiting the swinIR with fast fourier convolution and improved training for image super-resolution, arXiv preprint arXiv: 2208.11247 (2022)

2. Chen, L,, Chu, X., Zhang., X., et al.: Simple baselines for image restoration. In: European Conference on Computer Vision (ECCV), pp. 17–33. Springer, Israel (2022)
3. Chu, X., Chen, L., Yu, W.: Nafssr: stereo image super-resolution using nafnet. In: Proceedings of Conference on Computer Vision and Pattern Recognition (CVPR), pp. 1239–1248. IEEE, New Orleans (2022)
4. Kim, J., Lee, J., Lee, K.: Accurate image super-resolution using very deep convolutional networks. In: Proceedings of Conference on Computer Vision and Pattern Recognition (CVPR), pp. 1646–1654. IEEE, Las Vegas (2016)
5. Lim, B., Son, S., Kim, H., Nah, S., Lee, K.: Enhanced deep residual networks for single image super-resolution. In: Proceedings of Conference on Computer Vision and Pattern Recognition (CVPR), pp. 136–144. IEEE, Hawaii (2017)
6. Zhang, Y., Tian, Y., Kong, Y., Zhong, B., Fu, Y.: Residual dense network for image super-resolution. In: Proceedings of Conference on Computer Vision and Pattern Recognition (CVPR), pp. 2472–2481. IEEE, Utah (2018)
7. Dai, Q., Li, J., Yi, Q., Fang, F., Zhang, G.: Feedback network for mutually boosted stereo image super-resolution and disparity estimation. In: Proceedings of 29th ACM International Conference Multimedia (MM), pp. 1985–1993. ACM, Chengdu (2021)
8. Zheng, P., Askham, T., Brunton, S.L., Kutz, J.N., Aravkin, A.Y.: A unified framework for sparse relaxed regularized regression: sr3. IEEE Access 7, 1404–1423 (2019)
9. Ho, J., Jain, A., Abbeel, P.: Denoising diffusion probabilistic models. In: Proceedings of the 34th Neural Information Processing System (NIPS), pp. 6840–6851. MIT Press, NY (2020)
10. Wang, Y., Yu, J., Zhang, J.: Zero-shot image restoration using denoising diffusion null-space model, arXiv preprint arXiv:2212.00490, (2022)
11. Zhang, Y., Li, K., Li, K., Wang, L., Zhong, B., Fu, Y.: Image super-resolution using very deep residual channel attention networks. In: Proceedings of the IEEE Conference on Computer Vision (ECCV), pp. 286–301. Springer, Munich (2018)

Virtual Reality-Based Medical Rehabilitation Assistance System

Xianyan Li[1], Yiqin Yao[2], Ping Liang[3], Yijing Guo[3], and Hao Gao[1(✉)]

[1] College of Automation, Nanjing University of Posts and Telecommunications, Nanjing, China
tsgaohao@gmail.com
[2] Department of Neurology, Nanjing Lishui People's Hospital, Nanjing, China
[3] Department of Neurology, Southeast University Zhongda Hospital, Nanjing, China

Abstract. Due to braking, pain, and psychological factors after severe hand injuries, based on the theory of "central nervous system-peripheral loop", hand injuries can affect the functional connections of the brain, thereby affecting the rehabilitation process. Therefore, guiding patients to actively participate in task-oriented functional training in a safe manner and promoting their safe return to work is a challenge faced by current occupational rehabilitation work. A virtual reality occupational rehabilitation system developed based on VR technology conducts rehabilitation training for patients in both real and virtual scenarios. This system is developed in cooperation with HTC-VIVE-Pro devices and some actual devices. We designed some experiments to evaluate the feasibility of this system, and the results show that it does indeed contribute to patient rehabilitation.

Keywords: Virtual Reality · Medical rehabilitation · Assistive system

1 Introduction

In today's society, with the continuous improvement of social and economic standards, public expectations for medical services [12, 19]are also rising. Beyond simply curing diseases, people now hope to quickly regain their ability to carry out daily activities. Economic growth has enabled more individuals to invest in higher-quality, more comprehensive healthcare services.

However, traditional medical rehabilitation systems [7] have several shortcomings. First, they lack personalization, making it difficult to meet the specific needs of different patients. Second, traditional rehabilitation methods are often monotonous and unengaging, making it hard for patients to stay motivated and stick to treatment plans. Additionally, these conventional approaches lack real-time feedback mechanisms, making it difficult for both patients and healthcare professionals to accurately assess rehabilitation progress, detect issues, and make timely adjustments.

In recent years, with the rapid advancement of virtual reality (VR) technology [5, 26], VR has demonstrated great potential in the field of medical rehabilitation. Through devices such as head-mounted displays, controllers, and sensors, VR creates immersive virtual environments, allowing personalized treatment plans tailored to the needs and abilities of each patient.

Through in-depth analysis of current hospital cases, we have found that the main causes of injuries are mainly divided into three situations: vehicle injuries [9, 17], mechanical injuries [14, 18], and falls from heights [21, 22]. Based on these findings, we developed an innovative medical rehabilitation assistance system [1, 2, 13] using advanced virtual reality (VR) technology in combination with HTC VIVE Pro equipment. This system allows patients to interact with real-world objects within a virtual environment and simulates various work scenarios to help them specifically recover the vocational skills that were impaired by their injuries. In this paper, we focus primarily on the development and research of scenarios related to mechanical injuries and fall injuries.

2   Related Work

Back in 2003, Burdea pointed out that VR could serve as an enhancement to conventional therapy, used for patients with musculoskeletal issues, hemiplegia caused by stroke, and those with cognitive deficits, even predicting that VR could completely replace traditional interventions [4].

In recent years, Virtual Reality (VR) technology has been widely applied in the medical field, providing more effective treatment and rehabilitation methods for patients. It has also made significant progress in medical education, surgical simulation, and other areas. Numerous experts and scholars have conducted investigations into the effectiveness of VR in medical rehabilitation. Rose conducted extensive research and reviewed 18 studies to understand the performance and health status of individuals in daily life after using VR rehabilitation systems [23]. Maier et al. evaluated the efficacy of specific VR (SVR) and non-specific VR (NSVR) systems in the recovery of upper limb function and activity after stroke, with results showing significant impacts of SVR on bodily functions [16].

In specific applications, Dias P developed VR mini-games to provide upper limb rehabilitation training for stroke patients [10]. Esfahlani et al. created a non-immersive virtual rehabilitation system called ReHabgame, designed for neurorehabilitation [11]. Bortone proposed an immersive VR training system aimed at children with neuromotor disorders, using multisensory feedback to assist in motor exercises [3]. Canning applied VR in studies on gait and balance for Parkinson's disease patients, helping to better understand related motor-cognitive neural circuits [6]. Lu applied deep learning in Parkinson's disease [27]. Tan used VR to construct specific scenarios to aid in restoring scene memory and cognitive abilities for patients with mild cognitive impairment (MCI) [25]. Choi's team combined VR with mobile phones to develop a mobile game for upper limb rehabilitation in stroke patients [8].

3 Method

3.1 Introduction to the Equipment

In developing this medical rehabilitation assistance system, we chose the HTC VIVE Pro Professional [15] Edition as the core device. Its high-resolution AMOLED screen (2880x1600) and 90Hz refresh rate provide a smooth and realistic visual experience. Utilizing SteamVR [20] tracking technology, the system accurately captures head and hand movements, ensuring real-time feedback and free interaction. HTC also provided the VIVE Focus 3 [24] eye tracker for attention assessment and the VIVE Wireless Upgrade Kit to eliminate cable constraints (Fig. 1).

Fig. 1. The overall schematic diagram of the equipment.

To enhance the integration of virtual and real environments, we introduced VR gloves, enabling more natural gesture control and improving immersion and intuitive operation (Fig. 2).

Fig. 2. VR Glove Schematic

3.2 VR Scene Development

In recent years, the XR industry has developed rapidly, with many manufacturers launching various XR devices. Initially, each manufacturer maintained their own SDKs, leading to compatibility issues for developers. Programs developed using the SDK from manufacturer A might not be compatible with devices from manufacturer B, increasing the complexity of development. To simplify the development process, OpenXR was introduced, and Unity's XR Interaction Toolkit (XRI) provides developers with features for movement, object interaction, and UI interaction.

This paper focuses on development using Unity 2021, OpenXR, and XRI 2.5.2 to create realistic VR scenarios that help patients undergo simulated training in a safe environment, gradually restoring their vocational skills. The system enhances the engagement and interactivity of rehabilitation, accelerating the restoration of patient confidence.

Development of Mechanical Injury Recovery Scene. Workers operating lathes may suffer injuries due to unfamiliarity with the equipment, neglect of safety protocols, lack of focus, and other factors. Additionally, lathe aging, damage, insufficient lighting, and poorly designed layouts can also lead to accidents. These injuries not only impact workers' health but can also cause work interruptions, economic losses, and long-term psychological trauma.

To address this, we have developed a workshop simulation and used eye-tracking devices to monitor workers' attention. According to national standards (e.g., GB 8176–2012), we have set various environmental difficulty levels in visual space, vision, and sound to realistically simulate the workshop environment.

The workers' task is to operate virtual hands to pick up metal sheets and place them accurately on a virtual punch press, then start the press for stamping and dispose of the waste in a bin. We record key metrics such as material handling and placement time, stamping operation time, and level of attention. Eye-tracking technology helps analyze the workers' blink rate and gaze concentration.

Fig. 3. Overview diagram of the workshop scene.

Additionally, we have designed emergency scenarios (e.g., abnormal sounds from the press, unusual blinking of indicator lights, or the press becoming suspended) requiring workers to react within a specified time. Failure to respond in time is recorded as a failure, and the reaction time is used as a scoring criterion.

In the scenario shown in Fig. 3, workers pick up metal sheets from the right side of their body and place them on the punch press for stamping. After stamping, they place the waste in a bin on the left side. When the bin is full, it must be moved to a shelf, and the worker returns to continue the task. Random emergencies occur, and workers must handle them correctly; incidents and reaction times are recorded, with failure to respond or incorrect handling considered as rule violations (Fig. 4).

In terms of visual tracking, we use the HTC SRanipal Runtime SDK to obtain data on eye openness, gaze direction, and other metrics via its API. This information is used to

Fig. 4. Diagram illustrating eye tracking

render gaze lines in the virtual world to assess accuracy. The scene is divided into work and non-work areas to evaluate the worker's focus. We assign tags to all work-related objects and use hidden gaze lines during system operation to read the tags of objects that the gaze interacts with. If the gaze remains outside the work area for too long, it is considered a sign of inattention (Fig. 5).

Fig. 5. UI interface and environmental comparison diagram

For environmental control, we created a UI interface to manage three indicators: visual, auditory, and visual spatial elements. Visual spatial elements primarily refer to the width of pathways. Users can press a button on the controller to automatically display the UI interface in front of them, with a ray appearing on the virtual hand to interact with the UI. The image below shows a comparison of the UI interface with different lighting and pathway widths.

Development of High Altitude Fall Injury Recovery Scene. Falls from heights are a common type of accident in high-altitude work, potentially caused by unstable work platforms, lack of railings, or barriers. Other risks include dizziness from heights, adverse weather conditions (e.g., strong winds, rain, or snow), and human error.

To improve safety in high-altitude work, we have set up a virtual reality (VR) scene on a construction site. Workers must use a virtual elevator to reach the high-altitude work area and perform tasks. This design simulates a real work environment to reduce potential injury risks. We use eye-tracking devices to monitor workers' attention levels in real time and evaluate their task performance. This precise monitoring helps enhance safety and provides personalized feedback to help workers manage risks and challenges (Fig. 6).

Fig. 6. Overview diagram of the construction site environment.

In high-altitude work, workers might encounter emergencies such as dizziness, changing weather conditions, or falling materials. Workers need to respond quickly and maintain a stable psychological state. We assess their response speed, problem-solving abilities, and task completion rates while applying visual tracking technology. The system provides voice alerts when attention lapses are detected and records data for evaluation (Fig. 7).

Fig. 7. The environmental changes under different weather conditions.

To simulate a realistic construction site environment, we researched actual construction sites and used 3Dmax to model the site. Considering the impact of distant views on immersion during high-altitude work, we employed Unity's skybox technology to set the virtual background and adjusted the map scale to create an immersive scene. Additionally, to enhance realism, we incorporated a weather system that randomly generates weather changes (e.g., rain, snow, sunny, cloudy) based on the program.

4   Experimental Results

This section summarizes the development of two VR scenarios and the actual experiences of patients. We conducted experiments with 20 workers who had never used VR before, and more than half had never used a computer. The age distribution of the patients is as follows (Fig. 8):

4.1   System Performance Evaluation

The experiment was divided into three scenarios, each involving ten injured workers. We introduced five evaluation criteria for patients to rate their experience with the VR

Age distribution

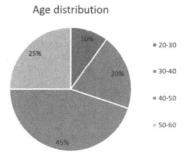

Fig. 8. Age distribution chart.

system: system smoothness, system stability, user acceptance, maximum acceptance time, and recovery assistance, with scores ranging from 1 to 10, where a score of 6 or above is considered passing.

During the experiment, patients were taken to a recovery room where they received brief training and an introduction to the system. After donning the VR headset and entering the virtual world, patients engaged in the tasks. After a few minutes of adaptation, all patients showed a strong interest, finding the treatment method both engaging and effective. Due to the randomness of scenario events, each patient had a slightly different experience, minimizing the overall impact on the scores. The scoring results for the mechanical injury recovery scenario are shown in the Table 1 below:

According to the experimental results, all scores for system smoothness, stability, and patient assistance exceeded the passing threshold, and the patients generally recognized the system positively. However, after using the system for more than 15 min, patients experienced fatigue and increased 3D dizziness, suggesting that each treatment session should be kept within 15 min. Some users reported feeling restricted by the VR equipment, which affected immersion. Despite these issues, participants remained optimistic about the approach, and the overall results were satisfactory. Most participants expressed a willingness to continue using this treatment method, indicating that VR therapy effectively engaged patients and enhanced their motivation.

Table 1. Patient evaluation form for rehabilitation system.

	System fluency	Stability	User acceptance	Recovery assistance	acceptance time
User1	8	9	8	8	18 min
User2	6	8	9	9	16 min
User3	7	8	8	8	15 min
User4	8	9	7	7	13 min
User5	9	7	6	9	20 min

4.2 System Rating

The text mentions that our medical rehabilitation assistance system evaluates patients' performance in virtual scenarios mainly based on the following aspects: task completion, reaction speed, attention concentration, work proficiency, and rehabilitation progress. These indicators are also rated on a scale of 10 points. The scoring results for the high-altitude scenario are shown in the Table 2 below:

Table 2. Rehabilitation System Rating Form for Patients.

	Task completion	Reaction speed	Attention concentration	Work proficiency	Rehabilitation progress
User1	7	7	8	7	8
User2	6	7	9	8	8
User3	6	8	7	9	8
User4	8	7	7	8	7
User5	6	7	8	8	9

As shown in the Table 2, our medical rehabilitation assistance system is capable of comprehensively monitoring worker performance in the virtual environment and providing reasonable scores to quantify rehabilitation progress. The task completion rate indicates that the difficulty level is moderate, as all participants achieved high scores, but none received a perfect score, suggesting that the system offers an appropriate level of challenge. Overall, the VR rehabilitation system has had a positive effect on supporting rehabilitation training; however, there is noticeable score homogenization with minimal variation. To further enhance effectiveness, we need to more carefully consider individual patient differences and adjust the training programs based on specific performance, while increasing the system's randomness and personalization.

5 Conclusion

This study developed a VR-based medical rehabilitation assistance system designed to aid patients with hand injuries in their recovery through task-oriented training. The system integrates VR technology with HTC-VIVE-Pro equipment, creating a combined virtual and real rehabilitation environment that emphasizes personalization and interactivity. By simulating work scenarios, the system enhances patient focus and engagement, while providing real-time feedback to help medical professionals monitor rehabilitation progress more accurately. Experimental results indicate that the system significantly improves rehabilitation efficiency and patient participation.

Looking ahead, we plan to optimize the system to adapt to the needs of different patients and develop additional application scenarios to assist a wider range of injured workers in their recovery. As technology advances, this system will play an even greater role in the field of occupational rehabilitation.

References

1. Anthes, C., García-Hernández, R.J., Wiedemann, M., Kranzlmüller, D.: State of the art of virtual reality technology. In: 2016 IEEE Aerospace Conference, pp. 1–19. IEEE (2016)
2. Baños, R.M., et al.: A positive psychological intervention using virtual reality for patients with advanced cancer in a hospital setting: a pilot study to assess feasibility. Support. Care Cancer **21**, 263–270 (2013)
3. Bortone, I., et al.: Wearable haptics and immersive virtual reality rehabilitation training in children with neuromotor impairments. IEEE Trans. Neural Syst. Rehabil. Eng. **26**(7), 1469–1478 (2018)
4. Burdea, G.C.: Virtual rehabilitation–benefits and challenges. Methods Inf. Med. **42**(05), 519–523 (2003)
5. Burdea, G.C., Coiffet, P.: Virtual Reality Technology. Wiley (2024)
6. Canning, C.G., Allen, N.E., Nackaerts, E., Paul, S.S., Nieuwboer, A., Gilat, M.: Virtual reality in research and rehabilitation of gait and balance in Parkinson disease. Nat. Rev. Neurol. **16**(8), 409–425 (2020)
7. Chang, L.H., Wang, J.: Integration of complementary medical treatments with rehabilitation from the perspectives of patients and their caregivers: a qualitative inquiry. Clin. Rehabil. **23**(8), 730–740 (2009)
8. Choi, Y.H., Paik, N.J.: Mobile game-based virtual reality program for upper extremity stroke rehabilitation. J. Vis. Exp. JoVE (133) (2018)
9. Conroy, C., et al.: The influence of vehicle damage on injury severity of drivers in head-on motor vehicle crashes. Accid. Anal. Prev. **40**(4), 1589–1594 (2008)
10. Dias, P., et al.: Using virtual reality to increase motivation in poststroke rehabilitation. IEEE Comput. Graphics Appl. **39**(1), 64–70 (2019)
11. Esfahlani, S.S., Thompson, T., Parsa, A.D., Brown, I., Cirstea, S.: Rehabgame: a non-immersive virtual reality rehabilitation system with applications in neuroscience. Heliyon **4**(2) (2018)
12. Jones, J., Hunter, D.: Consensus methods for medical and health services research. BMJ. Br. Med. J. **311**(7001), 376 (1995)
13. Kim, W.S., et al.: Clinical application of virtual reality for upper limb motor rehabilitation in stroke: review of technologies and clinical evidence. J. Clin. Med. **9**(10), 3369 (2020)
14. Knee, M., Miller, A.R.: Mechanical injury. Fruit quality and its biological basis pp.157–179 (2002)
15. Le Chénéchal, M., Chatel-Goldman, J.: Htc vive pro time performance benchmark for scientific research. In: Icat-Egve 2018 (2018)
16. Maier, M., Rubio Ballester, B., Duff, A., Duarte Oller, E., Verschure, P.F.: Effect of specific over nonspecific VR-based rehabilitation on poststroke motor recovery: a systematic meta-analysis. Neurorehabil. Neural Repair **33**(2), 112–129 (2019)
17. Mayou, R., Tyndel, S., Bryant, B.: Long-term outcome of motor vehicle accident injury. Psychosom. Med. **59**(6), 578–584 (1997)
18. Miyake, K., McNeil, P.L.: Mechanical injury and repair of cells. Crit. Care Med. **31**(8), S496–S501 (2003)
19. Mosadeghrad, A.M.: Factors affecting medical service quality. Iran. J. Public Health **43**(2), 210 (2014)
20. Murray, J.W.: Building virtual reality with unity and steamvr. CRC Press (2020)
21. Nadhim, E.A., Hon, C., Xia, B., Stewart, I., Fang, D.: Falls from height in the construction industry: a critical review of the scientific literature. Int. J. Environ. Res. Public Health **13**(7), 638 (2016)

22. Newaz, M.T., Ershadi, M., Carothers, L., Jefferies, M., Davis, P.: A review and assessment of technologies for addressing the risk of falling from height on construction sites. Saf. Sci. **147**, 105618 (2022)

23. Rose, T., Nam, C.S., Chen, K.B.: Immersion of virtual reality for rehabilitation-review. Appl. Ergon. **69**, 153–161 (2018)

24. Schuetz, I., Fiehler, K.: Eye tracking in virtual reality: vive pro eye spatial accuracy, precision, and calibration reliability. J. Eye Movement Res. **15**(3) (2022)

25. Tan, W., et al.: A method of vr-eeg scene cognitive rehabilitation training. Health Inf. Sci. Syst. **9**, 1–9 (2021)

26. Hageman, A.: Virtual reality. Nursing **24**(3), 3–3 (2018). https://doi.org/10.1007/s41193-018-0032-6

27. Wang, X., et al.: A parkinson's auxiliary diagnosis algorithm based on a hyperparameter optimization method of deep learning. In: IEEE/ACM Transactions on Computational Biology and Bioinformatics (2023)

IPSTT: Intention-Based Transformer for Multivariate Time Series Forecasting

Jingwei Wang[1,2], Jianmei Tan[1,2(✉)], Chang Lu[1,2], and Mengci Zhao[1,2]

[1] Chinese Aeronautical Establishment, Beijing 100029, China
tanjianmei123@163.com
[2] China Aviation System Engineering Institute, Beijing 100029, China

Abstract. Multivariate time series (MTS) forecasting has important application value in fields such as finance, healthcare, and meteorology. In recent years, forecasting models based on the Transformer architecture have received widespread attention. However, existing Transformer-based models often treat each variable sequence as an independent single variable sequence, ignoring the dependency relationships between variables. In addition, the self-attention mechanism faces limitations of quadratic time complexity and high memory usage when dealing with long sequence time-series forecasting (LSTF). Therefore, we propose the Intention-based Multivariable Time Series Forecasting Transformer (IPSTT). Specifically, IPSTT captures the temporal and inter variable dependencies of MTS through a spatial-temporal Transformer. We also use probsparse self-attention mechanism to reduce the time complexity of LSTF. In addition, pre trained GRU provides predictive intent for spatial-temporal Transformers. The experimental results show that the proposed method achieves a 50% and 20% improvement compared to the conventional methods on benchmark datasets and aviation datasets.

Keywords: Multivariate Time Series · Long Sequence Time-series Forecasting · Spatial-temporal Transformer · Self-attention

1 Introduction

Time-series forecasting is one of the important applications of time-series analysis. By analyzing and extracting features from existing time-series data, it predicts the trend of data changes and development in the future. With the development of neural network technology, time-series forecasting based on deep learning is widely applied in various fields, such as finance [1], transportation [2,3], healthcare [4], weather [5,6], etc.

In practical application scenarios, time-series exhibit diverse and complex characteristics, and the industry has further proposed the concept of Multivariate Time Series (MTS), which is a set of observations of multiple variables with time dependence [7]. These variables may have complex dynamic relationships, dependencies between data may be nonlinear, and there may be characteristics such as time lag effects and seasonality. Therefore, analyzing and forecasting MTS requires considering these characteristics and selecting appropriate methods.

In recent years, Transformer has been applied to the analysis and forecasting of MTS [8–10], achieving certain success. Transformer has good extraction ability for long-term dependencies in MTS, but in MTS, the dependency relationships between variables are equally important. Traditional Transformer-based models typically treat each variable sequence as an independent univariate sequence, ignoring the dependency relationships between variables. However, in practical applications, there are often complex interactions and correlations between variables, and ignoring these dependency relationships may lead to inaccurate prediction results. In addition, traditional Transformer models also face some challenges when dealing with long sequences. Mainly the quadratic time complexity and high memory usage required for model computation in Long Sequence Time-Series Forecasting (LSTF) [11].

To address the spatiotemporal dependency issue of Transformers, references [12,13] adopt the spatial-temporal Transformer architecture, mainly applied in human action recognition [14,15] and traffic flow prediction [16,17]. In human action recognition, spatial Transformer is responsible for processing spatial information of human body parts, while temporal Transformer is responsible for processing temporal relationships of actions. When applied to MTS tasks, the structure of spatial Transformer can extract dependencies between variables contained in MTS, while temporal Transformer can model time-series dependencies in LSTF. But with the addition of network structure, the issue of computational complexity remains unresolved.

This paper proposes an Intention-based Multivariate Time-Series Forecasting Transformer (IPSTT), which is a sparse model based on spatial-temporal Transformers. Specifically, IPSTT introduces a probsparse self-attention mechanism on the basis of spatial-temporal Transformer to replace the original self-attention mechanism, in order to reduce the time complexity of LSTF. At the same time, pre-training a GRU model for the last frame of the prediction sequence to provide prediction intent for the spatial-temporal Transformer can accelerate the convergence of the model and improve its stability. Finally, experiments on five benchmark datasets showed that IPSTT improved by up to 50% compared to state-of-the-art methods. Experiments on aviation datasets have shown that IPSTT improves aircraft state forecasting by up to 20%.

In this paper, we will discuss in the following structure. Section 1 introduces the background of the research. Section 2 will introduce the relevant work. Section 3 will provide a detailed description of the methodology used in this paper. Section 4 introduces the experimental setup. Section 5 presents and analyzes the experimental results. Finally, Sect. 6 provides a summary and outlook for this paper.

2   Related Work

2.1   Multivariate Time Series Forecasting

In MTS forecasting tasks, existing methods can be divided into two categories based on whether to consider the dependency relationships between variables. Zeng et al. [18] decomposes time-series into trend series and remainer series, and then models these two sequences using two single-layer linear networks, considering only the time dimension. Most Transformer based models also only consider modeling in the time dimension, compressing the multivariate variables at each time step into an embedding and then performing attention in the time dimension, thereby ignoring the dependency relationships between variables. A typical example is PatchTST [19], which treats each variable as an independent univariate time series and extracts local semantic information by patching the univariate time series. However, the dependency relationship between variables is equally important. Convolutional neural networks [20,21] and graph neural networks [22,23] can explicitly capture dependencies between variables. In Transformer-based models, Zhang et al. [9] embeds MTS into a two-dimensional vector array while preserving time and variable information. Then, two-stage attention (TSA) layers are used to capture dependencies across time and variables. Yu et al. [24] designed a temporal variable attention module, which utilizes both temporal and variable attention to extract key information from different dimensions.

2.2   Long Sequence Time-Series Forecasting

In LSTF tasks, existing transformer-based methods focus on improving the computational efficiency of self-attention mechanisms. Li et al. [25] proposed LogSparse attention, which only calculates the $O(\log L)$ dot product for each unit in each layer and stacks the $O(\log L)$ layer. The model can access the information of each unit, reducing complexity to $O(L(\log L)^2)$. Kitaev et al. [26] replaces point-wise attention with locality-sensitive hashing to reduce complexity to $O(L \log L)$. Informer [11] uses Kullback-Leibler divergence to select queries, only calculating the attention value of important queries and reducing complexity to $O(L \log L)$. In addition to directly changing the calculation of self-attention, there are also some methods that improve computational efficiency by changing the time-series dimension. Liu et al. [27] designed a pyramid attention module to capture features of different resolutions and model temporal dependencies across different ranges. Du et al. [28] segments time-series and replaces traditional point-wise attention with segment-wise attention, achieving practical efficiency that is more efficient than methods with complexity $O(L \log L)$ such as Informer and Autoformer [8]. PatchTST divides time-series into subsequence patches, which also improves computational efficiency and achieves better results than Preformer.

2.3   Application of Time-Series Forecasting in Aviation

In terms of aviation applications, Zhong et al. [29] used wind tunnel test data of a certain aircraft's large amplitude pitch oscillation to model the RBF (Radial

Basis Function) network, proving that the training speed of the RBF network is faster. He *et al.* [30] used LSTM recurrent neural networks to model the unsteady aerodynamic forces of oscillating delta wings, indicating that the LSTM neural network-based unsteady aerodynamic modeling method has fast convergence speed, high prediction accuracy, and good generalization performance. Chen *et al.* [31] validated the advantages of this time-dependent LSTM neural network model in unsteady aerodynamic modeling through forced motion wind tunnel tests and virtual flight tests. Zhang *et al.* [32] used a Transformer-based feature extraction model to process the historical trajectory sequence of the target aircraft, effectively improving the accuracy of trajectory prediction results. At present, there is no research on Transformer related models in the specific field of multivariable long sequence time series forecasting of aircraft trajectories. Therefore, this paper will also use the proposed model to address this issue.

3 Methodology

The IPSTT model architecture is shown in Fig. 1, which mainly consists of the GRU intent recognition module (GRU-IRM) and the probsparse self-attention spatial-temporal Transformer encoder module (PSTTEM). Among them, the GRU-IRM predicts the last frame of the subsequent forecasting sequence, and its role is to preliminarily predict the general trend of temporal changes. The PSTTEM extracts high-dimensional features, and performs residual connection with the interpolated GRU forecasting sequence, and then predicts the subsequent sequence.

The input data is the time-series data $S = \{S_1, S_2, \ldots, S_N\}$. For the i-th time-series data S_i, the data dimension is D and the sequence length is L. Take the data forecasting of a segment of $n+m$ frames as an example (n is the length of the previous input sequence, m is the length of the subsequent forecasting sequence), recorded as $P = \{P_1, P_2, \ldots, P_n, P_{n+1}, \ldots, P_{n+m}\}$. Next, perform feature grouping on P, taking P_i ($i \in [1, n+m]$) as an example, after feature grouping, time-series data $X_i \in R^{1 \times l \times d}$ is obtained, where l is the feature length after feature grouping, and d is the feature dimensions after grouping. After feature alignment and splicing, get $X = \{X_1, X_2, \ldots, X_n, X_{n+1}, \ldots, X_{n+m}\}$, where X_{n+1} to X_{n+m} are all 0 sequences.

In the process of model training, in the GRU-IRM training, S is sent to the GRU network to predict the last frame of each segment ($n+m$), and interpolate with the n-th frame and the $(n+m)$-th frame to obtain the $(n+1)$-th to $(n+m-1)$-th frames, and the last frame constitutes the GRU output X_{base}. During the PSTTEM training, X is sent to the PSTTEM to obtain the forecasting sequence X_{pre}, which is connected with X_{base} to obtain the forecasting sequence of the last m frames, and the forecasting results are output by segment ($n+m$).

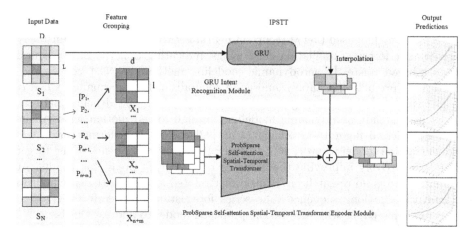

Fig. 1. Schematic diagram of the structure of the IPSTT. The colored squares in the figure indicate that there are specific values, and the white squares indicate that the value is 0.

3.1 GRU Intent Recognition Module

The GRU model only predicts the spatial position parameters (as mentioned above, the dimension is D), which is a typical res-GRU model. As shown in Fig. 2, GRU is an encode-decoder structure, and its decoder and encoder parameters are shared. GRU model input sequence $S_p \in R^{B \times n \times D}$. S_p is the previous input sequence. The process of obtaining the hidden state h through GRU encoding for S_p can be described as:

$$h_t = GRU(S_p) \tag{1}$$

Among them, h_t is the hidden state output by the encoder. In the decoding process, we use the last frame of the previous input sequence as the input of the decoder, and set the initial value of the hidden state of decoding as h_t. The remaining parameters of the GRU decoder are shared with the encoder, and the output is the last frame of the subsequent forecasting sequence, that is, the m-th frame. This process can be described as:

$$y = FC(GRU(S_p[-1:], h_t)) \tag{2}$$

where $y \in R^{B \times 1 \times D}$ is the predicted output of the decoder.

Since we want to predict the position of the last frame of the subsequent sequence as the intention information, we calculate the MSEloss of the last frame of the GRU forecasting sequence y and the true value sequence in the process of calculating the loss function. This process can be described as:

$$GRU Loss = MSE(y, GT_{trg}[-1:]) \tag{3}$$

GRU preliminarily predicts the last frame of the subsequent forecasting sequence, and can perform corresponding linear interpolation on the last frame

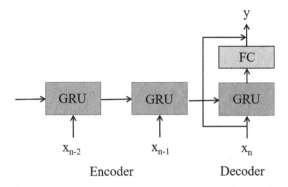

Fig. 2. Schematic diagram of Pre-trained GRU.

of the previous input sequence and the GRU forecasting output. The significance of the linear interpolation is to obtain the previous sequence to reach the nearest sequence predicted by the GRU. $X_{base} = \{X_{base_1}, X_{base_2}, \ldots, X_{base_m}\}$, this sequence can be used as the baseline of the forecasted sequence, this process can be described as:

$$X_{base_i} = src[:, -1 :, :] + \frac{y - src[:, -1 :, :]}{m} \times i \qquad (4)$$

where $src[:, -1 :, :]$ is the parameter of the last frame of the input sequence, y is the GRU forecasting parameter, $i \in [1, m]$. $X_{base} \in R^{B \times m \times D}$ is the interpolation intention sequence.

3.2 Probsparse Self-attention Spatial-Temporal Transformer Encoder Module

The backbone network uses a spatial-temporal Transformer with a probsparse self-attention mechanism. This module uses the probsparse self-attention mechanism to extract data features in the spatial and temporal dimensions, as shown in Fig. 3.

The input X of PSTTEM includes the previous input sequence and the same tensor marker as the predicted sequence. The network utilizes a probsparse self-attention mechanism to extract the spatial-temporal features of the input sequence, and finally directly reduces the dimension through a linear layer. We calculate the loss between the marker and the true value and perform backpropagation. After training, the tensor corresponding to the forecasting at the network marker is the subsequent forecasting sequence.

The following takes a certain $n + m$ sequence of X (n is the length of the previous input, m is the length of the subsequent forecasting) as an example to introduce in detail.

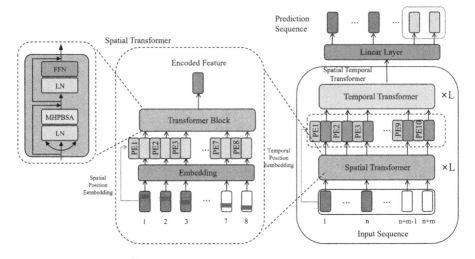

Fig. 3. ProbSparse Self-attention Spatial-Temporal Transformer Encoder Module.

Probsparse Self-attention Mechanism. For the traditional self-attention mechanism:

$$Attention(Q, K, V) = Softmax(\frac{QK^T}{\sqrt{d}})V \tag{5}$$

The calculation method of the original matrix is replaced by a sparse matrix. In the calculation of matrix Q and matrix K, due to the long-tailed distribution of the attention feature map, the non-zero value part of the sparse matrix is used to replace the QK calculation with the top-u selected in the original matrix Q. During the Attention calculation process, the QK calculation is performed simplifies to:

$$\bar{M}(q_i, K) = \max_j \left\{ \frac{q_i k_j^T}{\sqrt{d}} \right\} - \frac{1}{L_K} \sum_{j=1}^{L_K} \frac{q_i k_j^T}{\sqrt{d}} \tag{6}$$

Therefore, each head of the multi-head probsparse self-attention mechanism can be expressed as:

$$Attention(Q, K, V) = Softmax(\frac{\bar{Q}K^T}{\sqrt{d}})V \tag{7}$$

Spatial Transformer. As shown in Fig. 3, we utilize a Transformer module with probsparse self-attention to extract the relationship inside each frame feature, which consists of a multi-head probsparse self-attention mechanism (MHPBSA) and a feed-forward network (FFN). The spatial Transformer module is mainly used to extract spatial position features in the sequence. For spatial feature extraction, divide the D-dimensional data into l groups based on each d parameters, and the missing values are filled with 0, and the grouped data $X_{src} \in R^{B \times n \times l \times d}$.

For the subsequent forecasting sequence $X_{trg} = \{X_{n+1}, X_{n+2}, \ldots, X_{n+m}\}$, set its value to 0, and splice it after the previous input sequence $X_{src} \in R^{B \times n \times l \times d}$ as the input of the neural network. This process is described as:

$$X = Concat(X_{src}, X_{trg}) \tag{8}$$

The processed input sequence $X \in R^{B \times (n+m) \times l \times d}$, where B is the batch size.

For a given input tensor $X \in R^{B \times (n+m) \times l \times d}$, we introduce additional positional encodings to distinguish individual feature descriptions within each frame. Therefore, a trainable linear projection layer is first used to embed each labeled spatial position feature into the high-dimensional space, and then a learnable spatial position embedding is added to the markers in the projected space. This process can be described as:

$$X_{si} = X * W_s + E_s \tag{9}$$

where $X_{si} \in R^{B \times (n+m) \times l \times d_{model}}$ is used as the input of the spatial Transformer, W_s is the projection matrix, and E_s is the spatial position encoding. The spatial Transformer applies a probsparse self-attention mechanism to integrate spatial information between different frames. For each layer in the spatial Transformer module:

$$Z_s^{(layer+1)} = MHPBSA \left(LN \left(X_{si}^{layer} \right) \right) + X_{si}^{layer} \tag{10}$$

$$X_{so}^{(layer+1)} = FFN \left(LN \left(Z_s^{(layer+1)} \right) \right) + Z_s^{layer+1} \tag{11}$$

where $Z_s^{(layer+1)}$ is the MHPBSA output feature in the spatial Transformer, $X_{so}^{(layer+1)}$ is the output feature of the feedforward network, and the spatial Transformer is composed of L-layer Transformer stacked, in the process of feature extraction by spatial Transformer, it is calculated from the first time until all L blocks are completed. The output of the spatial transformation module is denoted as $H_{so} \in R^{B \times (n+m) \times l \times d_{model}}$. Where $layer \in [1, \ldots, L]$.

Temporal Transformer. The temporal Transformer focuses on establishing a time relationship between different frames of the input time-series sequences. It focuses on using the input time-series sequences to construct a time relationship. The temporal Transformer is also stacked by L-layer Transformer blocks. Reintegrate the output H_{so} tensor into $H_t \in R^{B \times (n+m) \times M} (M = l \times d_{model})$. Before feeding H_t into the temporal Transformer, we add a learnable temporal position embedding $E_T \in R^{(n+m) \times M}$ into the model training. Therefore, the input of the temporal Transformer X_{ti} can be described as:

$$X_{ti} = H_t + E_T \tag{12}$$

where $X_{ti} \in R^{B \times (n+m) \times M}$ is the input of the spatial Transformer, E_T is the temporal position encoding, and the temporal Transformer applies a probsparse self-attention mechanism to integrate information between all frames. For each layer in the temporal Transformer module:

$$Z_t^{(layer+1)} = MHPBSA\left(LN\left(X_{ti}^{layer}\right)\right) + X_{ti}^{layer} \qquad (13)$$

$$X_{to}^{(layer+1)} = FFN\left(LN\left(Z_t^{(layer+1)}\right)\right) + Z_t^{layer+1} \qquad (14)$$

where $Z_t^{(layer+1)}$ is the MHPBSA output feature in the temporal Transformer, $X_{to}^{(layer+1)}$ is the output feature of the feedforward network, and the temporal Transformer is also composed of L layers Transformers are stacked, and their output is $X_{to} \in R^{B \times (n+m) \times M}$. Since there is no decoder involved, the linear layer is directly used to reduce the dimensionality of the output of the temporal Transformer, and the final output $X_{pre} \in R^{B \times m \times D}$ is obtained.

Loss Function. Input the previous input sequence into the GRU model to predict Y, and obtain the corresponding X_{base}. At the same time, extract the spatial-temporal features of the sequence through the PSTTEM to obtain X_{pre}. Finally, the process of predicting the time-series sequence is as follows:

$$Y = X_{pre} + X_{base} \qquad (15)$$

The process of predicting time-series sequence is decomposed into GRU intention forecasting sequence X_{base} and SPTTEM forecasting residual term X_{pre}. In the process of backpropagation, the MES loss function between Y and the real time-series Trg_{truth} is calculated and the parameters of the SPTTEM network are updated. This process is described as:

$$Loss = MSE(Y, Trg_{truth}) \qquad (16)$$

4   Experiment Setup

4.1   Dataset

Benchmark Datasets: We tested our proposed IPSTT on 4 real-world benchmarks, which are: **1) ETTh1** (Electricity Transformer Temperature-hourly) dataset includes hourly oil temperature and 6 power load features collected by 2 electricity transformers over a period of 2 years, **2) ETTm1** (Electricity Transformer Temperature-minutely) dataset includes oil temperature and 6 power load features collected every 15 min from 2 electricity transformers over a period of 2 years, **3) WTH** (Weather) dataset contains hourly "wet bulb" values and 11 climate features from nearly 1600 locations in the United States from 2010 to 2013, **4) ECL** (Electricity Consuming Load) dataset contains the hourly electricity consumption of 321 customers from 2012 to 2014, **5) ILI** (Influenza-Like Illness) dataset includes weekly ILI patient data from the Centers for Disease Control and Prevention in the United States from 2002 to 2021. The train/val/test splits for the first three datasets are same as [11], the last two are same as [8].

Aviation Dataset: The aviation dataset in this paper is mainly composed of simulation data of a certain type of aircraft. The experimental dataset contains a total of 2000 time-series data files (each file contains 5000–8000 flight parameter frames). Among them, the flight state parameters include x(north position), y(east position), z(height), V(velocity), alpha(angle of attack), beta(side slip angle), roll(roll angle), pitch(pitch angle), yaw(yaw angle), p(roll rate), q(pitch rate), r(yaw rate), da(aileron deflection angle), de(elevator deflection angle), dr(rudder deflection angle), T(thrust), flag(type label), label(multi-class labels), except for id, there are 17 dimensions in total. The dataset has a total of 1,082,435 flight state frames, and the train/val/test splits are 7/2/1. The sampling rate is 2 frames/second (1 s contains 100 states, and every 50 states is sampled one).

4.2   Baselines

We selected five models for comparison on five benchmark datasets, including LSTMa, LSTnet, Transformer, Informant, and Pyraformer. We selected three models for comparison on aviation dataset, including LSTM, GRU, and Transformer.

4.3   Setup

Our pre-trained GRU model is a 1-layer GRU with 200 training epoches. Our main model consists of 3 layers of spatial encoders and 3 layers of temporal encoders, with 400 training epoches. Both models were optimized using the Adam optimizer with learning rates of 2e-4 and 3e-4, respectively. All experiments were implemented in PyTorch and conducted on a single NVIDIA A800 PCIe GPU. The dataset settings follow Zhou et al., train/val/test sets are zero mean normalized with the mean and std of training set on each dataset. We evaluate model performance by varying the predicted length. For the ILI dataset, the predicted length is {24, 36, 48, 60}, and for the other five datasets, the predicted length is {24, 48, 96, 168, 288, 336, 720, 960}. The input length is considered a hyperparameter. We use Mean Squared Error (MSE) and Mean Absolute Error (MAE) as evaluation metrics for each prediction length, and roll the entire dataset with a stride of 1. For aviation datasets, differential processing is performed on absolute numerical parameters such as spatial position parameters x, y, z, etc. in each frame of the sequence to transform non-stationary sequences into stationary sequences. Subsequently, MinMaxScaler is used to normalize the features. Set up five different sets of input and prediction windows for experiments. For step groups 1–5, the prediction lengths are {5, 10, 15, 10, 20}, and the corresponding input lengths are {10, 10, 10, 20, 20}. We use Root Mean Squared Error (RMSE) as the evaluation metric for each prediction length and roll the entire dataset with a stride of 1.

5   Experiments

5.1   Comparison Experiments of Benchmark Datasets

Table 1 presents the evaluation metric results (displayed in rows) for each dataset using the proposed method IPSTT and 5 baseline methods. As shown in Table 1, in the comparative experiments of each dataset row, IPSTT and the best/second performance among all baseline methods were highlighted in bold/underline IPSTT achieved leading performance in most prediction lengths on most datasets, with 29 top-1 and 7 top-2 in a total of 48 experimental settings. On the ETTm1 and ILI datasets, IPSTT achieved the best performance. Especially on the ILI dataset, IPSTT achieved a decrease of over 50% in MSE for all step sizes compared to the five methods, and a decrease of over 35% in MAE for all step sizes compared to the five methods. The prediction results obtained by IPSTT on the ETTh1 and WTH datasets are worse than those of Pyraformer. We analyze that this may be due to the introduction of the pyramid attention module in Pyraformer, which helps the model capture temporal dependencies of different ranges, thus achieving better performance on datasets of different time scales.

5.2   Comparison Experiments of Aviation Dataset

Table 2 shows the experimental results of RMSE for trajectory forecasting, bold/underline indicates the best/second. From the table, it can be seen that IPSTT has achieved leading performance in most prediction lengths on most datasets, with 12 top-1 and 3 top-2 in a total of 15 experimental settings. IPSTT achieved the best RMSE results in step groups 1, 3, and 5 in x, y, and z. And IPSTT has achieved a decrease of over 20% in its RMSE compared to the three methods in forecasting z. In addition, in step group 2, IPSTT is slightly inferior to Transformer in forecasting y, and in step group 4, IPSTT is also slightly inferior to Transformer in forecasting x and y. It can be seen that IPSTT improves its performance when the forecasting step is less than or greater than the input step. This long-distance prediction is exactly what is needed in practical applications.

In addition, we also visualized the forecasting results of all methods, and the 3D trajectories of some representative samples are shown in Fig. 4. As shown in the figure, the forecasting results of IPSTT are very continuous, almost consistent with the true value, and accurately capture the rotational details. In relatively simple trajectory forecasting (as shown in Figures (a) to (d)), all methods can fully predict subsequent trajectories; For more complex trajectory forecasting (such as Figure (e) and Figure (h)), when the step size is step group 1 (with a prediction step size of 5), LSTM performs better in trajectory forecasting, indicating that LSTM has certain advantages in short-term forecasting. In the other step size groups (with a prediction step size greater than 5), the Transformer's prediction performance is significantly better than LSTM and GRU, reflecting the advantage of the Transformer structure in capturing long-term features. Compared to Transformer, IPSTT clearly predicts more accurately. This

Table 1. Experimental results of IPSTT and comparative methods on the benchmark dataset. Bold/underline indicates the best/second.

Models		LSTMa MSE	LSTMa MAE	LSTnet MSE	LSTnet MAE	Transformer MSE	Transformer MAE	Informer MSE	Informer MAE	Pyraformer MSE	Pyraformer MAE	IPSTT MSE	IPSTT MAE
Metric		MSE	MAE	MSE	MAE	MSE	MAE	MSE	MAE	MSE	MAE	MSE	MAE
ETTh1	24	0.650	0.624	1.293	0.901	0.620	0.577	0.577	0.549	**0.493**	**0.507**	0.638	0.570
	48	0.720	0.675	1.456	0.960	0.692	0.671	0.685	0.625	**0.554**	**0.544**	0.732	0.620
	168	1.212	0.867	1.997	1.214	0.947	0.797	0.931	0.752	**0.781**	0.675	0.855	**0.673**
	336	1.424	0.994	2.655	1.369	1.094	0.813	1.128	0.873	**0.912**	0.747	0.919	**0.708**
	720	1.960	1.322	2.143	1.380	1.241	0.917	1.215	0.896	**0.993**	**0.792**	1.130	0.797
ETTm1	24	0.621	0.629	1.968	1.170	0.306	0.371	0.323	0.369	0.310	0.371	**0.300**	**0.356**
	48	1.392	0.939	1.999	1.215	0.465	0.470	0.494	0.503	0.465	0.464	**0.453**	**0.456**
	96	1.339	0.913	2.762	1.542	0.681	0.612	0.678	0.614	0.520	**0.504**	0.516	0.504
	288	1.740	1.124	1.257	2.076	1.162	0.879	1.056	0.786	0.729	0.657	**0.687**	**0.592**
	672	2.736	1.555	1.917	2.941	1.231	1.103	1.192	0.926	0.980	0.678	**0.827**	**0.671**
WTH	24	0.546	0.570	0.615	0.545	0.349	0.397	0.335	0.381	**0.301**	**0.359**	0.357	0.391
	48	0.829	0.677	0.660	0.589	0.386	0.433	0.395	0.459	**0.376**	**0.421**	0.450	0.458
	168	1.038	0.835	0.748	0.647	0.613	0.582	0.608	0.567	**0.519**	**0.521**	0.651	0.587
	336	1.657	1.059	0.782	0.683	0.707	0.634	0.702	0.620	**0.539**	**0.543**	0.727	0.632
	720	1.536	1.109	0.851	0.757	0.834	0.741	0.831	0.731	**0.547**	**0.553**	0.728	0.631
ECL	48	0.486	0.572	0.369	0.445	0.334	0.399	0.344	0.393	0.478	0.471	**0.233**	**0.341**
	168	0.574	0.602	0.394	0.476	0.353	0.420	0.368	0.424	0.452	0.455	**0.311**	**0.402**
	336	0.886	0.795	0.419	0.477	0.381	0.439	0.381	0.431	0.463	0.456	**0.345**	**0.424**
	720	1.676	1.095	0.556	0.565	0.391	0.438	0.406	**0.443**	0.480	0.461	**0.405**	0.465
	960	1.591	1.128	0.605	0.599	0.492	0.550	0.460	0.548	0.550	0.489	**0.423**	**0.472**
ILI	24	4.220	1.335	4.975	1.660	3.954	1.323	4.588	1.462	3.970	1.338	**1.381**	**0.720**
	36	4.771	1.427	5.322	1.659	4.167	1.360	4.845	1.496	4.377	1.410	**1.881**	**0.869**
	48	4.945	1.462	5.425	1.632	4.746	1.463	4.865	1.516	4.811	1.503	**1.410**	**0.729**
	60	5.176	1.504	5.477	1.675	5.219	1.553	5.212	1.576	5.204	1.588	**1.950**	**0.889**

Table 2. RMSE Results of IPSTT and comparison methods on x, y, z (Sg means step group). Bold/underline indicates the best/second.

Groups	Methods											
	LSTM			GRU			Transformer			IPSTT		
	x	y	z	x	y	z	x	y	z	x	y	z
sg 1	3.594	3.450	2.774	3.932	3.566	2.974	3.673	3.113	3.405	**3.034**	**2.972**	1.761
sg 2	9.336	8.910	7.598	11.076	10.672	7.873	9.920	8.361	7.968	**8.731**	8.397	5.335
sg 3	16.825	15.468	13.877	18.980	16.849	15.267	16.491	19.831	14.868	**15.291**	13.712	10.597
sg 4	11.655	10.195	7.806	11.932	10.89	8.336	7.808	6.959	7.580	9.661	9.043	5.362
sg 5	26.952	23.551	21.221	29.124	27.014	23.873	26.409	24.409	28.893	24.306	21.353	15.348

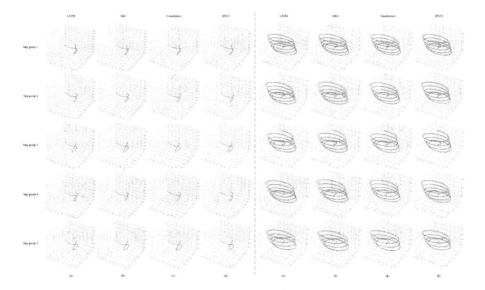

Fig. 4. Trajectory forecasting diagram of IPSTT and comparison methods (red represents the true value, blue represents the predicted value). (Color figure online)

clearly indicates that IPSTT provides good performance in capturing short-term to long-term trajectory features.

5.3 Ablation Study

The ablation experiment in this section removed the GRU intent recognition module (GRU) and the probsparse self-attention mechanism (PSM) from the IPSTT framework for performance comparison in time-series forecasting scenarios. Specifically, the two baseline methods are the IPSTT$_{w/o\ GRU}$ based solely on the probsparse self-attention mechanism, and the IPSTT$_{w/o\ PSM}$ model based solely on the GRU intent recognition module. To ensure fairness in the experiment, the training process of IPSTT$_{w/o\ GRU}$ and IPSTT$_{w/o\ PSM}$ is consistent with that described in Sect. 4.3.

Table 3 shows the results of our ablation experiments on the ETTm1 dataset. The best/second performance is highlighted in bold/underline. From the table, it can be seen that IPSTT has achieved leading performance in most forecasting lengths on most datasets, with 9 top-1 and 1 top-2 in a total of 10 experimental settings. When the forecasting step size is relatively short, the model using only the PSM can achieve top-2 experimental results. This may be because the difference between the short step size intention forecasting sequence and the input sequence is small, resulting in a smaller effect of the GRU intention recognition module. When the forecasting step size is long, the model using only the GRU intent recognition module can achieve slightly worse or even better results than IPSTT. This is because PSM focuses on reducing the time complexity of long sequence time-series forecasting, and does not use all queries for attention calculation during calculation. Therefore, it will accelerate training while leading to certain performance degradation. However, IPSTT still achieves optimal performance in most step size settings.

Table 3. Results of ablation experiments on ETTm1. Bold/underline indicates the best/second.

Models	IPSTT$_{w/o\ GRU}$		IPSTT$_{w/o\ PSM}$		IPSTT	
Metric	MSE	MAE	MSE	MAE	MSE	MAE
24	0.304	0.373	0.330	0.379	**0.300**	**0.356**
48	0.466	0.488	0.483	0.468	**0.453**	**0.456**
168	0.547	0.544	0.549	0.520	**0.516**	**0.504**
336	0.843	0.687	**0.675**	0.599	0.687	**0.592**
720	0.999	0.772	0.759	0.636	**0.719**	**0.623**

6   Conclusion

This paper introduces the Intention based Transformer for Multivariate Time series Forecasting (IPSTT) to enhance the accuracy of multivariate time-series forecasting. By pre-training a GRU, IPSTT provides predictive intent for subsequent spatial-temporal Transformer models, which capture the event history and inter-variable dependencies. IPSTT employs a probsparse self-attention mechanism to lower the time complexity in long sequence forecasting. Tests on five benchmark and aviation datasets demonstrate IPSTT's superiority over existing advanced models.

In our future research, we plan to further investigate the relationship between various parameters and enhance the design of data feature extraction networks to boost forecasting precision. Additionally, we aim to broaden our research domain to include comprehensive analysis of long sequence forecasting, equipping us to tackle more intricate time series forecasting challenges effectively.

Acknowledgments. This work was supported by the Aviation Fund, 2022Z071020002, Research on Endogenous Security Testing of Aviation Artificial Intelligence Frameworks and Software Systems.

Disclosure of Interests. The authors have no competing interests to declare that are relevant to the content of this article.

References

1. Patton, A.: Copula methods for forecasting multivariate time series. Handbook of economic forecasting (2013)
2. Yang, S., Lu, H., Li, J.: Multi-feature fusion-based object detection for intelligent transportation systems. IEEE Trans. Intell. Transp. Syst. **24**(1), 1126–1133 (2023). https://doi.org/10.1109/TITS.2022.3155488
3. Li, Y., et al.: Pose estimation of point sets using residual MLP in intelligent transportation infrastructure. IEEE Trans. Intell. Transp. Syst. **24**(11), 13359–13369 (2023). https://doi.org/10.1109/TITS.2023.3250604
4. Matsubara, Y., Sakurai, Y., van Panhuis, W.G., Faloutsos, C.: FUNNEL: automatic mining of spatially coevolving epidemics. In: ACM SIGKDD 2014, pp. 105–114 (2014)
5. Angryk, R.A., Martens, P.C., Aydin, B., et al.: Multivariate time series dataset for space weather data analytics. Sci. Data **7**, 221 (2020)
6. Gao, Z., Shi, X., Wang, H., et al.: EarthFormer: exploring space-time transformers for earth system forecasting[J]. Adv. Neural. Inf. Process. Syst. **35**, 25390–25403 (2022)
7. Oreshkin, B.N., Carpov, D., Chapados, N., Bengio, Y.: Nbeats: neural basis expansion analysis for interpretable time series forecasting. In: International Conference on Learning Representations (2019)
8. Wu, H., Xu, J., Wang, J., et al.: AutoFormer: decomposition transformers with auto-correlation for long-term series forecasting. Adv. Neural. Inf. Process. Syst. **34**, 22419–22430 (2021)
9. Zhang, Y., Yan, J.: CrossFormer: transformer utilizing cross-dimension dependency for multivariate time series forecasting. In: The Eleventh International Conference on Learning Representations (2022)
10. Gao, J., Hu, W., Chen, Y.: Client: Cross-variable Linear Integrated Enhanced Transformer for Multivariate Long-Term Time Series Forecasting. arXiv preprint arXiv:2305.18838 (2023)
11. Zhou, H., Zhang, S., Peng, J., et al.: Informer: beyond efficient transformer for long sequence time-series forecasting. Proc. AAAI Conf. Artif. Intell. **35**(12), 11106–11115 (2021)
12. Cong, Y., Liao, W., Ackermann, H., et al.: Spatial-temporal transformer for dynamic scene graph generation. In: Proceedings of the IEEE/CVF International Conference on Computer Vision, pp. 16372–16382 (2021)
13. Chen, K., Chen, G., Xu, D., et al.: NAST: non-autoregressive spatial-temporal transformer for time series forecasting (2021). arXiv preprint arXiv:2102.05624
14. Zhang, Y., Wu, B., Li, W., et al.: STST: Spatial-temporal specialized transformer for skeleton-based action recognition. In: Proceedings of the 29th ACM International Conference on Multimedia, pp. 3229-3237 (2021)
15. Gao, Z., Wang, P., Lv, P., et al.: Focal and global spatial-temporal transformer for skeleton-based action recognition. In: Proceedings of the Asian Conference on Computer Vision, pp. 382–398 (2022)
16. Xu, M., et al.: Spatial-Temporal Transformer Networks for Traffic Flow Forecasting. CoRR, arXiv:2001.02908 (2020)
17. Chen, C., Liu, Y., Chen, L., et al.: Bidirectional spatial-temporal adaptive transformer for Urban traffic flow forecasting. IEEE Trans. Neural Netw. Learn. Syst. **34**, 6913–6925 (2022)

18. Zeng, A., Chen, M., Zhang, L., et al.: Are transformers effective for time series forecasting? Proc. AAAI Conf. Artif. Intell. **37**(9), 11121–11128 (2023)
19. Nie, Y., Nguyen, N.H., Sinthong, P., et al.: A time series is worth 64 words: Long-term forecasting with transformers. arXiv preprint arXiv:2211.14730 (2022)
20. Lai, G., Chang, W.-C., Yang, Y., Liu, H.: Modeling long- and short-term temporal patterns with deep neural networks. In International ACM SIGIR Conference on Research & Development in Information Retrieval (SIGIR) (2018)
21. Deng, J., Chen, X., Jiang, R., et al.: Learning Structured Components: Towards Modular and Interpretable Multivariate Time Series Forecasting. arXiv preprint arXiv:2305.13036 (2023)
22. Xu, N., Kosma, C., Vazirgiannis, M.: TimeGNN: Temporal Dynamic Graph Learning for Time Series Forecasting. arXiv preprint arXiv:2307.14680 (2023)
23. Wu, Z., Pan, S., Long, G., Jiang, J., Chang, X., Zhang, C.: Connecting the dots: multivariate time series forecasting with graph neural networks. In: ACM SIGKDD International Conference on Knowledge Discovery & Data Mining (KDD) (2020)
24. Yu, C., Wang, F., Shao, Z., et al.: DSFormer: a double sampling transformer for multivariate time series long-term prediction. In: Proceedings of the 32nd ACM International Conference on Information and Knowledge Management, pp. 3062–3072 (2023)
25. Li, S., et al.: Enhancing the locality and breaking the memory bottleneck of transformer on time series forecasting. In: NeurIPS (2019)
26. Kitaev, N., Kaiser, L., Levskaya, A.: The efficient transformer. In ICLR, Reformer (2020)
27. Liu, S., Yu, H., Liao, C., et al.: PyraFormer: low-complexity pyramidal attention for long-range time series modeling and forecasting. In: International Conference on Learning Representations (2021)
28. Du, D., Su, B., Wei, Z.: PreFormer: predictive transformer with multi-scale segmentwise correlations for long-term time series forecasting. arXiv preprint arXiv:2202.11356v1 (2022)
29. Zhong, W., et al.: An unsteady high-angle-of-attack aerodynamic modeling method based on neural network. Chinese society of aeronautics and astronautics. In: Proceedings of the 9th China Aviation Society Youth Science and Technology Forum, pp. 478-485 (2020)
30. He, L., et al.: Unsteady aerodynamics modeling method based on long short-term memory neural network. Flight Dyn. **39**(5), 8–12 (2021)
31. Chen, X., et al.: Unsteady aerodynamic modeling research and virtual flight test verification. J. Exp. Fluid Mech. **36**(3), 65–72 (2022)
32. Zhang, B., Bi, W., Zhang, A., Mao, Z., Yang, M.: Transformer-based error compensation method for air combat aircraft trajectory prediction. Acta Aeronaut. Astronaut. Sin. **44**(9), 327413–327413 (2023)

A Segmentation-Based Approach for Lung Disease Classification Using Chest X-ray Images

Muhammad Rahman, Cao YongZhong, and Li Bin[✉]

College of Information Engineering, Yangzhou University, Jiangsu 225000, China
lb@yzu.edu.cn

Abstract. In the last decade, artificial neural networks and deep learning techniques have revolutionized the field of medical imaging by improving image segmentation, detection, and classification. This advancement has dramatically improved diagnosis speed and treatment efficiency, especially when interpreting chest X-ray images to detect abnormalities within the thoracic cavity. To improve patient outcomes, lung diseases must be diagnosed early and accurately. For the analysis of chest X-ray images, convolutional neural networks have been used in several studies, and their performance in this regard is quite good. However, convolutional neural networks have been criticized recently for learning from non-relevant areas of an image, which may pose a problem regarding their reliability. This problem can be overcome by image segmentation and image slicing. Therefore, this research study proposes a novel lung segmentation-based approach for diagnosing and classifying lung disease that relies on a combination of medical and vision transformer models. The medical transformer model is used for lung area segmentation from chest X-ray, followed by a vision transformer model for classifying various lung diseases based on the segmented lung areas. As a result, the proposed approach achieved an average accuracy of 0.9229 and an average area under the curve of 0.7612 on the NIH chest X-ray dataset segmented lung areas. Accuracy and area under the curve are improved by 0.07% and 0.57%, respectively, demonstrating the effectiveness of the segmentation-based approach for lung disease classification.

Keywords: Lung segmentation · lung disease classification · vision transformer for lung disease · chest X-ray segmentation · medical image processing

1 Introduction

Respiratory diseases are among the major causes of death globally. In the medical field, chest radiographs are widely used to diagnose these abnormalities in the chest area due to their cost efficacy and non-invasive nature [1]. However, manual chest X-ray (CXRs) interpretation is challenging, time-consuming, and subjective for radiology professionals without prior training and experience. Moreover, due to the similar appearance, it can also be challenging to differentiate between normal and infected individuals [2, 3]. However, automated CXRs image analysis can enhance the early diagnosis of lung disease, and reduce mortality rates.

© The Author(s), under exclusive license to Springer Nature Singapore Pte Ltd. 2025
H. Lu (Ed.): ISAIR 2024, CCIS 2402, pp. 172–185, 2025.
https://doi.org/10.1007/978-981-96-2911-4_17

Accurate segmentation of lungs from CXRs is critical for efficient diagnosis and treatment of lung abnormalities. Recently, Convolutional neural networks (CNNs) have been dominant in the field of image segmentation and classification [4, 5]. However, CNNs are used to selectively concentrate on specific regions of an input rather than analyzing the entire input equally. An approach that uses attention mechanisms, image segmentation, and image slicing or patching techniques can overcome this limitation [6]. As a result, the network can enhance its accuracy and reduce its computing requirements.

Since the emergence of transformer models, various artificial intelligence fields have been transformed due to their ability to capture long-range connections and represent relationships among distant elements. The transformer models offer considerable potential for medical image analysis [6, 7]. Therefore, this study proposed a two-step approach to utilize the transformer methods for lung image segmentation and disease classification from CXRs images. The Medical Transformer (MedT) model is used to segment and extract lung areas from CXRs images while the Vision Transformer (ViT) model is applied to classify the segmented lung regions into distinct diseases. The study investigates the following key objectives:

- An innovative approach that combines MedT and ViT transformer models for the segmentation and classification of CXRs images could accurately extract lung areas from CXRs images and significantly improve the classification performance.
- Fine-tuned the MedT model and analyzed the performance of the fine-tuned MedT model for the lung mask prediction.
- Fine-tuned the ViT model and tweaked the classification head layers to boost their performance for lung disease classification using the segmented lung regions.
- Evaluated and compared the proposed approach to other state-of-the-art learning techniques.

The article is organized as follows: Sect. 2 summarizes related works based on deep learning and transformers for lung segmentation disease classification. Section 3 discusses the proposed methodology, including datasets, preprocessing techniques, and the proposed approach. Experimental results and a discussion are conducted in Sect. 4. In Sect. 5, the paper is concluded and future research work is discussed.

2 Related Work

Recently, deep learning approaches have been extensively used in analyzing CXRs to detect lung disease. CNNs have been demonstrated to be effective for lung segmentation and disease classification. In the study [8], several deep learning pre-trained methods including VGGNet, AlexNet, ResNet50, and GoogleNet, were used to classify CXRs images into 15 classes, using two loss functions cross-entropy and weighted cross-entropy. Souid et al. [9] use the CXRs 14 dataset to assess lung disease using an Improved variant of MobileNetV2. According to their study, their proposed method obtained an Area Under the Curve (AUC) of 0.811 and outperformed other deep-learning strategies. In the study [10], the authors initially identified pneumonia cases from CXR images using a deep-learning model known as CheXNet. Later, they investigated the task of categorizing multilabel CXRs images into 14 different disease categories. Uswatun et al. [11], proposed the CheXNet as the backbone of the Feature pyramid network to classify thoracic diseases using CXRs. The Feature pyramid networks are designed to extract features from raw images and manage imbalanced data distributions. Combining CheXNet with the Feature pyramid network to improve the performance of CXRs classification. Aravind et al. [12] used a custom CNNs model and pre-trained Densenet121, Resnet50, Inception, and Vgg16 models to develop an efficient method for CXRs classification, they achieved an accuracy of 87% and an AUC value of 0.78%. The study [13] proposed a lung disease classification system containing four major components: alignment, comparison, segmentation, and classification. Traditional and deep learning approaches were compared.

However, CNNs may be unable to handle complex patterns in images. Recently, the transformer models have been demonstrated to be an effective alternative for an extensive range of image analysis tasks. Gabriel et al. [14], present and assess an input-enhanced ViT model for classifying CXRs images. The study [15], proposed an innovative multi-task ViT that utilizes lower-level CXRs features gathered via a backbone network to extract typical CXR findings. A versatile transformer model is created using the features obtained from the backbone network. Thanh et al. [16] developed a new deep-learning approach combining CNNs with ViT to enhance the accuracy of pneumonia detection. The study [17], analyzes a total of five models, two loss functions, and three benchmark datasets for the detection and segmentation of lung regions. Sangjoon et al. [18], proposed a self-training and self-supervised framework to improve ViT performance with self-training and self-supervision via knowledge distillation. In the study [19], the LT-ViT transformer has been developed to combine attention between image tokens and randomized auxiliary tokens representing labels. The proposed method achieved an AUC of 73.32% on the NIH dataset.

The ViT-based approaches have demonstrated good performance in image segmentation, detection, and classification tasks. However, the previously conducted research still has some shortcomings, such as its focus on the classification of disease classes while not giving sufficient concentration to classify the No Finding class. Furthermore, most multi-label CXRs image learning algorithms using ViT models fail to detect minor anomalies such as "nodules" in such complex cases. It should also be noted that other parts of the CXRs are irrelevant to diagnosing lung disease. Therefore, this study uses an approach that combines multiple transformer models for the segmentation of lung areas followed by the classification of lung disease. According to our knowledge, no studies have been conducted using the MedT to segment lung areas and used the ViT to classify lung diseases based on segmented lung regions.

3   Proposed Methodology

This section discusses the datasets, MedT, and ViT-based proposed approach used in this study.

3.1   Datasets

Four publicly available datasets are used to fine-tune the MedT and ViT for the segmentation and classification of lung diseases from CXRs images in the study.

Segmentation Datasets: The three distinct and publicly available CXRs and mask pairs datasets named Darwin, Montgomery, and Shenzhen datasets [20, 21], are used to fine-tune the MedT to predict the lungs mask. As the training data, the Darwin dataset which contains 6106 CXRs and mask pairs is utilized. The Shenzhen dataset, which contains 566 CXRs and mask pairs, is used as a testing dataset, whereas the Montgomery dataset, which includes 138 CXRs and mask pairs, is used as a validation dataset.

Classification Dataset: For classification, the ViT is fine-tuned on a sample dataset selected from the NIH dataset [22], which contains images related to lung diseases such as Emphysema, Nodule, Atelectasis, Mass, Edema, Consolidation, Infiltration, Fibrosis, Pneumonia, and No Finding. From the NIH dataset, the total number of 102316 instances is used as a classification dataset. Approximately 80% of the data from the selected sample is utilized for training, and 20% is used for testing. Training and testing data are preprocessed and normalized. In addition, image augmentation techniques are used to enhance the quality and quantity of the data, balance the class unbalances, enhance generalization capabilities, and resolve the overfitting problems. This study uses resizing, zooming, rotation, flipping, and cropping as augmentation techniques.

3.2 Proposed Approach

This study aims to propose a segmentation-based lung disease classification framework using transfer learning. In the first phase, the pre-trained MedT is fine-tuned to segment lung areas, while in the second phase, the pre-trained ViT is fine-tuned to perform classification. The following section discusses in detailed each phase.

Lung Segmentation: Most transformer-based approaches developed for vision tasks need a huge amount of data for appropriate training. However, the number of data instances for medical imaging applications is quite small, making it challenging to train transformers efficiently. MedT [23] is a gated axial-attention models that extend conventional architectures by including extra control mechanisms within their self-attention modules. The MedT also incorporates a Local-Global Training (LoGo) strategy that enables the model to be trained effectively on medical images, to further improve performance. Using the entire image and patches, it can learn both local and global features. A Gated Axial Attention U-Net model is used in the MedT for the LoGo training strategy to detect long-range relationships and contextual information within the image, allowing it for more accurate segmentation. Therefore, this study used a pre-trained MedT to fine-tune using the CXRs and mask pair datasets (Darwin, Montgomery, and Shenzhen). Following the fine-tuning of a pre-trained MedT, the authors applied the transfer learning technique to generate binary masks for lung regions to extract lung areas from CXRs images of the NIH dataset. Figure 1 illustrates the basic structure of the MedT model.

Disease Classification: Following the segmentation phase, in the second phase a pre-trained ViT-based transfer-learning approach is used to classify lung diseases into various categories. The ViT [24] divides images containing height, width, and number of channels into smaller patches. Before the patches are provided to the transformer encoder, vectorization, sequence embedding, learnable embedding, and patch embedding activities are carried out. In general, the ViT converts the input image into fixed-length vectors by dividing it into *16 x 16* patches. Upon receiving these vectors, a transformer performs further computations on them. In the subsequent encoder operations, a special token is

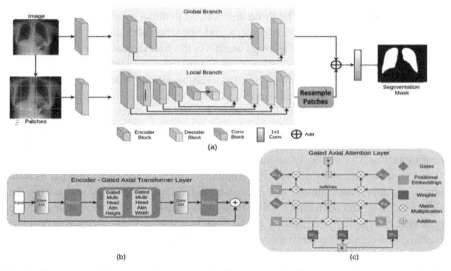

Fig. 1. The main architecture diagram for MedT uses the LoGo strategy for training. (b) The gated axial transformer layer is used in MedT. (c) The axial Attention Layer is a basic building block of both height and width gated multi-head attention blocks of the gated axial transformer.

included in the input sequence to facilitate image classification. An output that corresponds to this token is used to figure out the predicted class of the image. Additionally, positional information is included. A transformer encoder is used to encode all tokens. To determine the final classification result, the output of the special token for classification is fed into the Multi-Layer Perceptron (MLP) Head. The ViT architecture can be found in Fig. 2.

The pre-trained ViT model is used as an initial foundation approach for fine-tuning of ViT model on the segmented lung areas dataset. The pre-trained ViT model is modified by using a customized architecture that replaced the pre-trained ViT model prediction heads with two linear layers, two batch normalization layers, and two dropout layers, followed by a final classification layer. The input dimension for the first linear layer equals the input dimension of the ViT model head, and the output dimension is 512. After the first linear layer, a batch normalization layer, a ReLU activation function, and a dropout layer with a value of 0.3 are added. After this, the second linear layer is added with input dimensions of 512 and output dimensions of 256. A batch normalization layer, an activation function of ReLU, and a dropout layer with a value of 0.3 follow the second linear layer. Finally, the final classification layer has input dimensions of 256 and output dimensions equal to the number of classes. The pre-trained ViT model on ImageNet is utilized to minimize the objective function and training time. The newly added layers at the end of the ViT model remain trainable to learn from segmented lung areas.

This study uses transfer learning techniques to apply MedT for segmentation, followed by a ViT for the classification. In the first phase, the pre-trained MedT is fine-tuned on CXRs and mask pair datasets. The MedT model weights learned from CXRs and mask pairs data are saved and used to generate masks for the lung areas of the NIH

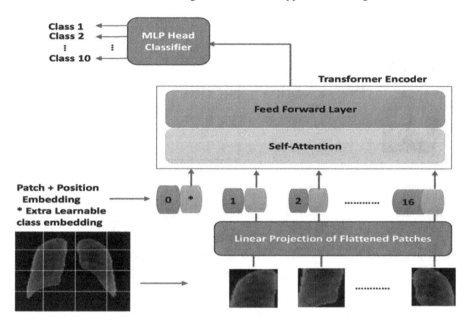

Fig. 2. The main architecture diagram of the ViT Model

dataset CXRs images. The masks obtained for the lung areas of the NIH dataset CXRs images, make it possible to extract the lung areas from the CXRs images by using these predicted lung masks. The extracted lung areas are normalized and used to fine-tune the pre-trained ViT model for disease classification. Figure 3 illustrates the proposed approach architecture.

3.3 Performance Metrics

The metrics used for segmentation are the intersection over union (IOU) and F1-score. These metrics measure the overlap between predicted masks and ground-truth lung regions. Three metrics are considered for classification performance evaluation: accuracy, loss, and AUC. Metrics such as these are used to evaluate whether the model is capable of accurately identifying and classifying lung diseases.

$$IOU = \frac{Overlap}{Union} \tag{1}$$

$$F1 = \frac{2 \times TP}{2 \times TP + FP + FN} \tag{2}$$

$$AUC = \frac{P_s \frac{P_n(N_n+1)}{2}}{P_n N_n} \tag{3}$$

$$Accuracy = \frac{TP + TN}{TP + FN + TN + FP} \tag{4}$$

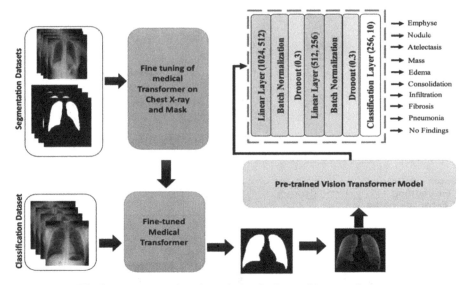

Fig. 3. The proposed MedT and ViT pipeline architecture diagram.

where TP represents the exact predicted positive, TN represents for true negative, FN indicates the false negative, and FP denotes the false positive. The P_n indicates the count of positive instances, N_n denotes the number of negative instances, and P_s indicates the total count of scored positive instances.

4   Experimental Setup, Results Analysis, and Discussion

The experimental setup, results analysis, and discussion is described in this section.

4.1   Experimental Setup

The experiment is conducted in two stages. Initially, the MedT is fine-tuned on three publicly available datasets. The Darwin dataset is used as training data, the Shenzhen dataset is used as a testing dataset, and the Montgomery dataset is used as a validation dataset. The images and masks are resized to 128 by 128 pixels and normalized, where the mean is 0.5, the standard division is 1.0, and the max pixel value is equal to 255.0. The batch size is 50, the loss function is LogNLLoss, the optimizer is Adam, and the learning rate is 1e-3. The MedT is trained for 20 epochs with pre-trained weights. In the second stage, the segmented lung areas are used to fine-tune the ViT model to classify lung diseases. The segmented lung areas are resized to 224×224 and normalized. The selected sample instances are 102316, from which 80% of the data are used as training, 20% as testing, and 20% of training data are used as validation data. The number of training instances is 65495, the validation instances number is 16404, whereas the testing instances are 20417. To conduct experiments the ViT_L_16 variant of the ViT model is selected. For comparison purposes, the Pyramid Vision Transformer (PVT) V2, and Data-Efficient Image Transformer (DEIT) are also fine-tuned in this study. For the classification model the loss function is BCEWithlogitsLoss, the learning rate is set to 1e-4, the optimizer is Adam, the batch size is 62, and the epochs are 20. All models were developed using Python and PyTorch version 2 on an Intel(R) Core (TM) i7-10700K 3.8 GHz processor. Furthermore, experiments were conducted using an NVIDIA RTX 2080 Ti GPU with 11 GB and 32 GB of RAM.

4.2 Result and Analysis

The following section discusses the experimental results achieved by the proposed method.

Segmentation Model Results: Three datasets containing CXRs with corresponding lung area masks are utilized to train and evaluate the proposed segmentation model. The performance of the segmentation model is measured using metrics such as IOU and F1-score. Table 1 demonstrates the performance results of the MedT model.

Table 1. The MedT model performance results.

Model	IOU	F1-Score
MedT	0.8118	0.8997

The MedT model, after being fine-tuned, is applied to predict the masks of lung areas for the NIH dataset CXRs images and extract the lung area from the images based on predicted masks. Figure 4 illustrates the sample CXRs, the predicted mask, and the lung areas extracted from the CXRs image.

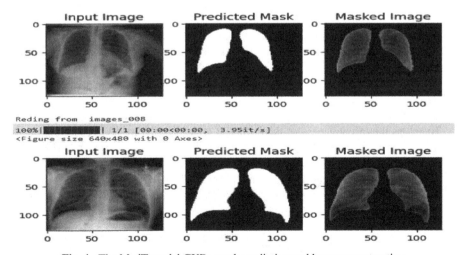

Fig. 4. The MedT model CXRs mask prediction and lung area extraction.

Classification Model Results: To evaluate the classification method described above, Table 2 presents the results of experiments conducted to classify lung disease. According to Table 2, the ViT model used as a classifier is capable of detecting lung diseases with high performance from segmented lung areas. The ViT model achieves an average training accuracy of 0.9215 and a loss of 0.2128, while in the testing phase, the average accuracy is 0.9229, and the loss is 0.2128. The performance measures such as training accuracy, training loss, testing accuracy, and testing loss achieved by the ViT model using the non-segmented CXRs images are 0.9209, 0.2180, 0.9222, and 0.2157, respectively. The results show that when the extracted lung areas are passed for classification, the performance of the ViT model is improved. The overall loss and accuracy are improved using the proposed model. The empirical evaluation indicates that segmented lung areas from CXRs are more effective in detecting lung disease. Furthermore, the extracted lung areas used for classification instead of the entire CXRs, lung disease can be detected more accurately with a lesser prediction error. The extracted lung areas serve as excellent reference points for improving the performance and model reliability.

Table 2. Average accuracy and loss of the proposed ViT model.

Images Type	Model	Training Accuracy	Training Loss	Testing Accuracy	Testing Loss
Whole non-segmented CXRs	PVT V2	0.9120	0.2336	0.9129	0.2335
	DEIT	0.9134	0.2290	0.9146	0.2286
	ViT	0.9209	0.2180	0.9222	0.2175
Segmented Lung Areas	PVT V2	0.9123	0.2337	0.9136	0.2306
	DEIT	0.9130	0.2307	0.9142	0.2274
	VIT	**0.9215**	**0.2148**	**0.9229**	**0.2128**

Additionally, we also consider calculating the accuracy for each disease class in the dataset. A total of 9 diseases that are related to lungs and normal images are selected. Based on the non-segmented CXRs and segmented lung areas, Table 3 shows each class accuracy for the proposed ViT model. According to Table 3, the accuracy achieved by ViT model for each class on segmented lung areas is higher than non-segmented CXRs images.

To assess the effectiveness of the proposed approach, the receiver operating curve (ROC) are plotted between the true-positive rate (TPR) and false-positive rate (FPR) for the non-segmented and the segmented lung areas CXRs images. According to Fig. 5, the ViT model has the highest AUC, which is 0.7612 on segmented lung areas, while achieved an AUC of 0.755 on the non-segmented CXRs images. Based on these findings, the ViT performed better on segmented lung areas than non-segmented CXRs for lung disease classification.

Furthermore, we also calculated the AUC value of each class for the proposed ViT model. Figure 6 a and b illustrate the graphical representation of the AUC for the ViT model using non-segmented and segmented lung areas CXRs images. The segmented

Table 3. Accuracy per class of proposed ViT Model.

Class Name	Non-segmented CXRs		Segmented Lungs areas	
	Training Accuracy	Testing Accuracy	Training Accuracy	Testing Accuracy
Emphysema	0.9771	0.9780	0.9797	0.9788
Nodule	0.9430	0.9420	0.9429	0.9418
Atelectasis	0.8944	0.8999	0.8946	0.8994
Mass	0.9477	0.9487	0.9476	0.9485
Edema	0.9790	0.9798	0.9790	0.9798
Consolidation	0.9574	0.9596	0.9574	0.9597
Infiltration	0.8203	0.8209	0.8186	0.8208
Fibrosis	0.9845	0.9856	0.9845	0.9855
Pneumonia	0.9871	0.9867	0.9871	0.9867
No Finding	0.6792	0.6811	0.6873	0.6899

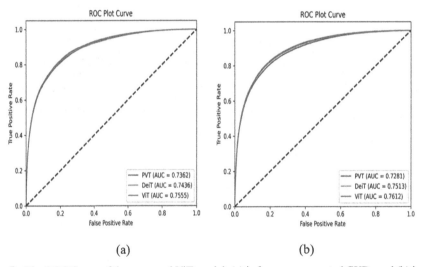

(a)   (b)

Fig. 5. The ROC Curve of the proposed ViT model, (a) is for non-segmented CXRs and (b) is for segmented lung areas.

lung areas achieved higher AUC values than the non-segmented CXRs image when compared to the AUC values.

Experimental results indicate that the ViT is capable of distinguishing between normal and various lung diseases with a high degree of accuracy and low loss using the segmented lung areas rather than the entire CXRs image. After experimental evaluation, the ViT model was found to have an overall training accuracy of 0.9209, a training loss of 0.2180, a testing accuracy of 0.9222, and a testing loss of 0.2157 on non-segmented CXRs

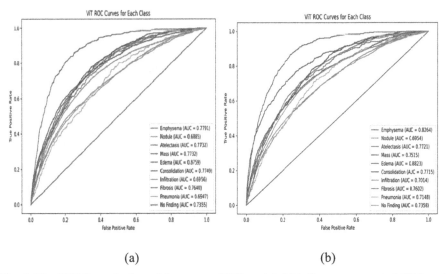

(a)   (b)

Fig. 6. The ROC for each class of the proposed ViT model, (a) is for non-segmented CXRs and (b) is for segmented lung areas.

images where on the segmented lung regions the training accuracy, training loss, testing accuracy, and testing loss are 0.9215, 0.2148, 0.9229, and 0.2128, respectively. The AUC value on the non-segmented CXRs is 0.7555, whereas the AUC value for segmented lung areas is 0.7612. Comparatively, the suggested segmentation-based framework for lung disease classification proved more effective.

4.3 Discussion

According to the results, the proposed MedT and ViT-based approach improved the efficiency and accuracy of lung disease image analysis. The fine-tuned MedT predicts more accurate masks for lung areas, as shown in Fig. 4. The results demonstrate that the transformer models can capture long-range dependencies in medical images and enhance the reliability of diagnosis. Additionally, the performance of the ViT model is improved when it is trained and tested on segmented lung areas rather than on non-segmented CXRs images. Based on segmented lung areas, the proposed approach achieves a prediction accuracy of 0.9229 and an AUC of 0.7612, compared to an accuracy of 0.922 and an AUC of 0.7555 obtained using non-segmented CXRs images. Based on the performance enhancement, it can be concluded that the segmented lung areas used to train a model for lung disease classification are more reliable, accurate, performed better, and robust than the non-segmented CXRs image.

Furthermore, the experimental results are compared to other recent and comparable approaches based on accuracy. The proposed approach outperforms other related and current approaches having more complex architectures. A comparison of our suggested approach with other related and recent approaches is presented in Table 4.

Table 4. The comparison of accuracy to other approaches.

Method	Accuracy
Wang et al. [8]	0.756
Bhusal et al. [26]	0.689
Chen et al. [27]	0.767
Souid et al. [9]	0.902
Chen et al. [28]	0.768
Chen et al. [29]	0.772
Rajpurkar et al. [10]	0.740
Aravind [12]	0.87
Uswatun Hasanah et al. [11]	0.914
Our Approach	**0.9229**

5 Conclusion

This research work proposed a MedT and ViT-based framework to segment CXRs and classify lung diseases. Demonstrates the effectiveness of transformer-based models for segmenting lung areas and classifying lung diseases. The proposed approach presents a promising solution for improving the automation of lung disease analysis, which could lead to earlier diagnosis and improved patient care. For the non-segmented CXRs images, the developed method achieves the highest average prediction accuracy of 0.9222, whereas the highest prediction accuracy of 0.9229 is achieved for segmented lung areas. The AUC value obtained for the non-segmented CXRs image is 0.7555, whereas the AUC value of 0.7612 is reported for the segmented lung areas. According to the results, segmentation of the lungs plays a critical role in accurate, reliable diagnosis of lung diseases.

Future work will involve training and fine-tuning the model using various training parameters and cost functions. Additionally, the segmented lungs will be used to fine-tune a multimodal image-to-text model to generate a more accurate and reliable report for lung disease.

References

1. Liu, W., Luo, J., Yang, Y., Wang, W., Deng, J., Yu, L.: Automatic lung segmentation in chest X-ray images using improved U-Net. Sci. Rep. **12**(1), 1–10 (2022). https://doi.org/10.1038/s41598-022-12743-y
2. Regmi, S., Subedi, A., Bagci, U., Jha, D., Campus, P.: Vision transformer for efficient chest x-ray and gastrointestinal image classification, April 2023, Accessed: 24 March 2024. https://arxiv.org/abs/2304.11529v1
3. Rahimiaghdam, S., Alemdar, H.: Evaluating the quality of visual explanations on chest X-ray images for thorax diseases classification. Neural Comput. Appl. 1–17 (2024). https://doi.org/10.1007/S00521-024-09587-0/TABLES/6

4. Sultana, S., Pramanik, A., Rahman, M.S.: Lung disease classification using deep learning models from chest x-ray images. In: 2023 3rd International Conference on Intelligent Communication and Computational Techniques, ICCT 2023 (2023) https://doi.org/10.1109/ICCT56969.2023.10075968

5. Dharmesh Ishwerlal, R., Agarwal, R., Sujatha, K.S.: lung disease classification using chest X ray image: an optimal ensemble of classification with hybrid training. Biom. Sig. Process Control **91**, 105941 (2024). https://doi.org/10.1016/J.BSPC.2023.105941

6. Singh, S., Kumar, M., Kumar, A., Verma, B.K., Abhishek, K., Selvarajan, S.: Efficient pneumonia detection using vision transformers on chest x-rays. Sci. Rep. **14**(1), 1–17 (2024). https://doi.org/10.1038/s41598-024-52703-2

7. He, K., et al.: Transformers in medical image analysis. Intell. Med. **3**(1), 59–78 (2023). https://doi.org/10.1016/J.IMED.2022.07.002

8. Wang, X., Peng, Y., Lu, L., Lu, Z., Bagheri, M., Summers, R.M.: ChestX-ray8: hospital-scale chest x-ray database and benchmarks on weakly-supervised classification and localization of common thorax diseases. pp. 2097–2106 (2017). Accessed 24 2024. https://uts.nlm.nih.gov/metathesaurus.html

9. Souid, N., Sakli, Sakli, H.: Classification and predictions of lung diseases from chest x-rays using MobileNet V2. Appl. Sci. **11**(6), 2751 (2021). https://doi.org/10.3390/APP11062751

10. Rajpurkar, P., et al.: CheXNet: radiologist-level pneumonia detection on chest x-rays with deep learning, November 2017, Accessed 24 Mar 2024. https://arxiv.org/abs/1711.05225v3

11. Hasanah, U., et al.: CheXNet and feature pyramid network: a fusion deep learning architecture for multilabel chest X-Ray clinical diagnoses classification. Int. J. Cardiovascular Imaging 1–14 (2023). https://doi.org/10.1007/S10554-023-03039-X/FIGURES/7

12. Pillai, S., Pillai, A.S.: Multi-label chest x-ray classification via deep learning. J. Intell. Learn. Syst. Appl. **14**(4), 43–56 (2022). https://doi.org/10.4236/JILSA.2022.144004

13. Yu, S.N., Chiu, M.C., Chang, Y.P., Liang, C.Y., Chen, W.: Improving computer-aided thoracic disease diagnosis through comparative analysis using chest x-ray images taken at different times. Sensors **24**(5), 1478 (2024). https://doi.org/10.3390/S24051478

14. Okolo, G.I., Katsigiannis, S., Ramzan, N.: IEViT: an enhanced vision transformer architecture for chest x-ray image classification. Comput. Methods Programs Biomed. **226**, 107141 (2022). https://doi.org/10.1016/J.CMPB.2022.107141

15. Park, S., et al.: Multi-task vision transformer using low-level chest X-ray feature corpus for COVID-19 diagnosis and severity quantification. Med. Image Anal. **75**, 102299 (2022). https://doi.org/10.1016/J.MEDIA.2021.102299

16. Pham, T.A., Hoang, V.D.: Chest X-ray image classification using transfer learning and hyperparameter customization for lung disease diagnosis. Journal of Information and Telecommunication (2024). https://doi.org/10.1080/24751839.2024.2317509

17. Ghali, R., Akhloufi, M.A.: Vision Transformers for Lung Segmentation on CXR Images. SN Comput Sci **4**(4), 1–14 (2023). https://doi.org/10.1007/S42979-023-01848-4/FIGURES/11

18. S. Park et al., "Self-evolving vision transformer for chest X-ray diagnosis through knowledge distillation," Nature Communications 2022 13:1, vol. 13, no. 1, pp. 1–11, Jul. 2022, https://doi.org/10.1038/s41467-022-31514-x

19. U. Marikkar, S. Atito, M. Awais, and A. Mahdi, "LT-ViT: A Vision Transformer for Multi-Label Chest X-Ray Classification," Proceedings - International Conference on Image Processing, ICIP, pp. 2565–2569, 2023, https://doi.org/10.1109/ICIP49359.2023.10222175

20. V. V. Danilov et al., "Automatic scoring of COVID-19 severity in X-ray imaging based on a novel deep learning workflow," Scientific Reports 2022 12:1, vol. 12, no. 1, pp. 1–22, Jul. 2022, https://doi.org/10.1038/s41598-022-15013-z

21. Jaeger, S., Candemir, S., Antani, S., Wáng, Y.-X.J., Lu, P.-X., Thoma, G.: Two public chest X-ray datasets for computer-aided screening of pulmonary diseases. Quant. Imaging Med. Surg. **4**(6), 47577–47477 (2014). https://doi.org/10.3978/J.ISSN.2223-4292.2014.11.20

22. "NIH Chest X-rays." Accessed: Mar. 24, 2024. [Online]. Available: https://www.kaggle.com/datasets/nih-chest-xrays/data

23. J. M. J. Valanarasu, P. Oza, I. Hacihaliloglu, and V. M. Patel, "Medical Transformer: Gated Axial-Attention for Medical Image Segmentation," Lecture Notes in Computer Science (including subseries Lecture Notes in Artificial Intelligence and Lecture Notes in Bioinformatics), vol. 12901 LNCS, pp. 36–46, 2021, https://doi.org/10.1007/978-3-030-87193-2_4/FIGURES/3

24. Dosovitskiy et al., "An Image is Worth 16x16 Words: Transformers for Image Recognition at Scale," ICLR 2021 - 9th International Conference on Learning Representations, Oct. 2020, Accessed: Mar. 24, 2024. [Online]. Available: https://arxiv.org/abs/2010.11929v2

25. M. Rahman, Y. Cao, X. Sun, B. Li, and Y. Hao, "Deep pre-trained networks as a feature extractor with XGBoost to detect tuberculosis from chest X-ray," Computers and Electrical Engineering, vol. 93, no. June, p. 107252, 2021, https://doi.org/10.1016/j.compeleceng.2021.107252

26. D. Bhusal and S. P. Panday, "Multi-Label Classification of Thoracic Diseases using Dense Convolutional Network on Chest Radiographs," Feb. 2022, Accessed: Mar. 24, 2024. [Online]. Available: https://arxiv.org/abs/2202.03583v3

27. Chen, J. Li, G. Lu, and D. Zhang, "Lesion Location Attention Guided Network for Multi-Label Thoracic Disease Classification in Chest X-Rays," IEEE J Biomed Health Inform, vol. 24, no. 7, pp. 2016–2027, Jul. 2020, https://doi.org/10.1109/JBHI.2019.2952597

28. Chen, J. Li, G. Lu, H. Yu, and D. Zhang, "Label co-occurrence learning with graph convolutional networks for multi-label chest X-ray image classification," IEEE J Biomed Health Inform, vol. 24, no. 8, pp. 2292–2302, Aug. 2020, https://doi.org/10.1109/JBHI.2020.2967084

29. Chen, B., Zhang, Z., Li, Y., Lu, G., Zhang, D.: Multi-Label Chest X-Ray Image Classification via Semantic Similarity Graph Embedding. IEEE Trans. Circuits Syst. Video Technol. 32(4), 2455–2468 (2022). https://doi.org/10.1109/TCSVT.2021.3079900

Dual-Stream Based Scene Text Manipulation Detection Method

Jiefu Chen and Guofeng Yi$^{(\boxtimes)}$

University of Electronic Science and Technology of China, Chengdu, China
790416231@qq.com

Abstract. In recent years, with the development of Deep Neural Network (DNN), Scene Text (ST) related research has made great progress. At the same time, many methods of Scene Text Manipulation (STM) are derived. However, from the perspective of the development of deepfake, this image manipulation technology has surpassed the human eye to distinguish between real and composite images. To prevent people from the malicious application, many anti-deepfake methods have been derived. Based on the lessons learned from deepfake, since the STM has now reached a level that is indistinguishable to the naked eye, it also faces the possibility of being used by people to maliciously guide behaviors (like interfering with automatic driving to recognize road signs, forging signatures, and modifying words to cause misunderstanding semantics, etc.). As far as we know, since STM has not formed a complete manipulated dataset, we are the first to explore the identification of image manipulation. We use mainstream manipulation methods to construct a new dataset, and we designed a model specially used to identify whether the scene text image is fake. Extensive experimental comparisons with mainstream anti-deepfake and image classification methods demonstrate the effectiveness of our method.

Keywords: Scene Text Manipulation · Deep Neural Network · Scene Text

1 Introduction

With the deepening of deep network research, various application scenarios have emerged, and image manipulation [4] has become a very hot topic. In the field of face recognition, there are DeepFake [1], Face2face [18],and FaceSwap [2]. In the field of image generation, there are models such as VAE [9], DDPM [6], etc. With the in-depth study of people, more and more scene text manipulation methods [24] have appeared. Considering that deepfakes were used to maliciously lead people to generate wrong video content, we believe that the current scene text manipulation will also face this risk. Even guide the visual system related to scene text to make wrong judgments.

This paper constructs a large number of high-quality manipulateed scene text images through the most advanced scene text manipulation model [13] (including erasure and modification) in the current open-source model, through our careful annotation and preprocessing, forming a dataset dedicated to scene text manipulation detection. At the

H. Lu (Ed.): ISAIR 2024, CCIS 2402, pp. 186–194, 2025.
https://doi.org/10.1007/978-981-96-2911-4_18

same time, we designed a model that can be used to detect scene text manipulation and compared the current advanced detection models and image classification models in the field of deepfake.

According to previous research in the field of image manipulation detection, high-frequency features can often retain more traces of image forgery, providing more detailed information for detection models. Therefore, our model uses the high-frequency features commonly used in the current image detection field as a guide to preserving the forgery traces of the image, while extracting the original visual features of the image. The cross-modal attention module makes the relevant representation information of the two features. They learn from each other so that they can pay more attention to the areas where there are fake traces, and then mix the visual features with the high-frequency features to calculate the final prediction result.

Our main contributions are as follows:

- We construct a dataset containing scene text manipulation images generated in various ways through careful annotation and preprocessing, and screening of manipulated images. This dataset provides the basis for our study of scene text manipulation.
- Through in-depth research on scene text manipulation images, we construct a detection model for scene text manipulation images. The model consists of three parts, a high-frequency feature extraction module, a visual feature extraction module, and a hybrid module of high-frequency features and visual features through a cross-modal attention mechanism.

2 Related Work

2.1 Scene Text Manipulation

Junyeop et al. [7] separately encodes the content features and style features of the input images by extracting the content features and style features of the scene text images, and by introducing a scene text recognizer. Finally, a text-manipulateed image is generated by combining the style features of the original image and the content features of the target text. Recently, Wu et al. [21] and Yang et al. [22] proposed word-level STE methods using text transformation, background inpainting and fusion modules. These methods attempt to train a model to separate text regions and background regions using text erasing images.

2.2 Image Manipulation Detection and Deepfake Detection

For the detection of deepfakes, since the face images of deepfakes are generated by people through the refinement operation of [1, 2, 17, 18], the traces of face forgery are difficult to detect, and the images of face forgery are very small, which makes it difficult to detect different deepfakes. The detection needs to add a corresponding special processing method to be able to detect the corresponding face forgery traces. For example, Qian et al. [12] uses a combination of global high-frequency noise and local noise to detect forgery traces, Li et al. [8] uses a method similar to X-ray to extract the mask information of the image to detect face forgery traces, and Luo et al. [11] proposes a method. A detection method was capable of generalization.

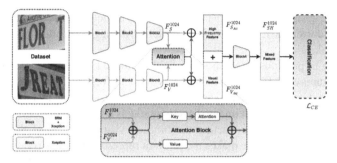

Fig. 1. Our Framework: Our model mainly consists of three parts 1. High- frequency feature extraction module. High-frequency information is obtained through SRM, and then feature extraction is performed through Xception; 2. RGB feature extraction module. Directly feed the original image into Xception to extract visual features; 3 cross-modal fusion attention modules. High-frequency features are mixed with visual features through our designed cross-modal attention fusion mechanism. Finally, the mixed features are sent to the classifier for classification.

3   Our Approach

In this section, we first introduce how we create a scene text manipulation dataset through existing scene text manipulation models and methods (erasing, editing, traditional editing). Then we introduce our proposed scene text tampering detection model, which includes 1. High-frequency feature extraction module; 2. RGB feature extraction module; 3. High-frequency features and RGB features through the cross-modal attention module.

3.1   Dataset Generation

Scene Text Erasure. The model [16] (STE) achieves the effect of erasing scene text through stroke mask prediction and background repair mechanism. Specifically, the model extracts the text part through the stroke mask by inputting a cropped scene text image with the bounding box and then uses the background repair module to restore the extracted text part through the background repair module to achieve the text erasing Effect. However, according to our experimental requirements, the manipulation of the scene text is by erasing part of the text images, to lead people to misunderstand, rather than erasing all the text. Therefore, we have made refined annotations for the scene text dataset, so that the model can generate scene text images that meet the requirements of our experimental standards.

Scene Text Manipulation. By inputting a scene text image with a bounding box and a target character, the model [13] (FANN) obtains the binarized target character image through the target character prediction and generation module of the model, and then combines the color background prediction module of the model to generate the target character image and The corresponding background, and finally paste it back into the original scene text image. This model can only replace and manipulate a single character

Fig. 2. This is a dataset we have built using the state-of-the-art open-source models available today and traditional image editing methods. The dataset contains a total of three classes, namely STE, FANN, and TIE. The first line is the STE class, which mainly uses the erasing model to erase the scene text, and the number of characters of the erased text is determined according to the bounding boxes. The second line is the FANN class, which is a single-character replacement operation for the scene text, and the target character of the replacement can be changed with our settings. The third row is the TIE class, which is generated by traditional image editing methods, such as rotating, flipping horizontally, flip- ping vertically, and adding noise.

image and has a good manipulation effect for the scene text of a single character. Therefore, we annotated the scene text images again, and each annotation box only contains one character to meet the input requirements of the model.

Traditional Image Manipulation to enrich the diversity of datasets, while Traditional Image manipulation (TIE) methods are also effective, datasets generated by traditional methods are also included in our experiments. We obtained the third scene text manipulation dataset by vertically flipping, horizontally flipping, blurring, and adding noise to the content in the manual annotation box (Fig. 3).

Fig. 3. Examples of the high-frequency features.

3.2 The Proposed Method

We selected the current mainstream classification models (VggNet [14], Resnet50 [5], Inception [15], Xception [3]) and deepfake detection models (CNNdetection [20], F3-NET [12], Face-Forge-Detection [11]) to conduct experiments on the generated datasets.

The experimental results show that the effect of the general classification model is not ideal, and the effect of the classification model for specific scenarios also has room for improvement. Considering that the scene text image is a sequence image, and the manipulateed area is often only a small part of the local area, we refer to the current methods commonly used in deepfake video detection and sequence recognition. First, extract the high frequency of the image. Information and visual information of the image, we use our well-designed cross-modal attention module to locate the feature attention area in the area where there may be forgery traces and then associate high-frequency noise features with visual features through the attention areas of shared weights. Combined, the combined features are mixed and processed through the convolution layer to obtain the final classification prediction result.

We design a detection model with three modules to specifically detect scene text tampering in images. The model mainly includes three modules: 1. High-frequency feature extraction module; 2. Visual feature extraction module; 3. Cross-modal attention fusion module. Our model is shown in Fig. 1.

High-frequency Features and High-frequency Feature Extraction. For image tampering, considering that the scene text image tampering operation is done by erasing the text, rebuilding the background, pasting the text, and other operations. Given that manipulation destroys the consistency of features in the original image, unique traces are often left in the noise space. Therefore, for the area between the text and the background, and the area where the background and the original image fit, there is forged information about the image. Therefore, we capture these forgery traces through high-frequency features.

We adopt Steganalysis Rich Model(SRM) [18] for high-frequency noise extraction to extract more accurate noise information. SRM has shown its superiority in high-frequency noise extraction in many fields. The SRM formula is as

$$x_h = SRM(x), \tag{1}$$

where x represents the original image and x_h represents the high-frequency image.

We refer to the noise information that SRM uses to extract images. SRM is composed of three specific Gaussian filters, a convolutional layer, and a Hard-tanh as the activation function. Finally, the x_h are sent to Xception for feature extraction to obtain the high frequency features F_h.

Visual Features Extraction. Considering that visual features can provide enough visual information, we use the current mainstream Xception as a feature extraction network to extract visual features F_v.

Cross-modal Attention Fusion Module. The visual feature information of scene text is continuous and sequential, and the high-frequency noise features are localized. We adopt the attention mechanism commonly used in the field of scene text recognition. Inspired by [23], we design a module that combines visual features and high-frequency features through cross-modal attention is used to guide the two features to learn their attention regions from each other, and finally, the two obtained feature information adjusted by the attention mechanism are fused to make Can more accurately focus on long-distance information and local area information. The operation of the whole module can be expressed by the following formula:

$$F_f = f_{CMAS}(F_h, F_v), \tag{2}$$

Table 1. Comparison of the results of various classification models and detection models.

	STE				STEFANN				TI			
Method	ACC	PR	RE	AUC	ACC	PR	RE	AUC	ACC	PR	RE	AUC
VGG19	0.813	0.933	0.753	0.872	0.575	0.341	0.642	0.617	0.522	0.168	0.577	0.602
ResNet50	0.878	0.915	0.851	0.924	0.773	0.952	0.701	0.818	0.758	0.847	0.719	0.826
Inception-V3	0.847	0.933	0.796	0.912	0.598	0.487	0.625	0.641	0.633	0.584	0.648	0.661
Xception	0.870	0.960	0.813	0.925	0.670	0.540	0.729	0.701	0.610	0.600	0.612	0.673
CNNdetection (CVPR'20)	0.860	0.884	0.844	0.920	0.794	0.958	0.721	0.857	0.811	0.874	0.776	0.871
F3-NET (only FAD) (CVPR'20)	0.900	0.920	0.884	0.958	0.860	0.980	0.790	0.921	0.880	0.960	0.827	0.934
F3-NET (both) (CVPR'20)	0.910	0.920	0.901	0.972	**0.940**	0.942	0.903	0.956	**0.911**	0.940	0.886	0.949
FFD (CVPR'21)	0.960	0.971	0.946	0.980	0.902	0.922	0.799	0.944	0.877	0.854	0.741	0.902
Ours	**0.982**	0.990	0.959	0.977	0.924	0.979	0.892	0.931	0.898	0.876	0.830	0.912

Loss Function. Inspired by the deepfake detection model, we use am-softmax and cross-entropy loss as the objective function. This loss function can increase the difference between classes and reduce the difference within, so it has better results in detection tasks.

4 Experiments

4.1 Datasets

In our experiments, we increase the diversity of manipulated images by using curved samples as manipulation objects. In the dataset used in the ICDAR [10] competition, all the data are collected in natural scenes, and the annotation frame of the text area is provided for researchers to extract the text area from the picture for identification. Among them, ICDAR 2003 contains 1113 images, ICDAR 2013 contains 1943 images, and ICDAR 2015 contains 6545 images, a total of 9601 scene text images that can be manipulated. IIIT5K provides real scene text images with richer backgrounds, which can effectively improve the diversity and robustness of the dataset. The dataset contains a total of 5,000 scene text images that can be manipulated by the model. SVT and SVT-Perspective [19] were obtained by shooting real street scenes, the two datasets contain a total of 1549 images. Through the introduction of the above dataset, we have a total of 16,438 scene text images that can be used for scene text manipulation.

Scene Text Manipulation Datasets. The STE model performs multi-character erasing and single-character erasing on scene text pictures. The STEFANN model performs single-character text manipulation on scene text pictures. Traditional image processing methods process bounding boxes whose lengths are randomly selected. The scene text manipulation image dataset contains three classes: text erasing, text modification, and traditional image processing. The text erasure class contains 11,979 images, the text modification class includes 14,469 images, and the traditional image processing class includes 10,000 images. We show some of the generated data in Fig. 2. The image sizes in this dataset are not consistent. In this paper, for the convenience of description, the images are adjusted to a uniform size.

4.2 Evaluation Metrics

In this section, we introduce the evaluation metrics we use in our experiments.

4.3 Model Evaluation Metrics

Evaluation metrics for classification and detection models. We use metrics commonly used to evaluate classification models, these metrics are Precision (PR), Recall (RE), Accuracy (ACC), and Area Under Curve (AUC).

Table 2. Comparison results of transfer experiments

Method	STE	STEFANN	TI
	ACC	ACC	ACC
VGG19	0.813	0.558	0.531
ResNet50	0.878	0.594	0.585
Inception-V3	0.847	0.604	0.582
Xception	0.870	0.630	0.590
CNNdetection (CVPR'20)	0.860	0.621	**0.599**
F3-NET (only FAD) (CVPR'20)	0.900	0.511	0.515
F3-NET (both) (CVPR'20)	0.910	0.532	0.580
FFD (CVPR'21)	0.960	**0.641**	0.593
Ours	**0.982**	0.629	0.580

4.4 Setting

We refer to Xception as the backbone network to extract high-frequency and visual features. All models are performed at epoch = 10, the optimizer uses adam, learning rate = 0.001, batchSize = 16, and the image resizes to 256*256.

4.5 Comparative Experiments

From the previous description, we obtained three datasets for scene text manipulation detection. For each dataset, we conduct experiments as a training set separately. As can be seen from Table 1, all classifiers without special improvement have a general effect on the detection of scene text manipulateed images. The models used for deepfake detection have a certain improvement in the detection effect on the STE dataset, and the classification model we designed has also achieved good results, especially on the STE dataset, we can see that The accuracy of our model is better than other models on the STE dataset, and the results are basically consistent with other models on other datasets.

We did a transfer experiment for each model, using STE and real images as the training set, and the other two invisible data sets as the test set, to explore the generalization ability and migration ability of each model. The experimental results are shown in

Table 2. The results of each model are not good, indicating that the differences between each data set are large, and the current models cannot effectively identify the distribution differences between classes.

5 Conclusion

In this paper, we propose an application scenario for scene text manipulation detection. We construct a multi-class scene text manipulation method by combining the existing state-of-the-art open-source scene text manipulation models and traditional image manipulation methods with the commonly used scene text data sets. New dataset. This dataset can be used to explore scene text manipulation detection. By comparing with the existing classification model and deepfake detection model, we found that the existing model cannot effectively detect scene text manipulation images. Therefore, we construct a new model for scene text manipulation detection, which consists of three modules, one is a high-frequency feature extraction module, one is a visual feature extraction module, and one is a cross-modal attention fusion module. Comprehensive experiments show the effectiveness of our model in scene text manipulation detection, and high-frequency features, visual features, and cross-modal attention fusion modules all contribute to the improvement of model performance.

References

1. Anonymous: Deepfakes (2017). https://github.com/iperov/DeepFaceLab
2. Anonymous: Faceswap (2017). https://github.com/MarekKowalski/FaceSwap
3. Chollet, F.: Xception: deep learning with depthwise separable convolutions. In: Proceedings of the IEEE Conference on Computer Vision and Pattern Recognition, pp. 125– 1258. IEEE, Piscataway, NJ (2017)
4. Delanoy, J., Lagunas, M., Condor, J., Gutierrez, D., Masiá, B.: A generative frame-work for image-based editing of material appearance using perceptual attributes. Comput. Graph. Forum **41**(1), 453–464 (2022)
5. He, K., Zhang, X., Ren, S., Sun, J.: Deep residual learning for image recognition. In: Proceedings of the IEEE Conference on Computer Vision and Pattern Recognition, pp. 770–778 (2016)
6. Ho, J., Jain, A., Abbeel, P.: Denoising diffusion probabilistic models. In: Larochelle, H., Ranzato, M., Hadsell, R., Balcan, M., Lin, H. (eds.) Advances in Neural Information Processing Systems 33: Annual Conference on Neural Information Processing Systems 2020, NeurIPS 2020, 6–12 December 2020, Virtual (2020)
7. Lee, J., Kim, Y., Kim, S., Yim, M., Shin, S., Lee, G., Park, S.: Rewritenet: realistic scene text image generation via editing text in real-world image. CoRR abs/2107.11041 (2021)
8. Li, L., et al.: Face x-ray for more general face forgery detection. In: Proceedings of the IEEE/CVF Conference on Computer Vision and Pattern Recognition, pp. 5001–5010 (2020)
9. Lin, Y., Liu, Z., Hwang, R., Nguyen, V., Lin, P., Lai, Y.: Machine learning with variational autoencoder for imbalanced datasets in intrusion detection. IEEE Access **10**, 15247–15260 (2022). https://doi.org/10.1109/ACCESS.2022.3149295
10. Lucas, S.M., et al.: ICDAR 2003 robust reading competitions: entries, results, and future directions. IJDAR **7**(2), 105–122 (2005)

11. Luo, Y., Zhang, Y., Yan, J., Liu, W.: Generalizing face forgery detection with high-frequency features. In: Proceedings of the IEEE/CVF Conference on Computer Vision and Pattern Recognition, pp. 16317–16326 (2021)
12. Qian, Y., Yin, G., Sheng, L., Chen, Z., Shao, J.: Thinking in frequency: face forgery detection by mining frequency-aware clues. In: European Conference on Computer Vision, pp. 86– 103. Springer (2020)
13. Roy, P., Bhattacharya, S., Ghosh, S., Pal, U.: STEFANN: scene text editor using font adaptive neural network. In: 2020 IEEE/CVF Conference on Computer Vision and Pattern Recognition, CVPR 2020, Seattle, WA, USA, 13–19 June 2020, pp. 13225– 13234. Computer Vision Foundation/IEEE (2020)
14. Simonyan, K., Zisserman, A.: Very deep convolutional networks for large-scale image recognition. arXiv preprint arXiv:1409.1556 (2014)
15. Szegedy, C., et al.: Going deeper with convolutions. In: Proceedings of the IEEE Conference on Computer Vision and Pattern Recognition, pp. 1–9 (2015)
16. Tang, Z., Miyazaki, T., Sugaya, Y., Omachi, S.: Stroke-based scene text erasing using synthetic data for training. IEEE Trans. Image Process. 30, 9306–9320 (2021)
17. Thies, J., Zollhöfer, M., Nießner, M.: Deferred neural rendering: image synthesis using neural textures. ACM Trans. Graph. 38(4), 66:1–66:12 (2019)
18. Thies, J., Zollhöfer, M., Stamminger, M., Theobalt, C., Nießner, M.: Face2face: real-time face capture and reenactment of RGB videos. In: 2016 IEEE Conference on Computer Vision and Pattern Recognition, CVPR 2016, Las Vegas, NV, USA, 27–30 June 2016, pp. 2387–2395. IEEE Computer Society (2016)
19. Wang, K., Belongie, S.: Word spotting in the wild. In: European Conference on Computer Vision, pp. 591–604. Springer (2010)
20. Wang, S.Y., Wang, O., Zhang, R., Owens, A., Efros, A.A.: Cnn-generated images are surprisingly easy to spot... for now. In: Proceedings of the IEEE/CVF Conference on Computer Vision and Pattern Recognition (CVPR), June 2020
21. Wu, L., et al.: Editing text in the wild. In: Proceedings of the 27th ACM International Conference on Multimedia, pp. 1500– 1508 (2019)
22. Yang, Q., Huang, J., Lin, W.: Swaptext: image based texts transfer in scenes. In: Proceedings of the IEEE/CVF Conference on Computer Vision and Pattern Recognition, pp. 14700–14709 (2020)
23. Ye, L., Rochan, M., Liu, Z., Wang, Y.: Cross-modal self-attention network for referring image segmentation. In: Proceedings of the IEEE/CVF Conference on Computer Vision and Pattern Recognition, pp. 10502–10511 (2019)
24. Zhang, J., et al.: Write-an-animation: high-level text-based animation editing with character-scene interaction. Comput. Graph. Forum 40(7), 217–228 (2021)

ECD: Event-Centric Disentangler for Weakly Supervised Video Anomaly Detection

Yi Qu[1]([✉]), Yixuan Zhou[1], and Guofeng Yi[2]

[1] University of Electronic Science and Technology of China, Chengdu 611731, Sichuan, China
iquyiiii@gmail.com, yxzhou@std.uestc.edu.cn
[2] Chengdu Koala Uran Technology Co., Ltd., Chengdu, China
yiguofeng@yourangroup.com

Abstract. Weakly supervised video anomaly detection (WVAD) aims to detect where abnormal events occur in videos using only video-level labels during training. Many existing WVAD methods concentrate on learning comprehensive representations for each frame, making them susceptible to interference from irrelevant backgrounds or scenes. In this paper, we address this challenge by introducing disentangled representation learning to WVAD, presenting a new modular component named the Event-Centric Disentangler (ECD). Specifically, our ECD incorporates an Event Focus Attention (EFA) module, estimating channel-wise attention to focus on event representations while filtering out irrelevant information from backgrounds or scenes. Alongside EFA, a Frame Importance Allocator (FIA) learns frame-wise weighting factors to aggregate frame-level predictions for the generation of video-level predictions. Furthermore, we introduce a video-level contrastive loss to provide disentanglement supervision for ECD training, within the constraints of weakly supervised settings. Integrating ECD into existing WVAD methods, we achieve state-of-the-art performance on two benchmark datasets, with 87.53% AUC and 81.61% AP on the UCF-Crime and XD-Violence datasets, respectively. Our code is available at https://github.com/quyiii/ECD.

Keywords: Disentangled Representation Learning · Video Anomaly Detection · Weakly Supervised Learning

1 Introduction

Video anomaly detection (VAD) aims to detect and localize abnormal events in untrimmed videos, holding significant potential in various applications [1, 2]. However, exploring VAD in a fully supervised manner at frame-level is impractical due to the high cost of collecting fully labeled anomaly videos. In recent years, weakly supervised video anomaly detection (WVAD), requiring only video-level labels indicating whether abnormal events occur, has been gaining popularity [3–10] and demonstrated significant performance improvements over unsupervised methods [11, 12].

Due to the absence of frame-level labels, most existing methods [3–5] borrow the idea of Multi-Instance Learning (MIL) [13, 14] to train their anomaly classifiers with

H. Lu (Ed.): ISAIR 2024, CCIS 2402, pp. 195–206, 2025.
https://doi.org/10.1007/978-981-96-2911-4_19

video-level labels. Within MIL frameworks, the positive (anomaly) bag is constituted by potential abnormal snippets, which are selected by customized abnormality criteria, e.g., feature magnitude [3]. However, the abnormality criteria are highly dependent on the occurrence of abnormal events, which are susceptible to interference from event-irrelevant backgrounds or scenes. As shown in Fig. 1, despite the divergence of feature distributions across normal and abnormal snippets, the features derived from the same video with identical scene are still mixed together, which makes anomaly detection intricate. In other words, the learned features are not only sensitive to the occurrence of abnormal events, but also entangled with irrelevant backgrounds or scenes, which is undesirable for anomaly detection.

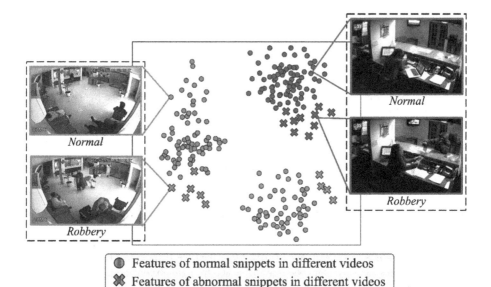

Fig. 1. The event-scene entangled feature distribution on UCF-Crime [1]

To mitigate the interference resulting from scenarios and enhance feature discrimination, we introduce disentangled representation learning (DRL) into WVAD and propose a novel Event-Centric Disentangler (ECD) for weakly supervised anomaly detection. Our ECD utilizes channel-wise attention calculated by the Event Focus Attention (EFA) module to filter out event-irrelevant information from backgrounds or scenes. Moreover, we design a Frame Importance Allocator (FIA) to generate frame-wise anomaly weight for bag- or video-level predictions constitution. To meet the constraints of weakly supervised settings, we introduce a video-level contrastive loss to provide disentanglement supervision for ECD training. Notably, serving as a plug-and-play module, our ECD can be seamlessly integrated into existing WVAD methods, resulting in further performance improvement.

Our main contributions are summarized as follows:

We propose a novel plug-and-play Event-Centric Disentangler (ECD), which first (to the best of our knowledge) introduces disentangled representation learning to extract event-centric features.

In the ECD, an Event Focus Attention (EFA) module estimates channel-wise attention focusing on event representations, and a Frame Importance Allocator (FIA) learns frame-wise weighting factors to aggregate frame-level predictions to video-level predictions.

We also present a video-level contrastive loss to provide disentanglement supervision for our ECD training, within the constraints of weakly supervised settings.

2 Related Work

In this section, we briefly review some prior and concurrent works related to the weakly supervised video anomaly detection task and disentangled representation learning theory.

2.1 Weakly Supervised Video Anomaly Detection

To reduce the difficulty of annotating abnormal events, weakly supervised video anomaly detection (WVAD) has been proposed, which utilizes both normal and abnormal videos with video-level labels during training and has attracted increasing attention. Multi-Instance Learning (MIL) is widely adopted in existing WVAD methods, which train their anomaly classifiers with video-level labels and selected scores generated by customized abnormality criteria like feature magnitude [3]. Other non-MIL based WVAD methods [6, 8] train their anomaly classifiers with pseudo frame-level labels whose quality is also highly dependent on the abnormality criteria. Despite these methods have explored various abnormality criteria and achieved significant performance, features discrimination still suffer from the interference of backgrounds or scenes and limits the reliability of abnormality criteria, which highly relates to feature. In this paper, we propose a novel ECD model to extract event-centric features and mitigate this interference.

2.2 Disentangled Representation Learning

Disentangled representation learning (DRL) [15] aims to learn the independent representations that are responsible for some specific attributes in the data. Single latent representation is only sensitive to variation in a single underlying attribute while being relatively invariant to changes in other attributes. With this property, DRL is widely used in generative applications such as style transfer [16, 17] and image editing [18, 19]. Take style transfer as an example, DRL can be used to transfer the style of the image by solely manipulating the representation that is responsible for the style attribute while keeping the attributes of content unchanged. Disentangled representation learning also has been used in other applications such as classification [20, 21] and retrieval [22, 23] tasks. In these recognition tasks, the semantic attributes of the image can be separated and learned by disentangling the latent representations. In this paper, we first (to the best of our knowledge) introduce the disentangled representation learning to the task of WVAD. We regard the attributes of events as the responsible factors in WVAD, and filter the attributes of events from irrelevant backgrounds or scenes through the channel-wise attention mechanism estimated by our proposed module EFA. With the disentangled representations of events, ECD can easily detect the target frames with abnormal events occurring, mitigating the influence of irrelevant background or scene variation.

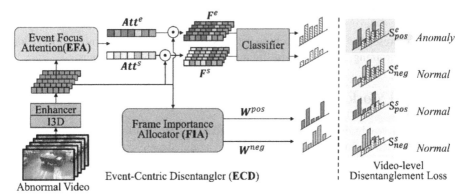

Fig. 2. The framework of our ECD model, which consists three parts: Event Focus Attention module (EFA), Frame Importance Allocator (FIA) and contrastive loss. EFA module utilizes channel-wise attention to extract event-focus features, FIA generates frame-wise anomaly weight for video-level predictions constitution, and contrastive loss provide disentanglement supervision for ECD training. Notably, the label of S_{pos}^e is set to 1 exclusively for abnormal videos.

3   Our ECD Approach

Similar to the previous works based on disentangle representation learning [16–19], we aim to disentangle event and scene presentations from the feature distribution where entangled presentations abound (see Fig. 1). To this end, we propose ECD.

In this section, we present a detailed introduction of the problem formulation and our proposed ECD framework, which consists of two stages, i.e., disentangled features extraction which contain event and scene presentation respectively, and video-level prediction construction which neglects the irrelevant snippets and emphasizes the important snippets, resulting in robustness and generalization capability improvement of the model.

3.1   Problem Setting

Following the setup for weakly supervised anomaly detection (WVAD) tasks. The training set consists of N untrimmed videos $V = \{V_i\}_{i=1}^N$, which can be divided into two subsets: normal set $V^n = \{V_i^n\}_{i=1}^{N^n}$ with video-level label $\{Y_i^n = 0\}_{i=1}^{N^n}$ and abnormal set $V^a = \{V_i^a\}_{i=1}^{N^a}$ with video-level label $\{Y_i^a = 1\}_{i=1}^{N^a}$, where $N^n + N^a = N$. In practice, each V_i is beforehand encoded into snippet features F_i by pre-trained backbones [24–27]. Our goal is to score each F_i^e according to $y_i = f(F_i^e)$ with the model $f(\cdot)$, where F_i^e is the enhanced feature of F_i by feature enhancer [3, 5].

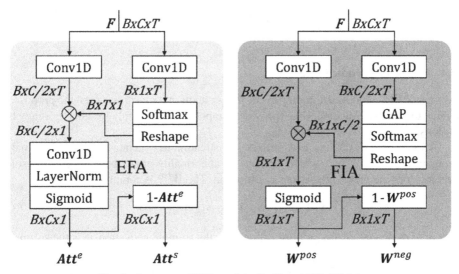

Fig. 3. Structure of EFA module (Left) and FIA (Right).

3.2 Event-Centric Disentangler

Our Event-Centric Disentangler (ECD) consists of two key components: Event Focus Attention (EFA) module and Frame Importance Allocator (FIA). Upon the video features, the EFA module first estimates channel-wise attention, which serves as soft mask to disentangle event representations from backgrounds or scenes. Parallel to EFA, the FIA module learns a set of frame-wise weighting factors for the aggregation of frame-level predictions to video-level predictions. Besides aggregating frame-level predictions, the introduction of FIA module also provides flexible loss composition for disentangled representation Learning of the proposed ECD, as shown in Fig. 2. With the EFA and FIA modules, we design a video-level contrastive loss to provide disentanglement supervision for ECD training, within the constraints of weakly supervised settings.

3.3 Event Focus Attention Module

To extract scene and event presentations from features, we propose our EFA module as shown in Fig. 3, which utilizes event attention to focus on the scene-irrelevant events. Consider a mini-batch of B videos, the hidden feature $\boldsymbol{F} \in \mathbb{R}^{B \times T \times C}$, the channel-wise event attention $\boldsymbol{Att}^e \in \mathbb{R}^{B \times 1 \times C}$ is computed through the following function:

$$\text{Att}^{\text{e}} = \sigma(\text{W}_z(\text{W}_v(\boldsymbol{F}) \otimes \phi(\text{W}_q(\boldsymbol{F})))) \tag{1}$$

where $\otimes$ means the matrix multiplication, σ is the sigmoid activation, ϕ is the softmax fucntion, and W_z, W_v, W_q are 1×1 convolution layers respectively.

With the event attention Att^e, we can extract event and scene presentations from features. The event-focus feature $\boldsymbol{F}^e \in \mathbb{R}^{B \times T \times C}$ and scene-focus feature $\boldsymbol{F}^s \in \mathbb{R}^{B \times T \times C}$ are computed as follows:

$$\boldsymbol{F}^{\text{e}} = \text{Att}^{\text{e}} \odot \boldsymbol{F}, \boldsymbol{F}^{\text{s}} = (1 - \textbf{Att}^{\textbf{e}}) \odot \boldsymbol{F} \tag{2}$$

where $\odot$ means the element-wise multiplication, and $1 - Att^e$ denotes the scene attention Att^s.

3.4 Frame Importance Allocator

Alongside EFA module estimating event-focus attention for each snippets, the proposed Frame Importance Allocator (FIA) provides temporal-wise anomaly weights for snippets to constitute video-level predictions.

AS shown in Fig. 3, our FIA utilizes self-attention to generate positive (abnormal) weights $W^{pos} \in \mathbb{R}^{B \times T \times 1}$, which denotes the abnormality of snippets and provide soft weights for video level predictions constitution. The W^{pos} is computed as follows:

$$W^{pos} = \sigma(W_v(F) \otimes \phi(g(W_q(F)))) \tag{3}$$

where $\otimes$ means the matrix multiplication, σ is the sigmoid activation, ϕ is the softmax function, $g(\cdot)$ is the global average pooling temporally, and W_v, W_q are 1×1 convolution layers respectively. Then, the negative (normal) weights are $W^{neg} = 1 - W^{pos}$.

Notably, with the event-focus feature F^e and scene-focus feature F^s, we calculate the video-level anomaly score as follows:

$$S^e_{pos} = \sum_{t=1}^{T}[c(F^e)_t \odot W^{pos}_t], S^e_{neg} = \sum_{t=1}^{T}[c(F^e)_t \odot W^{neg}_t] \tag{4}$$

$$S^s_{pos} = \sum_{t=1}^{T}[c(F^s)_t \odot W^{pos}_t], S^s_{neg} = \sum_{t=1}^{T}[c(F^s)_t \odot W^{neg}_t] \tag{5}$$

where $c(\cdot)$ denotes the anomaly classifier, $\odot$ is the element-wise multiplication operator, and S^e_{pos}, S^e_{neg}, S^s_{pos}, S^s_{neg} are the video-level predictions of event-focus abnormality score, event-focus normality score, scene-focus abnormality score, scene-focus normality score, respectively.

3.5 Video-Level Contrastive Loss

To encourage the separation between scene and event, we define a contrastive loss consists of four binary cross-entropy (BCE) losses based on the EFA module and FIA, which is formulated with abnormal videos as follows:

$$L^e_{pos} = BCE(S^e_{pos}, 1), L^e_{neg} = BCE(S^e_{neg}, 0) \tag{6}$$

$$L^s_{pos} = BCE(S^s_{pos}, 0), L^s_{neg} = BCE(S^s_{neg}, 0) \tag{7}$$

$$L^{abn}_{dis} = L^e_{pos} + \lambda_1 L^e_{neg} + \lambda_2 L^s_{pos} + \lambda_3 L^s_{neg} \tag{8}$$

where λ_1, λ_2, λ_3 are the hyper-parameters to balance the loss terms, L^e_{pos}, L^e_{neg}, L^s_{pos}, L^s_{neg} are video-level loss of prediction scores.

Particularly, the anomaly scores S_{pos}^e for abnormal videos are exclusively supervised to approach 1, as these scores capture features related to abnormal events. In the case of normal videos, S_{pos}^e should approach 0. Within these four losses, training EFA module with contrastive pair losses L_{pos}^e and L_{pos}^s can encourage the disentanglement capability of EFA, ultilizing L_{pos}^e and L_{neg}^e to train FIA can encourage its cpability of anomaly frame identification.

After integrating our ECD model into other methods, the overall loss function is defined as follows:

$$L = L_{ori} + \lambda_4 L_{dis} \tag{9}$$

where λ_4 is the hyper-parameter to balance the loss terms, L_{ori} is the original loss of adopted method, and L_{dis} is our contrastive loss for the EFA module and FIA.

4 Experiments

In this section, we give more details of our used datasets and results of the experiments compared with other state-of-the-art work [1–12], verifying the effectiveness of our proposed method.

Table 1. Comparison of AUC (%) on the UCF-Crime dataset [1]. Existing methods are divided into two categories: unsupervised (Un.) and weakly supervised (Weakly).

	Method	Venue	Feature	AUC (%)
Un	GCL [11]	CVPR'23	ResNext	74.20
	FPDM [12]	ICCV'23	Image	74.70
Weakly	Sultani et al. [1]	CVPR'18	C3D	75.41
	Sultani et al. [1]	CVPR'18	I3D	76.21
	GCN [8]	CVPR'19	TSN	82.12
	HL-Net [2]	ECCV'20	I3D	82.44
	CLAWS [7]	ECCV'20	C3D	83.03
	MIST [10]	CVPR'21	I3D	82.30
	MSL [9]	AAAI'22	I3D	85.30
	S3R [4]	ECCV'22	I3D	85.99
	CU-Net [6]	CVPR'23	I3D	86.22
	RTFM [3]	ICCV'21	I3D	84.30
	RTFM + **ECD**		I3D	**85.87**
	UR-DMU [5]	AAAI'23	I3D	86.97
	UR-DMU + **ECD**		I3D	**87.53**

4.1 Datasets and Setup

Datasets. Following previous works, we consider two prominent WVAD datasets: UCF-Crime [1] and XD-Violence [2], where only video-level labels are accessible during training.

UCF-Crime is a real-world surveillance video dataset, which contains 1900 videos with 13 different crime categories, e.g., abuse, explosion, and fighting. In the training set, there are 800 normal and 810 abnormal videos with video-level labels only. The testing set includes 140 normal and 150 abnormal videos with frame-level labels.

XD-Violence is the largest WVAD dataset with 4754 untrimmed videos collected from movies, surveillance, etc. It contains 6 categories of abnormal events, e.g., abuse, shooting, and car accident. With video-level labeled, the training set contains 1905 normal and 2049 abnormal videos. With frame-level labeled, the testing set includes 300 normal and 500 abnormal videos.

Evaluation Protocols.   To ensure a fair comparison with previous works, we employ the area under the curve (AUC) of the frame-level receiver operating characteristic (ROC) curve as primary metric for UCF-Crime. Meanwhile, the AUC of the frame-level precision-recall curve (AP) is used for XD-violence.

Implementation Details.   Our ECD is combined with existing WVAD methods to demonstrate its effectiveness, including the baseline RTFM [3] and the SOTA method UR-DMU [5] according to the official codes,[1,2] respectively. For fair comparison, we adopt features extracted by pretrained I3D [25] on Kinetics-400 following [5]. We utilize Adam optimizer to train the ECD-equipped models with a learning rate of 0.0001, a weight decay of 0.00005 and a batch size of 128 for 3000 iterations. Moreover, each mini-batch comprises 64 normal and abnormal videos, with each video being divided into $T = 200$ snippets during training. The hyperparameters of $(\lambda_1, \lambda_2, \lambda_3, \lambda_4)$ are set as $(0.1, 0.1, 1, 0.1)$ for UCF-Crime and $(0.1, 0.1, 0.5, 0.1)$ for XD-Violence. In the testing stage, we calculate the metrics by the mean anomaly scores of n-crops features, while the UCF-Crime is 10-crops and XD-Violence is 5-crops.

4.2 Comparison with the State-of-the-Arts

We experimentally evaluate the effectiveness of our proposed ECD on two datasets, i.e., a real-world surveillance video dataset UCF-Crime [1] and a multisource video dataset XD [2], and compare the results with other competitive methods [1–12].

Results on UCF-Crime.   As reported in Table 1, our ECD demonstrates consistently significant AUC improvement for the baseline (RTFM) and SOTA (UR-DMU) on this dataset. For RTFM, integrating with ECD results in a substantial performance improvement of 1.57%. Moreover, the ECD-equipped UR-DMU further achieves a novel SOTA performance with AUC 87.53%.

---

[1] https://github.com/tianyu0207/RTFM.
[2] https://github.com/henrryzh1/UR-DMU.

Table 2. Comparison of AP (%) on the XD-Violence dataset [2]. '✝' denotes the reproduced results of open-source code [5] by ourselves. '+ VGGish' means that methods use audio features as auxiliary information.

Method	Venue	Feature	AP (%)
Sultani et al. [1]	CVPR'18	I3D	73.20
HL-Net [2]	ECCV'20	I3D	73.67
HL-Net [2]	ECCV'20	I3D + VGGish	78.64
MSL [9]	AAAI'22	I3D	78.24
S3R [4]	ECCV'22	I3D	80.26
CU-Net [6]	CVPR'23	I3D	78.74
CU-Net [6]	CVPR'23	I3D + VGGish	81.43
RTFM [3]	ICCV'21	I3D	77.81
RTFM + **ECD**		I3D	**81.42**
UR-DMU ✝ [5]	AAAI'23	I3D	80.51
UR-DMU + **ECD**		I3D	**81.61**
UR-DMU [5]	AAAI'23	I3D + VGGish	81.77
UR-DMU + **ECD**		I3D + VGGish	**82.81**

Results on XD-Violence. On this largest WVAD dataset, our ECD also demonstrates superior performance gains. Specifically, Table 2 shows that the ECD-equipped RTFM exhibits competitiveness with SOTA methods, showcasing a significant AP improvement of 3.61%, while the ECD-integrated UR-DMU outperforms SOTA methods with AP 81.61%. Moreover, the performance of the ECD-equipped UR-DMU experiences further improvement when simply concatenating audio features with video features as the input, reaching an AP score of up to 82.81%.

Table 3. The Ablation of our proposed components on UCF-Crime [1] and XD-Violence [2] based on ECD-equipped UR-DMU. Despite AUC and AP, we also report the AUC_{abn} and AP_{abn}, which are the AUC and AP of abnormal videos, respectively.

Module				UCF-Crime				XD-Violence			
Base	EFA	FIA	L_{dis}	AUC	AP	AUC_{abn}	AP_{abn}	AUC	AP	AUC_{abn}	AP_{abn}
✓				86.47	31.32	69.91	32.09	93.02	80.32	79.89	81.44
✓	✓			86.53	31.41	70.12	32.40	93.43	80.81	80.58	81.63
✓	✓	✓		86.56	29.40	68.73	30.96	93.31	80.76	80.56	81.77
✓	✓		✓	86.57	30.35	69.21	31.36	93.22	81.24	80.59	81.91
✓	✓	✓	✓	**87.53**	**31.49**	**70.36**	**32.84**	**93.70**	**81.60**	**80.65**	**82.36**

Effectiveness of key components. To investigate the effectiveness of our key components, we conduct ablation experiments on UCF-Crime and XD-Violence datasets based on ECD-equipped UR-DMU. For comprehensive evaluation, we employ two additional indicators AUC_{abn} and AP_{abn}, the AUC and AP score of only abnormal videos as shown in * MERGEFORMAT Table 3. Baseline is the clean UR-DMU without our ECD and achieves the lowest performance. With the EFA module, all the metrics exhibit great improvement, which demonstrates the capability of our EFA to generate discriminative features. When FIA module is added, the performance gains tiny improvement, indicating that the FIA module can help to focus on the abnormal snippets. When add the EFA module with contrastive disentanglement loss implemented by top-K selection strategy, each metric gets further improvements. Finally, the full model, ECD-equipped UR-DMU, achieves the best performance, which demonstrates the effectiveness of our contrastive disentanglement loss and superiority of our FIA aggregation strategy compared to top-K selection. The t-SNE features visualization Fig. 4 intuitively demonstrates the effectiveness of our ECD and further proves the capability of EFA module to extract scene and event presentations from features.

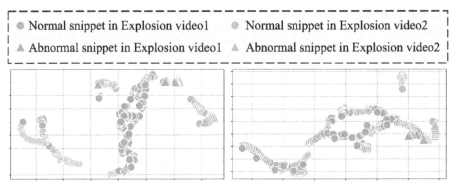

Fig. 4. The t-SNE visualization of UR-DMU hidden features with or without our ECD on UCF-Crime [1].

Effectiveness of Different Loss Terms. To explore the influences of four loss terms in our contrastive loss, we report the results of loss combinations based on ECD-equipped UR-DMU in Table 4. L_{ori} is the ECD-equipped UR-DMU without contrastive loss, which achieves the lowest performance as the baseline. When add contrastive loss L_{pos}^e and L_{neg}^e or L_{pos}^e and L_{pos}^s, the performance get further improvement, indicating the effectiveness of our contrastive loss. Moreover, integrating these two pairs contrastive losses simultaneously results a better performance. Finally, the comprehensive loss, which combines these four losses together, achieves the best performance, validating the effectiveness of our contrastive loss structure.

Table 4. The Ablation of different loss terms on UCF-Crime [3] and XD-Violence [2] based on ECD-equipped UR-DMU.

Loss terms					UCF-Crime		XD-Violence	
L_{ori}	L_{pos}^e	L_{neg}^e	L_{pos}^s	L_{neg}^s	AUC	AP	AUC	AP
$\checkmark$					86.56	29.40	93.31	80.76
$\checkmark$	$\checkmark$	$\checkmark$			86.64	30.76	93.59	80.86
$\checkmark$	$\checkmark$		$\checkmark$		86.68	30.71	93.57	80.84
$\checkmark$	$\checkmark$	$\checkmark$	$\checkmark$		86.85	31.39	93.61	81.22
$\checkmark$	$\checkmark$	$\checkmark$	$\checkmark$	$\checkmark$	**87.53**	**31.49**	**93.70**	**81.60**

5 Conclusions

In this paper, we introduced disentangled representation learning into WVAD and presented a novel ECD model to distill event-focus features from videos. The ECD consists of two modules: EFA decoupling features from event-irrelevant scenes, and FIA estimating temporal-wise anomaly weight for video-level prediction constitution. A video-level disentanglement loss was further proposed to encourage the feature separation between scene and event. The integration of ECD into existing methods demonstrated its effectiveness in learning event-focus features in WVAD.

References

1. Sultani, W., Chen, C., Shah, M.: Real-world anomaly detection in surveillance videos. In: CVPR, pp. 6479–6488 (2018)
2. Wu, P., Liu, J., Shi, Y., Shao, F., Wu, Z., Yang, Z.: Not only look, but also listen: learning multimodal violence detection under weak supervision. In: ECCV, pp. 322–339 (2020)
3. Tian, Y., Pang, G., Chen, Y., Singh, R., Verjans, J.W., Carneiro, G.: Weakly-supervised video anomaly detection with robust temporal feature magnitude learning. In: ICCV, pp. 4955–4966 (2021)
4. Wu, J.-C., Hsieh, H.-Y., Chen, D.-J., Fuh, C.-S., Liu, T.-L.: Self-supervised sparse representation for video anomaly detection. In: ECCV, pp. 729–745. Springer (2022)
5. Zhou, H., Yu, J.,Yang, W.: Dual memory units with uncertainty regulation for weakly supervised video anomaly detection (2023)
6. Zhang, C., et al.: Exploiting completeness and uncertainty of pseudo labels for weakly supervised video anomaly detection. In: CVPR, pp. 16271–16280 (2023)
7. Zaheer, M. Z., Mahmood, A., Astrid, M., Lee, S.-I.: Claws: clustering assisted weakly supervised learning with normalcy suppression for anomalous event detection. In: ECCV, 358–376 (2020)
8. Zhong, J., Li, N., Kong, W., Liu, S., Li, T. H., Li, G.: Graph convolutional label noise cleaner: train a plug-and-play action classifier for anomaly detection. In: CVPR, pp. 1237–1246 (2019)
9. Li, S., Liu, F., Jiao, L.: Self-training multi-sequence learning with transformer for weakly supervised video anomaly detection. In: AAAI, pp. 1395–1403 (2022)
10. Feng, J., Hong, F., Zheng, W.: Mist: multiple instance self-training framework for video anomaly detection. In: CVPR, pp. 14009–14018 (2021)

11. Zaheer, M. Z., Mahmood, A., Khan, M. H., Segu, M., Yu, F., Lee, S.-I.: Generative cooperative learning for unsupervised video anomaly detection. In: CVPR, pp. 14744–14754 (2022)
12. Yan, C., Zhang, S., Liu, Y., Pang, G., Wang, W.: Feature prediction diffusion model for video anomaly detection. In: ICCV, pp. 5527–5537 (2023)
13. Andrews, S., Tsochantaridis, I., Hofmann, T.: Support vector machines for multiple-instance learning. NIPS 15 (2002)
14. Li, W., Vasconcelos, N.: Multiple instance learning for soft bags via top instances. In: CVPR, pp. 4277–4285 (2015)
15. Bengio, Y., Courville, A., Vincent, P.: Representation learning: a review and new perspectives. PAMI 35(8), 1798–1828 (2013)
16. Zhang, J., Huang, Y., Li, Y., Zhao, W., Zhang, L.: Multi-attribute transfer via disentangled representation. AAAI 33(01), 9195–9202 (2019)
17. Dai, N., Liang, J., Qiu, X., Huang, X.: Style transformer: unpaired text style transfer without disentangled latent representation, arXiv preprint arXiv:1905.05621 (2019)
18. Jeon, I., Lee, W., Pyeon, M., Kim, G.: Ib-gan: Disentangled representation learning with information bottleneck generative adversarial networks. AAAI 35(9), 7926–7934 (2021)
19. Yao, X., Newson, A., Gousseau, Y., Hellier, P.: A latent transformer for disentangled face editing in images and videos. In: ICCV, pp. 13789–13798 (2021)
20. Tran, L., Yin, X., Liu, X.: Disentangled representation learning gan for pose-invariant face recognition. In: CVPR, pp. 1415–1424 (2017)
21. Kang, B., et al.: Decoupling representation and classifier for long-tailed recognition. In: ICLR (2019)
22. Wang, X., Chen, H., Zhou, Y., Ma, J., Zhu, W.: Disentangled representation learning for recommendation. PAMI 45(1), 408–424 (2022)
23. Hou, Y., Vig, E., Donoser, M., Bazzani, L.: Learning attribute-driven disentangled representations for interactive fashion retrieval. In: [ICCV, pp. 12147–12157 (2021)
24. Tran, D., Bourdev, L.D., Fergus, R., Torresani, L., Paluri, M.: Learning spatiotemporal features with 3d convolutional networks. In: ICCV, pp. 4489–4497 (2015)
25. Carreira, J, Zisserman, A.: Quo vadis, action recognition? A new model and the kinetics dataset. In: CVPR, pp. 4727–4733 (2017)
26. Xie, S., Girshick, R., Doll´ar, P., Tu, Z., He, K.: Aggregated residual transformations for deep neural networks. In: CVPR, pp. 1492–1500 (2017)
27. Gemmeke, J.F., et al.: Audio set: an ontology and human-labeled dataset for audio events. In: ICASSP, pp. 776–780. IEEE (2017)

Sequential Consistency Matters: Boosting Video Sequence Verification with Teacher Multimodal Transformer

Yaning Zhao[1]([✉]), Xun Jiang[1], Jingran Zhang[2], and Guofeng Yi[2]

[1] University of Electronic Science and Technology of China, Chengdu 611731, Sichuan, China
zhao802315@outlook.com
[2] Chengdu Koala Uran Technology Company, Chengdu 610000, Sichuan, China
yiguofeng@yourangroup.com

Abstract. Video sequence verification (SV), which aims to determine whether the procedures within two videos are consistent at the step level, has received significant attention in recent years. This paper introduces a novel approach to boost the SV task by leveraging multimodal data, including video frames and accompanying textual narrations. The core of the proposed method is the Teacher Multimodal Transformer, designed to facilitate the learning of matching information between different modalities and improve the SV task's performance through a pseudo-label generation algorithm. Additionally, a cross-grained contrastive learning loss is introduced to effectively capture relevant information between coarse-grained and fine-grained features. The paper demonstrates the efficacy of the proposed method on three widely used SV datasets, including CSV, Diving-SV, and COIN-SV. The proposed method has 2.23%, 1.56%, 2.6% improved to the conventional methods on these benchmarks under weakly supervised setting.

Keywords: Video Sequence Verification · Sequential Consistency · Teacher Multimodal Transformer · Cross-Grained Contrastive Learning

1 Introduction

Imagine you are assembling a television cabinet, a task comprising multiple complex steps that must be executed in sequence. Despite repeatedly consulting instructional videos to avoid failure, you inadvertently fail to follow the steps in order, resulting in an unsuccessful assembly. Evidently, the sequence of steps in completing a task is crucial. If you have sequential consistency with the instructional video, you can complete the task successfully. Based on this, we have explored video sequence verification (SV) [1] task.

The SV task aims to determine whether the procedures within two videos are consistent at the step level. The previous works [1, 2] only considered one modality, neglecting that sequential videos are generally accompanied by audio or textual explanations. Dong et al. [3] proposed a multimodal approach to enhance the quality of the generated representations, thereby improving the performance on the SV task.

© The Author(s), under exclusive license to Springer Nature Singapore Pte Ltd. 2025
H. Lu (Ed.): ISAIR 2024, CCIS 2402, pp. 207–219, 2025.
https://doi.org/10.1007/978-981-96-2911-4_20

A sequential video is composed of multiple frames accompanying with the textual narration which is composed of multiple sentences, some frames have low relevance to the narrative paragraph, and some sentences have low relevance to the video. However, the vast majority of existing studies primarily concentrate on either coarse-grained contrast [4], fine-grained contrast [5, 6], or a combination of both [3, 7], proving to be ineffective at eliminating these low relevance frames and sentences. To this end, we propose a cross-grained contrastive learning loss on the SV task, which includes video-sentences and paragraph-frames contrastive learning. (see Fig. 1).

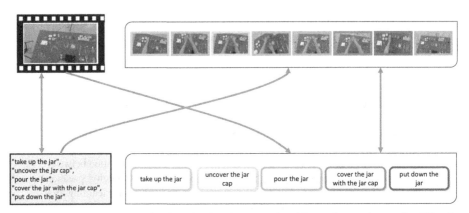

Fig. 1. Multi-grained contrastive learning loss between the video and narration on the SV task, including coarse-grained (video-paragraph), cross-grained (video-sentences, paragraph-frames) and fine-grained (frames-sentences).

In this paper, we propose a Teacher Multimodal Transformer (TMT) network and a pseudo-label generation algorithm to lead the vision transformer (ViT) network to generate high-quality representations. These two networks are intentionally built with complementary designs: TMT is designed to process and integrate visual and textual information simultaneously. It can effectively combine information from different modalities, and can better grasp contextual meanings. In contrast, the ViT network processes visual and textual modalities separately. It has a strong feature extraction ability and can capture subtle features. The outputs of the two networks serve as two distinct perspectives on the SV task, and their consensus is utilized to generate more plausible pseudo labels.

Our contributions can be summarized as follows:

- We propose a TMT network for the SV task. The ability of TMT to handle and integrate different modalities of data can be combined with the strong visual processing capabilities of the ViT. This combination can improve the generalization ability of the model.
- Based on this framework, we devise a pseudo-label generation algorithm to generate more plausible pseudo labels which help improve the performance of our framework on the SV task.
- We introduce cross-grained contrastive learning loss to capture the correlation between the coarse-grained feature and fine-grained feature on the SV task.

The rest of the paper is organized as follows. Some related works are given in Sect. 2. The proposed TMT architecture and multi-grained contrastive learning loss are detailed in Sect. 3. Experimental results and analysis are presented in Sect. 4. Finally, conclusion remarks are given in Sect. 5

2 Related Works

Sequential videos contain a wealth of "how-to" knowledge, allowing viewers to easily learn how to accomplish the task. Thus, many video datasets (e.g. CSV [1], Diving [8], EPIC-KITCHENS [9], COIN [10], HowTo100M [11]) related to sequential videos have proposed for researching, which are beneficial for the whole community. Different types of studies [12, 13] related to sequential videos have been proposed. Recently, Xu et al. [14] introduced the task of procedure-aware action quality assessment, aimed at evaluating diving sports videos by comparing them to a standard example video. Furthermore, the SV task was proposed by Qian et al. [1], which focuses on determining if two sequential videos follow the same sequence of steps. And they introduced the CosAlignment Transformer (CAT) and the sequence alignment loss to solve the task. In this field, Dong et al. [3] proposed a weakly supervised multimodal method to improve the quality of the representations, which uses the unaligned text and video frames, outperforms most of the other baselines. He et al. [2] proposed a weakly supervised collaborative procedure alignment (CPA) framework to achieve procedure-aware correlation learning for instructional videos.

The emergence and application of contrastive learning algorithms [15, 16], have markedly enhanced the quality of the generated representations [17]. CLIP [18] aims to train a model that understands the relationships between images and corresponding textual descriptions through large-scale multimodal contrastive learning. METIMT [19] utilized intra-modal which contains image-image and text-text contrastive learning and inter-modal which contains text-image contrastive learning to alleviate the modality gap for the text-image machine translation task. X-CLIP [20] introduced a method for video-text retrieval task based on contrastive learning that focuses on aligning semantics at multiple levels of granularity. Multimodal contrastive learning has significantly advanced multimodal tasks, but the exploration of cross-grained comparison remains limited in existing studies.

The idea of co-training and training two networks [21] to mutually enhance each other's performance has been explored in previous studies. Blum et al. [22] firstly proposed the concept of co-training. Han et al. [23] proposed TAN, eliminating the noisy labels for the networks so as to train the networks on the cleaner labels.

3 Proposal Method

3.1 Problem Statement

For a raw untrimmed sequential video, we divide the original video into N clips. From each clip, a single frame is randomly selected to create a sequence of N frames, denoted as $V = \{F_1, F_2, \ldots, F_N\}$. The corresponding procedural narration is represented as

$N = \{N_1, N_2, \ldots, N_T\}$, where N_i is a sentence of the narration. We need to note that the sentences and the frames do not have the timestamp-level or step-level annotations, they are only ordered by time separately. Following the SV task [1], our goal is to train an SV network, which can give embedding distance between each video pair and determine whether they are positive pair or negative pair. Therefore, in the training phase, the input paired sample can be represented as $\{X_1; X_2\}$, where $X = \{V, N\}$. In the testing phase, the input paired sample can be represented as $\{V_1; V_2\}$. The SV task can be formulated as $\mathcal{M}_\theta(V_1; V_2) \rightarrow \mathcal{D}$, where $\mathcal{D}$ is the distance between the two videos and θ is the parameters of our model. The overview of our framework is shown in Fig. 2.

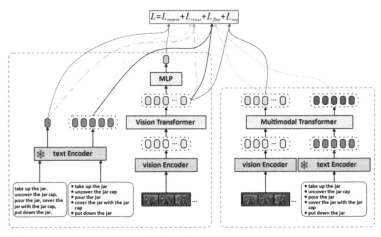

Fig. 2. The overview of our framework. Right: The TMT network. Left: The ViT network. Up: The loss module. The vision encoder takes the frames sampled from the untrimmed video as input. The text encoder takes the paragraph and the sentences as input, and outputs paragraph representation and sentence representations, separately. We get frame representations and video representation from ViT network. And We only get the frame representations from TMT network. At last, we feed the representations into the loss module.

3.2 Teacher Multimodal Transformer

Text and Vision Backbone. We leverage the pre-trained CLIP text encoder [18] to output the sentence-level feature $S = \{s_1, s_2, \ldots, s_T\} = \mathcal{F}_t(\{N_1, N_2, \ldots, N_T\}) \in \mathbb{R}^{T \times d}$. At the same time, we feed the paragraph p, which is obtained by simply concatenating the sequential sentences $\{N_1, N_2, \ldots, N_T\}$, into the text encoder to output the paragraph-level feature $P = \mathcal{F}_t(p) \in \mathbb{R}^d$. We leverage the pre-trained CLIP vision encoder [18] to output the frame-level feature $F = \{f_1, f_2, \ldots, f_N\} = \mathcal{F}_v(\{F_1, F_2, \ldots, F_N\}) \in \mathbb{R}^{N \times d}$. d denotes the dimension of the feature.

Multimodal Transformer. This module employs a multi-layer Transformer Encoder to process the visual and textual features (F, S) jointly. This module effectively builds the connection between text and video, as Eq. 1 shown:

$$\left[\widehat{F}; \widehat{S}\right] = \Phi_{MT}\left(\left[F + E_{pos}; S\right]\right) \tag{1}$$

where [.; .] denotes concatenation, Φ_{MT} represents Multimodal Transformer Encoder, E_{pos} refers to the temporal position embedding, $\widehat{F} = \left\{\widehat{f}_1, \widehat{f}_2, ..., \widehat{f}_N\right\} \in \mathbb{R}^{N \times d}$ and $\widehat{S} = \left\{\widehat{s}_1, \widehat{s}_2, ..., \widehat{s}_T\right\} \in \mathbb{R}^{T \times d}$. The similarity matrix $\widehat{M} \in \mathbb{R}^{N \times T}$ between the frame representations $\widehat{F}$ and the corresponding sentence representations $\widehat{S}$ is computed via Eq. 2:

$$\widehat{M}_{[i,j]} = \frac{\widehat{f}_i \cdot \widehat{s}_j}{\|\widehat{f}_i\| \|\widehat{s}_j\|} \tag{2}$$

Then, following WeakSVR [3], we use $Gumbel - Softmax$ [24] to get the first prediction between sentences and frames via Eq. 3:

$$\widehat{M}_{pred} = Gumbel - Softmax\left(\widehat{M}\right) \tag{3}$$

3.3 Co-training

Vision Transformer. As shown in Fig. 2, we leverage the same structure as WeakSVR[3] to obtain frame-level representation $\widehat{F}'$. As Eq. 4 shows:

$$\widehat{F}' = \Phi_{ViT}\left(F + E_{pos}\right) = \left\{\widehat{f}_1', \widehat{f}_2', ..., \widehat{f}_N'\right\} \in \mathbb{R}^{N \times d} \tag{4}$$

$$O = MLP\left(\widehat{F}'\right) \in \mathbb{R}^d \tag{5}$$

where E_{pos} refers to the temporal position embedding, and then we feed the feature $\widehat{F}'$ into the MLP module to obtain the video-level representation O by Eq. 5. The similarity matrix $\widehat{M}' \in \mathbb{R}^{N \times T}$ between the frame representations $\widehat{F}'$ and the corresponding sentence representations S is computed via Eq. 2 and the prediction $\widehat{M}'_{pred}$ can be computed by Eq. 3.

Pseudo-label Generation Algorithm. We obtain two fine-grained prediction similarity matrices $\widehat{M}_{pred}$ and $\widehat{M}'_{pred}$ from TMT and ViT, respectively. Following WeakSVR [3], we get the maximum index through argmax and sort the maximum-index list to an increasing order to generate pseudo labels. As Eq. 6 shows:

$$\widehat{M}_{pseudo} = sort\left[argmax_{k \in [1,T]}\left(\widehat{M}_{pred}\right)\right] \tag{6}$$

We can obtain $\widehat{M}'_{pseudo}$ too. We use the two pseudo-label matrices $\widehat{M}_{pseudo}, \widehat{M}'_{pseudo}$ to generate the more plausible ground truth. For the k-th frame, if the selected sentence is same in two matrices, we consider it to be the ground truth. If the selected sentence is different between two matrices, we randomly generate the corresponding sentence between the two selected sentences for the frame separately, then we sort the index list to an increasing order to generate the two pseudo ground truth matrices M_{pgt} and M'_{pgt} (see Fig. 3).

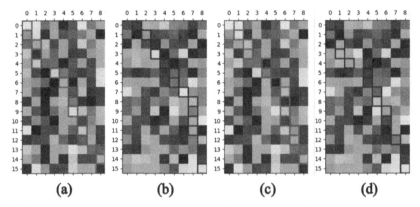

Fig. 3. Pseudo-label generation algorithm visualization. (a): A simulation of a pseudo-label matrix generated by ViT network. (b): A simulation of a pseudo-label matrix generated by TMT network. (c): The final pseudo ground truth matrix for ViT network. (d): The final pseudo ground truth matrix for TMT network.

Sequence Alignment Loss. For video1, we get $\widehat{F}'_{v1}$ from ViT and $\widehat{F}_{v1}$ from TMT. For video2, we can get $\widehat{F}'_{v2}$ and $\widehat{F}_{v2}$. The similarity matrix $C \in \mathbb{R}^{N \times N}$ between the two videos is computed via Eq. 2. Firstly, we apply the Softmax function across each row of the similarity matrix C, generating a matrix called C_r, across each column of C generating C_c. Then we take the average of C_r and C_c, naming the resulting matrix C_{avg}. Ideally, the diagonal entries of C_{avg} should approach 1, indicating high similarity, while the off-diagonal entries should be near 0, showing low similarity. We define our proposed sequence alignment loss like Eq. 7:

$$L_s^{v_1 v_2} = \| 1_N - f\left(C_{avg}^{v_1 v_2}\right) \| \tag{7}$$

where 1_N represents an N-dimensional vector filled with ones, and f is the function to extract the diagonal entries of a matrix. We can obtain four sequence alignment loss $L_s^{v_1^{ViT} v_2^{ViT}}, L_s^{v_1^{TMT} v_2^{TMT}}, L_s^{v_1^{ViT} v_2^{TMT}}, L_s^{v_1^{TMT} v_2^{ViT}}$. The finally sequence alignment loss can be defined as:

$$L_{seq} = \frac{L_s^{v_1^{ViT} v_2^{ViT}} + L_s^{v_1^{TMT} v_2^{TMT}} + L_s^{v_1^{ViT} v_2^{TMT}} + L_s^{v_1^{TMT} v_2^{ViT}}}{4} \tag{8}$$

3.4 Multi-grained Contrastive Learning

Video-Paragraph Loss. We obtain P from Sect. 3.2. And O from Sect. 3.3. Then, for a batch of BS data, we adopt the symmetric InfoNCE loss [25] to optimize our model:

$$L_{infoNCE}(V, P) = -\frac{1}{BS} \sum_{i=1}^{BS} log \frac{exp(s(O_i, P_i)/\tau)}{\sum_{j=1}^{BS} exp\left(s(O_j, P_j)/\tau\right)} \tag{9}$$

where τ is the temperature parameter [18], and $s(.,.)$ represents the cosine similarity. We adopt the symmetric InfoNCE loss, so the loss between video and paragraph can be formulated as:

$$L_{coarse} = L_{\text{InfoNCE}}(V, P) + L_{\text{InfoNCE}}(P, V) \tag{10}$$

Paragraph-Frame Loss and Video-Sentence Loss. The paragraph-level representation vector P is given in Sect. 3.2, and the frame-level representation vector $\widehat{F}'$ is given in Sect. 3.3. We calculate the cosine similarity $s_{P-F} \in \mathbb{R}^{N \times 1}$ between the paragraph representation and each frame representation. We consider the different similarity of the paragraph with each frame, firstly we use Softmax to obtain the original weights for the similarity vector, then we feed the vector to a linear layer to obtain the final similarity vector, which can be formulated as follow:

$$S_{PF} = Linear(Softmax(s_{P-F}))s_{P-F} \tag{11}$$

Similar to paragraph-frame loss, we can obtain the video-sentence similarity vector S_{VS} by Eq. 11. So, the cross-grained similarity scores can be represented as follow:

$$s(v_i, t_j) = \frac{S_{PF} + S_{VS}}{2} \tag{12}$$

Then, the loss L_{cross} can be computed by Eq. 10:

Frame-Sentence Loss. We symmetrically calculate the frame-sentence contrastive learning loss as follow, and the final fine-grained contrastive loss is shown in Eq. 15:

$$L_{TMT} = CE\left(\widehat{M}_{pred}(F, S), M_{pgt}(F, S)\right) + CE\left(\widehat{M}_{pred}(S, F), M_{pgt}(S, F)\right) \tag{13}$$

$$L_{ViT} = CE\left(\widehat{M}_{pred}'(F, S), M_{pgt}'(F, S)\right) + CE\left(\widehat{M}_{pred}'(S, F), M_{pgt}'(S, F)\right) \tag{14}$$

$$L_{fine} = L_{TMT} + L_{ViT} \tag{15}$$

3.5 Training and Inference

During training, our objective function can be formulated as:

$$L = L_{seq} + L_{coarse} + \lambda_1 L_{cross} + \lambda_2 L_{fine} \tag{16}$$

where λ_1, λ_2 are the hyperparameters, and we set $\lambda_1 = 1$, $\lambda_2 = 1$ in our experiments.

During inference, we use the normalized Euclidean distance between representations of the paired videos to distinguish positive pairs from negative pairs:

$$d = g(v_1, v_2) \tag{17}$$

$$y = \begin{cases} 0, d > threshold \\ 1, d \leq threshold \end{cases} \tag{18}$$

where $g(.,.)$ represents $l2$-normalization Euclidean distance function.

4 Experiments

4.1 Experimental Details

Datasets. We evaluate our model on the datasets CSV [1], Diving-SV [8] and COIN-SV [10]. CSV contains 1941 chemical experiment videos to complete 14 tasks. Diving48-SV contains 16997 diving competition videos and includes 48 procedures. COIN-SV contains 2114 comprehensive sequential videos, with highly complex backgrounds.

Implementation Details. Our visual backbone is the pre-trained CLIP [18] vision encoder based on ViT-B [26] and not frozen. Our language backbone is the pre-trained CLIP [18] text encoder and frozen. The different layers of our model are initialized by Kaiming and Xavier uniform initialization [27, 28]. We train our model on two RTX 3090TI GPUs with AdamW optimizer [29] with cosine annealing learning rate scheduler [30] with an initial learning rate of $5e - 4$, and weight decay 0.01. We set batch size, the video representations dimension, paragraph representations dimension and sampled frames number to 8, 512, 512, 16 for all three datasets. We use PyTorch [30] for all our experiments.

Evaluation Metrics. In all our experiments, we utilize the Area Under ROC Curve (AUC) as the metric for model evaluation. A higher AUC represents better performance.

4.2 Experimental Results

We compare our proposed model against some baselines on CSV, Diving-SV, COIN-SV. Our model achieves the state-of-the-art result under the weakly supervised setting on all three datasets. Under supervised setting, we incorporate the classification layer on the top of the video representation, in order to maintain a fair comparison with WeakSVR [3]. The performance comparisons are shown in Table 1 and Table 2.

Table 1. Results of our method and compared approaches on CSV, Diving-SV, and COIN-SV datasets under weakly supervised setting.

Method	Text Encoder	Weakly Supervised (w/o CLS)		
		CSV	Diving-SV	COIN-SV
MIL-NCE [13]	MLP	53.02	58.49	47.95
CAT [1]	CLIP [18]	70.63	77.87	47.70
VideoSwin [33] + MLP	CLIP [18]	62.48	60.88	54.73
CLIP [18] + TE [26] + Pool	CLIP [18]	58.67	72.13	49.79
CLIP [18] + TE [26] + MLP	CLIP [18]	74.82	81.47	50.13
WeakSVR [3]	CLIP [18]	79.80	85.19	52.56
Ours	CLIP [18]	**82.03**	**86.75**	**55.16**

Table 2. Results of our method and compared approaches on CSV, Diving-SV, and COIN-SV datasets under supervised setting.

Method	Pre-train	Supervised (w CLS)		
		CSV	Diving-SV	COIN-SV
MIL-NCE [13]	HowTo100M 11]	56.16	63.43	47.80
Swin [32]	K-400 [35]	54.06	73.10	43.70
TRN [33]	K-400 [35]	80.32	80.69	57.19
CAT [1]	K-400 [35]	83.02	83.11	51.13
CLIP [18] + TE [26] + MLP	CLIP [18]	79.38	83.48	48.50
WeakSVR [3]	CLIP [18]	86.92	86.09	59.57
CPA [2] + R50	K-400 [35]	88.14	84.29	57.57
CPA [2] + X3D	K-400 [35]	86.06	**88.11**	57.55
Ours	CLIP [18]	**88.82**	86.91	**60.79**

4.3   Further Analysis

Ablations on Main Components. We conduct an ablation analysis of the proposed TMT and cross-grained contrastive learning loss. Table 3 and Table 4 show that WeakSVR performs inferiorly on all datasets compared to our proposed approach under two settings. Under weakly supervised setting, removing the TMT or L_{cross} leads to a decrease in performance, highlighting the importance of main components in the model. Under supervised setting, the performance of our method is the same as under weakly supervised setting on CSV and COIN-SV datasets. However, on dataset Diving-SV, due to the tasks having overly similar backgrounds, L_{cross} leads to a decrease in the overall performance of our method.

Table 3. Ablation studies of our proposed TMT and cross-grained contrastive learning loss. To verify the effectiveness of *TMT* and L_{cross} separately, we conduct experiments on CSV, Diving-DV and COIN-SV under weakly supervised setting.

Method	TMT	L_{cross}	CSV	Diving-SV	COIN-SV
WeakSVR [3] (w/o CLS)	×	×	79.80	85.19	52.56
Ours (w/o CLS)	✓	×	81.91	86.29	54.82
Ours (w/o CLS)	×	✓	81.56	85.39	54.21
Ours (w/o CLS)	✓	✓	**82.03**	**86.75**	**55.16**

Table 4. Ablation studies of our proposed TMT and cross-grained contrastive learning loss. To verify the effectiveness of TMT and L_{cross} separately, we conduct experiments on CSV, Diving-DV and COIN-SV under the supervised setting.

Method	TMT	L_{cross}	CSV	Diving-SV	COIN-SV
WeakSVR [3] (w CLS)	×	×	86.92	86.09	59.57
Ours (w CLS)	✓	×	88.10	**86.96**	60.49
Ours (w CLS)	×	✓	87.28	86.30	59.71
Ours (w CLS)	✓	✓	**88.82**	86.91	**60.79**

Ablations on Paragraph-frames and Video-sentences Contrastive Loss. As shown in Table 5, our method obtains the best performance. The results indicate that paragraph-frames and video-sentences contrastive losses improve performance under weakly supervised setting on all three datasets. However, on Diving-SV, L_{vs} is more effective than L_{pf}.

Table 5. Ablation studies of our proposed paragraph-frames and video-sentences contrastive loss. To verify the effectiveness of L_{pf} and L_{vs} separately, we conduct experiments on CSV, Diving-DV and COIN-SV under no TMT setting.

Method	L_{pf}	L_{vs}	CSV	Diving-SV	COIN-SV
WeakSVR [3] (w/o CLS)	×	×	79.80	85.19	52.56
Ours (w/o CLS)	✓	×	79.32	85.90	51.57
Ours (w/o CLS)	×	✓	80.85	**86.19**	54.07
Ours (w/o CLS)	✓	✓	**81.56**	85.39	**54.21**

Ablation on Pseudo-label Generation Algorithm. We conduct ablation studies on all three datasets to investigate the effects of our proposed pseudo-label generation algorithm. As Table 6 shows, our proposed algorithm is crucial. It outperforms the situation without the algorithm by 1.99%, 0.01%, 2.89% on CSV, Diving-SV and COIN-SV.

Table 6. Ablation studies of our proposed pseudo-label generation algorithm (PGA). We conduct experiments on CSV, Diving-DV and COIN-SV under no L_{cross} setting.

Method	PGA	CSV	Diving-SV	COIN-SV
WeakSVR [3] (w/o CLS)	×	79.80	85.19	52.56
Ours (w/o CLS)	×	79.92	86.28	51.93
Ours (w/o CLS)	✓	**81.91**	**86.29**	**54.82**

5 Conclusions

In this paper, we studied the SV task. And our research contributes significantly to the field by proposing a TMT network, a pseudo-label generation algorithm and the cross-grained contrastive learning loss. Our method not only adapts to the complex variations of video sequences but also exhibits a strong understanding of the intricate relationship between visual content and its textual descriptions. The integration of the TMT network and the cross-grained contrastive learning strategy has shown a synergistic effect, leading to a robust model that generalizes well across different datasets and scenarios. The pseudo-labeling technique contributes to this by providing a reliable way to utilize unlabeled data, which is particularly valuable in real-world applications where annotated data may be scarce or expensive to obtain. Our method provides a comprehensive understanding of the content and the sequence of steps in a sequential video, which is crucial for tasks such as instructional video analysis and procedure verification. In the future, we will explore more effective methods to learn the video representation for sequential videos.

References

1. Qian, Y., Luo, W., Lian, D., Tang, X., Zhao, P., Gao, S.: Svip: sequence verification for procedures in videos. In: Proceedings of the IEEE/CVF Conference on Computer Vision and Pattern Recognition, pp. 19890–19902 (2022)
2. He, T., et al.: Collaborative weakly supervised video correlation learning for procedure-aware instructional video analysis. In: Proceedings of the AAAI Conference on Artificial Intelligence, vol. 38(3), 2112–2120 (2024)
3. Dong, S., Hu, H., Lian, D., Luo, W., Qian, Y., Gao, S.: Weakly supervised video representation learning with unaligned text for sequential videos. In: Proceedings of the IEEE/CVF Conference on Computer Vision and Pattern Recognition, pp. 2437–2447 (2023)
4. Luo, H., et al.: Clip4clip: an empirical study of clip for end to end video clip retrieval and captioning. Neurocomputing **508**, 293–304 (2022)
5. Lee, K.H., Chen, X., Hua, G., Hu, H., He, X.: Stacked cross attention for image-text matching. In: Proceedings of the European conference on computer vision (ECCV), pp. 201–216 (2018)
6. Yao, L., et al.: Filip: fine-grained interactive language-image pre-training. In: International Conference on Learning Representations (2021)
7. Yang, J., Bisk, Y., Gao, J.: Taco: token-aware cascade contrastive learning for video-text alignment. In: Proceedings of the IEEE/CVF International Conference on Computer Vision, pp. 11562–11572 (2021)
8. Li, Y., Li, Y., Vasconcelos, N.: Resound: towards action recognition without representation bias. In: Proceedings of the European Conference on Computer Vision (ECCV), pp. 513–528 (2018)
9. Damen, D., et al.: Scaling egocentric vision: the epic-kitchens dataset. In: Proceedings of the European conference on computer vision (ECCV), pp. 720–736 (2018)
10. Tang, Y., et al.: Coin: a large-scale dataset for comprehensive instructional video analysis. In: Proceedings of the IEEE/CVF Conference on Computer Vision and Pattern Recognition, pp. 1207–1216 (2019)
11. Miech, A., Zhukov, D., Alayrac, J.B., Tapaswi, M., Laptev, I., Sivic, J.: Howto100m: learning a text-video embedding by watching hundred million narrated video clips. In: Proceedings of the IEEE/CVF international conference on computer vision, pp. 2630–2640 (2019)

12. Lin, X., Petroni, F., Bertasius, G., Rohrbach, M., Chang, S.F., Torresani, L.: Learning to recognize procedural activities with distant supervision. In: Proceedings of the IEEE/CVF Conference on Computer Vision and Pattern Recognition, pp. 13853–13863 (2022)

13. Miech, A., Alayrac, J.B., Smaira, L., Laptev, I., Sivic, J., Zisserman, A.: End-to-end learning of visual representations from uncurated instructional videos. In: Proceedings of the IEEE/CVF Conference on Computer Vision and Pattern Recognition, pp. 9879–9889 (2020)

14. Xu, J., Rao, Y., Yu, X., Chen, G., Zhou, J., Lu, J.: Finediving: a fine-grained dataset for procedure-aware action quality assessment. In: Proceedings of the IEEE/CVF conference on computer vision and pattern recognition, pp. 2949–2958 (2022)

15. Grill, J.B., et al.: Bootstrap your own latent-a new approach to self-supervised learning. Adv. Neural. Inf. Process. Syst. **33**, 21271–21284 (2020)

16. He, K., Fan, H., Wu, Y., Xie, S., Girshick, R.: Momentum contrast for unsupervised visual representation learning. In: Proceedings of the IEEE/CVF conference on computer vision and pattern recognition, pp. 9729–9738 (2020)

17. Lu, H., Teng, Y., Li, Y.: Learning latent dynamics for autonomous shape control of deformable object. IEEE Trans. Intell. Transp. Syst. **24**(11), 13133–13140 (2023)

18. Radford, A., et al.: Learning transferable visual models from natural language supervision. In: International Conference on Machine Learning, pp. 8748–8763. PMLR (2021)

19. Ma, C., et al.: Modal contrastive learning based end-to-end text image machine translation. IEEE/ACM Trans. Audio Speech Lang. Process. (2023)

20. Ma, Y., Xu, G., Sun, X., Yan, M., Zhang, J., Ji, R.: X-clip: end-to-end multi-grained contrastive learning for video-text retrieval. In: Proceedings of the 30th ACM International Conference on Multimedia, pp. 638–647 (2022)

21. Ma, C., et al.: Visual information processing for deep-sea visual monitoring system. Cognitive Robot. **1**, 3–11 (2021)

22. Blum, A., Mitchell, T., "Combining labeled and unlabeled data with co-training. In: Proceedings of the Eleventh Annual Conference on Computational Learning theory, pp. 92–100 (1998)

23. Han, T., Xie, W., Zisserman, A.: Temporal alignment networks for long-term video. In: Proceedings of the IEEE/CVF Conference on Computer Vision and Pattern Recognition, pp. 2906–2916 (2022)

24. Jang, E., Gu, S., Poole, B.: Categorical reparameterization with gumbel-softmax. In: ICLR (2017)

25. Oord, A.v.d., Li, Y., Vinyals, O.: Representation learning with contrastive predictive coding. arXiv preprint arXiv:1807.03748 (2018)

26. Dosovitskiy, A., et al.: An image is worth 16x16 words: Transformers for image recognition at scale. In: ICLR (2021)

27. He, K., Chen, X., Xie, S., Li, Y., Dollár, P., Girshick, R.: Masked autoencoders are scalable vision learners. In: Proceedings of the IEEE/CVF Conference on Computer Vision and Pattern Recognition, pp. 16000–16009 (2022)

28. He, K., Zhang, X., Ren, S., Sun, J.: Delving deep into rectifiers: surpassing human-level performance on imagenet classification. In: Proceedings of the IEEE International Conference on Computer Vision, pp. 1026–1034 (2015)

29. You, Y., Liet al.: Large batch optimization for deep learning: Training bert in 76 minutes. In: ICLR (2020)

30. Loshchilov, I., Hutter, F.: SGDR: Stochastic gradient descent with warm restarts. In: ICLR (2017)

31. Paszke, A., et al.: Pytorch: an imperative style, high-performance deep learning library. Advances in Neural Inform. Process. Syst. **32** (2019)

32. Liu, Z., et al.: Swin transformer: hierarchical vision transformer using shifted windows. In: Proceedings of the IEEE/CVF International Conference on Computer Vision, pp. 10012–10022 (2021)
33. Liu, Z., et al.: Video swin transformer. In: Proceedings of the IEEE/CVF Conference on Computer Vision and Pattern Recognition, pp. 3202–3211 (2022)
34. Zhou, B., Andonian, A., Oliva, A., Torralba, A.: Temporal relational reasoning in videos. In: Proceedings of the European conference on computer vision (ECCV), pp. 803–818 (2018)
35. Carreira, J., Zisserman, A.: Quo vadis, action recognition? a new model and the kinetics dataset. In: Proceedings of the IEEE Conference on Computer Vision and Pattern Recognition, pp. 6299–6308 (2017)

A Violent Language Detection Model Based on Short Text

Dongfang Li[1], Li Tan[1(⊠)], Boya Zou[1], and He Liu[2]

[1] School of Computer Science and Engineering, Beijing Technology and Business University,
Beijing 100048, China
tanli@btbu.edu.cn
[2] Chongqing Academy of Educational Science, Chongqing, China

Abstract. In recent years, with the proliferation of Internet platforms, each striving to enhance user engagement, corresponding social channels have been established to facilitate user expression of personal opinions and viewpoints. However, this openness has also provided a platform for some individuals to flout platform regulations and disseminate toxic content laden with violent tendencies. Such behavior undermines the stability of these platforms, jeopardizes national unity, and poses risks to societal cohesion and individual well-being. Recognizing and addressing the toxicity of online speech is paramount for enhancing user experience, fostering a healthier online environment, and advancing societal development. This paper introduces BLAM, an online speech toxicity detection model built upon deep learning principles. Leveraging TEDA training data on toxic speech instances, we propose a deep neural network model, BLAM, integrating bidirectional long short-term memory networks, self-attention mechanisms, and global maximum pooling layers. Our approach demonstrates an 8% improvement over traditional methods in accurately identifying toxic speech.

Keywords: Deep learning · cyber violence speech · NLP · self attention

1 Introduction

With the advancement of society, people's lives have significantly improved. The rise of the Internet has not only met people's needs but also provided numerous platforms for daily life [1], social interaction, and entertainment. To enhance user engagement and foster closer interaction between applications and users, these platforms have incorporated comment and communication features [2]. Consequently, every netizen can express their opinions freely, essentially making everyone a media outlet. Individual voices can reach wide audiences through Internet platforms, ensuring that no one's voice goes unheard [3].

However, within the realm of transparency, convenience, and freedom of expression on Internet platforms, some users have abused this privilege by making inappropriate, violent, harassing, discriminatory, and toxic remarks. Such behavior not only impedes social development but also threatens national security, unity, and societal stability. Studies have revealed alarming statistics, with half of minors encountering toxic comments and a significant portion of Internet users experiencing verbal abuse, insults, threats, and stalking. Toxic speech has become an escalating societal issue exacerbated by the expanding reach of the Internet[4].

Consequently, the identification and detection of toxic speech play crucial roles in maintaining social harmony, fostering a positive online environment, ensuring a pleasant user experience, and safeguarding the well-being of individuals[5]. However, manual detection alone is insufficient to effectively combat toxic speech in the absence of robust management measures. Hence, there's an urgent need to explore online speech toxicity detection using deep learning methodologies.

Researchers such as Betty [6] van Aken and Julian Risch have compared various deep learning and shallow methods on large datasets, proposing ensemble learning to optimize classifier combinations. Additionally, Ghosh et al. [7, 8] analyzed conversational context for irony detection, while Badjatiya et al. focused on uncivilized language detection. Furthermore, L et al. established a parallel convolutional neural network model for feature extraction. Inspired by AlphaGo's design, Nie introduced policy and valuation networks for text classification and bad word detection [9].

This paper contributes to the field by proposing BLAM, a deep neural network model trained on TEDA toxic scene data. BLAM integrates bidirectional long short-term memory networks, self-attention mechanisms, and global maximum pooling layers, exhibiting strong performance in identifying violent short texts. It is well-suited for social platforms such as Weibo, Douyin, and Bilibili, offering promising potential for mitigating toxic speech online.

2 Model

2.1 Long Short-Term Memory Network

Recurrent neural network (RNN) In order to effectively solve the problem of gradient explosion or disappearance, a long short-term memory network (LSTM) is constructed by introducing a gating mechanism [10, 13]. LSTM network can be regarded as a special case of RNN, only the main part of data is passed to the next layer instead of the whole data. The main improvements are in the following two aspects: new internal state: $h_t \in R^D$ circular information storage, hidden layer $h_t \in R^D$.

C_t calculated according to the following formula:

$$C_t = f_t \cdot C_{t-1} + i_t \cdot C_t \tag{1}$$

$$h_t = o_t \odot \tanh(C_t) \tag{2}$$

The LSTM consists of a forgetting door, an input door and an output door. The Forget gate f_t determines how much information is discarded in a $t - 1$ moment. Enter the gate i_t to determine how much information will be stored in the t slot. (3) The output gate O_t determines how much information needs to be given to h_t. The forgetting door, input door and output door are calculated as follows:

$$f_t = \sigma\left(W_{f_1} h_{t-1} + W_{f_2} X_t + b_f\right) \tag{3}$$

$$i_t = \sigma\left(W_{i_1} h_{t-1} + W_{f_2} X_t + b_i\right) \qquad (4)$$

$$o_t = \sigma\left(W_{o_1} h_{t-1} + W_{o_2} X_t + b_0\right) \qquad (5)$$

where $\sigma(\cdot)$ is the Logistic function whose output interval is (0,1), X_t is the input at the current time, and $h_t - 1$ is the external state at the previous time. The frame diagram of LSTM is shown in Fig. 1.

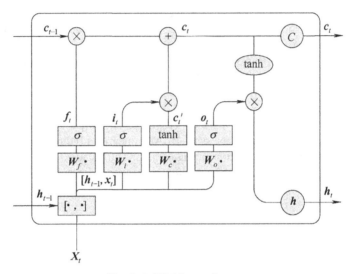

Fig. 1. LSTM frame diagram.

The cyclic unit structure of the LSTM network is shown in Fig. 1. The calculation process is as follows: (1) Firstly, using $h_t - 1$ and x_t, three gates are calculated according to formulas 1–3, and the candidate states c_t; (2) Update the memory unit c_t by combining the forgetting gate f_t and the input gate i_t; (3) Pass the memory unit c_t in combination with the output gate O_t to the external state h_t. LSTM overcomes the problem of gradients through a gating mechanism, for example, given sentences such as "I play cricket and I'm good at bowling," the word "bowling" depends on the word "cricket," which lags far behind the former. As the distance between the two subordinate words increases, the performance of the RNN usually decreases, and the gradient value also significantly disappears. Long-term short-term memory (LSTM) copes with this problem and performs well in cases of long-term dependence [12, 13].

2.2 Attention Mechanism

NLP attention mechanism, therefore, according to the requirements of the task distribution of vector in different weights, thus achieve the goal of information selection, use $X = [x_1, \cdots, x_N] \in R^{D \times N}$ said information matrix, including $x_n \in R^D$ for D dimensional vector, n ∈ [1, N] says a word vector in NLP. In the information matrix, the attention distribution is calculated on the word embedding matrix first, and then the weighted average of each word vector is calculated according to the attention distribution.

Attention distribution in NLP a_n In order to select the required information from the word vector matrix X, the query word vector q related to the target task is introduced and the correlation between each word vector and the query word vector is calculated through a scoring function s(x, q). The index position of the selected information is represented by the attention variable z ∈ [1, N], i.e. z = n indicates that the n word vector is selected. First calculate the probability of choosing the first i word vector αn given q and x.

$$a_n = \text{softmax}(s(x, q)) \tag{6}$$

Compared with the additive model, the dot product model can improve the computational efficiency by using matrix computation. However, when the D-dimension is too large, the variance of the computational model will be increased, and the gradient of attention distribution will be relatively small. The dot product of the matrix can solve the above problems, so we use dot product to scale the model. The formula of the dot product model is as follows (Fig. 2):

$$s(x, q) = xTq \tag{7}$$

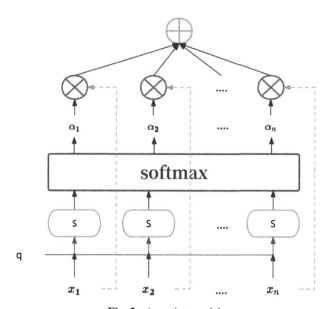

Fig. 2. Attention model.

2.3 TEDA Model

TEDA is a language pre-training model released by Google in 2018. It emphasizes that the traditional one-way language model or the shallow splicing method of two one-way language models is no longer used for pre-training, but the bidirectional Transformer structure is adopted, among which Transformer is originally developed by Jacob Devlin, Ming-Wei Chang, Kenton Lee, Kristina Toutanova [14] and others have proposed to provide a dense vector representation for natural language by using a deep neural network with Transformer architecture.

TEDA is a multi-task Model that utilizes the self-supervised nature of large-scale text data to construct the Next Sentence Prediction (NSP) and Masked Language Model(MLM) self-supervised tasks. The idea of MLM is to randomly [15] mask some words from the input corpus and then predict the word from the context. However, MLM is unable to understand the relationship between sentences. In order to obtain sentence-level representations and enable the model to judge whether sentence B is the context of sentence A, TEDA uses the NSP task for pre-training to generate deep bidirectional language representations that can integrate the left and right context information.

TEDA input content consists of word embeddings [16] composed of word vectors of text as shown in Fig. 3. The token CLS at the beginning is used to represent the vector of the entire text, the positional embeddings used to represent the position information of words, and the segmentation embeddings used to distinguish the text belonging to two sentences. These three embeddings combine to form TEDA input vector. The maximum length of joint eigenvectors accepted by TEDA is 512.

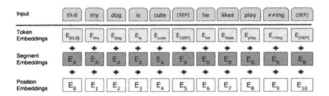

Fig. 3. TEDA input.

2.4 BLAM Model

In this paper, the multi-task toxic speech detection model BLAM constructed by TEDA is constructed by multi-task structure based on hierarchical sharing mechanism. The shared network layer is TEDA word embedding layer and bidirectional LSTM layer respectively, and the multi-task is identity recognition task and speech toxicity detection task respectively. In the task of speech toxicity detection, in order to improve the performance of speech toxicity recognition to some extent, self-attention mechanism and maximum pooling layer are added to the model to deal with this challenge. In the identification task, CRF is applied after bidirectional LSTM [17], and the model parameters are updated by backpropagation.

This paper uses two layers of Bi_LSTM as the shared layer of multi-task learning. On the one hand, Bi_LSTM is recognized in entity recognition performance; on the other hand, BI_LSTM is used to extract the semantic information features of speech, and can better extract the context information of words, so as to obtain the semantic meaning of speech and enhance the ability of the network. In a bidirectional LSTM, the direction of one LSTM is the positive sequence direction of the input sequence, and the other is the reverse sequence direction of the input sequence. When feature extraction is carried out for speech, LSTM in the two directions do not share the statev [18]. LSTM state in the positive sequence direction is transmitted only in the positive sequence direction, and LSTM state in the reverse sequence direction is transmitted only in the reverse direction, but it will be spliced at the same time afterwards as the output of the entire Bi_LSTM. Due to the capacity of information transmission and the disappearance of gradient, Bi LSTM layer, the upper layer of the model, can only establish short-distance dependency[19]. If long-distance dependency between input words is to be established, there are two ways to realize it. One is to establish deep network, but the computing cost will increase. However, the length of the speech text in this paper is uncertain, and the full connection layer cannot handle the variable length of the input sequence. In practical applications, the size of the connection weight is also different for different input lengths. In this case, the attention force mechanism can be used to "dynamically" generate the weights of different connections. Finally, the overall output of the model looks like this:

$$c_t = f_t \cdot c_{t-1} + i_t \cdot c_t \tag{8}$$

$$o_t = \sigma\left(W_{o1}c_{t-1} + W_{o2}f_t + X_t\right) \tag{9}$$

3 Experiment

3.1 Data Set

At the end of 2017, CivilComments shut down and opted to transfer its 2 million public comments from its platform to an enduring open archive5 so that researchers can understand and improve civility in online conversations for years to come. Jigsaw sponsored the work and expanded the human raters' data annotation of various toxic conversation attributes [20], where the text of each comment is in the comment_text column. Each piece of data in the Train(training set) carries a toxicity label (target). For evaluation purposes, a target value of target $>= 0.5$ would be considered violent speech (toxic). The data display is shown in Fig. 4.

The distribution of target predicted in this paper is shown in Fig. 5. This data also has several other subtype toxicity properties. The model does not need to predict these properties; they are used as additional avenues for research. In addition, subsets of comments [21] have been marked with various identity attributes that represent the identities mentioned in the text.

3.2 Optimizer Selection

The updating direction of Adam parameters can be used to calculate the exponential weighted average of gradient g_t according to formula 10, and the learning rate can be adaptively adjusted according to the exponential weighted average of gradient squared

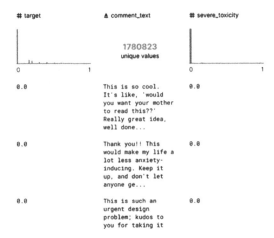

Fig. 4. Data set information.

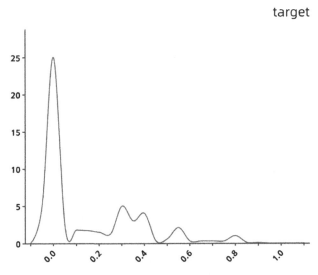

Fig. 5. Target value distribution.

g^2 calculated from 11. Adam adaptive momentum estimation algorithm can be regarded as a combination of momentum method and RMSprop algorithm, which not only uses momentum as the parameter updating direction, but also adaptively adjusts the learning rate. Adam algorithm computes the exponential weighted average of the gradient squared g^2 on one hand and the exponential weighted average of the gradient g on the other hand.

$$Mt = \beta 1 Mt - 1 + (1 - \beta 1)gt \qquad (10)$$

$$Gt = \beta 2 Gt - 1 + (1 - \beta 2)gt \odot gt \qquad (11)$$

where β_1 and β_2 are the decay rates of the two moving averages respectively. In this paper, $\beta_1 = 0.9$ and $\beta_2 = 0.99$ are set. The mean of the gradient is M_t and the variance of the gradient without subtracting the mean is G_t.

3.3 Experimental Result

There was serious imbalance in the data in this paper. In order to explore the performance ability of the model under different data distributions, the original data set, the data set with different weights for positive and negative samples, and the balanced data set after downsampling were used to conduct corresponding experiments respectively. The Batch size was 512 and the Epoch was 8 rounds. The changes of LOSS, AUC, and AUC during model training in each case are shown in Figs. 6 and 7.

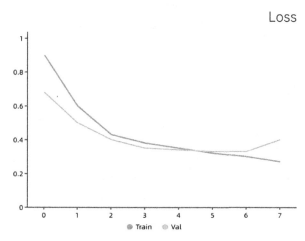

Fig. 6. Loss changes.

According to the above training results, compared with the weighted and sampled data, the initial loss value of the original data is small, but the convergence is slower. The Recall value of the model trained by the down-sampled data presents a linear increase, while the recall value of the original data and the weighted data is low, and the value fluctuates greatly. The AUC value of the data after downsampling performs better and has a good trend compared with the other two. The model trained with the data after downsampling is superior to the other two in all aspects. According to the above training results, it can be inferred that if the Epoch value is increased, the value of each index will be better.

According to Table 1, it can be seen that the BLAM model proposed in this paper has better performance than other models. Although the machine learning methods such as logistic regression (LR) and XGBoost have solid mathematical foundation and relatively simple algorithms, they cannot automatically extract text features and have certain limitations, so the experimental effect cannot reach the best. LSTM network has the memory ability to receive not only its own information, but also historical information, which

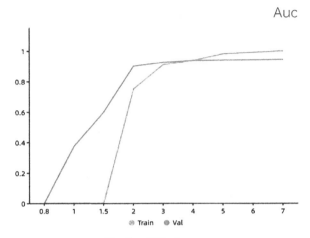

Fig. 7. AUC changes.

Table 1. Toxicity detection performance of different models.

Model	Accuracy	Precision	Recall	Auc	F1
LR	0.75	0.79	0.50	0.85	0.61
XGBoost	0.80	0.77	0.76	0.90	0.73
LSTM	0.81	0.86	0.78	0.92	0.83
OUR	0.89	0.90	0.88	0.98	0.89

has long-term dependence, so it is more suitable for short text tasks than convolutional networks. Although LSTM can establish long-distance dependence in theory, it can only establish short-distance dependence in practice due to the capacity of information transmission and the disappearance of gradient. In order to better establish long-distance dependence between input sequences and obtain long-distance information interaction, BLAM establishes long-distance dependence by adding self-attention mechanism. The self-attention mechanism calculates attention for every word and all words, so the maximum path length is only 1, capturing long distance dependencies, no matter how long distances are between them.

In summary, it can be seen that each layer of BLAM model has a certain positive effect on the detection of violent speech.

4   Conclusion

In recent years, with the opening of Internet platforms, each platform has opened corresponding social channels in order to improve its stickiness with users, and the majority of users can freely express their personal opinions and views. However, some users make use of the characteristics of the Internet platform, such as trans-time and transparency, to make violent remarks, which seriously endangers the network environment and social security. Based on this, this paper proposes a new attention-based BLAM model based on long short-term memory network combined with TEDA model, and proves the reliability of the model through experiments.

Acknowledgment. This work was supported by the Ministry of Education Humanities and Social Sciences Fund (23YJAZH129) and the Chongqing Education Science "14th Five-Year Plan" (K23YG6020127) .

References

1. Pose Estimation of Point Sets Using Residual MLP in Intelligent Transportation Infrastructure.IEEE Transactions on Intelligent Transportation Systems (2023)
2. Botella-Gil, B., Sepúlveda-Torres, R., Bonet-Jover, A., Martínez-Barco, P., Saquete, E.: Semiautomatic dataset annotation applied to automatic violent message detection. IEEE Access **12**, 19651–19664 (2024). https://doi.org/10.1109/ACCESS.2024.3361404
3. Wang, L., Islam, T.: Automatic detection of cyberbullying: racism and sexism on twitter. In: Jahankhani, H. (eds.) Cybersecurity in the Age of Smart Societies. Advanced Sciences and Technologies for Security Applications. Springer, Cham (2023)
4. Underwater Visibility Enhancement IoT System in Extreme Environment. IEEE Internet of Things Journal (2023)
5. Deep Fuzzy Hashing Network for Efficient Image Retrieval: IEEE Trans. Fuzzy Syst. (2020). https://doi.org/10.1109/TFUZZ.2020.2984991
6. Visual information processing for deep-sea visual monitoring system: Cognitive Robotics **1**, 3–11 (2021)
7. Learning Latent Dynamics for Autonomous Shape Control of Deformable Object. IEEE Transactions on Intelligent Transportation Systems (2022)
8. Brain-Inspired Perception Feature and Cognition Model Applied to Safety Patrol Robot. IEEE Transactions on Industrial Informatics (2023)
9. Li, J., Li, S., Cheng, L., et al.: BSAS: a blockchain-based trustworthy and privacy-preserving speed advisory system. IEEE Trans. Veh. Technol. **71**(11), 11421–11430 (2022)
10. Byon, H.D., Harris, C., Crandall, M., Song, J., Topaz, M.: Identifying Type II workplace violence from clinical notes using natural language processing. Workplace Health Safety. **71**(10), 484–490 (2023)
11. Yan, L., Chao, L., Zhongxiong, L., Wentao, L.: Aspect level sentiment analysis using fused multi attention neural networks. Comput. Eng. Design **44**(03), 894–900 (2023). https://doi.org/10.16208/j.issn1000-7024.2023.03.035
12. Aydin, C.R., Gungor, T.: Combination of recursive and recurrent neural networks for aspect-based sentiment analysis using inter-aspect relations. IEEE Access **8**, 77820–77832 (2020)
13. Li, Y., Yin, C., Zhong, S.-H.: Sentence constituent-aware aspect category sentiment analysis with graph attention networks. Nat. Lang. Process. Chin. Comput. **12430**, 815–827 (2020)
14. Sangeetha, K., Prabha, D.: Sentiment analysis of student feedback using multi-head attention fusion model of word and context embedding for LSTM. J. Ambient. Intell. Humaniz. Comput. **12**(6), 4117–4126 (2021)
15. Yin, D., Meng, T., Chang, K.W.: SentiBERT: a transferable transformer-based architecture for compositional sentiment semantics. In: Proceedings of the 58th Annual Meeting of the Association for Computational Linguistics, pp. 3695–3706. Association for Computational Linguistics, Stroudsburg, PA (2020)

16. Grover, A., Leskovec, J.: node2vec: scalable feature learning for networks. In: Proceedings of the 22nd ACM SIGKDD International Conference on Knowledge Discovery and Data Mining, pp. 855–864 (2016)

17. Schlichtkrull, M., Kipf, T.N., Bloem, P., et al.: Modeling relational data with graph convolutional networks. In: The Semantic Web: 15th International Conference, ESWC 2018, Heraklion, Crete, Greece, 3–7 June Proceedings 15, pp. 593–607. Springer International Publishing, (2018)

18. Chen, Y., Mishra, P., Franceschi, L., et al.: Refactor gnns: revisiting factorisation-based models from a message-passing perspective. Adv. Neural. Inf. Process. Syst. **35**, 16138–16150 (2022)

19. Zhao, T., Yang, C., Li, Y., et al.: Space4hgnn: a novel, modularized and reproducible platform to evaluate heterogeneous graph neural network. In: Proceedings of the 45th International ACM SIGIR Conference on Research and Development in Information Retrieval, pp. 2776–2789 (2022)

20. Ahn, H., Yang, Y., Gan, Q., et al.: Descent steps of a relation-aware energy produce heterogeneous graph neural networks. Adv. Neural. Inf. Process. Syst. **35**, 38436–38448 (2022)

21. Wang, X., Ji, H., Shi, C., et al.: Heterogeneous graph attention network. In: The World Wide Web Conference, pp. 2022–2032 (2019)

Underground Temperature Prediction Based on LSTM Neural Network and Embedded System Reasoning

Jie Li, Mei Wang[✉], ZhiBo Gong, and LiZhi Li

Xi'an University of Science and Technology, Xi'an 715100, Shaanxi, China
23208223079@stu.xust.edu.cn

Abstract. This study enhances underground mine temperature prediction using Long Short-Term Memory (LSTM) neural networks, achieving a 34% improvement over traditional methods. Extensive training with ample temperature datasets shows the LSTM model's robust real-world performance. To tackle underground environment challenges, an Embedded System RK3588 is introduced, optimizing and extending performance for scenarios with only temperature data. The integration of RK3588 with the LSTM model enables continuous, accurate, and robust temperature prediction, improving adaptability to complex conditions and supporting comprehensive safety assessments. This synergy enhances real-time inference, significantly advancing mine safety management by improving fire prediction and prevention.

Keywords: Underground Scene · LSTM Neural Networks · Temperature Prediction · Continuous Reasoning · Mine Safety Management

1 Introduction

Temperature anomalies in coal mines have significant implications for safety, economy, and worker welfare, causing a large proportion of accidents and economic losses. IoT technology enables extensive data collection from mining operations, highlighting the importance of analyzing this data for safety measures. Deep learning, particularly LSTM neural networks, enhances predictive capabilities for temperature anomaly detection. This study utilizes LSTM networks to improve prediction accuracy and enable real-time safety assessments by integrating temperature, humidity, and gas concentration data. Integration with the RK3588 system enhances adaptability to underground conditions, enabling real-time, accurate, and robust inference for mine safety management. The findings offer new insights and solutions for predicting temperature anomalies and enhancing safety management through continuous reasoning.

The paper is organized as follows. Section 2 covers the temperature prediction model. Section 3 focuses on model optimization. Section 4 discusses embedded systems inference. Finally, Section 5 contains the conclusion.

© The Author(s), under exclusive license to Springer Nature Singapore Pte Ltd. 2025
H. Lu (Ed.): ISAIR 2024, CCIS 2402, pp. 231–236, 2025.
https://doi.org/10.1007/978-981-96-2911-4_22

2 Temperature Prediction Model

Underground mining experiences fluctuating temperatures due to various factors like mining conditions, depth, wind speed, and CO concentration. These factors interact to create a complex temperature system, but limited sensor data impedes a thorough understanding. This study utilizes the LSTM algorithm with extensive time-series data to predict temperature trends accurately. The model enhances early warning and management of underground fires, promoting a safer working environment [1] (Fig. 1).

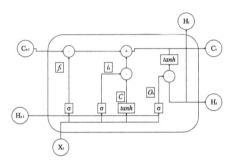

Fig. 1. Structure of LSTM cells

The study uses LSTM, an advanced RNN variant, to predict underground temperatures in three steps:

Step 1: Processing original data by filtering and de-noising temperature data;

Step 2: Employing an LSTM model to predict temperatures, with input in (X, Y) format;

Step 3: Fine-tuning parameters for accurate temperature trend forecasting and comprehensive predictions.

LSTM Fig. 2 framework diagram shows its unique recurrent neural network structure, providing an intuitive perspective for us to analyze its internal mechanism for processing sequence data [2].

The processed time series gas, temperature and wind speed data are sent to the LSTM network for training and prediction, and in the LSTM network node, the data are transmitted to the state node through the input gate, calculated by the Sigmoid function and the tanh function, and then the information to be discarded and retained by the forgetting gate and the memory gate is calculated according to Eqs. (1) and (2) respectively.

$$f_t = sigmoid\left(W_{xf}x_t + W_{hf}h_{t-1} + b_f\right) \tag{1}$$

$$i_t = sigmoid(W_{xi}x_t + W_{hi}h_{t-1} + b_i) \tag{2}$$

Temporary unit state Ct' calculates and stores the temporary state information of gas, temperature and wind speed data at time t by Eq. (3), after completing the information memory and updating, the output gate calculates how much information can be output

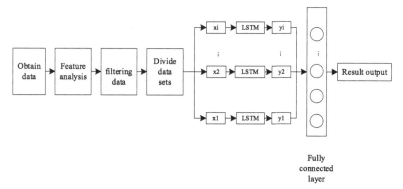

Fig. 2. LSTM model framework

to the current control unit according to Eq. (4), h_t and is used as the input of the next moment [3].

$$\tilde{c}_t =\sim \tanh\left(W_{xg}x_t + W_{hg}h_{t-1} + b_g\right) \tag{3}$$

$$o_t = sigmoid\left(W_{xo}x_t + W_{ho}h_{t-1} + bo\right) \tag{4}$$

The state of the element Ct and the state node of the hidden layer, h-t. information is calculated according to Eqs. (5) and (6).

$$c_t = f_t.c_{t-1} + i_t.\,\tilde{c}_t \tag{5}$$

$$h_t = o_t \times \tanh(c_t) \tag{6}$$

3   Model Optimization

Time-series temperature datasets often contain noise from various sources, such as measurement errors and environmental disturbances, impacting the accuracy of temperature change capture by the model. Hence, wavelet denoising plays a critical role in this context. The temperature time series is initially decomposed into wavelet coefficients of different scales and frequencies using wavelet decomposition, employing the wavelet basis function $\psi_{a,b}^{*}(t)$. Subsequently, these wavelet coefficients are tholder, and the thresholds are used to filter out the low-amplitude high-frequency noise components. The process of threshold processing helps to retain the main components of the temperature signal and suppress the noise [4]. Finally, the processed wavelet coefficients are reconstructed into a temperature time series with noise removal by inverse wavelet transform.

$$W(a, b) = \int_{-\infty}^{\infty} x(t)\psi_{a,b}^{*}(t)\,dt \tag{7}$$

Equation (7) decomposes the temperature time series $x(t)$ into wavelets to obtain wavelet coefficients $W(a, b)$, where a and b represent the scale and displacement, $\psi_{a,b}^{*}(t)$ are the wavelet basis functions.

$$x(t) = \sum_{a} \sum_{b} W_{thresh}(a,b) \psi_{a,b}(t) \tag{8}$$

Equation (8) uses the wavelet coefficient after threshold processing to perform the inverse wavelet transform to obtain the denoised temperature time series x(t).

By removing noise, the true pattern of temperature changes can be more clearly identified, improving the prediction accuracy of the model [5]. As shown in Fig. 3.

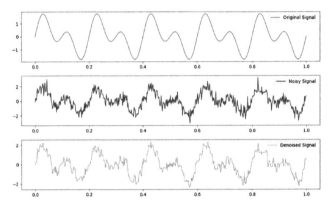

Fig. 3. Wavelet denoising

Processed with wavelet denoising, a stable and accurate temperature prediction model adapts well to real-world data scenarios. The results of the experiment are shown in Figure 3 and Figure 4, displaying the comparative outcomes of the LSTM、GRU、Bi-LSTM and RNN prediction models on the same dataset in this study (Figs. 5, 6 and 7):

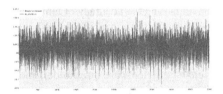

Fig. 4. LSTM prediction result graph   **Fig. 5.** GRU prediction result graph

In the result graph, the expectation is for the model LSTM, after comparing GRU, Bi-LSTM and RNN, to accurately capture temperature trends and predict future changes [6]. Comparative observations indicate that LSTM achieves an accuracy of 99%, with measures such as MSE, RMSE, MAE, and MAPE below 5%, and R^2 exceeding 99%.

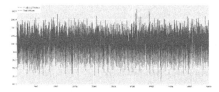

Fig. 6. Bi-LSTM prediction result graph   **Fig. 7.** RNN prediction result graph

4   Embedded Systems Inference

The RK3588 processor seamlessly integrates with the LSTM model via interface adaptation. PyTorch models are converted to ONNX format for RK3588 deployment, ensuring optimal performance. ONNX facilitates smooth conversion between deep learning frameworks and adapts to RKNN format for RK3588 devices [7]. This integration effectively deploys deep learning models on the RK3588 processor for tasks like temperature prediction in embedded systems. Figure 8 shows the hardware inference flowchart:

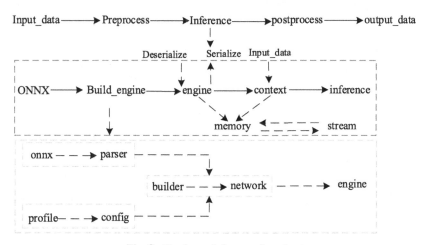

Fig. 8. Hardware inference flowchart

The integration of the RK3588 processor with the LSTM model offers enhanced accuracy in underground temperature predictions. Through interface adaptation and model conversion to ONNX and RKNN formats, seamless deployment and optimized system performance are achieved. Hardware simulation and board inference validate model functionality, ensuring reliable performance in real-world scenarios [8]. This integrated approach provides a robust framework for leveraging deep learning in embedded systems, particularly for tasks like temperature prediction.

5 Conclusion

The study underscores the significance of developing and continuously refining temperature prediction models in underground mine settings, while also offering insights for future research. Firstly, while acknowledging the model's strong performance in training and validation, the potential limitations imposed by data quality and quantity are recognized. Hence, expanding data collection across diverse mining environments and exploring additional data features can enhance model generalization and prediction accuracy.

Secondly, while the focus lies on single-variable temperature prediction, the complexity of underground environments is acknowledged, incorporating factors like humidity and gas concentration. Extending the model to multi-variable prediction while considering more environmental parameters can enhance prediction comprehensiveness and accuracy.

Furthermore, while hardware simulation and board testing were conducted on the RK3588 embedded system, real-world applications may encounter diverse environmental conditions. Therefore, future efforts should focus on validating and optimizing RK3588's adaptability and stability in actual mining environments to ensure reliability and effectiveness underground.

Acknowledgments. This work is supported by the National Science and Technology Major Project of China under grant 2022ZD0119005, and the Core Technology Research project of Key Industrial Chains of Xian City under grant 23ZDCYJSGG0025–2022, the Natural Science Foundation of Shaanxi Province under grant 2024JC-YBMS-539.

References

1. Yang, X.: Application of high-strength support technology in coal mining face. Manag. Technol. Small Medium-sized Enterprises (Second Edition) **11**, 163–164 (2020)
2. Guo, X.: Coal mine excavation support technology under complex geological conditions. China Petrol. Chem. Ind. Stan. Qual. **40**(21), 180–182 (2020)
3. Wang, B.: Application of high-strength support technology in coal mine mining and tunneling. Mining Equipment **6**, 34–35 (2020)
4. Jun, Z.: Coal mine mining and tunneling support technology under complex geological conditions. Mining Equipment **6**, 90–91 (2020)
5. Xue, Y., Bahrami, D., Zhou, L.: Identification of location and size of underground mine fires using simulated ventilation data and random forest model. Mining, Metallurgy Explor. **40**, 1399–1407 (2023)
6. Li, H., Guo, G., Zheng, N.: New evaluation methods for coal loss due to underground coal fires. Combust. Sci. Technol. **193**(6), 1022–1041 (2021)
7. Jiang, F., Qu, X., Wang, Y., et al.: Research on coal mine rock burst monitoring and early warning technology based on cloud computing. Coal Sci. Technol. **46**(1), 199–206, 244 (2018)
8. Chen, X.: Analysis of the causes and treatment measures of coal mine water disaster accidents. Shandong Indust. Technol. (10), 94, 93 (2019)
9. Qi, Q., Li, Y., Zhao, S., et al.: 70 years of development of rockburst in my country's coal mines: establishment and thinking of theoretical and technical systems. Coal Sci. Technol. **47**(9), 1–40 (2019)

PointPET: A Novel Network for 6D Pose Estimation of Industrial Components Using Smart Data Driven Modeling

Jintong Cai[1]([⊠]), Yujie Li[2,3], and Huimin Lu[1,4]

[1] School of Automation, Southeast University, Nanjing, China
jintongcai@seu.edu.cn
[2] School of Information Engineering, Yangzhou University, Yangzhou, China
[3] School of Engineering, Kyushu Institute of Technology, Fukuoka, Japan
[4] Institute for Advanced Ocean Research, Southeast University, Nantong, China

Abstract. Smart data-driven modeling has significantly advanced algorithm research in industrial applications by enabling data collection in virtual environments, effectively addressing the challenges of data labeling in real-world scenarios. Our research focuses on utilizing deep learning techniques to estimate the 6D pose of components in industrial settings. Traditional RGB-D-based pose estimation methods have struggled to meet the high-precision demands of these industrial scenarios. In contrast, point cloud-based approaches have shown promising potential in addressing these challenges. In this study, we introduce PointPET, a novel Transformer-based network designed for 6D pose estimation. PointPET leverages a self-attention mechanism to encode local features, facilitating end-to-end prediction of an object's 6D pose from input data. Our evaluation of the ICD-4 dataset demonstrates that PointPET can predict position with an accuracy of 1 mm and rotation angles within $5°$, meeting the stringent precision requirements of industrial applications.

Keywords: Smart data-driven modeling · 6D pose estimation · ICD-4 dataset · Transformer · Self-attention module

1 Introduction

The rapid advancement of artificial intelligence, big data, and mobile edge computing technologies [1, 2] has driven the transformation of traditional manufacturing into an intelligent, digital industrial system. At the same time, deep learning technologies [2] have enabled industrial robots to mimic human cognition and behavior, tackling complex pattern recognition tasks and fostering algorithmic innovation in the industrial domain. However, the effectiveness of deep learning is highly dependent on the availability of large datasets, and domain-specific data distribution can limit model predictive capabilities. To ensure optimal real-world performance, vast amounts of real-world data must be collected and manually labeled, a process that is both time-consuming and costly. Smart Data-Driven Modeling (SDDM) [3] technology addresses this challenge by enabling

© The Author(s), under exclusive license to Springer Nature Singapore Pte Ltd. 2025
H. Lu (Ed.): ISAIR 2024, CCIS 2402, pp. 237–249, 2025.
https://doi.org/10.1007/978-981-96-2911-4_23

efficient data collection and labeling. Using of Simulation-to-Reality (Sim2Real) technology [4], simulation data obtained through efficient sampling in virtual environments can be leveraged to generalize perception models for deployment in physical environments. In this paper, we focus on the visual perception challenges related to the grasping capabilities of industrial robots, specifically addressing the problem of 6D pose estimation of industrial components using SDDM and deep learning techniques [5, 6].

6D pose estimation involves determining an object's 6D pose within the camera coordinate system, encompassing its 3D position and 3D orientation. Accurate visual perception allows robots to interpret their surroundings, providing precise pose information for tasks such as grasping, assembly, and collision avoidance. Earlier approaches relied on RGB data to represent an object's geometry, texture, and color, utilizing manual feature matching techniques [8, 9]. PoseNet [10] was the first approach to leverage Convolutional Neural Networks (CNNs) for 6D pose estimation from RGB images. However, RGB-based methods depend heavily on object textures and inherently lack 3D spatial information, making them ill-suited for handling complex scenes. With advancements in sensor technology, RGB-D-based methods [7] have gained popularity for 6D pose estimation. PoseCNN [11], for example, integrates color and depth information to predict object centers and 3D rotations via regression. Nonetheless, both RGB and RGB-D based methods face challenges in accurately predicting the pose of symmetrical objects [7], which are common in industrial environments.

With the introduction of PointNet [12], which utilizes symmetric functions to address the challenge of feature extraction from unordered point clouds, point cloud-based methods have increasingly been adopted for pose estimation tasks in industrial environments. PoseMLP [13] is notable for being the first method to incorporate a point cloud-based backbone network for 6D pose estimation, regressing the translation and rotation of industrial components in an end-to-end manner. Well-designed local feature modules can further enhance the backbone network's ability to extract fine geometric features from point clouds, thereby directly improving the predictive accuracy of pose estimation networks. Recognizing the potential of this approach, we are exploring ways to incorporate these techniques into our work.

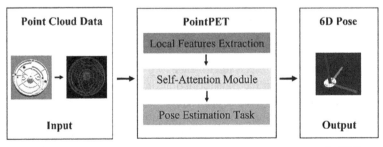

Fig. 1. Overview of PointPET: For point clouds of industrial components, PointPET encodes the input using a local feature module and a self-attention module, enabling direct, end-to-end 6D pose estimation.

In this study, we address the challenge of 6D pose estimation for industrial components using a point cloud-based approach. Our method, named PointPET, is inspired by PoseMLP [13] and incorporates a Transformer-based architecture to effectively encode local features of the point cloud via a well-designed self-attention module [14, 15]. As shown in Fig. 1, industrial components are input into the network in point cloud format. Fine local texture information is extracted through the local feature module and encoded using the point cloud-based self-attention mechanism, which generates an attention feature matrix. The 6D translation and rotation of industrial components are then predicted directly in an end-to-end manner through a regression-based approach. We evaluate the performance of our method on the ICD-4 dataset [13], the first dataset of industrial components constructed using SDDM for pose estimation tasks.

Our main contributions are as follows:

- We propose a novel framework for 6D pose estimation, named PointPET, which integrates Transformer-based methods into a point cloud-based backbone network, enabling end-to-end 6D pose prediction.
- We redesign the self-attention mechanism specifically for point clouds to encode local features, resulting in more discriminative feature representations.
- Our approach is trained and evaluated on the ICD-4 dataset, and when compared to other point cloud-based 6D pose estimation methods, it demonstrates superior performance.

2 Related Work

2.1 Non-learning-Based Methods

Pose estimation using RGB images captured by cameras has a long history of development [7]. RGB images provide geometric, texture, and color information about objects. Early research often relied on methods like SIFT and SURF to design pose estimation algorithms based on physical texture [5]. Vachetti et al. [16] used 2D descriptors to establish correspondences between 2D and 3D points, employing the Perspective-n-Point (PnP) algorithm to calculate the 6D pose of objects. However, this method requires extensive texture information. Ulrich et al. [18] developed a template-based approach using 3D models to enhance the accuracy and robustness of pose estimation by combining geometric and color information. Lin et al. [19] introduced the Fine Pose Part-Based Model (FPM) to localize objects in images, estimating object poses through carefully designed templates. Despite their strengths, model-based methods rely heavily on precise models, which limits the generalization capability of the algorithms.

The advent of depth cameras and 3D scanners has made it easier to capture 3D scene information [20], providing rich geometric, shape, and scale features that enhance pose estimation methods. Some local descriptor approaches employ the Iterative Closest Point (ICP) algorithm [21] to match offline-calculated local descriptors with online-generated global descriptors, establishing pose relationships between two coordinate systems. These descriptors are invariant to rotation and translation, improving pose estimation accuracy. David et al. [22] designed descriptors based on scene fragments and model views to extract features from scenes, enhancing performance in scene understanding tasks. However, these methods are limited by the offline-generated local descriptors and can be computationally expensive.

2.2 Learning-Based Methods

Recent research in vision tasks has been dominated by learning-based methods [5], which typically involve training a high-performing CNN to extract features from 2D images. Peng et al. [23] proposed a two-stage approach called PVNet, which first generates a semantic segmentation of the target object and then uses a keypoint detection method to create a vector field pointing to the object's keypoints. The keypoints are determined through voting within the vector field, and the object's 6D pose is subsequently solved. Parker et al. [24] utilized an autoencoder to predict pixel-to-3D coordinate correspondences, followed by the RANSAC iterative PnP [17] algorithm to directly compute the pose. However, learning-based methods are often limited by the availability of training data. When the predicted pose does not exist in the training set, the model's performance may degrade. Moreover, accurately estimating poses for symmetric and occluded objects remains a challenge for these methods.

2.3 Point-Cloud-Based Methods

Pose Estimation Using Point Clouds. Point clouds are a crucial representation format for describing 3D scenes, capable of conveying color, intensity, and other object-related information. However, their sparse and discrete nature makes it challenging to apply CNNs directly to point cloud data, as voxelizing point clouds can lead to the loss of geometric information [25]. Qi et al. [12] addressed this issue by employing simple symmetric functions to extract features from unordered point clouds, using a T-Net to learn a transformed feature matrix, thereby enhancing the model's transformation invariance. This straightforward yet effective approach has inspired advancements in point cloud-based scene understanding tasks [15, 26]. PoseMLP [13] is the first method to utilize point cloud data as input for pose estimation. It employs a well-designed residual multi-layer perceptron to extract multi-scale features from input industrial component point clouds, generating a fine-grained feature matrix. Simple parallel branches are then utilized to directly predict accurate 6D poses. Leveraging Smart Data-Driven Modeling (SDDM) and Simulation-to-Reality (Sim2Real) technology, PoseMLP is trained and tested on the ICD-4 industrial components dataset constructed in a simulated environment, further enhancing the model's generalization capability.

Transformer in Point Cloud. The success of the Transformer architecture [27] in natural language processing has encouraged researchers in the vision community to investigate its application in point cloud scene understanding tasks. The core component of the Transformer, the self-attention module, is permutation-invariant and can effectively handle unordered point clouds, leading to the development of various Transformer-based architectures for point cloud feature extraction [14, 15, 28]. In this paper, we explore the potential of the Transformer to enhance prediction results in 6D pose estimation tasks.

3   Method

Our proposed method, PointPET, takes point cloud data of industrial components as input and accurately estimates component translation and rotation in an end-to-end manner. As shown in Fig. 2, we build upon the PoseMLP approach [13] to leverage the rich geometric information and spatial scale preservation inherent in point cloud data. The input point cloud undergoes local feature encoding through feature embedding and grouping operations based on the K-nearest neighbor (KNN) algorithm. Subsequently, four stacked self-attention modules encode these local features to compute attention features. These attention features are then fused with the local features and fed into two parallel task heads via MLP and max pooling operations to predict translation and rotation. The task heads consist of fully connected layers with ReLU activations. In the following sections, we will provide a detailed description of the main components.

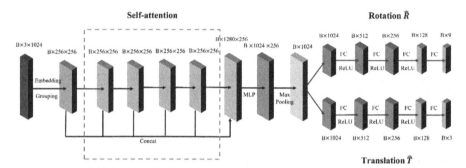

Fig. 2. PointPET structure. The input point cloud undergoes feature embedding before local features are encoded using KNN and MLP. A well-designed self-attention module is applied repeatedly to enhance these local features. Finally, the aggregated global features are passed to the task head, which predicts translation and rotation in parallel.

3.1   Local Feature Extraction

Given a point cloud $P \in \mathbb{R}^{N \times d}$ representing an industrial component, where N is the number of points and d is the feature dimension of each point, PointPET first performs feature mapping to transform the input features of P into a high-dimensional space to capture semantic similarities between points. Previous methods, such as PointNet [12], utilized MLPs for global-scale feature mapping, often neglecting object features at different scales. However, industrial components frequently exhibit varying shapes and sizes, necessitating a feature mapping approach that effectively captures discriminative features within an appropriate feature space. This represents the first challenge that must be addressed.

As shown in Fig. 3, we carefully designed the local feature encoding module by drawing inspiration from the approach used in PointNet++ [29]. For a given point cloud P, we enhance the model's generalization by discarding color features and using only positional information for encoding, resulting in input features $F_p \in \mathbb{R}^{N \times 3}$. These

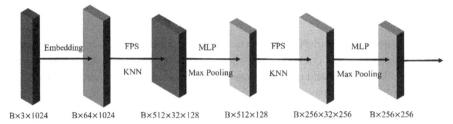

Fig. 3. Local Feature Extraction Process. For the input feature F_p, the embedded feature F_e is first calculated. Then, neighbor features F_N are aggregated using farthest point sampling (FPS) and K-nearest neighbors (KNN). This process is repeated to ultimately obtain the local feature F_L.

input features are then embedded to obtain the embedded feature F_e through a feature embedding operation, as shown in Eq. (1):

$$F_e = MLP(F_p) \tag{1}$$

where the resulting embedded feature $F_e \in \mathbb{R}^{N \times 64}$ is obtained through a multi-layer perceptron (MLP) that includes 1D convolution, batch normalization (BN), and ReLU activation layers. The core operation is described by Eq. (2):

$$MLP = ReLU(BN(Conv1d)) \tag{2}$$

For the input feature F_p, we compute F_e using two MLP operations. Subsequently, to reduce the size of the scene and ensure a more uniform distribution of the constituent point clouds, we apply the Farthest Point Sampling (FPS) algorithm to sample the original point cloud. We use the K-nearest neighbor (KNN) algorithm to find K neighbors for each point P_i from the sampling result, aggregating their features to obtain the neighborhood feature F_N:

$$F_N = KNN(FPS(F_e)) \tag{3}$$

where the number of neighbors is set to $K = 32$. Subsequently, we apply maximum pooling and multi-layer perceptron (MLP) operations to the local area feature F_N to obtain the local feature F_L:

$$F_L = MaxPooling(MLP(F_N)) \tag{4}$$

We reduce the dimensionality of the feature matrix through max pooling, enhancing the reusability of the modules. As illustrated in Fig. 3, we apply Eqs. (3) and (4) twice to obtain the final output of local feature extraction, $F_m \in \mathbb{R}^{N' \times d_m}$, where $d_m = 256$. The matrix F_m contains local features at multiple scales, and this fine feature encoding is advantageous for subsequent self-attention feature computation.

3.2 Self-attention Module

The traditional Transformer [27] employs a multi-layer perceptron (MLP) to design core components, including input embedding, positional encoding, and self-attention modules. Unlike convolutional neural networks (CNNs), Transformers are order-independent, meaning the order of the input does not affect the output. MLP-based components align well with the characteristics of point clouds. The second challenge that needs to be addressed is how to integrate the core operations of the Transformer into a point cloud-based backbone network. During local feature extraction, we performed feature embedding on the input feature F_p. Given that point clouds inherently contain positional information, we follow the approach in [14] and omit the additional positional embedding operation to reduce computational complexity. Our goal is to develop an improved self-attention module capable of effectively encoding point cloud features.

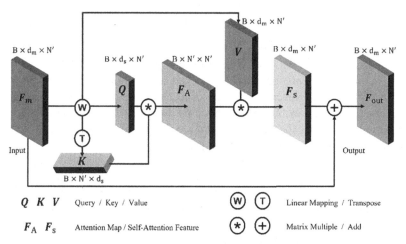

Fig. 4. Self-attention module. Through the combination of Q, K, and V, the global context information of point cloud data is obtained. Q, K, and V are all obtained by a linear transformation of the input.

The self-attention module calculates the semantic similarity between different items in a data sequence, as illustrated in Fig. 4. In our design, the self-attention module takes local features $F_m \in \mathbb{R}^{N' \times d_m}$ as its input. We first apply a linear transformation to F_m to obtain the query matrix $Q \in \mathbb{R}^{N' \times d_s}$, the key matrix $K \in \mathbb{R}^{N' \times d_s}$, and the value matrix $V \in \mathbb{R}^{N' \times d_m}$:

$$Q = F_m \cdot W_{query} \tag{5}$$

$$K = F_m \cdot W_{key} \tag{6}$$

$$V = F_m \cdot W_{value} \tag{7}$$

where $W_{query} \in \mathbb{R}^{d_m \times d_s}$, $W_{key} \in \mathbb{R}^{d_m \times d_s}$ and $W_{value} \in \mathbb{R}^{d_m \times d_m}$ are shareable weights that the network needs to learn. Then, we compute the scaled dot-product attention map $F_A \in \mathbb{R}^{N' \times N'}$ as the normalized matrix product of Q and K transpose:

$$F_A = Softmax\left(\frac{Q \cdot K^T}{\sqrt{d_1}}\right) \tag{8}$$

The matrix $Q \cdot K^T$ represents the pairwise similarity between each query vector in Q and each key vector in K. The function $Softmax(./\sqrt{d_1})$ acts as an activation function that normalizes the similarity scores into a probability distribution for each query. Finally, we obtain the self-attention feature $F_s \in \mathbb{R}^{N' \times d_m}$: by multiplying F_A and the value matrix V:

$$F_s = F_A \cdot V \tag{9}$$

To combine the information from the input features F_m and the self-attention features F_s, we perform a channel-wise addition to obtain the final output $F_{out} \in \mathbb{R}^{N' \times d_m}$:

$$F_{out} = F_m + F_A \tag{10}$$

Note that F_m and F_s have the same size, so can be added directly. The final output F_{out} has the same size as the input F_m, so it is natural to consider stacking. As shown in Fig. 2, in our implementation, we use 4 stacked self-attention modules for encoding. The input F_m in the first layer is the result of local feature extraction, and in the next three layers, F_m is the previous self-attention module. The encoding result F_{out} of the attention module. In the experiment, we set $d_m = 256$ and $d_s = 64$.

In our approach, we removed the local position encoding operation and integrated the self-attention module of the Transformer with a point cloud-based backbone network. The input features were linearly transformed to obtain the Q, K, and V, which were then used to compute the self-attention features through the dot product. Our method is straightforward and effective. Since the operators used in these operations are permutation invariant, they are well-suited for our purposes.

3.3 Feature Fusion

After obtaining the local features F_m and the four attention features F_{out}, we concatenate these features following the approach described in [12, 29]. The final output feature F_B of the backbone network is then obtained through MLP and maximum pooling operations. In our implementation, F_B is a linear vector of length 1024. Unlike segmentation tasks, our pose estimation task addresses unordered point-wise features, so a linear F_B is sufficient to meet the requirements of the task.

3.4 Task Heads

Our goal is to perform pose estimation on the input point cloud. For the output F_B of the backbone network, we design two parallel branches to predict translation and rotation. As shown in Fig. 2, these branches consist of repeated applications of fully connected layers and ReLU activations, progressively decreasing the number of feature channels. In the translation branch, we predict the position vector of the object's 3D centroid coordinates (x, y, z). In the rotation branch, we predict the rotation matrix between the component frame and the world frame, resulting in an output dimension of 9. Both branches utilize a Smooth L1 loss as their evaluation function during training.

4 Experiment

4.1 Dataset

We use the ICD-4 dataset [13] to train and test our approach. This dataset provides detailed information about several industrial components. The data collection process is based on Smart Data-Driven Modeling (SDDM) and involves loading STL templates into the Robot Operating System (ROS), with random orientation changes applied to the components in the Gazebo simulation environment. An automated script saves the point cloud and ground truth pose information for each frame. As a result, the ICD-4 dataset contains 20,000 training samples for each component.

For our experiments, we selected three representative models, as shown in Fig. 5. Model A is a circular component with a central cylindrical protrusion. Model B is a "V"-shaped component capable of rotating around an axis. Model C is also circular but features numerous irregular protrusions and surface cavities. These models were chosen to provide a diverse range of shapes and features for comprehensive testing.

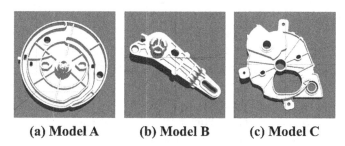

| (a) Model A | (b) Model B | (c) Model C |

Fig. 5. Visualization of some components in the ICD-4 dataset [13].

4.2 Training and Inference Details

We conduct experiments on an NVIDIA GeForce RTX 2080 GPU and split the training and testing sets in a 9:1 ratio. During the offline training phase, we trained PointPET on Models A, B, and C separately, using the same training parameters as in [13] for ease of comparison. In the online testing phase, we followed a four-step process: (a) loading the scene and test components into the Gazebo simulation environment; (b) using the ROS monitoring node to obtain the pose of the current frame component as ground truth; (c) sending the current frame's point cloud to PointPET to obtain predicted translation and rotation results; and (d) calculating the errors.

To assess the efficacy of our proposed approach, we compute the errors in both translation and rotation predictions and analyze their impact on the overall accuracy of our method. For translation, the network predicts the offset (x, y, z) of the center point coordinates, and we calculate the translation error by subtracting the ground truth from the predicted value. For rotation, the network predicts a transformation matrix, which must be converted into Euler angles $(roll, pitch, yaw)$ to compute the angular error between the predicted and ground truth values. To enhance the credibility of our results, we report the largest error that occurs within a fixed period. Additionally, to reduce computational complexity, we downsampled the input point cloud to 1024 points during both the training and testing phases.

Table 1. Quantitative results on Model A.

Method	Translation (Max error)			Rotation (Max error)			Time(s)
	X (mm)	Y(mm)	Z(mm)	Roll(deg)	Pitch(deg)	Yaw(deg)	
PointNet [12]	2.52	1.65	1.10	15.26	10.77	5.80	**0.02**
PointNet++ [29]	0.79	1.55	1.02	33.01	29.25	40.74	0.26
PoseMLP [13]	0.10	1.03	**0.07**	2.24	4.70	11.19	0.72
PoseMLP-F [13]	0.15	1.39	0.16	**0.87**	10.19	8.68	0.72
PoseMLP-N [13]	0.22	1.44	0.43	1.59	3.95	**3.36**	0.72
PoseMLP-D [13]	0.11	1.27	0.17	2.36	8.55	8.26	0.77
PointPET (Ours)	**0.07**	**0.39**	0.30	2.12	**0.88**	3.39	0.50

Table 2. Quantitative results on Model B.

Method	Translation (Max error)			Rotation (Max error)			Time(s)
	X (mm)	Y(mm)	Z(mm)	Roll(deg)	Pitch(deg)	Yaw(deg)	
PointNet [12]	12.9	4.36	3.54	4.20	**0.28**	6.66	**0.02**
PointNet++ [29]	8.07	4.47	7.20	2.95	8.14	14.52	0.26
PoseMLP [13]	2.83	0.92	0.87	0.37	0.64	2.78	0.72
PoseMLP-F [13]	0.52	1.66	2.59	1.75	6.27	4.24	0.72
PoseMLP-N [13]	**0.20**	3.28	1.38	**0.20**	5.69	3.40	0.72
PoseMLP-D [13]	0.83	2.10	2.67	2.49	0.29	2.35	0.77
PointPET (Ours)	0.70	**0.39**	**0.71**	0.86	1.16	**0.44**	0.50

4.3 Quantitative Results

We conducted tests to evaluate the pose estimation performance of various artifacts, using PoseMLP [13], PointNet [12], and PointNet++ [29] as control groups. For each component's test results, we report the maximum translation error, maximum angular error, and average prediction time for a single frame input.

Model A: As shown in Table 1, for translation prediction, our method achieved the best results for the X and Y components and performed comparably to the PoseMLP series of algorithms for the Z component, outperforming PointNet and PointNet++. For rotation

Table 3. Quantitative results on Model C.

Method	Translation (Max error)			Rotation (Max error)			Time(s)
	X (mm)	Y(mm)	Z(mm)	Roll(deg)	Pitch(deg)	Yaw(deg)	
PointNet [12]	5.92	3.52	2.17	2.98	1.59	2.66	**0.02**
PointNet++ [29]	**0.02**	3.28	1.38	**0.02**	5.69	3.40	0.26
PoseMLP [13]	2.36	0.45	1.13	4.68	7.11	7.28	0.72
PoseMLP-F [13]	1.21	**0.12**	**0.30**	1.38	**0.03**	4.13	0.72
PoseMLP-N [13]	0.92	0.95	0.69	3.27	4.32	4.26	0.72
PoseMLP-D [13]	1.45	1.45	1.60	2.41	3.61	6.31	0.77
PointPET (Ours)	0.86	0.42	0.37	4.39	2.88	**1.28**	0.50

prediction, PointPET achieved a pitch error of only 0.88°, significantly better than the comparison methods. The errors for the other components were also stable, all within 4°. In terms of average prediction time, PointPET required only 0.50 s, outperforming the PoseMLP series and achieving a prediction speed of less than 0.30 s with fewer parameters than PointNet and PointNet++.

Model B: As shown in Table 2, PointPET achieved the best performance for the Y and Z components, with translation errors of less than 0.90 mm. The error for the X component was also significantly better than that of the PointNet series. The angular error was below 1.20°, demonstrating greater stability compared to PoseMLP. These results indicate that the well-designed backbone network of PointPET is highly adaptable to artifacts with asymmetric structures.

Model C: As shown in Table 3, after downsampling, Model C became more similar to a symmetric model. Our PointPET method continued to demonstrate stable prediction performance, with translation errors of less than 0.9 mm and rotation errors within 4.4°, indicating good stability.

5   Conclusion

In this work, we introduced a new point-based feature extraction network, PointPET, for 6D pose estimation of industrial components. Our approach integrates the Transformer architecture with a well-designed local feature extractor to capture fine-grained features of industrial components. The self-attention module encodes local features and computes attention feature maps through linear transformation, dot product, and normalization operations. For pose estimation, we directly obtain rotation and translation information through parallel branches. We evaluated our approach on the ICD-4 dataset, constructed using SDDM technology. Our results demonstrate that PointPET achieves strong performance in translation prediction and outperforms PointNet series methods in rotation prediction.

In future work, we plan to enhance the generalization ability and robustness of PointPET to enable accurate 6D pose estimation in complex real world industrial scenarios.

Acknowledgment. This work was supported by the National Natural Science Foundation of China (NSFC) Young Scientists Fund (No. 62206237).

References

1. Khan, W.Z., et al.: Edge computing: a survey. Future Gener. Comput. Syst. **97**, 219–235 (2019)
2. Wang, F., Zhang, M., Wang, X., Ma, X., Liu, J.: Deep learning for edge computing applications: a state-of-the-art survey. IEEE Access **8**, 58322–58336 (2020)
3. Ren, J., et al.: A survey on end-edge-cloud orchestrated network computing paradigms: transparent computing, mobile edge computing, fog computing, and cloudlet. ACM Comput. Surv. (CSUR) **52**(6), 1–36 (2019)
4. Höfer, S., et al.: Sim2Real in robotics and automation: applications and challenges. IEEE Trans. Autom. Sci. Eng. **18**(2), 398–400 (2021)
5. Du, G., et al.: Vision-based robotic grasping from object localization, object pose estimation to grasp estimation for parallel grippers: a review. Artif. Intell. Rev. **54**(3), 1677–1734 (2021)
6. Cordeiro, A., et al.: Bin picking approaches based on deep learning techniques: a state-of-the-art survey. In: 2022 IEEE International Conference on Autonomous Robot Systems and Competitions (ICARSC). IEEE (2022)
7. He, Z., et al.: 6D pose estimation of objects: recent technologies and challenges. Appl. Sci. **11**(1), 228 (2020)
8. Bay, H., et al.: Speeded-up robust features (SURF). Comput. Vis. Image Understanding **110**(3), 346–359 (2008)
9. Zhang, X., et al.: Vision-based pose estimation for textureless space objects by contour points matching. IEEE Trans. Aerosp. Electron. Syst. **54**(5), 2342–2355 (2018)
10. Kendall, A., Matthew, G., Roberto, C.: PoseNet: a convolutional network for real-time 6-dof camera relocalization. Proceedings of the IEEE International Conference on Computer Vision (2015)
11. Xiang, Y., et al.: PoseCNN: a convolutional neural network for 6D object pose estimation in cluttered scenes. arXiv preprint arXiv:1711.00199 (2017)
12. Qi, C.R., et al.: PointNet: deep learning on point sets for 3D classification and segmentation. In: Proceedings of the IEEE Conference on Computer Vision and Pattern Recognition (2017)
13. Li, Y., et al.: Pose estimation of point sets using residual MLP in intelligent transportation infrastructure. IEEE Trans. Intell. Transp. Syst. (2023)
14. Guo, M.-H., et al.: PCT: point cloud transformer. Comput. Vis. Media **7**, 187–199 (2021)
15. Li, Y., Cai, J.: Point cloud classification network based on self-attention mechanism. Comput. Electr. Eng. **104**, 108451 (2022)
16. Vacchetti, L., Lepetit, V., Fua, P.: Stable real-time 3D tracking using online and offline information. IEEE Trans. Pattern Anal. Mach. Intell. **26**(10), 1385–1391 (2004)
17. Lepetit, V., Moreno-Noguer, F., Fua, P.: EP n P: an accurate O (n) solution to the P n P problem. Int. J. Comput. Vis. **81**, 155–166 (2009)
18. Ulrich, M., Wiedemann, C., Steger, C.: Combining scale-space and similarity-based aspect graphs for fast 3D object recognition. IEEE Trans. Pattern Anal. Mach. Intell. **34**(10), 1902–1914 (2011)

19. Lim, J.J., Aditya, K., Antonio, T.: FPM: fine pose parts-based model with 3D cad models. In: Computer Vision–ECCV 2014: 13th European Conference, Zurich, Switzerland, September 6–12, 2014, Proceedings, Part VI 13. Springer International Publishing (2014)

20. Guo, Y., et al.: Deep learning for 3D point clouds: a survey. IEEE Trans. Pattern Anal. Mach. Intell. **43**(12), 4338–4364 (2020)

21. Chen, Y., Medioni, G.: Object modelling by registration of multiple range images. Image Vis. Comput. **10**(3), 145–155 (1992)

22. Nospes, D., et al.: Recognition and 6D pose estimation of large-scale objects using 3D semi-global descriptors. In: 2019 16th International Conference on Machine Vision Applications (MVA). IEEE (2019)

23. Peng, S., et al.: Pvnet: pixel-wise voting network for 6dof pose estimation. In: Proceedings of the IEEE/CVF Conference on Computer Vision and Pattern Recognition (2019)

24. Park, K., Timothy, P., Markus, V.: Pix2pose: pixel-wise coordinate regression of objects for 6d pose estimation. In: Proceedings of the IEEE/CVF International Conference on Computer Vision (2019)

25. Yang, S., Huimin, L., Li, J.: Multifeature fusion-based object detection for intelligent transportation systems. IEEE Trans. Intell. Transp. Syst. **24**(1), 1126–1133 (2022)

26. Li, Y., et al.: Joint semantic-instance segmentation method for intelligent transportation system. IEEE Trans. Intell. Transp. Syst. (2022)

27. Vaswani, A., et al.: Attention is all you need. In: Advances in Neural Information Processing Systems, vol. 30 (2017)

28. Zhao, H., et al.: Point transformer. In: Proceedings of the IEEE/CVF International Conference on Computer Vision (2021)

29. Qi, C.R., et al.: Pointnet++: deep hierarchical feature learning on point sets in a metric space. In: Advances in Neural Information Processing Systems, vol. 30 (2017)

PD-SLAM: A Visual SLAM for Dynamic Environments

Chenghao Xu[1], Qingxiao Zou[1,2], and Wankou Yang[1(✉)]

[1] Southeast University, Nanjing, China
wkyang@seu.edu.cn
[2] School of Cyber Science and Engineering, Xuzhou, China

Abstract. This article presents PD-SLAM, a visual SLAM (Simultaneous Localization and Mapping) system designed specifically for dynamic environments. Accurately self-positioning and mapping the environment are crucial capabilities for intelligent robots. However, most existing SLAM systems assume static environments, which may lead to reduced robustness of the system in the presence of moving objects. PD-SLAM, built upon the ORB-SLAM3 framework, addresses this challenge by integrating a semantic segmentation module and optical flow techniques to filter out features from moving regions. Additionally, PD-SLAM utilizes a geometric feature-based method to eliminate outlier features, thereby effectively removing dynamic objects from the environment. Performance evaluations conducted on the TUM RGB-D dataset have demonstrated that PD-SLAM significantly improves absolute trajectory accuracy in dynamic environments.

Keywords: Dynamic Environments · Semantic Segmentation · Optical Flow · SLAM

1 Introduction

Simultaneous Localization and Mapping (SLAM) is the ability of a mobile robot to determine its position and construct a map of an unknown environment simultaneously, which is crucial in fields such as robotics, autonomous driving, and augmented reality [1].

Visual SLAM (VSLAM) has been extensively researched in recent years, and its technological framework has become quite mature. Advanced SLAM algorithms like ORB-SLAM3 [2] and LSD-SLAM [3] have achieved satisfactory results. However, traditional VSLAM frameworks still face challenges when applied in new environments [4], particularly in dynamic settings where their localization and mapping capabilities are significantly impaired. This is primarily because most VSLAM systems assume that the environment is static [5]. When dynamic objects are present, this assumption leads to inaccuracies in pose estimation and errors in map points.

In this paper, we developed a visual SLAM system named PD-SLAM based on ORB-SLAM3, which effectively reduces the impact of dynamic objects on the pose

H. Lu (Ed.): ISAIR 2024, CCIS 2402, pp. 250–257, 2025.
https://doi.org/10.1007/978-981-96-2911-4_24

estimation of the SLAM system in dynamic environments. As shown in Fig. 1(a), PD-SLAM integrates a semantic segmentation module and an optical flow module for filtering out moving regions, combined with a feature-point-based geometric consistency check module to further filter out feature points that do not meet the requirements. Experiments on the TUM-RGBD dataset [6] show that PD-SLAM performs significantly better than ORB-SLAM3, especially in handling dynamic objects with greater accuracy and robustness.

The main contributions of this paper are as follows:

- We introduce a lightweight semantic segmentation network into the SLAM system to effectively filter out dynamic objects in the scene, such as pedestrians and moving vehicles.
- We present a combined approach that utilizes optical flow computation and semantic segmentation to accurately filter and match feature points in areas with dynamic targets. We eliminate unsuitable feature points within the tracking component of ORB-SLAM3 to enhance tracking precision.

2 Related Works

2.1 SLAM in Dynamic Environments

SLAM in dynamic environments remains a formidable challenge within the field of robotics research. Presently, the mainstream solutions are divided into two categories: geometric information-based methods and semantic information-based methods.

Geometric information-based methods rely on optical flow and scene flow to identify and filter dynamic objects within the environment. For example, Daniela Esparza [4] uses optical flow, SegNet, and depth maps to detect dynamic objects, while QH Cheng [7] uses optical flow to detect dynamic feature points. Although optical flow is primarily used to check motion consistency, its effectiveness in removing dynamic objects is limited due to low accuracy.

Semantic information-based methods primarily use semantic segmentation [20] or object detection to filter out dynamic objects. For instance, Berta [8] effectively identifies dynamic objects using Mask R-CNN and geometric methods. F Zhong [9] enhances SLAM accuracy by integrating object detection algorithms based on deep neural networks. Runz M [10] uses instance-level semantic information to create maps that include objects, achieving commendable results but facing challenges in real-time performance.

2.2 Selection of Semantic Segmentation Models

In current SLAM systems, using semantic segmentation models to mitigate the impact of moving objects in dynamic environments has become a common practice. In early research, models chosen for their accuracy and robustness, such as Mask R-CNN [8] and DeepLab v2 [10], were often preferred. While these models provide accurate segmentation, their high computational cost makes real-time processing challenging. For example, C Yu [11] used SegNet, which attempts to balance response time while maintaining reasonable accuracy, but still does not fully meet real-time processing needs.

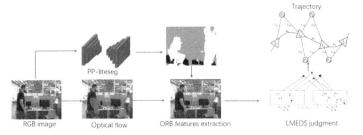

(a) The overview of PD-SLAM

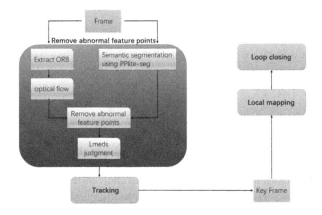

(b) The framework of PD-SLAM

Fig. 1. The overview and framework of PD-SLAM. (a) The overview of PD-SLAM. (b) The framework of PD-SLAM

In recent years, several lightweight semantic segmentation models have emerged, such as ENet [12], MobileNet [13], ShuffleNet [14], ESPNet [15], and ICNet [16]. These models are specifically suited for real-time tasks and devices with limited computational resources, ensuring low latency and adequate accuracy.

These models not only accelerate the segmentation process but also enhance performance, making them ideal choices for SLAM systems in dynamic environments. This paper will integrate an advanced lightweight semantic segmentation network into the SLAM system to significantly enhance its real-time performance.

3   System Introduction

3.1   The Framework of PD-SLAM

ORB-SLAM3 are distinguished by their high accuracy, robustness, practicality, and efficiency, establishing it as the system of choice for a variety of practical application scenarios [2]. Consequently, PD-SLAM selects ORB-SLAM3 as its foundational SLAM framework, with modifications to detect and exclude dynamic objects.

The PD-SLAM system operates four parallel threads: feature point removal in dynamic areas, tracking, local mapping, and loop closure processing. As shown in Fig. 1(b), the process begins with raw RGB images captured from a camera, which are first fed into the feature point removal module for dynamic areas. This module executes two synchronized threads that perform semantic segmentation and optical flow detection simultaneously.

In the optical flow detection thread, the system identifies feature points from the RGB images and uses optical flow technology to determine target areas where the movement distance between two frames exceeds the normal range. Combining the results of semantic segmentation, the system eliminates feature points within the identified dynamic areas. The remaining feature points are then filtered from a geometric perspective, primarily using transformation matrices to select static feature points that are suitable for subsequent processing steps. In the tracking, local mapping, and loop closure stages, the PD-SLAM system follows processing methods same to those used in ORB-SLAM3. This includes tracking the camera's movement path, constructing a local map of the environment, and optimizing map consistency through loop closure detection. This approach significantly enhances the performance and accuracy of the SLAM system in dynamic environments.

3.2 Semantic Segmentation Model

The PD-SLAM system is designed with real-time operational requirements in mind, utilizing the lightweight semantic segmentation model PP-LiteSeg [18] provided by PaddlePaddle [17], which achieves a good balance between realtime performance and accuracy. PaddlePaddle also offers a variety of semantic segmentation models, facilitating future replacements. In practical applications, especially in indoor environments, PD-SLAM primarily filters out humans as dynamic objects.

3.3 Identifying Moving Objects with Optical Flow

Considering the processing time demands of semantic segmentation algorithms, this study proposes a method that combines ORB feature points with optical flow computation to identify feature points in areas containing moving objects. This method serves as a redundant solution for environments where fast semantic segmentation inference is not feasible. Additionally, since semantic segmentation may not fully extract all moving targets, such as a person holding a book where the book might not be recognized as part of the moving region, this method can also act as an auxiliary means to filter moving areas. To reduce time consumption, this study adopts a parallel processing strategy, simultaneously running semantic segmentation, feature point extraction, and optical flow selection to optimize the workflow and ensure the efficiency and feasibility of the algorithm in resource-constrained environments.

The main steps include:

– Feature Point Extraction: Using the ORB feature extraction function of ORB-SLAM3 to extract feature points from the current frame image.

- Optical Flow Point Matching: Comparing feature points and their surroundings in the current and previous frames to identify the most similar matching points.
- Calculation of Optical Flow Values: Calculating the positional differences between each pair of matched feature points across two frames.
- Elimination of Feature Points in Moving Regions: Based on the subtle movements between two frames, assuming that the movement of static objects is minimal, set a threshold to filter out feature points located in moving regions. Although this method avoids the high computational cost of semantic segmentation, the sparse optical flow method cannot completely replace semantic segmentation because it does not comprehensively identify and remove all moving objects. Therefore, this method should be considered as an auxiliary or redundant option.

3.4 Least Median of Squares Discrimination

After processing images using semantic segmentation and optical flow techniques, it is necessary to identify and remove some imperfectly processed feature points. To eliminate these residual feature points, this paper introduces a geometric consistency check method based on the Least Median of Squares (Lmeds) algorithm:

- Feature Point Matching: Receive processed ORB feature points and descriptors from the above process and match them using descriptors.
- Anomalous Feature Point Identification: Find the best matching feature points by comparing the Hamming distance. If a feature point does not have a corresponding match in the other frame, it is considered anomalous.
- Seek Transformation Matrix: Use the Lmeds method to find an optimal transformation matrix for matched pairs of feature points.
- Consistency Check with the Global Motion Model: Eliminate feature points that do not conform to the transformation matrix, retaining only those that do.
- Applicability Conditions: The effectiveness of this method may be limited when the proportion of moving objects in the image is high. It is best applied in scenarios where the scene has been made predominantly static through preprocessing with semantic segmentation or optical flow techniques.

4 Experimental

In this section, we conducted experiments on PD-SLAM to verify its accuracy and responsiveness. We tested the semantic segmentation module of PD-SLAM and the time it takes to process a single image. Additionally, we used the TUM RGB-D dataset to test camera trajectory accuracy in dynamic environments. All experiments were conducted on a computer equipped with an Intel i7 CPU, a 3060ti GPU, and 32GB of RAM.

4.1 Tests on TUM RGB-D Dataset

PD-SLAM modifies the ORB-SLAM3 system and compares it with ORB-SLAM3 and the classical dynamic SLAM system DS-SLAM to validate PD-SLAM's performance advantages. The evaluation uses two metrics: Absolute Trajectory Error (ATE)

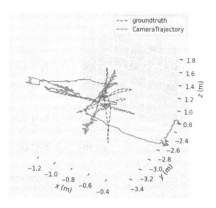
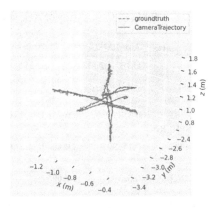

(a) Trajectory plot of ORB-SLAM3   (b) Trajectory plot of PD-SLAM

Fig. 2. The comparison of ORB-SLAM3 and PD-SLAM on the TUM RGB-D fr3-walking-xyz dataset. (a) Trajectory plot of ORB-SLAM3. (b) Trajectory plot of PD-SLAM

and Relative Pose Error (RPE), which measure global trajectory consistency and drift, respectively.

As shown in Fig. 2, Tests show that in dynamic environment like the TUM RGB-D fr3-walking-xyz dataset, ORB-SLAM3 demonstrates limitations in camera trajectory estimation, while PD-SLAM shows greater advantages when processing the same dataset. PD-SLAM effectively filters out dynamic feature points and relies on static regions of the environment to estimate camera trajectories. This improves the accuracy of trajectory estimation, making PD-SLAM's camera trajectory much closer to the original trajectory.

PD-SLAM's algorithmic design focuses on static features and filters out dynamic feature points, enhancing system performance in dynamic environments. This not only increases accuracy but also enhances the system's robustness, making it a more suitable SLAM solution for dynamic settings.

As shown in Table 1, during the evaluation of Absolute Trajectory Error (ATE), PD-SLAM outperforms ORB-SLAM3 and DS-SLAM across various TUM datasets, particularly in datasets heavily affected by dynamic elements. However, in the SITTING-STATIC dataset, improvements of PD-SLAM over ORB-SLAM3 are minimal, possibly because the dataset contains fewer potentially moving objects. In the evaluation of Relative Pose Error (RPE), PD-SLAM also surpasses DS-SLAM, with some fluctuations compared to ORB-SLAM3 in certain datasets, but overall performance remains within a normal range.

4.2 Time Costs

The lightweight semantic segmentation model used in this paper operates at a frame rate close to 70 frames per second under actual conditions, significantly improving over the visual SLAM in dynamic environments. The PD-SLAM system requires about 15 ms to process the semantic segmentation module for a single frame, and the entire tracking part

Table 1. Comparison of ATE and RPE for Different SLAM Methods

Test Sequences	ATE RMSE			RPE RMSE		
	ORB-SLAM3	DS-SLAM	PD-SLAM	ORB-SLAM3	DS-SLAM	PD-SLAM
SITTING STATIC	0.007424	0.0065	**0.006052**	**0.005147**	0.0078	0.005762
WALKING HALFSPHERE	0.154780	0.0303	**0.028606**	0.020188	0.0297	**0.017236**
WALKING RPY	0.152904	0.4442	**0.073977**	0.028081	0.1503	**0.036305**
WALKING STATIC	0.023904	**0.0081**	0.009659	0.019586	0.0102	**0.007328**
WALKING XYZ	0.270320	0.0247	**0.012346**	0.021777	0.0333	**0.011694**

takes approximately 30 ms per frame. The overall frame rate reaches about 33 frames per second, sufficient to provide a smooth visual experience and can be considered to have achieved real-time performance.

5 Conclusion

In this paper, we developed a visual SLAM system named PD-SLAM based on ORB-SLAM3, which effectively reduces the impact of dynamic objects on the system's pose estimation in dynamic environments. PD-SLAM integrates a semantic segmentation module, optical flow technology, and geometric consistency checks to remove outlier feature points. Performance tests on the TUM-RGBD dataset demonstrate that PD-SLAM's pose estimation performance significantly surpasses that of ORB-SLAM3, and it also shows improvements when compared with DS-SLAM.

References

1. Bresson, G., Alsayed, Z., Yu, L., Glaser, S.: Simultaneous localization and mapping: a survey of current trends in autonomous driving. IEEE Trans. Intell. Veh. **2**(3), 194–220 (2017)
2. Campos, C., Elvira, R., Rodríguez, J.J.G., Montiel, J.M., Tardós, J.D.: ORB-SLAM3: an accurate open-source library for visual, visual–inertial, and multimap slam. IEEE Trans. Rob. **37**(6), 1874–1890 (2021)
3. Engel, J., Schöps, T., Cremers, D.: LSD-SLAM: large-scale direct monocular SLAM. In: European Conference on Computer Vision, pp. 834–849. Springer (2014)
4. Esparza, D., Flores, G.: The STDyn-SLAM: a stereo vision and semantic segmentation approach for VSLAM in dynamic outdoor environments. IEEE Access **10**, 18201–18209 (2022)
5. Wen, S., Li, P., Zhao, Y., Zhang, H., Sun, F., Wang, Z.: Semantic visual SLAM in dynamic environment. Auton. Robot. **45**(4), 493–504 (2021)
6. Sturm, J., Engelhard, N., Endres, F., Burgard, W., Cremers, D.: A benchmark for the evaluation of RGB-D SLAM systems. In: 2012 IEEE/RSJ International Conference on Intelligent Robots and Systems, pp. 573–580 (2012)

7. Cheng, Q.H.: Improving monocular visual SLAM in dynamic environments: an optical-flow-based approach. Adv. Robot. Int. J. Robot. Soc. Japan **33**(11–12) (2019)
8. Bescos, B., Fácil, J.M., Civera, J., Neira, J.: DynaSLAM: tracking, mapping, and inpainting in dynamic scenes. IEEE Robot. Autom. Lett. **3**(4), 4076–4083 (2018)
9. Zhong, F., Wang, S., Zhang, Z., Wang, Y.: Detect-SLAM: making object detection and SLAM mutually beneficial. In: 2018 IEEE Winter Conference on Applications of Computer Vision (WACV), pp. 1001–1010 (2018)
10. Runz, M., Buffier, M., Agapito, L.: Maskfusion: real-time recognition, tracking and reconstruction of multiple moving objects. In: 2018 IEEE International Symposium on Mixed and Augmented Reality (ISMAR), pp. 10–20 (2018)
11. Yu, C., et al.: DS-SLAM: a semantic visual SLAM towards dynamic environments. In: 2018 IEEE/RSJ International Conference on Intelligent Robots and Systems (IROS), pp. 1168–1174 (2018)
12. Paszke, A., Chaurasia, A., Kim, S., Culurciello, E.: ENet: a deep neural network architecture for real-time semantic segmentation. arXiv preprint arXiv:1606.02147 (2016)
13. Sinha, D., El-Sharkawy, M.: Thin MobileNet: an enhanced mobilenet architecture. In: 2019 IEEE 10th Annual Ubiquitous Computing, Electronics & Mobile Communication Conference (UEMCON), pp. 0280–0285 (2019)
14. Zhang, X., Zhou, X., Lin, M. Sun, J.: ShuffleNet: an extremely efficient convolutional neural network for mobile devices. In: Proceedings of the IEEE Conference on Computer Vision and Pattern Recognition, pp. 6848–6856 (2018)
15. Mehta, S., Rastegari, M., Caspi, A., Shapiro, L., Hajishirzi, H.: ESPNet: efficient spatial pyramid of dilated convolutions for semantic segmentation. In: Proceedings of the European Conference on Computer Vision (ECCV), pp. 552–568 (2018)
16. Zhao, H., Qi, X., Shen, X., Shi, J., Jia, J.: ICNet for real-time semantic segmentation on high-resolution images. In: Proceedings of the European Conference on Computer Vision (ECCV), pp. 405–420 (2018)
17. Liu, Y., et al.: Paddleseg: a high-efficient development toolkit for image segmentation. arXiv preprint arXiv:2101.06175 (2021)
18. Peng, J., et al.: Pp-liteseg: a superior real-time semantic segmentation model. arXiv preprint arXiv:2204.02681 (2022)
19. Zhang, Z., Scaramuzza, D.: A tutorial on quantitative trajectory evaluation for visual(-inertial) odometry. In: IEEE/RSJ International Conference on Intelligent Robots and Systems, pp. 7244–7251 (2018)
20. Zhou, Q., et al.: Multi-scale deep context convolutional neural networks for semantic segmentation. World Wide Web **22**, 555–570 (2019)

The Requirements and Constraints of Self-built Data Set on Detection Transformer in Complex Scenario

Junjie Shi, Mei Wang$^{(\boxtimes)}$, Xinyu Liu, Yonggao Zhang, and Yuancheng Li

School of Computer Science and Technology, Xi 'an University of Science and Technology, Xi'an 715100, China

23208223084@stu.xust.edu.cn, wangm@xust.edu.cn

Abstract. As the core task in the field of computer vision, object detection has made great progress in recent years. In recent years, a target Detection model based on Transformer architecture-DETR (Detection Transformer), has attracted wide attention. The purpose of this paper is to introduce and analyze the characteristics of the earth observation self-built data set, and then use DETR model to train the earth observation self-built data set and evaluate and analyze the experimental results. The challenges of target detection and the limitations of traditional methods are reviewed, followed by an introduction to the Transformer model. Then, the structure, training flow and key components of DETR model are discussed in detail. We experiment the DETR model on common target detection datasets and compare its performance with traditional target detection methods. Under the premise of certain advantages, the model achieves an average precision of more than 40%, which is comparable to the performance of traditional models.

Keywords: Self-built data set · Object detection · Transformer

1 Introduction

Target observation is not only a key topic in traffic monitoring, driving assistance system, city traffic control and other fields, but also a hot research content in the field of computer vision.

The DETR model selected in this paper uses transformer as the architecture, which abandons the anchor prior commonly used in previous algorithms and eliminates the NMS post-processing method, so as to truly realize the end-to-end target detection. The types of detection objects mainly include car, person, motorcycle, bike, truck and bus.

In the specific application of object detection, the research faces many challenges. For example, in harsh environments, resulting in the loss of the target, misjudgment or missed detection; At different altitudes, the size of the target changes in real time. This paper aims to study the latter, to ensure the detection ability of small targets, but also to ensure the accuracy in complex scenes [1].

First we introduce the model architecture of Transformer and DETR, and then describe the preparation and characteristics of self-built data set. Finally, different models are used to perform comparative experiments on different data sets.

H. Lu (Ed.): ISAIR 2024, CCIS 2402, pp. 258–264, 2025.
https://doi.org/10.1007/978-981-96-2911-4_25

2   Cognitive Model Architecture

2.1   Transformer

Structure and Working Principle of Transformer Model

The Transformer model is a deep neural network architecture based on a Self-Attention Mechanism that was originally used for natural language processing tasks but has since been successfully applied to image processing as well (Fig. 1).

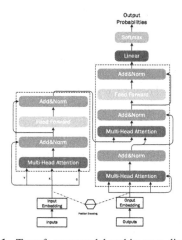

Fig. 1. Transformer model architecture diagram

The Transformer model is a self-attention-based deep learning model architecture that is widely used in natural language processing and other sequential data processing tasks. The core idea is to abandon the sequence dependence of traditional recurrent neural networks (RNNs) and long term memory networks (LSTMs), and adopt a self-attention mechanism, which enables the model to process all the position information of the input sequence at the same time, so as to capture semantic relations over a longer distance. The working principles of Transformer include multi-head self-attention mechanisms, where multi-head attention allows the model to encode information in multiple subspaces, and feedforward neural networks, which are responsible for nonlinear transformations of features at each location. By stacking multiple layers, the Transformer model can learn more complex semantic representations, and through parallel computation of the self-attention mechanism, the model also achieves better training and inference efficiency. Transformer's innovative design makes significant achievements in tasks such as machine translation, text generation and language modeling, making it one of the major milestones in the field of deep learning [2].

Overall, the Transformer model models long-term dependencies in sequence data through a multi-layer encoder-decoder structure and self-attention mechanism, resulting in significant success in tasks such as natural language processing and image processing. The Transformer architecture also provides important ideas and inspiration for subsequent model design.

2.2   Constraints and Architecture of DETR Model

Working Constraints of DETR Model

DETR uses the Transformer architecture, a neural network architecture based on a self-attention mechanism, which is commonly used for sequence-to-sequence tasks such as machine translation. Transformer consists of multiple encoders and decoders for encoding inputs and generating outputs.

No anchor and no NMS design: DETR does not use traditional anchor and non-maximum suppression techniques. It turns the object detection problem into a set prediction problem that directly outputs the positions and categories of all objects in the image, eliminating hand-designed anchor boxes.

Attention mechanism: DETR uses a self-attention mechanism to capture the relationships between the elements in the input sequence, enabling the model to analyze the global relevance of different areas of the image.

Loss function design: DETR uses a joint loss function to transform the object detection problem into a set prediction problem.

a. Classification Loss

DETR uses Cross Entropy Loss to measure the accuracy of a model's predictions for a target class. The cross entropy loss is defined as follows:

$$classification\ loss = -\frac{1}{N} \sum_{i=1c=1}^{N} \sum_{i=1c=1}^{c} y_{i,c} \cdot \log(p_{i,c}) \tag{1}$$

N is the number of samples and represents the number of targets in the image. C is the number of categories for the target. $y_{i,c}$ is a binary label that indicates whether the i object belongs to class c.

b. Box Regression Loss

DETR uses Smooth L1 Loss to measure the accuracy of the bounding box position. The smooth L1 loss for the predicted bounding box at the first position versus the true bounding box at the first position is defined as follows:

$$box\ regression\ loss = -\frac{1}{N} \sum_{i=1}^{N} \sum_{i \in (z,y,w,h)} smooth\_L1(\overline{t_{ij}} - t_{ij}) \tag{2}$$

N is the number of samples and represents the number of targets in the image. $\overline{t_{ij}}$ is the j component in the bounding box parameter of the i target predicted by the model. t_{ij} is the j component of the true bounding box parameter of the i target predicted by the model. smooth_L1(x) is smoothing out the loss of L1,

$$L_1 = \begin{cases} 0.5x^2, if\ |x| < 1 \\ |x| - 0.5, otherwise \end{cases} \tag{3}$$

c. Hungarian matching

The Hungarian matching algorithm mainly solves the assignment problem, that is, given two sets of points (usually two sets of equal length), find a one-to-one correspondence that minimizes the total matching cost. In DETR, this algorithm is used to determine the best match between the predicted frame and the real frame for calculating losses [3].

Overall Network Architecture of the DETR Model

The overall framework of DETR is as follows: First, image features are extracted by CNN; Then it is fed into transformer encoder-decoder. The structure of the encoder and decoder is basically the same as transformer, which is mainly modified in the input part and the output part. Finally, the prediction of class and b box is obtained, and the loss is calculated by binary matching to optimize the network (Fig. 2).

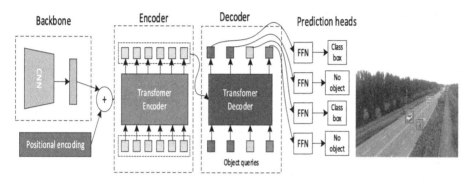

Fig. 2. DETR model network architecture

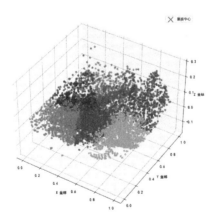

Fig. 3. Clustering result

For example, input a 3*800*1066 input image size (3 → RGB channel), through the CNN convolutional network into 2048*25*34(800 and 1066 1/32), through 1*1 dimensional reduction operation into 256*25*34, position coding (256*25*34), Input straightening vector (850*256) into encoder, output through six encoders (850*256); Enter decoder, object queries(100*256), 850*256 and 100*256 repeatedly perform self-attention operations to get 100*256 features; Enter the full connection layer prediction,

FFN(feed forward network) makes two predictions [category prediction (6), box prediction (x, y, width, height)], and then uses Hungarian algorithm to do box matching and gradient reverse backpass to update the model [4].

3 Preparation and Characteristics of Self-built Data Set

3.1 Composition and Collection Method of Data Set

The data used in this experiment are all from the self-built data set of earth observation. The scenes are respectively public road sections and campus scenes are divided into six categories, as shown in the Table 1. The data acquisition method is manually operated by the DJI INSPIRE 1 UAV in different time periods and scenarios. The captured video is cut every 5 s and a picture is generated for the next annotation.

Table 1. Self-built data set composition.

Label name	Number of images
Car	1000 (training set)
Person	
Motorcycle	
Bike	100 (validation set)
Truck	
Bus	

3.2 Requirements for Data Set and Feature Analysis

We chose to save the pictures after annotation as YOLO format [6, 7], but this experiment required us to use coco format data sets for training and reasoning, so the next work was to convert the divided training set and verification set into the format required by our experiment.

We use K-means algorithm to cluster these data sets through the annotation files of data sets and their coordinate information, and study their characteristics through the clustering results in Fig. 3 [5].

4 Experimental Results and Performance Analysis

4.1 The Detection Effect of the Model on the Self-built Data Set

We selected all the targets of the picture and trained 65 rounds under different IOU for the experiment. The experimental results are shown in Table 2, and the results are shown in Fig. 4.

Table 2. The AP and AR rate after 65 training epochs.

AR	AP	IoU	area
0.167	0.213	0.50:0.95	all
0.275	0.439	0.50	all
0.319	0.191	0.75	all

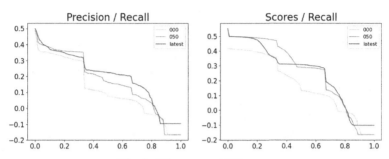

Fig. 4. P/R curve and S/R curve

4.2 Contrast Experiment

In this paper, we first do a comparison experiment with Fast-RCNN on COCO data set [6]. Find that DETR achieves AP value comparable with Fast-RCNN when the number of parameters is small.

To consolidate the results, we ran another set of experiments. In this set of experiments, we use two different object detection models, DETR and YOLOv5, based on which the application of COCO dataset and our own dataset are fully compared and evaluated. This series of experiments aims to more fully demonstrate and validate the model's performance on different data sets, thereby more convincingly explaining the model's strengths, weaknesses and applicability. The results are shown in Tables 3 and 4.

Table 3. Comparative experiments of DETR and FAST-RCNN

Data set	Model	Parameter	AP (%)
COCO data set	Fast-RCNN	166 M	41.1
	DETR	41 M	44
Self-built data set	Fast-RCNN	166 M	47.2
	DETR	41 M	43.9

Table 4. Comparative experiments of DETR and YOLOv5

Data set	Model	AR (%)	AP (%)
COCO data set	YOLOv5	45.6	35.7
	DETR	42.4	44
Self-built data set	YOLOv5	39.5	48.0
	DETR	31.9	43.9

5 Conclusion

The purpose of this study is to achieve more accurate and efficient target detection through DETR model training of self-built data set. Through different epochs of training, we have successfully applied DETR model to self-built data set and obtained good experimental results. The key performance indicators show that our model performs well in target detection tasks, achieving good accuracy and mAP values. The discussion of experimental results shows that DETR model has good generalization ability. However, in some specific scenarios, there is still room for improvement, perhaps due to special features or uneven categories in the data set.

Acknowledgments. This work is supported by the National Science and Technology Major Project of China under grant 2022ZD0119005, and the Core Technology Research project of Key Industrial Chains of Xian City under grant 23ZDCYJSGG0025–2022, the Natural Science Foundation of Shaanxi Province under grant 2024JC-YBMS-539.

References

1. Zou, Z., et al.: Object detection in 20 years: a survey. Proc. IEEE **111**(3), 257–276 (2023)
2. Vaswani, A., et al.: Attention is all you need. In: Advances in Neural Information Processing Systems, vol. 30 (2017)
3. Stewart, R., Mykhaylo, A., Andrew, Y.N.: End-to-end people detection in crowded scenes. In: Proceedings of the IEEE Conference on Computer Vision and Pattern Recognition (2016)
4. Carion, N., et al.: End-to-end object detection with transformers. In: European Conference on Computer Vision. Springer International Publishing, Cham (2020)
5. Ahmed, M., Seraj, R., Islam, S.M.S.: The k-means algorithm: a comprehensive survey and performance evaluation. Electronics **9**(8), 1295 (2020)
6. Lin, T.-Y., et al.: Microsoft coco: common objects in context. In: Computer Vision–ECCV 2014: 13th European Conference, Zurich, Switzerland, September 6–12, 2014, Proceedings, Part V 13. Springer International Publishing (2014)
7. Lu, H., Li, Y., Mu, S., Wang, D., Kim, H., Serikawa, S.: Motor anomaly detection for unmanned aerial vehicles using reinforcement learning. IEEE Internet Things J. **5**(4), 2315–2322 (2017)
8. Wang, S.H., et al.: Multiple sclerosis detection based on biorthogonal wavelet transform, RBF kernel principal component analysis, and logistic regression. IEEE Access **4**, 7567–7576 (2016)

Self-supervised Contrastive Learning With Similarity-Based Sample Judgment

Zheng Jiang[1,2], Quan Zhou[1,2(✉)], Xiaofu Wu[1], Zhiyi Mo[2], Suofei Zhang[3], and Bin Kang[3]

[1] National Engineering Research Center of Communications and Networking, Nanjing University of Posts and Telecommunications, Nanjing, People's Republic of China
quan.zhou@njupt.edu.cn
[2] Guangxi Colleges and Universities Key Laboratory of Intelligent Software, Wuzhou University, Wuzhou, People's Republic of China
[3] Department of Internet of Things, Nanjing University of Posts and Telecommunications, Nanjing, People's Republic of China

Abstract. Self-supervised learning can assist neural network models in automatically learning knowledge and patterns from a large amount of unlabeled data. Recently, self-supervised learning has garnered significant attention and has made substantial progress. Contrastive learning, as an effective method within self-supervised learning, enhances the model's ability to model training images by increasing inter-class distances and decreasing intra-class distances. In this work, we propose a novel self-supervised deep learning paradigm with similarity-based sample judgement to choose reliable positive/negative samples, thereby avoiding cases where samples of the same class are mistakenly classified as negative sample. Specifically, we use a teacher-student network to generate multi-view features for self-supervised contrastive learning and make robust positive/negative sample judgments based on the similarity information between samples. Finally, we conduct training based on the results of reliable sample judgments. Extensive experimental results demonstrate that the proposed method achieves satisfactory performance in terms of classification accuracy on the ImageNet dataset and various downstream tasks.

Keywords: Image Classification · Self-supervised Learning · Contrastive Learning

1 Introduction

Self-supervised learning is an integral part of the field of computer vision, enabling computer systems to autonomously acquire knowledge and patterns

Q. Zhou–This work is partly supported by NSFC (No. 61876093,62171232), Postgraduate Research & Practice Innovation Program of Jiangsu Province(No. KYCX22_0962), and open funding project of Guangxi Colleges and Universities Key Laboratory of Intelligent Software (No. 2023B01).

H. Lu (Ed.): ISAIR 2024, CCIS 2402, pp. 265–279, 2025.
https://doi.org/10.1007/978-981-96-2911-4_26

from a large volume of unlabeled data. This capability is crucial for numerous computer vision tasks(e.g., [1–7]), including image segmentation, image retrieval, and object recognition. Many tasks in computer vision rely on some form of annotated data to supervise the training of neural network models, such as fully supervised, semi-supervised, and weakly supervised training methods. However, the manual annotation of each image incurs significant human and material resources due to the vast scale of the data. In contrast, self-supervised learning can uncover the intrinsic characteristics or patterns of image features without the need for annotated data. Recently, self-supervised representation learning has made steady advances and has demonstrated promising results across multiple visual tasks. Contrastive learning [8], as a form of self-supervised learning, requires the model to compare different samples in the data during the learning process, thereby promoting the model to learn data representations and features. Specifically, contrastive learning increases inter-class distance while reducing intra-class distance, enhancing the model's ability to model the training images.

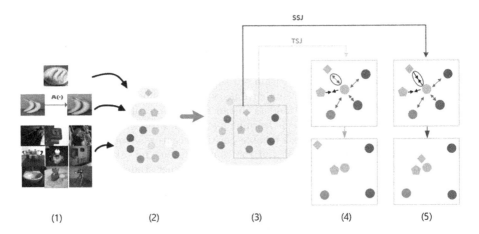

Fig. 1. Motivation and Idea. We provide a specific example to illustrate the issue of same-class images being misclassified as negative sample. Subfigure (1) is divided into three parts, showing an image of a banana, another image of a banana along with its augmented $A(\cdot)$ version, and several images of different categories. Projecting these images into the feature space, as shown in subfigures (2) and (3). Subfigure (4) includes the Traditional Sample Judgment (TSJ) and Subfigure (5) includes the Similarity-based Sample Judgment (SSJ). In TSJ, the misclassification of the two banana images as a negative sample pair results in an inaccurate expansion of their distance within the feature space, consequently causing dispersion in the intra-class distances. Conversely, SSJ effectively avoids this issue.

Recently, the significant success of self-supervised learning, particularly self-supervised contrastive learning, can be attributed to various outstanding learning strategies. Currently, the InfoNCE loss [9]is the most commonly used loss function in self-supervised contrastive learning, which aims to maximize the similarity of positive sample pairs while minimizing the similarity of negative sample pairs, enabling the model to learn more discriminative representations. InstDisc [10] introduced a large-scale memory bank for storing image features to Increase the scale of negative samples. MoCo [2] conceptualized contrastive learning as a dictionary learning problem and maintained an online queue for storing negative samples, achieving decoupling of the number of negative samples from the batch size, outperform the fully supervised ResNet-50 [11] in Classification task on the ImageNet dataset [12] and segmentation tasks. SimCLR [3] utilized larger batch sizes, longer training times, and more complex data augmentations, and added an extra linear classifier (i.e., a fully connected layer and ReLU activation) used only during pretraining and not during prediction. BYOL [4] no longer utilizes negative samples and learned solely from positive sample, training by pulling the feature representations of two views of an image closer together. SwAV [5] fused contrastive learning and clustering methods, gathering similar objects around a cluster center while pushing dissimilar objects toward other cluster centers. SimSiam [6] simplifies the aforementioned approach, demonstrating that satisfactory results can be achieved even without the need for negative samples, large batch size, and momentum encoders.

However, the performance evaluation of all contrastive learning strategies depends on the accurate determination of positive and negative sample, which is crucial for the model's ability to learn effective representations. To achieve better feature representation, contrastive learning generally assumes that images with the same category are positive sample, while Images with different categories are negative sample, and then trains the model based on these positive/negative samples. Therefore, accurately determining which images are positive samples and which are negative samples is crucial for the training process. However, in unsupervised conditions, the training dataset's images lack category information, making it impossible to determine positive and negative sample based on category information. Therefore, traditional contrastive learning methods assume that any training image and its augmented version belong to the same category, considering them as positive sample pairs, while other training images are considered as negative samples. Although this method of positive and negative sample determination is widely adopted in existing self-supervised contrastive learning mechanisms, it still has the following drawback: traditional contrastive learning methods use data augmentation to obtain positive samples and treat other images as negative samples, thus overlooking the possibility that certain training images may objectively belong to the same category as the current image. In such cases, traditional methods may erroneously classify these images and the current image as negative samples, as illustrated in Fig. 1.

In this work, we propose a new self-supervised contrastive learning paradigm by introducing an effective and reliable positive/negative sample judgment mechanism within the contrastive learning framework. The judgement mechanism is plug-and-play, and its universality implies that it can be readily applied to various contrastive learning methods. Specifically, we introduce a teacher-student network to obtain multi-view feature representations of the data. To learn more efficiently from unlabeled data, we obtain more reliable sample judgments through a sample judgment, which is based on the similarity of sample features for decision-making, and train based on these judgments.

In order to evaluate the proposed method, we conducted extensive experiments on various datasets, including linear evaluation tasks, transfer learning, and ablation studies. The proposed method, using a ResNet-50 encoder pretrained on the ImageNet dataset, achieved a top-1 accuracy of 71.712% in the linear evaluation, which is 1.112% higher than previous state-of-the-art. Specifically, our main **contributions** can be summarized as follows:

- First, We have proposed a novel and effective self-supervised contrastive learning method. Specifically, We obtain reliable sample judgments through the Similarity-based Sample Judgment Module (SSJM) and use these reliable positive/negative samples for model training. Additionally, we weight the negative samples to optimize the feature space distribution of these samples. This approach mitigates the problem of images from the same category being mistakenly classified as negative samples, and enhances the robustness of the model.
- Second, the SSJM module features plug-and-play capabilities, allowing seamless integration into any framework based on contrastive learning with positive and negative samples.
- Finally, The extensive experimental results demonstrate that the proposed method outperforms previous methods in linear evaluation when self-supervised contrast learning is performed on ImageNet datasets.

2   Related Work

2.1   Self-learning

Self-supervised learning aims to learn representations of data from unlabeled data without relying on manual labels. In self-supervised tasks, models are trained by generating labels automatically, instead of relying on label information in the dataset. Self-supervised learning achieves this by designing a proxy task that assists the model in learning useful representations. Proxy tasks are typically constructed by applying some form of transformation or prediction to the data. These tasks aim to simulate real supervised tasks without requiring actual labels. There are various variations of proxy tasks in self-supervised learning, including autoencoder tasks [13–16], contrastive learning tasks [3–6], generative tasks [17,18], and more. By leveraging a large amount of unlabeled data, self-supervised learning can effectively pretrain models and demonstrate strong performance in various downstream tasks.

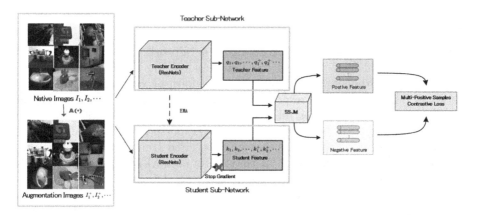

Fig. 2. The architecture of Self-supervised Contrastive learning with Similarity-based Sample Judgment.

2.2   Contrastive Learning

Contrastive learning [8], as a self-supervised learning method, aims to train models by learning the similarities and differences between samples. Contrastive loss is a loss function used in contrastive learning to measure the similarity and dissimilarity between pairs of samples. The objective of contrastive loss is to maximize the similarity between positive samples and minimize the similarity between negative samples. In recent years, this method has been widely used in unsupervised/self-supervised representation learning tasks [1,3,4,9,10,19–23] and is superior to pretext task-based other unsupervised/self-supervised methods [24–28].

2.3   MoCo

In MoCo [2] (Momentum Contrast) , the goal of contrast learning is to learn the representation of images by building a dynamic dictionary.For image data, a standard positive sample sampling strategy [19] involves creating multiple views of each image data using data augmentation, where all views except the current image are treated as negative samples. The number of negative samples and the consistency between features play important roles in the contrastive learning process. MoCo framework utilizes a teacher-student network, where the student network encoder employs stop-gradient operations and momentum updates [10,23]. To store more negative samples during contrastive computation, MoCo maintains an online queue that stores image features from multiple iterations, constructing a large and consistent dictionary. Providing more negative samples and more consistent feature representations is crucial for contrastive learning, a fact confirmed by recent research [29–31].

3 Our Method

The architecture consists of a Teacher-Student Network and a Similarity-based Sample Judgment Module(SSJM), as illustrated in Fig. 2. The encoder model of the Teacher-Student Network can take the form of various types of neural networks [11,32–37] and is responsible for generating feature vectors of input images. The SSJM generates reliable positive and negative sample judgments based on the similarity between image features, and the model is trained based on these judgments. To stabilize the self-supervised training of the model, we prevent gradient backpropagation for the student network and utilize exponential moving average (EMA) to update its parameters, thereby stabilizing the self-supervised training of the model.

3.1 Student-Teacher Network

Self-supervised learning tries to learn the underlying structure and useful feature representations of data from a large scale unlabeled dataset $D = \{I_1, I_2, I_3, \cdots, I_N\}$, where I_i represents each image in the dataset. For each image in the dataset $I_i \in D$, we can obtain two views through data augmentation $X = \{x_1, x_2, x_3, \cdots, x_N,\}$, $X^+ = \{x_1^+, x_2^+, x_3^+, \cdots, x_N^+,\}$, which are then used as inputs for the teacher $f_T(\cdot, \theta_t)$ and student networks $f_S(\cdot, \theta_s)$. The teacher sub-network $f_T(\cdot, \theta_t)$ consists of a backbone, a feature projection head, and a prediction head, while the student sub-network $f_S(\cdot, \theta_s)$ consists of a backbone and a feature projection head. For the inputs to the teacher network, we applied techniques such as random horizontal flipping, random cropping, color jittering, and Gaussian blurring during data augmentation $A(\cdot)$. Through the teacher-student network, we can obtain four distinct feature representations for image I_i as

$$q_i = f_T(x_i, \theta_t), \quad q_i^+ = f_T(x_i^+, \theta_t) \tag{1}$$

$$k_i = f_S(x_i, \theta_s), \quad k_i^+ = f_S(x_i^+, \theta_s) \tag{2}$$

where q_i and is q_i^+ the feature representation from the teacher sub-network and k_i and is k_i^+ is the feature representation from the student sub-network.

In the teacher-student network, the teacher sub-network updates its parameters θ_t through gradient backpropagation. To stabilize the training of the self-supervised network model [2], we have implemented a strategy of preventing gradient backpropagation for the student sub-network. Additionally, we use exponential moving average (EMA) for updating the parameters of the student sub-network θ_s as,

$$\theta_s \leftarrow (1 - \sigma) \times \theta_t + \sigma \times \theta_s \tag{3}$$

where σ represents the momentum smoothing coefficient, which is used to control the update speed of the student sub-network.

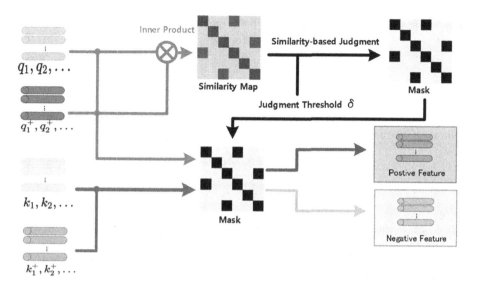

Fig. 3. Overview of the proposed Robust Sample Judgment Module.

3.2 Similarity-Based Sample Judgment Module(SSJM)

Currently, contrastive learning focuses on using strategies such as large batch sizes [3], memory banks [10], or large dynamic dictionaries [2,4,6] to obtain as many contrastive samples as possible in order to achieve more effective results. However, these learning strategies overlook a potential issue: the selected negative samples may be unreliable, as images from the same class could inadvertently be treated as negative samples. Training with more robust positive/negative samples can significantly improve the training effectiveness of self-supervised learning models. Therefore, we propose the Similarity-based Sample Judgment Module (SSJM), as illustrated in Fig. 3.

We heuristically select robust positive/negative samples within the self-supervised learning framework by leveraging the similarity between different image features. Specifically, for two distinct images I_i and I_j, we measure the similarity between the two images by calculating their inner product in the feature space.

$$Sim(i,j) = q_i \cdot q_j^+ \tag{4}$$

where $q_i = f_T(x_i, \theta_t)$, $q_j^+ = f_T(x_j^+, \theta_t)$.

Next, we establish a similarity-based sample judgment threshold δ as

$$\delta = \alpha \times Sim(i,i) \tag{5}$$

where, $Sim(i,i)$ represents the similarity between an image and its data-augmented version. α is a constant coefficient hyperparameter. δ is used to determine whether two image features form a positive/negative sample pair. By calculating $Sim(i,j)$ for $i \in [1,N]$ and $j \in [1,N]$, we can obtain a similarity map with a shape of $N \times N$. Then, by using the similarity map and threshold δ, we can obtain the judgment mask $Mask\,(i,j)$, as shown in Equation (6).

$$Mask(i,j) = \begin{cases} 1, & \text{if } \text{Sim}(i,j) \geq \delta \ or \ i = j \\ 0, & \text{otherwise} \end{cases} \tag{6}$$

For all images in the dataset $I_i \in D$, we make the judgment based on the following inequality:

$$\tilde{P}_i = \{I_j \mid I_j \in D, Mask(i,j) = 1\} \tag{7}$$

$$\tilde{N}_i = \{I_j \mid I_j \in D, Mask(i,j) = 0\} \tag{8}$$

where $\tilde{P}_i$ represents the selected positive sample set for image I_i, and $\tilde{N}_i$ represents the selected negative sample set for image I_i. By dynamically selecting robust positive/negative sample in each iteration, we can effectively train the self-supervised contrastive learning network. In fact, SSJM accomplishes the task of generating pseudo-labels in self-supervised learning.

By utilizing a similarity-based sample judgment threshold δ to address the misclassification of images within the same category as negative samples, we aim to further optimize the distribution of negative samples in the feature space. We believe that negative samples with higher similarity are relatively harder to distinguish. Therefore, during the model training process, we aim to assign higher weights to these relatively "challenging" samples to increase the model's sensitivity to these negative samples, as shown in Eq. (9).

$$\lambda_{i,j} = K \times Sim(i,j) \tag{9}$$

where λ represents the weight assigned to the image I_j from the negative sample set $\tilde{N}_i$ when calculating the loss function with respect to the current image I_i, where K is a constant hyperparameter.

3.3 Multi-positive Samples Contrastive Loss

In our method, we utilize a robust sample judgement module to select reliable positive and negative samples during training. We then employ a Multi-Positive samples Contrastive Loss L to minimize the similarity between negative samples and maximize the similarity between positive samples. Specifically, our multi-positive samples contrastive loss function L is derived from the traditional InfoNCE loss L_{NCE} , which is defined as follows:

$$L_{NCE}\,(a,b) = -\log \frac{\exp\left(\frac{a_i \cdot b_i}{\gamma}\right)}{\sum_{j=1}^{K} \exp\left(\frac{a_i \cdot b_j}{\gamma}\right)} \tag{10}$$

where a_i and b_i represent the feature vectors generated from different views of image $I_i \in D$, λ is the weight of the negative sample, and γ is the temperature coefficient, which is used to smooth the distribution of similarities, making the training process more stable.

For the InfoNCE loss, we have made the following improvements:

(1) We transform the logarithmic numerator from a monomial to a polynomial, enabling its applicability in scenarios where there are multiple images of the same class in the training set, i.e. in the context of multi-positive samples contrastive learning.

(2) We introduce a mechanism for negative sample weighting, which enhances the sensitivity of the model to challenging negative samples by increasing the weight of similar negative samples. This method effectively enhances the robustness of the model.

(3) We integrate symmetry into the InfoNCE loss. Symmetric contrastive loss compels the model to consider both directions of a pair, promoting a more comprehensive exploration of the feature space. This approach enables the capture of complex patterns that might be overlooked when only a single direction is considered, thereby enhancing the model's consistency and robustness.

Specifically, Multi-Positive Samples Contrastive Loss L is defined as follows,

According to Eq. (1) and (2), we can yield four sets of feature vectors $q_i = f_T(x_i, \theta_t), q_i^+ = f_T(x_i^+, \theta_t), k_i = f_S(x_i, \theta_s), k_i^+ = f_S(x_i^+, \theta_s)$ when both X and X^+ are input into the teacher sub-networks and student sub-networks, respectively.

$$L_{NCE}^{plus}(a, b) = -\log \frac{\sum_{j=1}^{K} 1_{(b_j \in \hat{P}_i)} \exp\left(\frac{a_i \cdot b_i}{\gamma}\right)}{\sum_{j=1}^{K} 1_{(b_j \in \hat{N}_i)} \lambda_{i,j} \exp\left(\frac{a_i \cdot b_i}{\gamma}\right) + \sum_{j=1}^{K} 1_{(b_j \in \hat{P}_i)} \exp\left(\frac{a_i \cdot b_i}{\gamma}\right)} \tag{11}$$

Equation (10) represents an improved InfoNCE loss, where the logarithmic numerator part is no longer a monomial but a polynomial that can dynamically change based on the number of positive samples. This new loss L_{NCE}^{plus} function is suitable for scenarios involving multi-positive pair contrastive learning.

$$L = \frac{1}{2} \times \left(L_{NCE}^{plus}(q, k^+) + L_{NCE}^{plus}(q^+, k) \right) \tag{12}$$

Equation (11) represents the final loss function that has integrated symmetry. This symmetric contrastive loss possesses symmetry and is applicable to scenarios involving multi-positive samples.

4   Experiments

4.1   Implementation Details

To generate multi-view data representations, we employed sophisticated data augmentation techniques to model various transformation strategies for different views. For the teacher sub-network, we initially perform random cropping and resize the images to 224×224. Subsequently, we apply color jitter operations with brightness of 0.4, contrast of 0.4, saturation of 0.2, and hue of 0.1, with a probability of 0.8. Additionally, with a 0.2 probability, we convert the image to grayscale. Finally, we apply Gaussian blur with a blur radius ranging from 0.1 to 2.0 and randomly flip the images horizontally. For the student sub-network, in addition to the aforementioned data augmentation, we further include a step of applying the Solarize operation with a probability of 0.2. Finally, we normalize the RGB channels using a mean of $[0.485, 0.456, 0.406]$ and a standard deviation of $[0.229, 0.224, 0.225]$.

We use the ResNet-50 [11] network as the backbone for both the teacher and student sub-networks, and after feature projection, the final output feature dimension is 256. The LARS optimizer is utilized to minimize the loss function in Eq. (9), with an initial learning rate of 4, weight decay of 1e-6, momentum of 0.9, and a batch size of 1024. Additionally, we employ cosine annealing to adjust the learning rate for a maximum of 200 iterations. In Eq. (3), For the student subnetwork, exponential moving average (EMA) with a momentum smoothing coefficient σ of 0.99 is applied. In Eq. (9), the constant hyperparameter K is set to 20.0. And in Eq. (11), the temperature coefficient γ is set to 1.0.

After a period of pre-training, the ResNet-50 model has already acquired a certain level of feature representation capability. At this stage, we introduce the Similarity-based Sample Judgment Module (SSJM) to enable the model to learn more precise feature representations. The timing of introducing SSJM into the model training is crucial for its effectiveness, and we will demonstrate this in the subsequent ablation study section.

4.2   Linear Evaluation

Linear evaluation is a commonly used evaluation method to assess the quality of the feature representations learned by a self-supervised learning (SSL) model. After freezing the backbone of the SSL model, a separate linear classifier is trained in a supervised manner to evaluate the effectiveness of self-supervised learning [2–4,6]. In Table 1, utilizing the ResNet-50 encoder as the backbone network on the ImageNet dataset, we compared our method with previous state-of-the-art SSL methods in terms of accuracy, listing the top-1 and top-5 accuracy.

4.3   Ablation Study

Ablation Study is a scientific research method aimed at evaluating the impact of systematically removing or disabling models, variables, or components on the overall performance of a system. We trained the ResNet-50 model on the ImageNet dataset to investigate the effect of the following parameters on the model.

Firstly, we investigate the impacts of incorporating similarity judgment and weighting of negative samples in Table 2.

Table 1. The accuracy of self-supervised learning methods, based on linear evaluation using the **ImageNet**, is compared with that of a **ResNet-50** encoder.

Method	200ep
SimCLR [3]	66.5
MoCo [2]	67.5
SWAV [5]	69.1
SimSiam [6]	70.0
BYOL [4]	70.6
OUR(no RSJM)	**71.050**
OUR(with RSJM)	**71.712**

Table 2. Explore the influence of similarity-based sample judgment threshold δ and negative sample weighting in linear evaluation.

Similarity Judgment	Negative sample weighting	Top-1(%)
		71.050
✓		71.280(↑**0.23**)
	✓	71.218(↑**0.168**)
✓	✓	71.502(↑**0.452**)

Constant coefficient hyperparamete α of sample judgment threshold δ. The selection of positive and negative samples by SSJM is related to the constant coefficient hyperparameter α in Table 3, which determines the size of the sample judgment threshold δ. A larger α leads to a larger sample judgment threshold, indicating a stricter selection of positive samples. For example, when $\alpha = 1$, this means that we select all samples with similarity greater than or equal to the current sample and its data-augmented version as positive samples. We employed the ResNet-50 encoder and conducted a total of 200 epochs of pre-training. Constant coefficient hyperparametes α used are 0.6, 0.7, 0.8, and 0.9, and their performance was tested through linear evaluation on the ImageNet dataset.

Table 3. The effect of the Constant coefficient hyperparamete α in the sample judgment threshold δ on the ResNet-50 encoder based on linear evaluation.

α	0.6	0.7	0.8	0.9
Top-1(%)	71.424	71.454	**71.502**	71.358

The timing of integrating SSJM. The timing of integrating SSJM is crucial. If SSJM is introduced too early, the limited modeling capabilities of the encoder at that stage may lead to errors in the positive and negative sample judgments based on similarity. Conversely, introducing SSJM too late may result in SSJM occupying too little time during training. In Table 4, We employed the ResNet-50 encoder, the constant coefficient hyperparameter $\alpha = 1$, and conducted a total of 200 epochs of pre-training. SSJM was introduced at the 50th, 100th, 150th, and 175th epochs, and their performance was tested through linear evaluation on the ImageNet dataset.

Table 4. The timing of integrating SSJM on the ResNet-50 encoder based on linear evaluation.

timing of introduction	50	100	150	175
Top-1(%)		71.052	71.384	**71.502**	71.322

4.4 "Plug-and-Play" Module Validation

We will validate the plug-and-play nature of our proposed similarity-based sample judgment module (SSJM). We demonstrate the flexibility and universality of this module in various scenarios to prove its plug-and-play characteristics. Therefore, We have selected several recent self-supervised contrastive learning strategies, integrated SSJM into them, and performed performance comparisons to showcase the plug-and-play nature of this module, as shown in Table 5.

Table 5. Experimental Results of Integrating **SSJM** into SimCLR and MoCo Models.

Method	Top-1(%)
SimCLR [3]	66.512
MoCo [2]	67.548
SimCLR+OUR	**66.857(↑0.345)**
MoCo+OUR	**67.932(↑0.384)**

5   Conclusion Remarks and Future Work

This paper presents a self-supervised contrast learning framework with robust sample pair judgment. In contrast to previous self-supervised contrastive learning methods that utilize the judgement of positive and negative samples, our approach introduces a similarity-based sample judgment module(SSJM). This module utilizes a similarity-based sample judgment threshold δ to classify similar samples as positive and dissimilar samples as negative, based on the similarity of image sample features. This effectively prevents the issue of misclassifying multiple images of the same class in the training set as negative samples during the training process. Additionally, the similarity-based sample judgment module is designed to be plug-and-play, offering flexibility and universality across various contrastive learning strategies. Extensive experiments demonstrate impressive results in both linear evaluation and various transfer tasks.

In the future, we are interested in integrating SSJM into supervised, semi-supervised, and weakly supervised learning methods that utilize contrastive learning, as well as various downstream tasks.

References

1. Bachman, P., Hjelm, R.D., Buchwalter, W.: Learning representations by maximizing mutual information across views. In: Advances in Neural Information Processing Systems, vol. 32 (2019)
2. He, K., Fan, H., Wu, Y., Xie, S., Girshick, R.: Momentum contrast for unsupervised visual representation learning. In: Proceedings of the IEEE/CVF Conference on Computer Vision and Pattern Recognition, pp. 9729–9738 (2020)
3. Chen, T., Kornblith, S., Norouzi, M., Hinton, G.: A simple framework for contrastive learning of visual representations. In: International Conference on Machine Learning, pp. 1597–1607. PMLR (2020)
4. Grill, J.-B., et al.: Bootstrap your own latent-a new approach to self-supervised learning. In: Advances in Neural Information Processing Systems, vol. 33, pp. 21 271–21 284 (2020)
5. Caron, M., Misra, I., Mairal, J., Goyal, P., Bojanowski, P., Joulin, A.: Unsupervised learning of visual features by contrasting cluster assignments. Adv. Neural. Inf. Process. Syst. **33**, 9912–9924 (2020)
6. Chen, X., He, K.: Exploring simple Siamese representation learning. In: Proceedings of the IEEE/CVF Conference on Computer Vision and Pattern Recognition, pp. 15 750–15 758 (2021)
7. Zhu, W., Liu, J., Huang, Y.: HNSSL: hard negative-based self-supervised learning. In: Proceedings of the IEEE/CVF Conference on Computer Vision and Pattern Recognition, pp. 4777–4786 (2023)
8. Hadsell, R., Chopra, S., LeCun, Y.: Dimensionality reduction by learning an invariant mapping. In: IEEE Computer Society Conference on Computer Vision and Pattern Recognition (CVPR 2006), vol. 2. IEEE 2006, pp. 1735–1742 (2006)
9. Oord, A., Li, Y., Vinyals, O.: Representation learning with contrastive predictive coding. arXiv preprint arXiv:1807.03748 (2018)
10. Wu, Z., Xiong, Y., Yu, S.X., Lin, D.: Unsupervised feature learning via non-parametric instance discrimination. In: Proceedings of the IEEE Conference on Computer Vision and Pattern Recognition, pp. 3733–3742 (2018)
11. He, K., Zhang, X., Ren, S., Sun, J.: Deep residual learning for image recognition. In: Proceedings of the IEEE Conference on Computer Vision and Pattern Recognition, pp. 770–778 (2016)
12. Russakovsky, O., Deng, J., Su, H., Krause, J., Satheesh, S., Ma, S., Huang, Z., Karpathy, A., Khosla, A., Bernstein, M., et al.: Imagenet large scale visual recognition challenge. Int. J. Comput. Vision **115**, 211–252 (2015)

13. Vincent, P., Larochelle, H., Bengio, Y., Manzagol, P.-A.: Extracting and composing robust features with denoising autoencoders. In: Proceedings of the 25th International Conference on Machine Learning, pp. 1096–1103 (2008)
14. Pathak, D., Krahenbuhl, P., Donahue, J., Darrell, T., Efros, A.A.: Context encoders: feature learning by inpainting. In: Proceedings of the IEEE Conference on Computer Vision and Pattern Recognition, pp. 2536–2544 (2016)
15. Zhang, R., Isola, P., Efros, A.A.: Colorful image colorization. In: Leibe, B., Matas, J., Sebe, N., Welling, M. (eds.) ECCV 2016. LNCS, vol. 9907, pp. 649–666. Springer, Cham (2016). https://doi.org/10.1007/978-3-319-46487-9_40
16. Zhang, R., Isola, P., Efros, A.: A Split-brain autoencoders: Unsupervised learning by cross-channel prediction. In: Proceedings of the IEEE Conference on Computer Vision and Pattern Recognition, pp. 1058–1067 (2017)
17. Chen, X., Duan, Y., Houthooft, R., Schulman, J., Sutskever, I., Abbeel, P.: Infogan: interpretable representation learning by information maximizing generative adversarial nets. In: Advances in Neural Information Processing Systems, vol. 29 (2016)
18. Salimans, T., Goodfellow, I., Zaremba, W., Cheung, V., Radford, A., Chen, X.: Improved techniques for training Gans. In: Advances in Neural Information Processing Systems, vol. 29 (2016)
19. Hjelm, R.D., et al.: Learning deep representations by mutual information estimation and maximization. arXiv preprint arXiv:1808.06670 (2018)
20. Ye, M., Zhang, X., Yuen, P.C., Chang, S.-F.: Unsupervised embedding learning via invariant and spreading instance feature. In: Proceedings of the IEEE/CVF Conference on Computer Vision and Pattern Recognition, pp. 6210–6219 (2019)
21. Henaff, O.: Data-efficient image recognition with contrastive predictive coding. In: International Conference on Machine Learning, pp. 4182–4192. PMLR (2020)
22. Tian, Y., Krishnan, D., Isola, P.: Contrastive multiview coding. In: Vedaldi, A., Bischof, H., Brox, T., Frahm, J.-M. (eds.) ECCV 2020. LNCS, vol. 12356, pp. 776–794. Springer, Cham (2020). https://doi.org/10.1007/978-3-030-58621-8_45
23. Misra, I., Maaten, L.: Self-supervised learning of pretext-invariant representations. In: Proceedings of the IEEE/CVF Conference on Computer Vision and Pattern Recognition, pp. 6707–6717 (2020)
24. Dosovitskiy, A., Springenberg, J.T., Riedmiller, M., Brox, T.: Discriminative unsupervised feature learning with convolutional neural networks. In: Advances in Neural Information Processing Systems, vol. 27 (2014)
25. Larsson, G., Maire, M., Shakhnarovich, G.: Learning representations for automatic colorization. In: Leibe, B., Matas, J., Sebe, N., Welling, M. (eds.) ECCV 2016. LNCS, vol. 9908, pp. 577–593. Springer, Cham (2016). https://doi.org/10.1007/978-3-319-46493-0_35
26. Gidaris, S., Singh, P., Komodakis, N.: Unsupervised representation learning by predicting image rotations," arXiv preprint arXiv:1803.07728 (2018)
27. Doersch, C., Gupta, A., Efros, A.A.: Unsupervised visual representation learning by context prediction. In: Proceedings of the IEEE International Conference on Computer Vision, pp. 1422–1430 (2015)
28. Noroozi, M., Favaro, P.: Unsupervised learning of visual representations by solving jigsaw puzzles. In: Leibe, B., Matas, J., Sebe, N., Welling, M. (eds.) ECCV 2016. LNCS, vol. 9910, pp. 69–84. Springer, Cham (2016). https://doi.org/10.1007/978-3-319-46466-4_5
29. Khosla, P., et al.: Supervised contrastive learning. Adv. Neural Inf. Process. Syst. **33**, 18661–18673 (2020)

30. Robinson, J., Chuang, C.-Y., Sra, S., Jegelka, S.: Contrastive learning with hard negative samples. arXiv preprint arXiv:2010.04592 (2020)
31. Kalantidis, Y., Sariyildiz, M.B., Pion, N., Weinzaepfel, P., Larlus, D.: Hard negative mixing for contrastive learning. Adv. Neural Inf. Process. Syst. **33**, 21798–21809 (2020)
32. Simonyan, K., Zisserman, A.: Very deep convolutional networks for large-scale image recognition. arXiv preprint arXiv:1409.1556 (2014)
33. Szegedy, C., et al.: Going deeper with convolutions. In: Proceedings of the IEEE Conference on Computer Vision and Pattern Recognition, pp. 1–9 (2015)
34. Dosovitskiy, A., et al.: An image is worth 16×16 words: Transformers for image recognition at scale. arXiv preprint arXiv:2010.11929 (2020)
35. Wang, W., et al.: Pyramid vision transformer: A versatile backbone for dense prediction without convolutions. In: Proceedings of the IEEE/CVF International Conference on Computer Vision, pp. 568–578 (2021)
36. Ren, S., Zhou, D., He, S., Feng, J., Wang, X.: Shunted self-attention via multi-scale token aggregation. In: Proceedings of the IEEE/CVF Conference on Computer Vision and Pattern Recognition, pp. 10 853–10 862 (2022)
37. Wang, W., et al.: Crossformer++: a versatile vision transformer hinging on cross-scale attention. arXiv preprint arXiv:2303.06908 (2023)

A Combined Model Based on the Signal Decomposition Method, Optimization Method, and Machine Learning for Wind Speed Predicting

Anfeng Zhu[1], Qiancheng Zhao[1(✉)], Tianlong Yang[1], and Ling Zhou[2]

[1] Engineering Research Center of Hunan Province for the Mining and Utilization of Wind Turbines Operation Data, Hunan University of Science and Technology, Xiangtan 411201, China
hnustzaf@mail.hnust.edu.cn

[2] College of Electrical and Information Engineering, Hunan University of Technology, Zhuzhou 412002, China

Abstract. The stochastic and changing characteristics of wind speed signals can pose a great challenge to the accuracy of wind speed forecasting. Therefore, this work proposes a wind speed forecasting method founded on singular spectrum analysis (SSA) and ALO-LSSVM. The method firstly uses SSA to decompose the original sequence, then builds the least squares support vector machine (LSSVM) for each part separately, and finally superimposes the forecast outcomes of every component to determine the predicted wind speed value. To improve the prediction performance, the ant-lion algorithm (ALO) is applied in optimize the settings of the LSSVM. The data from a wind farm in southern China are analyzed, and the outcomes reveal that the suggested approach has greater prediction accuracy.

Keywords: Singular spectrum analysis · Ant-lion algorithm · machine learning · Wind speed prediction

1 Introduction

Due to the widespread use of fossil fuels, the imminent extinction of fossil energy sources and the resulting environmental issues are becoming increasingly serious. Clean and sustainable wind energy is becoming a high priority for all countries. However, the intermittent, random and uncontrollable nature of wind energy makes it a great challenge to connect wind power to the grid on a large scale, so accurate and effective forecasting of wind speed is of major essential for the smooth running of the electricity system.

Researchers have studied wind speed forecasting extensively in the past few years. At present, the approaches used for wind speed forecasting mainly include regression analysis, time series, Markov chain, support vector machine [12] and neural network [1–5]. However, in the reality of wind speed prediction, through the above single forecasting

H. Lu (Ed.): ISAIR 2024, CCIS 2402, pp. 280–289, 2025.
https://doi.org/10.1007/978-981-96-2911-4_27

method often can not achieve the desired prediction effect, to the single prediction approach to raise the forecasting accuracy of wind speed by certain improvements. Literature [6] compares the LMD and empirical modal decomposition (EMD) from four points, and the results show that the LMD can effectively eliminate modal aliasing compared with the EMD to obtain more accurate instantaneous frequencies. Literature [7] shows that SSA outperforms wavelet analysis and empirical modal decomposition analysis methods in removing noise. Literature [8] used the multivariate universe optimization (MVO) algorithm to optimize parameters of the LSSVM, and achieved high modeling accuracy.

In view of the advantages of LSSVM with strong generalization ability and sample problem processing ability, this paper adopts ALO to optimize the settings of LSSVM, and combines with SSA method to propose a wind speed prediction model founded on SSA-ALO-LSSVM. Through experimental simulation analysis, the suggested method significantly raises the accuracy of wind speed prediction.

2   Methodology

2.1   SSA

SSA combines components of time series, multiple statistics, multiple geometry, and singular value decomposition to extract trends, periodic oscillations, and noise components from signals, and is suitable for analyzing non-stationary time series that contain underlying structure [9]. The number of observed one-dimensional time series is selected by choosing an appropriate embedding dimension d. A K-column trajectory matrix consisting of K vectors $X_i(i = 1,2,\cdots, K = N-d + 1)$ is shown in the following equation:

$$X = [X_1, \cdots X_K] = \left(X_{ij}\right)_{i,j=1}^{d,K} = \begin{pmatrix} x_1 & x_2 & x_3 & \cdots & x_K \\ x_2 & x_3 & x_4 & \cdots & x_{K+1} \\ \vdots & \vdots & \vdots & \cdots & \vdots \\ x_d & x_{d+1} & x_{d+2} & \cdots & y_N \end{pmatrix} \quad (1)$$

The covariance XX^T is calculated to find the d eigenvalues $\lambda_1 \geq \lambda_2 \geq, \cdots, \geq \lambda_d \geq 0$, $U_1, \cdots, U_d$ as their corresponding orthogonal eigenvectors.

$$E_i = \sqrt{\lambda_i} U_i V_i, i = 1, 2, \cdots, d' \quad (2)$$

$$V_i = X^T U_i / \sqrt{\lambda_i} \quad (3)$$

$$X = E_1 + E_2 + \cdots + E_i \quad (4)$$

where X_i is the i-th SVD component; U represents the empirical orthogonal function of matrix X; and V_i represents the principal element of X.

Divide Eq. (4) into m different groups and sum the matrices included in each group, where α represents the contribution rate of each group.

$$X_I = X_{i_1} + \cdots + X_{i_0} \tag{5}$$

$$X = X_{I_1} + \cdots X_{I_m} \tag{6}$$

$$\alpha = \frac{\lambda_i}{\sum\limits_{i=1}^{d} \lambda_i} \tag{7}$$

The grouped matrix X represents transformed into a matrix of length N using diagonal averaging. The matrix Y is transformed to $Y = \{y_1, y_2, \cdots, y_N\}$:

$$y_k = \begin{cases} \frac{1}{k} \sum\limits_{m=1}^{k} y^*_{m,k-m+1}, & 1 \le k < d^* \\ \frac{1}{d^*} \sum\limits_{m=1}^{L^*} y^*_{m,k-m+1}, & d^* \le k < K^* \\ \frac{1}{N-k+1} \sum\limits_{m=k-K^*+1}^{N-K^*+1} y^*_{m,k-m+1}, & K^* \le k < N \end{cases} \tag{8}$$

Applying Eq. (8) to obtain the matrix, generates the sequence $X^{(k)} = \left(x_1^{(k)}, \cdots, x_N^{(k)} \right)$, which is in the original sequence:

$$x_i = \sum\limits_{k=1}^{m} x_N^{(k)}, i = 1, 2, \cdots, N \tag{9}$$

2.2 ALO

2.2.1 Ants Wandering Randomly

Ants wandering randomly are normalized to:

$$X_i^t = \frac{\left(X_i^t - a_i\right) \times \left(d_i^t - c_i^t\right)}{(b_i - a_i)} + c_i t \; x_i = \sum\limits_{k=1}^{m} x_N^{(k)}, i = 1, 2, \cdots, N \tag{10}$$

where a_i represents the minimum value of the arbitrary tour for the i-th variable; d_i^t represents the maximum value of the i-th variable for the t-th iteration; c_i^t represents the minimum value of the i-th variable for the t-th repetition; and b_i represents the maximum value of the random tour for the i-th variable.

2.2.2 Impact of Ant-Lion Traps

The erratic wandering routes of the ants are impacted by the ant-lion traps as shown in the following equation.

$$c_i^t = A_j^t + c^t \tag{11}$$

$$d_i^t = A_j^t + d^t \tag{12}$$

where c^t represents the minimum value of all variables in the t-th repetition; A_j^t represents the position of the j-th ant lion chosen in the t-th repetition.

2.2.3 Ant-Lion Capture Mechanism

Ant lions are capable of constructing traps commensurate with their fitness, and ants falling into the traps adaptively reduce the radius of the ants' randomized walking hypersphere [10], as shown in the formula below.

$$c^t = \frac{c^t}{I}, d^t = \frac{d^t}{I} \tag{13}$$

$$I = \begin{cases} 1, & t \le 0.1T \\ 10^v \times \frac{t}{T}, & t > 0.1T \end{cases} \tag{14}$$

where I denotes the scaling factor; T represents the maximum number of repetitions; and v represents the number that varies with increasing iterations.

When the ant adaptation value is less than the ant lion, then the ant is captured, at this point, the ant lion location will be updated founded on the location of the ant as given in the equation below.

$$A_j^t = Ant_i^t, \quad f\left(Ant_i^t\right) < f\left(A_j^t\right) \tag{15}$$

2.2.4 Elitism

The best adapted ant lions were selected as elite ant lions with ant positions:

$$Ant_i^t = \frac{R_A^t + R_E^t}{2} \tag{16}$$

where R_A^t is the randomized swim surrounding the ant lion picked by the roulette wheel in the t-th repetition; R_E^t represents the randomized swim surrounding the elite ant lion in the t-th repetition.

2.3 LSSVM

For a given training set:

$$T = x_1, y_1, x_2, y_2, \cdots x_n, y_n \tag{17}$$

Assume that its regression function is

$$y = f(t) = \boldsymbol{\omega}^{\mathrm{T}} x + b \tag{18}$$

where x represents the sample input; y represents the sample output; In the high-dimensional space, the standard vector and intercept of the hyperplane are denoted by ω and b, respectively.

The regression issue can be changed into a constraint problem by applying the risk minimization concept [11].

$$\min_{\omega,b,e} J(\boldsymbol{\omega}, e) = \frac{1}{2}\boldsymbol{\omega}^{\mathrm{T}}\boldsymbol{\omega} + \frac{1}{2}\gamma\sum_{i=1}^{N} e_i^2 \tag{19}$$

With the introduction of the Lagrange multiplier α, the problem mentioned above becomes:

$$L(\boldsymbol{\omega}, b, e, \alpha) = J(\boldsymbol{\omega}, e) - \sum_{i=1}^{N} \alpha_i \boldsymbol{\omega}^{\mathrm{T}} \varphi(x_i) + b + e_i - y_i \tag{20}$$

Partial differentiation of ω, b, e, α, respectively, yields the optimal value, which in turn establishes the regression function:

$$y(x) = \sum_{i=1}^{N} \alpha_i K(x, x_i) + b \tag{21}$$

where $K(x, x_i)$ is the kernel function.

3 Experimental Settings

3.1 Evaluation Indicators

The following calculation formula is applied to assess the modeling accuracy: mean absolute error (MAPE), root mean square error (RMSE), and mean absolute percentage error (MAPE).

$$\mathrm{MAE} = \frac{1}{n}\sum_{i=1}^{n} \left| \widehat{y}_i - y_i \right| \tag{22}$$

$$\mathrm{RMSE} = \sqrt{\frac{1}{n}\sum_{i=1}^{n} \left(\widehat{y}_i - y_i \right)^2} \tag{23}$$

$$\text{MAPE} = \frac{1}{n} \sum_{i=1}^{n} \left| \frac{\widehat{y}_i - y_i}{y_i} \right| \tag{24}$$

where y_i represents the real value; $\widehat{y}_i$ represents the predicted value.

3.2 Model Structure

In this work, a wind speed prediction method founded on SSA-ALO-LSSVM is proposed. First, the original sequence is decomposed using singular spectrum analysis. Then, the components are modeled as LSSVM separately, and finally the forecasted wind speed values are obtained by superimposing the forecasting results of every component. To increase the prediction performance, ALO is applied in optimize the LSSVM settings. The flowchart of the research's primary components is displayed in Fig. 1.

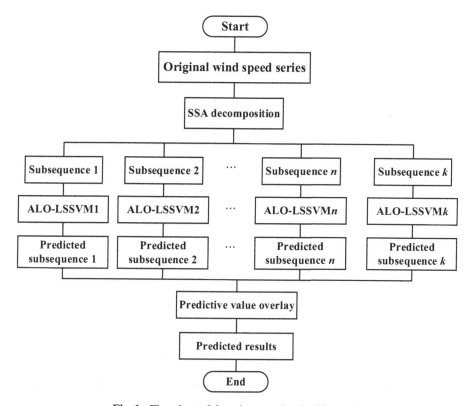

Fig. 1. Flowchart of the primary points in this work.

4   Results and Analysis

In this section, it is discussed whether SSA-ALO-LSSVM is better than other models. The different approaches are SSA-GA-LSSVM, SSA-PSO-LSSVM and SSA-ALO-LSSVM. The outcome of the model evaluation is demonstrated in Table 1, from which SSA-ALO-LSSVM outperforms the other models in any number of prediction stages. Figure 2 compares different approaches for one-step prediction.

Table 1. Comparison of the different approaches.

Model	MAE			RMSE			MAPE		
	1-Step	2-Step	3-Step	1-Step	2-Step	3-Step	1-Step	2-Step	3-Step
SSA-GA-LSSVM	0.2488	0.3529	0.4573	0.2876	0.4241	0.5425	3.2584	4.5047	6.7046
SSA-PSO-LSSVM	0.2193	0.3051	0.3724	0.2556	0.3527	0.4579	2.7432	3.7152	5.6083
SSA-ALO-LSSVM	**0.1876**	**0.2235**	**0.2648**	**0.2127**	**0.2547**	**0.3135**	**2.3218**	**2.7456**	**4.1068**

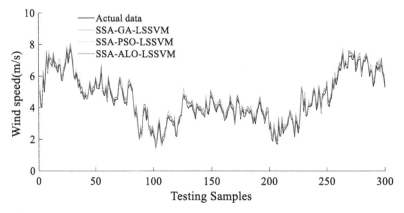

Fig. 2. Comparison of the different approaches.

Regarding one-step forecasting, SSA-ALO-LSSVM achieves satisfactory results: MAE = 0.1876, RMSE = 0.2127, and MAPE = 2.3218. When the prediction step is two, the MAE values of SSA-GA-LSSVM, SSA-PSO-LSSVM, and SSA-ALO-LSSVM are 0.3529, 0.3051, and 0.2235. When the prediction step is three, the RMSE values of SSA-GA-LSSVM, SSA-PSO-LSSVM, and SSA-ALO-LSSVM are 0.5425, 0.4579, and 0.3135. Figures 3, 4 and 5 shows the results of evaluation indicators generated by employing different approaches.

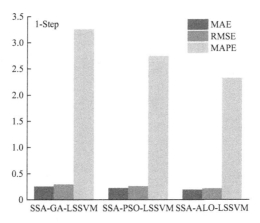

Fig. 3. Model error analysis 1-Step Prediction.

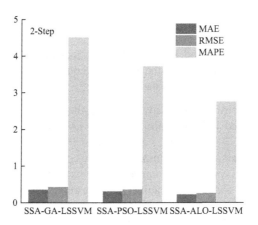

Fig. 4. Model error analysis 2-Step Prediction.

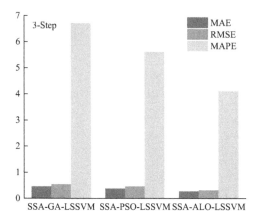

Fig. 5. Model error analysis 3-Step Prediction.

5   Conclusion

In this work, a multi-step wind speed forecasting technology is proposed by combining SSA and ALO-LSSVM, and the following conclusions are obtained from the comparative study with the measured data:

(1) Using singular spectrum analysis to decompose the original sequence can decrease the difficulty caused by wind speed volatility and intermittency on wind speed prediction.
(2) Improved ALO is adopted to optimize the settings of LSSVM model, and the precision of forecasting is enhanced. It can accurately predict the wind speed at different time intervals with good vanning ability, and the efficiency of the approach applied in this work is further confirmed by comparing the prediction findings with the measured data.

Acknowledgments. This work is supported by National Key Research and Development Program of People's Republic of China (grant number 2022YFF0608700) and Hunan Provincial Education Department Youth Project (No. 22B0590).

References

1. Zhu, A, Zhao, Q., Wang, X., Zhou, L.: Ultra-short-term wind power combined prediction based on complementary ensemble empirical mode decomposition, whale optimisation algorithm, and elman network. Energies **15**(9), 3055 (2022)
2. Liu, H., Chen, C.: Data processing strategies in wind energy forecasting models and applications: a comprehensive review. Appl. Energy **249**, 392–408 (2019)
3. Zhu, A., Zhao, Q., Yang, T., Zhou, L., Zeng, B.: Condition monitoring of wind turbine based on deep learning networks and kernel principal component analysis. Comput. Electr. Eng. **105**, 108538 (2023)

4. Pieraccini, M., Parrini, F., Fratini, M., Atzeni, C., Spinelli, P.: In-service testing of wind turbine towers using a microwave sensor. Renew. Energy **33**(1), 13–21 (2008)
5. Zhu, A., Zhao, Q., Yang, T., Zhou, L., Zeng, B.: Wind speed prediction and reconstruction based on improved grey wolf optimization algorithm and deep learning networks. Comput. Electr. Eng. **114**, 109074 (2024)
6. Wang, Y., He, Z., Zi, Y.: A comparative study on the local mean decomposition and empirical mode decomposition and their applications to rotating machinery health diagnosis. J. Vib. Acoust. **132**(2), 613–624 (2010)
7. Du, W., Zhou, J., Wang, Z., Li, R., Wang, J.: Application of improved singular spectrum decomposition method for composite fault diagnosis of gear boxes. Sensors **18**(11), 3804 (2018)
8. Yu, W., Yan, W., Ji, Z.: Research on modeling and process parameters optimization of GlcN fermentation process. J. Syst. Simul. **32**(10), 1895–1902 (2020)
9. Golyandina, N., Nekrutkin, V., Zhigljavsky, A.A.: Analysis of Time Series Structure: SSA and Related Techniques. CRC Press (2001)
10. Mirjalili, S.: The ant lion optimizer. Adv. Eng. Software **83**, 80–98 (2015)
11. Yuan, X., Chen, C., Yuan, Y., Huang, Y., Tan, Q.: Short-term wind power prediction based on LSSVM–GSA model. Energy Convers. Manage. **101**, 393–401 (2015)
12. Soomro, A.A., Mokhtar, A.A., Kurnia, J.C., Lashari, N., Lu, H., Sambo, C.: Integrity assessment of corroded oil and gas pipelines using machine learning: a systematic review. Eng. Fail. Anal. **131**, 105810 (2022)

Improved YOLOv8 Modeling for Earth Observation

Haoyang Zhao, Mei Wang$^{(\boxtimes)}$, Kangle Li, Kun Yang, Lizhi Li, and Zhibo Gong

College of Computer Science and Technology, Xi'an University of Science and Technology,
Xi'an 710699, China
wangm@xust.edu.cn

Abstract. With the continuous development of deep learning, various new object detection models continue to emerge, among which the YOLOv8 model has attracted a large number of researchers in this field due to its excellent performance. The proposal of various new models has become particularly important for the application of object detection in various complex scenes. This article mainly discusses the introduction of a more focused bounding box loss function Focaler-IoU in the YOLOv8 model to improve its detection ability in Earth observation scenarios. The dataset of Earth observation scenes usually faces problems such as small targets, uneven distribution, and difficulty in annotation. These issues result in low accuracy of the trained model in practical detection tasks, making it difficult to meet the needs of practical applications. To address these issues, we chose to replace the original loss function of YOLOv8 with the Focaler-IoU loss function. The Focaler-IoU loss function improves the model's performance in small object detection and imbalanced data distribution by better focusing on the accuracy of bounding boxes, enhancing the model's learning ability for samples. The experimental results show that our proposed method improves mAP and mAP50:95 by about 3.5% compared to traditional methods, and both Precision and Recall are improved. This indicates that the improved model can be more effectively applied to object detection tasks in Earth observation scenes.

Keywords: Object detection · Self built dataset · YOLOv8

1 Introduction

In recent years, with the rapid development and widespread application of drone technology, object detection technology based on Earth observation perspective has shown enormous potential and application value in multiple fields [1]. It has played an important role in many scenarios such as traffic monitoring, agricultural monitoring, and safety patrols. However, object detection tasks from the perspective of Earth observation face challenges such as small image targets, dense distribution, and uneven categories. Therefore, the selection of detection models is also an important task.

Among numerous object detection models, the YOLO (You Only Look Once) series of models have received widespread attention and application due to their efficient detection speed and high accuracy [2]. Each version of the YOLO model [9] has improved

© The Author(s), under exclusive license to Springer Nature Singapore Pte Ltd. 2025
H. Lu (Ed.): ISAIR 2024, CCIS 2402, pp. 290–295, 2025.
https://doi.org/10.1007/978-981-96-2911-4_28

in accuracy and speed, especially the latest YOLOv8 model, which performs well on multiple public datasets and demonstrates strong detection capabilities [3]. However, in the scenario of ground observation, the YOLOv8 model still has some shortcomings, especially in dealing with small targets and imbalanced data distribution, and there is still significant room for improvement in detection performance.

To address these issues, we have introduced a new bounding box loss function Focaler-IoU in the YOLOv8 model. The Focaler-IoU loss function enhances the model's learning ability for small targets and imbalanced data by focusing on difficult to detect samples, thereby improving detection accuracy and recall. Traditional loss functions often fail to fully utilize the complexity of ground observation scenarios, while Focaler-IoU adapts better to these complex scenarios by adjusting the loss distribution [4].

In the following chapters, we will introduce the Focaler-IoU loss function, the network topology and working principle of the yolov8 model, explore its application in Earth observation scenarios, and demonstrate its performance through multiple rounds of training using self built datasets.

2 Related Work

2.1 Overview of Object Detection

Object detection is an important task in the field of computer vision, which is to find all the interesting objects (objects) in the image, determine their categories and positions. In the field of object detection, algorithms are mainly divided into two categories: single-stage method and two-stage method. The YOLOv8 used in our paper belongs to single-stage method. Their difference lies in the two-stage method, which first generates candidate regions and then classifies and regresses them. It has high accuracy but also requires a larger computational load and slower speed, making it more suitable for application scenarios that require high detection accuracy. The single-stage method directly predicts object categories and bounding boxes from images, with high computational efficiency and fast speed, but relatively lower accuracy compared to the two-stage method [5]. It is suitable for applications with high real-time requirements such as ground observation.

3 Research Method

3.1 Focaler-IoU Loss Function

In the field of object detection, the accuracy of object detection depends on the loss function of bounding box regression. The traditional loss function is sensitive to outliers and has unstable performance, while IoU (Intersection over Union), as a more suitable evaluation indicator, significantly improves accuracy in object detection. However, there is a gradient vanishing problem with IoU loss when there is no overlap in the boxes. For this purpose, researchers have proposed a series of IoU based loss functions that optimize loss calculation in different ways to improve detection accuracy and convergence speed. However, the imbalance of training samples still affects the performance of edge regression. Focaler-IoU combines Focal Loss and IoU loss functions to solve the problem of imbalanced positive and negative samples and bounding box regression in object detection tasks by focusing on different regression samples, thereby improving the performance of detectors in different detection tasks. The formula for the Focaler-IoU loss function is as follows:

$$IoU^{focaler} = \begin{cases} 0, & IoU < d \\ \frac{IoU-d}{u-d}, & d \ll IoU \ll u \\ 1, & IoU > u \end{cases} \tag{1}$$

where $IoU^{focaler}$ is the reconstructed Focaler-IoU, IoU is the original IoU value, and [d, u] ∈ [0, 1]. By adjusting the values of d and u, we can make $IoU^{focaler}$ focus on different regression samples. Its loss is defined below [4]:

$$L_{\text{Focaler-IoU}} = 1 - IoU^{focaler} \tag{2}$$

3.2   Yolov8 Model Network Structure

YOLOv8 achieves efficient object detection through an improved backbone network, feature fusion mechanism, and anchor free detection method. The model preprocesses input images, extracts features, fuses features, directly predicts targets, and ultimately outputs accurate target detection results through reasonable loss functions and post-processing steps (Fig. 1).

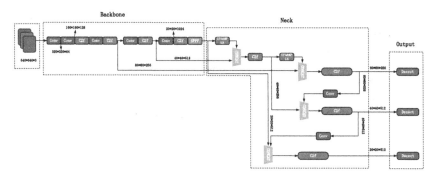

Fig. 1. YOLOv8s Network Architecture

The model structure of YOLOv8 mainly consists of three parts:

As the backbone of the YOLOv8 model, Backbone's main function is to extract multi-scale features from input images. As the foundation of the entire network, it is responsible for extracting the feature information of the input image, and the extracted features are also the basis for subsequent network layer object detection [6].

The Neck layer is a feature fusion layer mainly used to fuse multi-scale features extracted by Backbone, enhancing the model's detection ability for targets of different scales [7]. This level can fuse feature maps of different scales, enabling the network to simultaneously detect targets of different sizes.

The function of the Head section is to convert the fused feature map into the final detection result. In the YOLOv8 model, the Head section typically contains multiple detection heads, each responsible for predicting targets of a specific scale to achieve detection of targets of different sizes [8].

4 Experiments

4.1 Self Built Dataset

The dataset used in our experiment is a self built dataset, which is usually collected in scenes with high personnel flow and vehicles such as campuses, highways, and blocks. The detection targets are mainly six categories: pedestrians, cars, electric vehicles, motorcycles, buses, and trucks. Using DJI drones as the raw video capture tool, the scene is recorded at a height of approximately 40m. After the video collection is completed, use a cropping tool to crop and save the video every 5 s. The saved images are manually annotated using the labelimg tool. The number of images in the training set of the dataset is 910, and the number of images in the test set is 166.

4.2 Experimental Environment

The GPU used in the experiment is NVIDIA RTX 4090-24G, with Pytorch framework version 2.0.0 + cu118, Python version 3.8.0, and Cuda version 11.8.

4.3 Contrast Test

Our improved method and traditional method were trained for 192 rounds under the same parameters and dataset conditions. The changes in mAP and loss function are shown in the following Fig. 2:

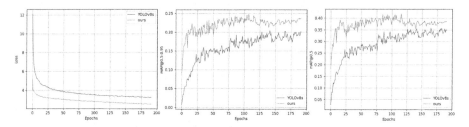

Fig. 2. Comparison of Improvement Effects

It can be clearly seen that the improved model has a faster and smoother convergence speed of the overall Loss function compared to the traditional model, and the mAP is also higher than the traditional model. The overall performance of the improved model is better than the former.

Table 1 shows the comparison of all categories and indicators between our model and traditional models on the same dataset.

Table 1. Comparison of All Category Indicators.

Data set	Model	Class	P	R	mAP	mAP50:95
Self built dataset	YOLOv8	all	0. 398	0.387	0.351	0.202
	Ours	all	**0. 422**	**0. 403**	**0.399**	**0. 238**

4.4 Visualization of Detection Results

The following figure shows the comparison of detection performance between the improved yolov8s model and the yolov8s model with added Focaler-IoU loss function in dense and sparse scenes under the same parameter settings and training rounds. The left side shows the detection performance of the original yolov8s model, and the right side shows the detection performance of the improved yolov8s model.

In dense scenes, the pre improved model missed detection of distant vehicles, covered vehicles, and pedestrians. The improved model has a higher overall confidence in vehicle and pedestrian detection, and most pedestrians and covered vehicles can be correctly detected after adding the Focaler-IoU loss function. In sparse scenes, the improved model can better recognize distant vehicles, and the overall detection confidence is better than before, but pedestrians in the distance are still not detected. From this, it can be seen that the improved model can effectively reduce the occurrence of false positives and missed detections. The addition of the Focaler-IoU loss function does indeed improve the detection performance of small targets in Earth observation scenarios (Figs. 3 and 4).

Fig. 3. Comparison of object detection in dense scenes

Fig. 4. Comparison of sparse scene object detection

5   Conclusion

This article provides an in-depth exploration and analysis of the YOLOv8 object detection model in Earth observation scenarios. Through a series of experiments and comparative analysis, we have verified that the YOLOv8 model with the addition of Focaler-IoU loss function effectively improves the detection accuracy of small targets in this scenario, and can effectively improve the occurrence of false positives and missed detections. Although the improved model has achieved significant results in object detection tasks in Earth observation scenarios, there are still some challenges and limitations. There are still many small targets in the distance that cannot be fully detected, and the accuracy of pedestrian detection is also lower. Therefore, the model still needs further improvement and optimization.

Acknowledgments. This work is supported by the National Science and Technology Major Project of China under grant 2022ZD0119005, and the Core Technology Research project of Key Industrial Chains of Xian City under grant 23ZDCYJSGG0025–2022, the Natural Science Foundation of Shaanxi Province under grant 2024JC-YBMS-539.

References

1. Lu, H., Zhang, M., Xu, X., Li, Y., Shen, H.T.: Deep fuzzy hashing network for efficient image retrieval. IEEE Trans. Fuzzy Syst. (2020). https://doi.org/10.1109/TFUZZ.2020.2984991
2. Ma, C., et al.: Visual information processing for deep-sea visual monitoring system. Cogn. Robot. **1**, 3–11 (2021)
3. Lu, H., Teng, Y., Li, Y.: Learning latent dynamics for autonomous shape control of deformable object. IEEE Trans. Intell. Transp. Syst. (2022)
4. Zhang, H., Zhang, S.: Focaler-IoU: more focused intersection over union loss. arXiv preprint arXiv:2401.10525 (2024). Accessed 15 May 2024
5. Li, Y., Cai, J., Zhou, Q., Lu, H.: Joint semantic-instance segmentation method for intelligent transportation system. IEEE Trans. Intell. Transp. Syst. (2022)
6. Zhao, X., Zhang, W., Zhang, H., Zheng, C., Ma, J., Zhang, Z.: ITD-YOLOv8: an infrared target detection model based on YOLOv8 for unmanned aerial vehicles. Drones (2024)
7. Huangfu, Z., Li, S.: Lightweight you only look once v8: an upgraded you only look once v8 algorithm for small object identification in unmanned aerial vehicle images. Appl. Sci. (2023)
8. Lan, K., Jiang, X., Ding, X., Lin, H., Chan, S.: High-efficiency and high-precision ship detection algorithm based on improved YOLOv8n. Mathematics (2024)
9. Koga, S., Hamamoto, K., Lu, H., Nakatoh, Y.: Optimizing food sample handling and placement pattern recognition with YOLO: advanced techniques in robotic object detection. Cogn. Robot. (2024)

Semantic Guided Multi-feature Awared Network for Self-supervised Learning

Yuhan Li[1], Ningyuan Li[1], Xipeng Pan[2], Wenyi Zhao[1], Weidong Zhang[3], Lingqiao Li[2], Mu Yang[4], and Huihua Yang[1(✉)]

[1] Beijing University of Posts and Telecommunications, Beijing, China
{yuhanli,yhh}@bupt.edu.cn
[2] Guilin University of Electronic Technology, Guilin, China
[3] Henan Institute of Science and Technology, Henan, China
[4] Techmach (Beijing) Industrial Technology Co. Ltd., Beijing, China

Abstract. Contrastive learning is a mainstream method of self-supervised learning, which has achieved excellent performance recently. It refers to learning representative features by discriminating the similarities and dissimilarities between images without labels. However, contrastive learning focuses more on the deep semantic information, it falls short in terms of spatial sensitivity. Besides, neural networks with different depths extract different information, all of which is critical for models to perform decision-making. Nevertheless, traditional contrastive learning methods do not sufficiently utilize the input features. To address these issues, we propose SGMNet, which adopts a cross-space mutual optimization structure combining contrastive learning with position prediction task. Moreover, to improve the utilization of information, SGMNet integrates features from different levels so that it can obtain texture and semantic information. In addition, considering the high redundancy of shallow feature, in order to make the model focus on the important parts and avoid it learning some meaningless "shortcuts", we design a feature fusion module to extract the information in the shallow feature map with deep feature map, which enables the model to focus on the semantic-related important detail features. Experimental results show that SGMNet gives competitive performance on multiple datasets.

Keywords: Contrastive Learning · Self-supervised Learning · Pretext Task · Information Fusion · Hybrid Task

1 Introduction

Recently, deep learning has been widely used in various fields, such as deep-sea visual monitoring systems [1, 2], intelligent transportation systems [3], robot perception [5, 6, 8], and crowd counting during the coronavirus [7]. Due to the large amount of manual annotation required for supervised deep learning methods, it not only causes significant annotation costs, but also often leads to mislabeling and omissions, which consequently, results in decreased accuracy of the models. As self-supervised learning (SSL) can learn unlabeled data and obtain label-independent, generalizable feature, it has recently become a popular pre-training paradigm. Contrastive learning [4, 9, 10] is a mainstream training method of SSL, which is based on the invariance of image views. In the absence of labels, the model learns advanced semantic features by discriminating the differences between images, effectively separating the representation of different images, so that models can learn high quality representations. Before the advent of contrastive learning, pretext tasks are widely employed to assist training on target tasks. Since these methods focus on specific tasks, the resulting representation are task-dependent and limited. Nevertheless, they perform well in some specific aspects: for instance, using rotation as an auxiliary task enables the model to better identify the subject of images by accurately judging the degree of rotation, while position prediction as an auxiliary task helps the model learn the logical relationships within the image, thereby enhancing spatial sensitivity. In recent years, many approaches have attempted to combine contrastive learning with pretext tasks to obtain representations with stronger semantic expression capabilities and more detailed information within the image [23]. Therefore, how to properly combine a suitable pretext task with the contrastive learning, and efficiently utilize information remain crucial problems to be addressed.

In addition to this, existing models only use the features output from the last layer of the backbone network for contrastive learning or pretext tasks, resulting in a waste of important information. In fact, the shallow layers produce low-level features, capturing texture and edge details, whereas the deeper layers extract high-level semantic information, which is crucial for a wide range of downstream tasks. When humans carry out classification tasks, they first make a rough classification based on high-level features, and then make a fine-grained classification based on color, texture, and details. Using shallow information also presents some challenges. The shallow feature is highly redundant. If these complex and useless information from the shallow feature cannot be properly filtered out, the models may learn some meaningless "shortcuts", making it more difficult for the models to obtain more robust representations. Furthermore, since contrastive learning focuses more on the overall view and neglects the internal correlations of images, such as positional structure and texture details, it performs well in semantic alignment but lacks spatial sensitivity [11].

To address these issues, we propose SGMNet. By designing a feature fusion module, SGMNet achieves the fusion of low-level and high-level features. This module first extracts feature maps at different levels generated by the encoder, and then uses the deep feature map as a guidance to generate a feature extractor for extracting useful information from the shallow features. This feature extractor effectively filters out those complex and useless information, and makes the model focus on semantically guided important detail information. Finally, the deep features are fused with the extracted shallow features, which results in the representations including information of different levels. In addition, we propose cross-space mutual optimization to encourage the model to learn more effectively based on the information provided by the feature space by introducing a position prediction task in embedding space, which improves the spatial sensitivity of our model while maintains the semantic alignment. In order to make the model learn the internal spatial structure and improve the information utilization, we use the spatially-coupled sampling manner to crop a set of images with spatial constraints from the original images.

Our contributions can be summarized as follows:

(1) In order to improve the utilization of information and obtain representations with strong semantic alignment and spatial sensitivity, we propose SGMNet which adopts a hybrid task structure combining contrastive learning with position prediction task. SGMNet can effectively integrate features from different levels with a feature fusion module. Experimental results show that our model has significant improvements on multiple datasets.
(2) We are the first to propose the feature fusion module to achieve the fusion of multi-level features for self-supervised learning. This module leverages an extractor to acquire critical information from the redundant shallow feature map. It can effectively prevent the model from learning "shortcuts" and improve the generalization ability of our model. Besides this module has strong flexibility and can be utilized on various contrastive learning methods for improvements.
(3) We propose a cross-space mutual optimization structure for the first time, which jointly optimizes the feature space and embedding space. The feature space provides more information of different levels to the embedding space and the embedding space optimization drives the model to learn more sufficiently by performing a position prediction task. As a result, SGMNet gains better semantic alignment and spatial sensitivity.

2 Proposed Method

2.1 Overall Framework

The overall structure of the model is shown in Fig. 1. Generally, SGMNet leverages cross-space mutual optimization. The feature space refers to the space where the feature map obtained by the backbone is located. While the embedding space denotes the space where the representations that are utilized for pretext tasks locate. The feature space provides extra information from different levels to the embedding space and the embedding space optimization drives the model to learn more effectively by performing a position prediction task.

To be specific, SGMNet adopts a Siamese network structure for the pre-training process, which is divided into a base encoder $f_\theta(.)$ and a derived encoder $f_\phi(.)$. Entering a mini-batch images into the sampling module, the sampled images are then shuffled and stitched, then processed by the base encoder and the derived encoder. The derived encoder is a momentum encoder, and its parameters are updated through momentum from the base encoder $f_\theta(.)$. The output feature map is divided into shallow and deep parts and we use r to denote the fusion ratio between deep and shallow layers and $r = 1/2$ by default. Suppose the backbone of this network consists of b blocks, then with the output of the $r \times b$-th block being the shallow feature map, and the output of the last block is the deep feature map. These two feature maps are input into the feature fusion module to obtain the fused feature vector for subsequent tasks. The subsequent tasks involve position prediction of the feature vectors to determine the relative positions of different crops from the same image. The feature vectors are then passed through multi-layer perceptrons (MLPs) to obtain latent vectors, which are used for contrastive learning. Crops from the same image are considered positive, while crops from different images are considered negative.

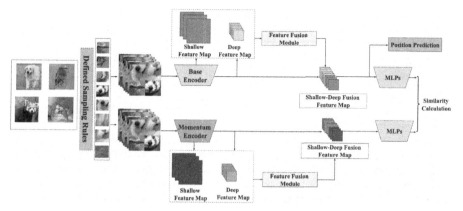

Fig. 1. Illustration of the overall framework. SGMNet adopts a Siamese network structure for the pre-training process. The images are separately processed by the base encoder and the derived encoder which is updated by the momentum of base encoder. The output feature map is divided into shallow and deep parts. These two feature maps are then input into the feature fusion module to obtain the fused feature vector for subsequent tasks, including position prediction and contrastive learning.

2.2 Spatially-Coupled Sampling Manner

The conventional sampling method suffers from a lack of diversity and fails to provide the model with an understanding of the internal spatial structure of the image. Therefore, we propose a spatially-coupled sampling manner, which involves sampling a set of images with position constraints. This method preserves the spatial relationships within the images, enabling the model to learn location information and ultimately improving information utilization. The illustration of this method is shown in Fig. 5. Assuming the image resolution is $H \times W$, two coupled crops of size $w \times h$ are sampled from the image, with the overlap ratio between the two crops set to cr. In order to ensure the diversification of sampling information, the cr setting should not be too large, and its interval should be $0 \leq cr \leq 0.3$, and the default value of cr in this paper is 0.2 in subsequent experiments.

2.3 Feature Fusion Module

The feature fusion module is guided by deep semantic information to extract important parts from shallow low-level features. Then it fuses deep features with extracted shallow features to provide the model with richer features of multiple levels. We denotes the deep features as $F_d \in R^{X_1 \times X_1 \times C_d}$ and $F_s \in R^{X_2 \times X_2 \times C_s}$ represents the shallow features, which are generated by the same base-encoder but processed by different numbers of convolution layers. We then divide the shallow feature map into $r = (X_2 / X_1)^2$ patches $\{p_{(i,j)} | 0 \leq i,j \leq (X_2 / X_1)\}$.

To obtain the feature extractor for extracting shallow features, each patch first undergoes similarity calculation with the deep feature map. The similarity between the (i,j)-th

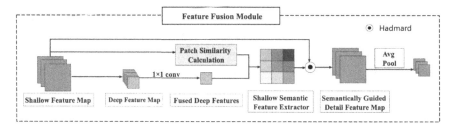

Fig. 2. Illustration of the Feature Fusion Module. We first aggregate the deep feature map into a one channel feature map. Then divide the shallow feature map into patches, each patch undergoes similarity calculation with the deep feature map to obtain the feature extractor for extracting shallow features. Subsequently, the feature extractor is used to extract critical information from the shallow features, which is then concatenated with the deep features for further processing.

patch and the deep feature map is calculated as:

$$Sim_{(i,j)} = \sum_p \sum_q [I(p,q) - F\prime_d(p,q)]^2 \tag{1}$$

where (m,n) denotes the size of each patch, (p,q) represents the pixel at the p-th row and q-th column in the patch, and $I(p,q)$ represents the corresponding pixel value of the patch of shallow feature map. The similarity obtained from this calculation represents the weight of the (i,j)-th patch in the feature extractor. As a result, the weights of $(X_2/X_1)^2$ patches together form the feature extractor. Subsequently, the feature extractor is used to extract critical information from the shallow features, which is then concatenated with the deep features for further processing. The illustration of this process is shown in Fig. 2.

For simplicity, we aggregate the deep feature map into a one channel feature map before the similarity calculation process mentioned above:

$$F_{d\prime} = f(F_d) \tag{2}$$

where $f{:}(X_1 \times X_1 \times C_d \to X_1 \times X_1)$ is a (1×1) convolution operator in our model.

2.4 Loss Function

The loss function is divided into two parts to efficiently utilize the fused features of deep and shallow layers, which are corresponding to the two tasks of position prediction and contrastive learning. First, the feature vectors obtained from the fusion module are used for position prediction. Specifically, pseudo-labels are assigned to two crops of the same image, for example, the label for the upper crop is **0** and the label for the lower crop is **1**. The fused features are processed by the dense partition pooling, and then a binary classification loss function is used to predict the target, which aims at training the model to distinguish the relative positions of the crops. The loss of position prediction is calculated as:

$$L_D = -\sum_c y_c log(p_c) \tag{3}$$

where y_c is the label of position and p_c is the probability given by the model.

The feature vectors are then input into MLPs to obtain latent vectors, which are then used for the contrastive learning task. Crops from the same image are considered positive, while those from different images are considered negative. The objective is to maximize the similarity between positive samples. The loss function for contrastive learning is represented as:

$$L_C = \sum_{i \in I}(-1/|P(i)|)\sum_p log[(exp(z_i z_p / \tau)) / \sum_\alpha exp(z_i z_\alpha / \tau)] \qquad (4)$$

In order to optimize the above two tasks, the two objective functions are jointly optimized. The joint optimization objective is:

$$L = L_c + \mu L_D \qquad (5)$$

where μ denotes the weight of position prediction loss.

3 Experiments

In this section, we first introduce the benchmark datasets, experimental settings, and parameter details, and then conduct experiments on five datasets to demonstrate the effectiveness and robustness of SGMNet.

Subsequently, ablation experiments are carried out, where the feature fusion module and position prediction module are separately removed for experiments and the results demonstrate the effectiveness of the two modules. We also study the influence of different fusion ratio on the performance of our model and provide reasonable analysis for the results.

3.1 Datasets

To test classification performance of SGMNet, we conduct extensive experiments on five benchmark datasets: STL-10, CIFAR-100, CIFAR-10, Tiny-ImageNet, ImageNet-100. The ImageNet [12] dataset contains 14197122 images with a total of 1000 categories, which cover most of the picture categories contained in real-life scenarios. The ImageNet-100 and Tiny-ImageNet that we use are two subsets of ImagNet. The ImageNet-100 dataset has 100 classes, each with 1000 training images and 300 test images. While, the Tiny-ImageNet contains 100000 images of 200 classes, each of them has 500 training images, 50 validation images and 50 test images. The STL-10 dataset has ten classes of RGB images, with a resolution of 96 × 96. It contains a training set of 5000 images and a test set of 8000 images. The CIFAR-10 [13] dataset has a total of 50000 training images and 10000 test images, which are divided into ten categories. CIFAR-100 [13] is divided into 100 categories (a total of 20 superclasses, each superclass has five subclasses), each class has 600 images, including 500 training images and 100 test images.

3.2 Experimental Setup

We implement SGMNet with PyTorch and train SGMNet using RTX 3090 GPU. As for the implementation details, we use ResNet-50 [14] as the backbone and select LARS optimizer schedulers and cosine learning rate scheduler, with an initial learning rate of 0.6, momentum of 0.9. The temperature is set to 1.0. We pre-train 100 epochs for SSL stage on each dataset, and train a linear classification model for 100 epochs subsequently. The experiment on ImageNet-100 is run on a single RTX 3090 GPU and experiments on other datasets are run with two RTX 3090 GPUs.

3.3 Comparison with State-of-the-Art Methods

Table 1. Results of SGMNet on CIFAR-10, CIFAR-100, STL-10, Tiny-ImageNet, ImageNet-100. Best results are in bold and second best results are underlined. All the results are obtained under the training settings of 100 epochs for SSL stage and 100 epochs for linear classification stage.

Model	CIFAR-10		CIFAR-100		STL-10		Tiny-ImageNet		ImageNet100	
	Top@1	Top@5	Top@1	Top@5	Top@1	Top@5	Top@1	Top@5	Top@1	Top@5
MoCo-v1	74.5	98.2	48.1	75.2	76.6	98.6	39.6	62.8	58.8	81.6
SimCLR	85.3	–	57.4	–	82.9	–	49.0	–	72.7	–
MoCo-v2	73.9	97.9	45.3	72.5	76.2	98.9	38.5	62.0	55.6	79.9
SimSiam	56.3	95.3	21.1	47.3	64.7	97.6	30.7	56.4	50.1	79.0
JigCLu	86.6	98.9	51.5	79.4	88.7	99.7	50.2	76.3	76.0	93.4
Barlowtwins	81.4	99.1	52.8	78.7	80.7	99.2	44.0	68.3	70.0	89.7
MoCo-v3	86.1	99.5	53.3	80.9	85.5	99.4	47.5	72.8	73.1	92.2
W2SSL	90.8	99.8	60.5	85.4	90.7	99.7	56.6	80.3	81.1	95.2
SGMNet	**92.6**	99.8	60.8	**86.1**	**92.4**	99.7	**57.0**	**81.1**	81.6	**95.8**
SGMNet (BS = 128)	92.2	**99.9**	**61.0**	85.8	92.1	**99.8**	56.2	80.1	81.1	95.6

In this part, we conduct self-supervised pre-training with batch size of 256 for 100 epochs, followed by 100 epochs of fine-tuning for linear classification.

We select some of the most advanced and representative methods for comparison, including MoCo-v1 [15], SimCLR [16], SimSiam [17], MoCo-v2 [8], JigCLu [18], BarlowTwins [19], MoCo-v3 [20] and W2SSL [21]. MoCo-v3 explores the training of ViT [22] under the contrastive learning paradigm, and on the basis of MoCo-v2, the memory queue is removed and a large batch size is adopted. JigClu proposes a single-batch self-supervised task pretext task Jigsaw Cluster, which divides, shuffles and reorganizes images. Compared with the dual-batches method, the computational effort is reduced to a certain extent. BarlowTwins focuses on the relationships within different representations and use cross-correlation matrix to reduce redundancy. This method does not require negative samples. W2SSL is the most advanced method at the moment. The performance of our model compared to state-of-the-art methods is shown in Table 1. As we can see, SGMNet outperforms traditional methods based on pretext tasks and contrastive learning models, which demonstrates the superiority of our method. We also train SGMNet with batch size of 128 during self-supervised pre-training. As we can see in the last row of the table, SGMNet still outperforms most of the baseline models with a smaller batch size.

3.4 Ablation Study

We conduct ablation study on CIFAR-10 and ImageNet-100 to demonstrate the effectiveness of each module of SGMNet. Experimental results are shown in the Table 2. As we can see, on CIFAR-10, the feature fusion module is more effective; on ImageNet-100, the position prediction module gains more improvements; the cross-space mutual optimization structure gives the best performance on both datasets. We speculate that when there are fewer categories, feature space optimization makes considerable improvements through directly providing the model with abundant information without interfering with optimization goals. When it comes to fine-grained classification, it requires the model to capture more detailed information and learn more sophisticated representations. Thus, new optimization goals need to be introduced to drive the model to more sufficiently leverage the input information and improves spatial sensitivity to assist decision-making, which makes embedding space optimization play more critical roles. When using the cross-space mutual optimization structure, feature space provides embedding space with information from different levels, and the embedding space encourages the model to learn more efficiently by incorporating extra tasks, which together gives optimal results.

Table 2. Influence of feature fusion module and position prediction. ResNet-50 is used for backbone, which is trained with a batch size of 256 for 100 epochs in the SSL stage, followed by 100 epochs of fine-tuning for linear classification. P, F and CS denote that the model adopts the position prediction module, the feature fusion module and cross-space mutual optimization.

Module	CIFAR10	ImageNet100
Baseline	74.5	58.8
P	90.8	81.1
F	92.6	80.3
CS	**92.6**	81.6

3.5 Analysis

Fusion Ratio Analysis. We also study the effect of fusing features of different levels to find the best combinations for efficient utilization of information. The results are shown in Table 3. Specifically, we take the fusion ratio $r = \{0.25, 0.5, 0.75\}$, which means that we fuse the feature maps from the first, second, and third layers with the feature map of the last layer (the fourth layer) respectively. The results indicate that the combination of feature maps from the second layer and the last layer is the most effective. Besides, we can see that the result of the first layer fused with the last layer is better than that of the fusion of the third layer and the last layer. We speculate the probable reason is that the feature map of the third layer is almost as abstract as the feature map of the last layer which cannot fuse the semantic information with details information as expected. However the feature map of the first layer contains redundant detail information which still cannot avoid the model learning some "shortcuts" even if we utilize the high level semantic information for extraction. Hence it is crucial for the feature fusion module to choose a proper combination of features from different levels.

Table 3. Influence of fusion ratio. ResNet-50 is used for backbone, which is trained with a batch size of 256 for 100 epochs and 200 epochs in the SSL stage, followed by 100 epochs of fine-tuning for linear classification on STL-10.

Fusion Ratio	100 Epochs	200 Epochs
0.25	91.3	92.4
0.5	**92.1**	**93.0**
0.75	90.5	91.2

4 Conclusion

In this paper, we propose SGMNet, which employs the Siamese network and integrates the advantages of position prediction and contrastive learning tasks to capture comprehensive features. Under a cross-space mutual optimization framework, our model generates fused features to learn and capture distinctive information from different levels within the images. We introduce the feature fusion module to achieve the fusion of deep and shallow features, which uses deep semantic information as guidance to extract important detailed features from shallow features. Meanwhile, our feature fusion module can be used as a plug-and-play component in various models to enhance performance, offering flexibility. We conduct thorough experiments on five datasets, and the results indicate that our model achieves competitive performance. As for future work, we think it is necessary to continue exploring the interpretability of the optimal combination of deep and shallow layers and further enhance training efficiency.

Acknowledgements. This work is supported by the National Natural Science Foundation of China (Grant No. 62176026).

References

1. Ma, C., et al.: Visual information processing for deep-sea visual monitoring system. Cogn. Robot. **1**, 3–11 (2021)

2. Li, Y., et al.: Underwater visibility enhancement IoT system in extreme environment. IEEE Internet Things J. (2023)
3. Li, Y., et al.: Brain-inspired perception feature and cognition model applied to safety patrol robot. IEEE Trans. Ind. Inf. (2023)
4. Chen, X., et al.: Improved baselines with momentum contrastive learning. arXiv preprint arXiv:2003.04297 (2020)
5. Yang, S., Huimin, L., Li, J.: Multifeature fusion-based object detection for intelligent transportation systems. IEEE Trans. Intell. Transp. Syst. **24**(1), 1126–1133 (2022)
6. Li, Yujie, et al. "Joint semantic-instance segmentation method for intelligent transportation system." IEEE Transactions on Intelligent Transportation Systems 24.12 (2022): 15540–15547
7. Dong, L., et al.: CCTwins: a weakly supervised transformer-based crowd counting method with adaptive scene consistency attention. IEEE Trans. Consum. Electron. **70**(1), 22–35 (2023)
8. Zheng, Y., et al.: Global-PBNet: a novel point cloud registration for autonomous driving. IEEE Trans. Intell. Transp. Syst. **23**(11), 22312–22319 (2022)
9. Seyfi, M., Banitalebi-Dehkordi, A., Zhang, Y.: Extending momentum contrast with cross similarity consistency regularization. IEEE Trans. Circuits Syst. Video Technol. **32**(10), 6714–6727 (2022)
10. Tao, L., Wang, X., Yamasaki, T.: An improved inter-intra contrastive learning framework on self-supervised video representation. IEEE Trans. Circuits Syst. Video Technol. **32**(8), 5266–5280 (2022)
11. Tao, C., et al.: Siamese image modeling for self-supervised vision representation learning. In: Proceedings of the IEEE/CVF Conference on Computer Vision and Pattern Recognition (2023)
12. Deng, J., et al.: Imagenet: a large-scale hierarchical image database. In: 2009 IEEE Conference on Computer Vision and Pattern Recognition. IEEE (2009)
13. Krizhevsky, A., Geoffrey, H.: Learning multiple layers of features from tiny images 7 (2009)
14. He, K., et al.: Deep residual learning for image recognition. In: Proceedings of the IEEE Conference on Computer Vision and Pattern Recognition. (2016)
15. He, K., et al.: Momentum contrast for unsupervised visual representation learning. In: Proceedings of the IEEE/CVF Conference on Computer Vision and Pattern Recognition (2020)
16. Chen, T., et al.: A simple framework for contrastive learning of visual representations. In: International Conference on Machine Learning. PMLR (2020)
17. Chen, X., Kaiming, H.: Exploring simple siamese representation learning. In: Proceedings of the IEEE/CVF Conference on Computer Vision and Pattern Recognition (2021)
18. Chen, P., Shu, L., Jiaya, J.: Jigsaw clustering for unsupervised visual representation learning. In: Proceedings of the IEEE/CVF Conference on Computer Vision and Pattern Recognition (2021)
19. Zbontar, J., et al.: Barlow twins: self-supervised learning via redundancy reduction. In: International Conference on Machine Learning. PMLR (2021)
20. Chen, X., Saining, X., Kaiming, H.: An empirical study of training self-supervised vision transformers. In: Proceedings of the IEEE/CVF International Conference on Computer Vision (2021)
21. Zhao, W., et al.: Learning what and where to learn: a new perspective on self-supervised learning. IEEE Trans. Circuits Syst. Video Technol. (2023)
22. Dosovitskiy, A.: An image is worth 16×16 words: transformers for image recognition at scale. arXiv preprint arXiv:2010.11929 (2020)
23. Cong, D., et al.: CAN: contextual aggregating network for semantic segmentation. In: ICASSP 2019–2019 IEEE International Conference on Acoustics, Speech and Signal Processing (ICASSP), pp. 1892–1896. IEEE (2019)

Author Index

© The Editor(s) (if applicable) and The Author(s), under exclusive license
to Springer Nature Singapore Pte Ltd. 2025
H. Lu (Ed.): ISAIR 2024, CCIS 2402, pp. 307–309, 2025.
https://doi.org/10.1007/978-981-96-2911-4

Printed in the United States
by Baker & Taylor Publisher Services